What Is a Person?

PRAISE PAGE

This book is not an imposition of "thick" Western moral universalism onto Africa. Instead, it presents an authentic conversation between Africa and the West, exploring what a person is amidst complex ethical challenges. The book will undoubtedly captivate readers, particularly those of us in Asia, who are intrigued by the diverse understandings of personhood across different cultures and borders. It provides a valuable opportunity to delve into these perspectives in depth.

Ruiping Fan, City University of Hong Kong

This book is a must-read for anyone who wants to engage in philosophy across the borders of their own time and place. It models a way to collaborate on a more global scale as it engages beyond Western thought with the idea of personhood. Jecker and Atuire explored African and Western views regarding personhood without assuming Western supremacy. It is historically rich and suggestive. *What is a Person?* offers readers an innovative pioneering of the methods of contemporary philosophical research and a compelling vision of persons.

Akira Akabayashi, M.D., Ph.D.
Professor Emeritus, University of Tokyo
Research Professor, New York University

Jecker and Atuire have produced a volume that could not be more timely or useful. As debates rage about the definition of a person fueled by disputes over abortion, embryonic research, and the definition of death, to mention but a few, it is crucial that disputants attend to rich traditions of thinking about the issue in Africa. Personhood is a concept that ought be rooted globally not parochially as this book thoughtfully shows.

Arthur Caplan Ph.D.
Mitty Professor of Bioethics and
Head of the Division of Medical Ethics
NYU Grossman School of Medicine

It is impossible not to be intrigued by the potential of a relational account of personhood that includes all human beings; is held equally by all humans, but in degrees by non-humans; cannot be diminished in humans; and grounds duties towards others. Add an audacious claim that African philosophy provides a plausible, secular foundation for personhood—rivalling what the soul once did to ground superlative moral worth—and you have a must-read book. *Emergent Personhood* brilliantly brings African and Western ideas into conversation, and the result is compelling.

Kevin Behrens, University of the
Witwatersrand, South Africa.

or

Kevin Behrens, Director: Steve Biko
Centre for Bioethics, Johannesburg.

In studying a new language, you learn things about your native tongue that had never occurred to you. So, too, Jecker and Atuire show that "person" is both a richer and a more ambiguous concept when African ideas are laid alongside those found in Euro-American traditions, whose complexities and contradictions thereby become more apparent. The breadth and depth of their book manifests the immense benefit of truly crossing borders when thinking afresh about a concept as central as personhood is not only for philosophy but for what we do—or, morally, should do—in many, varied domains of life.

—*Alexander Morgan Capron*, Former Director of Ethics, Trade, Human Rights and Law, World Health Organization, and University Professor Emeritus, University of Southern California

Philosophy Across Borders

Series Editors:

Bronwyn Finnigan, Australian National University
Nilanjan Das, University of Toronto
Evan Thompson, University of British Columbia
Amy Olberding, University of Oklahoma

Published in the Series:

What Is a Person? Untapped Insights from Africa
Nancy S. Jecker and Caesar A. Atuire

What Is a Person?

Untapped Insights from Africa

NANCY S. JECKER
AND
CAESAR A. ATUIRE

OXFORD
UNIVERSITY PRESS

Oxford University Press is a department of the University of Oxford. It furthers the University's objective of excellence in research, scholarship, and education by publishing worldwide. Oxford is a registered trade mark of Oxford University Press in the UK and certain other countries.

Published in the United States of America by Oxford University Press
198 Madison Avenue, New York, NY 10016, United States of America.

© Oxford University Press 2025

All rights reserved. No part of this publication may be reproduced, stored in a retrieval system, or transmitted, in any form or by any means, without the prior permission in writing of Oxford University Press, or as expressly permitted by law, by license, or under terms agreed with the appropriate reproduction rights organization. Inquiries concerning reproduction outside the scope of the above should be sent to the Rights Department, Oxford University Press, at the address above.

You must not circulate this work in any other form
and you must impose this same condition on any acquirer.

CIP data is on file at the Library of Congress

ISBN 978-0-19-769092-5

DOI: 10.1093/oso/9780197690925.001.0001

Printed by Integrated Books International, United States of America

To my mother, Mae Driscoll Silbergeld, for introducing me to fundamental questions of philosophy,
To my father, Sam Silbergeld, for supporting me as a writer from the start,
To my husband, Barry Aaronson, for love beyond words.
—NSJ

To my parents, Martha Akosua and John Akanyaachaab, for life and much more,
To my Builsa people, for moulding my identity and purpose,
To Philosophy, for ushering me into the quest for meanings.
—CAA

Contents

List of Tables   xi
Preface   xiii
List of Abbreviations   xv

Introduction: Philosophy Across Borders   1

PART I: HUMAN PERSONS

1. A Conversation between Africa and the West   11
   1.1 Introduction   11
   1.2 Key Concepts   12
   1.3 Contemporary African and Western Views   16
   1.4 Precursors of Contemporary African and Western Views   31
   1.5 Conclusion   46

2. Emergent Personhood   47
   2.1 Introduction   47
   2.2 Five Features   48
   2.3 Emergent Personhood   61
   2.4 Abortion   79
   2.5 Conclusion   84

3. Personhood Across the Lifespan   86
   3.1 Introduction   86
   3.2 African and Early Greek Personhood Across the Lifespan   87
   3.3 Contemporary Western Personhood Across the Lifespan   96
   3.4 Emergent Personhood Across the Lifespan   100
   3.5 Replies to Objections   106
   3.6 Conclusion   111

4. Becoming a Non-Person 113
   4.1 Introduction 113
   4.2 The Death of Persons and Human Beings 114
   4.3 Replies to Objections 129
   4.4 Hastening Death 135
   4.5 Conclusion 143

PART II: NON-HUMAN PERSONS

5. Zombies and Robots 147
   5.1 Introduction 147
   5.2 Are Zombies Persons? 148
   5.3 Could Machines Be Persons? 158
   5.4 Replies to Objections 172
   5.5 Conclusion 176

6. Animals and Nature 178
   6.1 Introduction 178
   6.2 Animals 178
   6.3 Non-Animal Nature 193
   6.4 Replies to Objections 206
   6.5 Conclusion 209

7. Space Aliens and Terraforming 210
   7.1 Introduction 210
   7.2 Space Aliens and Extraterrestrial Life 211
   7.3 Terraforming Mars 227
   7.4 Conclusion 240

Epilogue 243
Notes 247
Bibliography 285
Name Index 313
Subject Index 317

Tables

1.1	African and Contemporary Western Views of Persons	30
1.2	African and Early Western Views of Persons	45
2.1	Advantages/Disadvantages of African and Early Greek Personhood	60
2.2	Advantages/Disadvantages of Judeo-Christian Personhood	61
2.3	Emergent Personhood's Analysis of Human and Non-human Personhood	72
2.4	What Is 'Speciesism'?	72
3.1	Inequalities in Moral Standing across the Lifespan	100
4.1	The Cessation of Persons	129
4.2	Five Frameworks for Supporting Voluntary Active Euthanasia for a Patient Near Death with Advanced Dementia Who Suffers Unrelenting Pain	143
5.1	Three Types of Zombies	151
5.2	Are Zombies Persons?	157
5.3	Sufficient Conditions for Non-human Personhood	161
5.4	Sufficient Conditions for Human Personhood	161
5.5	Qualities Conferring Moral Status on AI	170
5.6	Are LaMDA, ChatGPT, Samantha, Hal, David, and Ava Persons?	171
6.1	Are Animals Persons?	192
6.2	Emergent Personhood in Humans versus Animals	192
6.3	Emergent Personhood in Humans versus Nature	205
6.4	Are Things in Nature, Besides Animals, Persons?	206
7.1	Should We Save Humans or ETs?	227
7.2	Can Lands on Mars Have Moral Standing or Personhood?	239

Preface

As the first in Oxford University Press's new series, *Philosophy Across Borders*, this book arrives at a pivotal moment—just as the world emerges from the height of the coronavirus disease 2019 (COVID-19) pandemic. During the pandemic, those of us fortunate enough to remain healthy and able to pursue philosophy found ourselves engaged in virtual collaborations. We (the authors) have never met in person. We composed this entire book, start to finish, by 'zooming.' As we pen its final touches, still never having met in person, we are struck that philosophy across borders is not only more widely accessible than ever before but also is deeply enriching for anyone who embarks on it with a desire to learn. We are more convinced than ever that the moment is ripe for philosophers to cross borders.

The optics of our collaboration on personhood might seem straightforward. One of us is white and the other Black; hence, it might be assumed that the white person (NSJ) contributed expertise about Western approaches to personhood while the Black person (CAA) brought knowledge of the African tradition. Yet, appearances are deceiving. African philosophy holds special significance for each of us. For one of us, a white American from the United States, the North American continent links to a history of profound injustice and slavery, which reverberates today in structural racism and Black Lives Matter. For the other, a Black African from Ghana, African philosophy's significance is more obvious. Each of us also identifies with the Western tradition. For one of us, with European ancestry, the linkage is more apparent. For the other, ties to the West trace to early post-colonial education in Africa and later, to formative years spent living and studying in Europe and to dual citizenship in both Ghana and Italy. Our identities are more complex than meets the eye. So too are the traditions we write about, which we call—imperfectly—'African' and 'Western' philosophy. At the same time that we invite the reader into a cross-border conversation about personhood, we will be deconstructing borders and interrogating difference. What we call 'African' and 'Western' personhood are strands in a larger human narrative about what it means to be a person—a narrative that traverses the borders of many traditions and runs across all human history.

"Wisdom is not in the head of one person" (*nyansa nni onipa baako ti mu*).[1] We acknowledge, with gratitude, the wisdom of many people who helped us with this book. The following (listed alphabetically) read draft chapters and offered valuable feedback: Kevin Behrens, Jantina De Vries, Paul Menzel, Thaddeus Metz, and Chris Wareham.

Abbreviations

AI	artificial intelligence
ChatGPT	Chat Generative Pre-trained Transformer
COVID 19	Coronavirus Disease 2019
ET	extraterrestrial
LaMDA	Language Model for Dialog Applications
NASA	National Aeronautics and Space Administration
PVS	persistent vegetative state
UDDA	Uniform Determination of Death Act
US	United States

Introduction
Philosophy Across Borders

Philosophers invoke the concept of a 'person' widely—not only as a basic building block for normative theories prescribing conduct but also to furnish a conceptual grounding for political and social philosophies about a just state.[1,2,3,4] The concept is legion in philosophy and across a wide swath of disciplines, including psychology,[5,6,7] law,[8,9,10] biomedicine,[11,12,13] anthropology,[14,15,16] and others.[17] The oldest known meaning of the word 'person' relates to performance before others in fiction or real life: the Latin *persōna*, referred to a "mask used by a player, character in a play, dramatic role," or "the part played by a person in life, character, role, position."[18]

Today, broad agreement about personhood exists at a high level of abstraction, yet sharp divisions emerge as we move closer to the ground. Philosophers generally agree that to be a person differs from being a member of a species, and most often they characterize 'person' in normative rather than purely biological terms. By and large, philosophers converge in thinking that 'person' indicates a being of superlative moral worth, variously expressed as deserving of dignity, rights, or respect. However, little consensus exists in delineating necessary and sufficient conditions for personhood or determining whether particular beings (or things) count as persons. Are fetuses, cows, great apes, trees, soils, ecosystems, or artificially intelligent social robots 'persons'? People holding religious views may ask, 'Is God(s) a person?' Views diverge.

2 WHAT IS A PERSON?

As we cross borders not only of time but also of culture, accounts of personhood splinter further. Compare the account of persons frequently espoused by people indigenous to sub-Saharan Africa with the one predominant in the West today. African personhood often underscores that persons exist only within "the nexus of their communal relationships."[19] This idea finds expression in pithy sayings, such as *a person is a person through other persons*,[20] and *I am because we are, and because we are, therefore I am*.[21] According to this way of thinking, "without incorporation into this or that community, individuals are considered to be mere danglers to whom the description 'person' does not fully apply."[22] Western personhood differs strikingly, stressing that persons hold the source of their exceptional moral worth inside themselves, in capacities such as sentience, consciousness, self-consciousness, reason, self-motivated activity, or language.[23] Unlike both African and Western personhood, some societies in Melanesia and India regard persons as "permeable or partible."[24] For example, the Nakaya, a hunter-gatherer community in the Nilgiri region of south India, reportedly consider 'person' to be an abstraction, referring to human forms (or to other non-human beings or objects) that we relate to in certain ways. The attribution itself serves not to differentiate solitary 'individuals' but to recognize a relational composite or 'dividuals.' According to Bird-David, "When I individuate a human being I am conscious of her 'in herself' (as a single separate entity); when I dividuate her I am conscious of how she related with me."[25] 'Individual' is literally an indivisible thing, referring to "existing as a separate indivisible entity; numerically one";[26] by contrast, 'dividual' indicates those "capable of being divided into parts."[27] According to this analysis, 'person' is an abstract idea composed of base-level relationships. This approach reflects an ontology that decenters individuals while centering relationships.

This book navigates distinct and culturally complex philosophies of persons by bringing them into conversation, focusing on the two philosophies that we, the authors, know best: African and Western.

It explores these philosophies as moving pictures rather than stills, crossing not only boundaries of society and culture but also of historical time. Drawing insights from each tradition, we formulate and defend a new philosophy, *Emergent Personhood*. Emergent Personhood borrows from African philosophy the insight that social relational qualities undergird personhood. From Western philosophy, it takes the conception that all humans are moral equals. Building on these ideas, Emergent Personhood offers a new philosophy of persons.

As we launch our inquiry into personhood, some of our staunchest critics are philosophers who doubt that 'person' can do the heavy lifting assigned to it. Some proclaim "the end of personhood," arguing that "at best the concept is unhelpful to much of bioethics today and at worst it is harmful and pernicious."[28] Their argument turns on showing first, that personhood functions as a conversation stopper. It "flatten[s] the normative conversation" by functioning as a sorter, putting people into boxes labeled 'has serious rights' or 'does not have serious rights,' which squelches debate.[29] Second, the concept is offensive. For example, disability scholars have pointed out that labeling a cognitively impaired human being a 'non-person,' or even asking whether individuals with disabilities count as 'persons,' demeans them; it is "substantively problematic."[30] Third, 'person' is a blunt instrument for working through complex, cutting-edge challenges. In a 2021 book, *Rethinking Moral Status*, thirty influential moral philosophers wrestled with cases involving brain organoids,[31] digital minds,[32,33] monkeys,[34] and invertebrates.[35] They contended that in these instances, entities might have a *measure* of moral status and should not be discounted morally if they do not qualify as full-fledged persons.

These issues merit careful attention, and we agree with many of the concerns raised. Yet, we take issue with the conclusion that applied fields like bioethics should abandon 'personhood.'[36] First, the all-or-nothing approach to persons that leads to conceptual sorting might indeed be a conversation stopper; yet this way of rendering persons is hardly inevitable. As we will show in the chapters that follow, sub-Saharan African philosophy understands personhood *as a matter of degree*, something someone (or something) can have more or less of. Had we stayed solidly within the Western tradition, we too might have concluded that personhood should be left out of practical ethics debates at the frontiers of science and technology. Doing philosophy across borders allows us to draw a different conclusion. Second, we agree that it is substantively problematic to ask whether a human being with cognitive impairment is a 'person.' We reject this approach; Our account, Emergent Personhood, establishes that all human beings are persons from birth to death by virtue of being in human-human relationship. Finally, we concur that the future is daunting. Grappling with complex new cases will challenge moral concepts like never before. Yet moral notions are hardly fixed; they bend and flex to meet the needs of a particular time and place. As we will show throughout the book, the notion of 'person' has evolved appreciably throughout history. Ancient and medieval thinkers, for example, believed in the existence of celestial beings and angels; they dedicated energies to deciphering the personhood of such beings. Many religious people today say that their god is a person. Later debates, which we will canvass in this book, address the personhood of robots and artificial intelligences. These debates shift understandings of what it means to be a person, and the notion of being a person evolves. Our task, as philosophers, is to shape and reshape how we think about personhood in ways that speak to problems at hand.

This book tackles these and other concerns by beginning a conversation between Africa and the West about what a 'person' is. As the conversation gets under way, a central aim will be to look for a philosophically compelling vision of personhood that incorporates insights from each tradition. Since the meanings of terms like *person* are never settled, our goal is not to put to rest debate about what a 'person' is. Instead, it is to shift the direction future debates take.

- *Chapter 1: A Conversation between Africa and the West.* After clarifying key concepts, Chapter 1 characterizes the philosophies of persons ascendant in Africa and the West today. It identifies differences along five key parameters: extrinsic/intrinsic, earned/unearned, scalar/binary, changing/stable, and foundational/derived. We ask when these differences emerged and trace their origins from the early Patristic era to the Middle Ages, and the predominance of Christianity in the West. We point out that strong affinities existed between Africa and the West before the rise of Christianity, noting similarities between African philosophy and early Greek and Roman views.
- *Chapter 2: Emergent Personhood.* Chapter 2 asks, What led the West to abandon the older Greek and Roman view of persons? What was gained and what was lost? After weighing this, we set forth five requirements that an adequate account of personhood must meet. This lays the groundwork for introducing a new philosophy of persons, *Emergent Personhood.* Emergent Personhood distills the most compelling insights from African and Western views and sets forth a sufficient condition for personhood that builds on these insights. We distinguish human and non-human persons and unpack the notion of 'speciesism.' Chapter 2 closes by examining the implications of Emergent Personhood for the moral standing of prenatal human life.
- *Chapter 3: Personhood Across the Lifespan.* Chapter 3 explicates Emergent Personhood further, considering its implications for human beings across the lifespan. We distinguish our view from contemporary African and Western approaches. Unlike some African accounts, Emergent Personhood commits to the moral equality of human beings. In contrast to some utilitarian and Kantian approaches, it rejects the position that older adults with intellectual impairment have less moral status or are not persons.

- *Chapter 4: Becoming a Non-Person.* Chapter 4 delves into the question of how human personhood ends. After clarifying the distinction between biological death and the death of a person, we distinguish Emergent Personhood's account from African and Western views. We consider the proposal to hasten death for people who request it, and we explore moral duties toward the newly dead and ancestors.
- *Chapter 5: Zombies and Robots.* Chapter 5 shifts the focus to non-human persons. It brings to light affinities between Emergent Personhood and some African views: both share the belief that consciousness is not necessary for being a person. This opens the door to greater inclusivity and personhood for artificial intelligences. After engaging with a series of objections, the chapter concludes that artificial entities that relate to us but lack conscious states can be persons if they stand in sufficiently close, pro-social relationships with human beings.
- *Chapter 6: Animals and Nature.* Chapter 6 considers whether animals, soils, rocks, or ecosystems could have the high moral status we associate with persons. We argue that Emergent Personhood can countenance personhood for varied types of beings and objects, yet prioritizes humans. It offers an approach that purports to be compelling for human beings, rather than aspiring to a 'view from nowhere,'[37] or an ethics for all living things, rational beings, or creatures that can suffer.
- *Chapter 7: Space Aliens and Terraforming.* Chapter 7 thinks expansively about the world beyond Earth. It applies Emergent Personhood to extraterrestrial life and lands and considers what duty, if any, calls for protecting pristine extraterrestrial environments for their own sakes. We explore extremophiles (organisms that thrive in environments hazardous to humans) and illustrate ethical challenges using science fiction examples. The chapter concludes that if they exist, extraterrestrial creatures, and the lands and planets they live on, can

acquire personhood in the same ways that non-human terrestrial beings and lands can.

Stepping back, it should be apparent that our book does philosophy differently. It breaks ground by engaging the concept of 'person' across borders. Rather than cordoning off one tradition and using it as a point of contrast or difference, our technique showcases both African and Western thought, revealing both affinities and differences. Weaving them together into a new philosophy, Emergent Personhood, we show how untapped insights from Africa contribute to a more enlightened view of persons, one less tethered than mainstream alternatives to the particular cultural, economic, and historical moorings of contemporary Western thought. We are convinced that as more philosophers engage in cross-border philosophizing, it will spur progress and enrich the field.

PART I
HUMAN PERSONS

1
A Conversation between Africa and the West

1.1 Introduction

We tend to think of ourselves as 'persons' in a moral sense, as beings with a certain dignity or worth, entitled to others' respect. Yet just beneath the surface of this seemingly simple belief, philosophical questions churn. What makes an entity a person? How does an individual become one? What does it mean for personhood to end? Are all humans persons? Are any non-humans persons? Could we ever build an artificial person? What do we owe persons and what do persons owe us?

In this chapter, we engage these perennial philosophical problems across borders. As philosophers immersed in both sub-Saharan African and Western ways of thinking, we bring these distinct traditions into conversation with one another. After briefly introducing key concepts (in Section 1.2), we begin, in Section 1.3, by characterizing the contemporary personhood debate in sub-Saharan African and Western philosophy. As will quickly become apparent, these views offer strikingly different visions. However, since sub-Saharan African and Western philosophers have generally not engaged with one another, few attempts to probe differences have occurred—no philosophers from Africa and the West that we are aware of have worked collaboratively on personhood. In Section 1.4, we entertain a provocative proposal, which we explore in greater depth throughout the book: *striking differences between sub-Saharan African and Western views about personhood* were not always present, are hardly inevitable, and can and should be bridged. Section 1.5 gives a glimpse of how we will defend this provocative proposal, setting forth an overarching plan for the book.

A brief word about nomenclature. Going forward, we identify, imperfectly, certain views as 'African' and others as 'Western.' We do not intend to 'essentialize' African or Western views or to represent these nuanced philosophical traditions as univocal. Instead, our aim is to characterize views *widely* held among people in those regions. We do not mean to imply that all or only people in these regions hold the views in question or that such views are 'pure' and untouched by outside influences. Inevitably, we gloss over exceptions within each tradition in order to furnish general characterizations. Unless otherwise indicated, 'African' is shorthand for the region of Africa located south of the Sahara, and 'African philosophy' refers to ideas prominent among black peoples indigenous to that region as captured in the works of academic philosophers.[i] Individuals south of the Sahara who descended from native sub-Saharan Africans include diverse peoples, with different languages and dialects, distinctive beliefs, and different ethnic groups—among them the Akan, Igbo, and Yoruba of West Africa; the Shona of East Africa; the Zulu of Southern Africa; and the Hutu, Chewa, Kanuri, Kongo, and Luba of Central Africa.

1.2 Key Concepts

Westerners and Africans have reason to ask how and why their views differ only if it can first be established that they are talking

---

[i] The academic philosophers we have in mind are black African scholars and others who have engaged with African ideas but are not indigenous to the African continent. Some of the earliest contributors to African philosophy such as Placide Tempels and Barry Hallen and, more recently, well-known contributors such as Helen Lauer, Thaddeus Metz, and Kevin Behrens are considered white.

about the same thing. We therefore begin by setting forth working definitions of key terms that will help us navigate the waters: *person, moral subject, mere object, valuing-as-an-end, valuing-as-a-mean, intrinsic value,* and *extrinsic value.*

When we call someone a *person*, the intuitive idea is that they have an exceptionally high moral status.[ii] Someone who qualifies has standing to demand that others treat them with respect and see them in a certain way.[1] This is variously expressed as having a right or entitlement to life, a superlative value or dignity, or value for one's own sake. Being a person is often thought to imply a stringent presumption against interference; it is sometimes associated with a strong reason to offer aid or ensure fair treatment.[2] Philosophical debates about personhood often start with a shared assumption that a 'normal' adult human being represents a clear case of someone who counts as a person. These debates begin to diverge when it comes to saying why normal adult humans qualify and who or what others might. As we use the term, 'person' captures these general ideas, while leaving open substantive questions about what the source of a person's value is, allowing for a range of reasonable views.

Short of full-fledged personhood, a being may merit moral concern to a lesser extent, or not at all. Objects that have some

---

[ii] While there is wide agreement about this definition of 'person,' not everyone subscribes to it. For example, Molefe and Muade interpret the African conception of 'person' as equating personhood with moral character, not moral status (Molefe M, Muade E, 2023, An Appraisal of 'African Perspectives of Moral Status: A Framework for Evaluating Global Bioethical Issues,' *Arumaruka: Journal of Conversational Thinking* 3(1): 25–50, DOI: 10.4314/ajct.v3i2.2). Yet, other philosophers working in the African tradition, such as Gyekye and Wiredu, explicitly decouple moral status from social status, identifying personhood with moral status and linking character with social status (see Gyekye K, 2010, Person and Community in African Thought, in Wiredu K, Gyekye K, eds., *Person and Community: Ghanaian Philosophical Studies, I,* Council for Research in Values and Philosophy (Washington, DC), 101–122, https://www.crvp.org/publications/Series-II/1-Contents.pdf.Wiredu K, 1992, The Moral Foundations of African Culture, in Flack HE, Pellegrino ED, eds., *African-American Perspectives on Biomedical Ethics,* Georgetown University Press, 80–93). Our aim is not to settle this debate, which we deal with in greater detail elsewhere (Jecker NS, Atuire CA, 2024. Personhood: An Emergent View from Africa and the West, *Developing World Bioethics,* ahead of print, DOI: 10.1111/dewb.12461).

moral standing, with or without full personhood, we refer to as *moral subjects*. By contrast, objects with no moral value we refer to as *mere objects*. For example, if human beings are persons, they qualify as moral subjects, and if sentient non-human animals have some moral value short of personhood, they also qualify as moral subjects. Mere objects may be useful or be a means to valuable things yet are not themselves morally valuable. For example, tables and chairs are useful and money is a means to valuable things, yet most people would say that tables, chairs, and money lack any value in themselves apart from this.

We use the phrases *moral considerability*, *moral standing*, and *moral status* interchangeably as overarching terms referring to moral worth. For example, on most interpretations of African ethics, all human beings are morally considerable, which means they have some moral worth. According to several contemporary Western accounts (discussed in Chapter 6, Section 6.2), the capacity for consciousness is necessary for being morally considerable, but being a human being is not.[3,4,5] These examples make evident that our use of these terms is indeterminate with respect to substantive requirements for moral worth, leaving open the question of what the necessary and sufficient conditions for moral worth are.

While the above designations indicate an object's value, valuing *as-an-end* or *as-a-means* indicates the way in which people value objects. When we value an object as-an-end, we value it for its own sake rather than merely using it for our own purposes. For example, Kant regards rational agents as deserving to be valued as-an-end, not merely used to achieve someone else's goals. When we value someone as-a-means only, we use them solely to achieve our own (or someone else's) aims.

A final distinction is between *intrinsic* and *extrinsic value*. These terms refer metaphorically to the location or source of value. To say that something has intrinsic value means that it carries the source of its value in itself. For example, if being alive has intrinsic value, then it is valuable itself, irrespective of what it accomplishes or achieves. By contrast, a ticket to a ball game has extrinsic value, because it derives its value entirely from some outside source, i.e., its ability to get us into a ballgame.

Various combinations of means/end and intrinsic/extrinsic value are possible. Both intrinsically and extrinsically valuable objects can be valued as ends or as means. For example, intrinsically valuable things, like persons, can be treated either as means only or as ends. Likewise, instrumentally valuable things, like money, can be sought as ends-in-themselves or as means. Korsgaard holds that we frequently make the mistake of assuming that only intrinsically valuable objects deserve to be treated as ends and notes that many extrinsically valuable objects also deserve to be valued as ends.[6] For example, a work of art may have no intrinsic value yet deserve to be valued as-an-end (not a means only), because it comprises part of an intrinsically valuable whole, such as an aesthetic experience or a flourishing human life. These working definitions of types of value (intrinsic/extrinsic) and ways of valuing (ends/means) abstract away from substantive claims about what has value and how different kinds of valuable things should be treated. Together with the definitions of person, moral subject, and mere object, they form a basic structure or critical perspective that will help us to organize ethical deliberation across a range of views.

These working definitions (of *person, moral subject, mere object, valuing-as-an-end, valuing-as-a-means, intrinsic value,* and *extrinsic value*) are widely used in Africa and the West. However, they are not universally shared. Molefe and Muade, for example, argue that in the African tradition, 'personhood' is an assessment of character, not moral status.[7] We proceed on the assumption that the basic structure we set forth is *sufficiently* widespread in both traditions that it can function as a common currency. It furnishes the best available framework for the purpose of cross-border conversation.

1.3 Contemporary African and Western Views

With these preliminaries addressed, we circle back to our starting question, 'What is a person?'[iii] A standard answer given in contemporary African philosophy is that personhood is fundamentally *relational*: what makes a person a person is their interconnection with others and a community rather than any standalone quality a person possesses independent of that. Since African philosophy has characteristically been an oral tradition, these ideas often find expression in pithy sayings, such as "a person is a person through other persons" (*umuntu ngumuntu ngabantu*),[8] and "I am because we are, and because we are, therefore I am."[9] These sayings convey the thought that persons become persons through participating in social roles and relationships.

On some African accounts, personhood is something human beings achieve through relating to others in morally excellent ways.[10] Thus, Ikuenobe argues that a plausible African view of dignity requires attaining moral excellence and holds that the mere capacity for such attainment is insufficient and only instrumentally good.[11] Menkiti regards the enactment of moral excellences through social practices constitutive of personhood, not merely evidence of its presence.[12] For others, the font of dignity is people's *capacity* for relating or relating in morally excellent ways, irrespective of whether they in fact relate in that way. For example, Metz grounds a theory of moral status on the capacity to relate in a certain way and characterizes this in terms of "being able in principle, i.e., without changes to a thing's nature," to be a subject or object of communality.[13] Likewise, Molefe grounds a conception of dignity in the capacity for pro-social virtues, specifically sympathy, and explicitly criticizes performance-based views of dignity.[14] Despite

---

[iii] We do not purport to give a comprehensive account of either tradition named in the head, and we note exceptions to our general characterizations throughout the book.

their differences, all these African renderings of personhood prize relational values, holding that what is special and inviolable about human beings is how they interact with others and a community.

Underpinning these diverse relational accounts is a metaphysical picture that portrays human beings as fundamentally social and takes for granted "the givenness of a human intertwined existence."[15] For Gyekye, "Living in relation to others... immediately plunges [individuals]... into a moral universe."[16] Characterizing the natural state of humankind as a family, or a community considered to be an extension of the family, Ahiauzu depicts relationships between persons as familial, as opposed to contractual:

> the relationship is not one based on a conception of fair play... but on a sense of concern for others. It is not borne out of an idea of implicit consent or ahistorical actual consent but on the humanity of persons and the implication of that humanity for normativity.[17]

Mbiti puts the point this way: "the individual does not and cannot exist alone except corporally. [The individual] ... owes [their] existence [as a person] to other people, including those of past generations and their contemporaries. [The individual] is simply part of the whole."[18] Gyekye expresses it thus: "when a [human being] descends from heaven, [the human being] descends into a human society (*onipa firi soro besi a, obesi onipa kurom*)," explaining that "Akan thought... sees humans as originally born into a human society (*onipakurom*), and therefore as social beings from the outset."[19]

Salient differences come to light when one sets these contemporary African views of persons alongside Western accounts. Unlike African philosophy's embrace of community, a dominant strand in Western moral and political philosophy is to be cautious about community. Unlike their African counterparts, Western scholars tend to regard society as a potential intrusion and threat. Respecting persons requires minimizing such incursions. Rather than regarding human social existence as given, contemporary Western views more typically require people to consent to society, at least hypothetically, and to its associated restrictions. For example, the social contact tradition of Hobbes, Locke, Rousseau, and Kant regards human beings as primordially separate from civil society and choosing in some sense whether to enter society and abide by its constraints. Kant, for example, holds that social rules must be justifiable to all those who are subject to them, and holds that it violates the dignity of persons to force them to act against their own reasons. For Hobbes, societal restrictions are a necessary evil, accepted only to avoid a "war of all against all" and a life that is "nasty, brutish, and short."[20]

Unlike their African counterparts, Western approaches often home in on qualities that individuals could in theory possess independent of standing in social relationships or belonging to a society. Kant, for example, compares the dignity (*würde*) of human beings to a jewel that dazzles us and says it "shine[s] by its own light as a thing which has its whole value *in itself*."[21] The metaphor signals the Kantian idea that persons have an inner worth (*inneren Wert*), which consists of their capacity to be rational end-setters: "It is our capacity to set ends—to freely choose what shall be an end by means of reason, that not only makes every rational being an end in itself, but which forms the only possible final purpose of nature."[22] For Kant, this capacity relies on our reasoning faculty and is something we carry with us under any and all circumstances.

Like Kant, the Akan people of Ghana compare the superlative value of human beings to objects that bedazzle us. Gyekye, for example, invokes the maxim, "The human being is more beautiful than gold (*Onipa ye fe sen sika*),"[23] and elucidates it by saying, "It is the human being that counts: I call upon gold, it answers not; I call upon cloth, it answers not; it is the human being that counts (*Onipa ne asem: mefre sika a, sika nnye so, mefre ntama a, ntama nnye so; onipa ne asem*)."[24] In this juxtaposition, while gold has intrinsic qualities we value, it lacks the responsiveness to human calling, which is the hallmark of being a person in the African sense. Comparing the two traditions, the source of bedazzlement differs: for Kant, it is an internal light within the jewel; for Gyekye, it is responsiveness to human calling.

With this general comparison as backdrop, we flesh out the comparison further by asking five questions: are the properties that confer personhood (1) intrinsic or extrinsic; (2) earned or unearned; (3) binary or scalar; (4) mostly stable or mostly changing; and (5) foundational or derivative?[iv] In making these comparisons, our aim is to consider contemporary African and Western personhood from a high-altitude—offering a general picture, yet inevitably, missing significant details and nuances[v].

1. Intrinsic or extrinsic? Beginning with the intrinsic/extrinsic distinction, we note that overall, African approaches hold that the conditions qualifying someone for personhood are not properties 'inside' a person, but 'outside,' consisting in relationships with others and the community.[vi] According to Gbadegesin, "the 'I' is just a 'We' seen from another perspective."[25] Shutte explains the point this way:

> In European philosophy of whatever kind, the self is always envisaged as something 'inside' a person, or at least as a kind of container of mental properties and powers. In African thought it is seen as 'outside,' subsisting in relationship to what is other, the natural and social environment. In fact, the sharp distinction between self and world, ... so characteristic in European philosophy, disappears.[26]

Menkiti likewise asserts that "in the African view it is the community which defines the person as person, not some *isolated* quality of rationality, will or memory."[27] Menkiti goes on to explain, "it is not

---

[iv] Our discussion of five questions draws on Jecker NS, Atuire CA, 2024, Personhood: An Emergent View from Africa and the West (Developing World Bioethics, ahead of print, DOI: 10.1111/dewb.12461).

[v] The fivefold framework we introduce to compare African and Western personhood can serve as a general tool to compare other conceptions of personhood across borders.

[vi] An exception is Matolino, who rejects relational ontology as a meaningful way of thinking about African conceptions of the self. (See Matolino B, 2009, Radical versus Moderates: A Critique of Gyekye's Moderate Communitarianism, *South African Journal of Philosophy* 28(2): 160–170, DOI: 10.4314/sajpem.v28i2.46674.)

enough to have before us the biological organism, with whatever rudimentary psychological characteristics are seen as attaching to it. We must also conceive of this organism as going through a long process of social and ritual transformation until it attains the full complement of excellences" seen as definitive of persons.[28] Metz summarizes the differences between African and Western views by noting that in the Western philosophical tradition, "the self or person is usually identified with something internal, either a soul that contains mental states, a brain that contains mental states or, most common these days, a chain of mental states themselves, some of which are self-aware"; by contrast, in the African tradition, "the essence of any concrete, natural object is, at least in part, necessarily constituted by its relationships with elements of the world beyond the thing's intrinsic properties."[29]

In comparison to African accounts, contemporary Western stances often locate persons' superlative value in intrinsic attributes, not relations to outside objects.[vii] This trademark feature of Western views is on full display in practical debates about personhood. For example, discussing abortion and the moral status of the fetus, Warren begins with the question of what qualities a hypothetical alien would require to count as a person, arguing that aliens are not persons if they lack certain innate properties that (Western) philosophers have proposed for personhood, such as sentience, consciousness, self-awareness, reason, self-motivated activity, and the capacity for language.[30]

In keeping with this approach, Kantian ethics identifies the inner capacity of the will to act based on moral laws it gives itself to be the hallmark of having high moral worth and dignity.[viii] For

---

[vii] An important exception is contemporary feminist ethics. For a general overview, see Norlock K, 2019, Feminist Ethics, in Zalta EN, ed., *Stanford Encyclopedia of Philosophy*, https://plato.stanford.edu/archives/sum2019/entries/feminism-ethics/.

[viii] We refer to 'Kantian' views to indicate how this view is standardly represented and taught in universities. We acknowledge diverse renderings of Kantian philosophy as well as disputes among Kant scholars about how Kant is best understood. Addressing this issue falls outside the scope of our inquiry.

Kant, 'autonomy of the will' indicates the capacity of a rational will, uninfluenced by outside sources, to choose the moral laws to which it will be subject. Korsgaard surmises that for Kant, "Any attempt to control the actions and reactions of another by any means except an appeal to reason treats her as a mere means, because it attempts to reduce her to a mediate cause."[31] Similarly, Schneewind interprets Kant as saying that

> there is no place for others to tell us what morality requires, nor has anyone the authority to do so—not our neighbor, not the magistrates and their laws, not even those who speak in the name of God. Because we are autonomous, each of us must be allowed a social space within which we may freely determine our own action.[32]

According to Kantian ethics, pro-social virtues like generosity and charity are problematic as a source of value, because they can render beneficiaries dependent, hinge on a do-gooder's involuntary temperament, and often reflect debts benefactors owe, not magnanimity.[33]

Another leading contemporary Western account, utilitarianism, holds that 'being morally considerable' depends on the internal psychological ability to suffer or have enjoyments.[ix] Utilitarian ethics is often associated with the claim that any being with this ability deserves to have their interests (e.g., the intensity, duration, etc. of one's pleasure or pain) factored into the calculus that determines which action brings about the greatest good.[34] Bentham, for example, held that the relevant question for determining moral considerability was "not, Can they *reason*? nor Can they *talk*? but, Can they *suffer*?"[35]

[ix] We refer to utilitarian philosophy to indicate how this view is standardly represented and taught in universities. We acknowledge diverse renderings of it as well as disputes among utilitarians about how the view is best understood. Addressing this falls outside the scope of our inquiry.

Contemporary utilitarians, such as Singer, contrast beings with the capacity to suffer or experience enjoyments with those that lack it, claiming, "It would be nonsense to say that it was not in the interests of a stone to be kicked along the road by a schoolboy. A stone does not have interests because it cannot suffer."[36] For Singer, all beings that have an equal capacity to suffer deserve to have their interests considered equally, irrespective of the kinds of beings they are. Singer's position prioritizes non-humans over humans in cases where non-humans have a greater capacity for suffering and enjoyment. For Singer, the special status assigned to humans in the West today is the relic of a religious orthodoxy that should be abandoned: "During the centuries of Christian domination of European thought the ethical attitudes of [Christian] doctrines became part of the unquestioned moral orthodoxy of European civilization."[37] Singer's utilitarianism implies that human life, and human-human relationships, have no special value aside from the pleasurable states they produce.

2. *Earned or unearned?* A second point of comparison comes to light when we raise the question, are the traits that confer personhood earned or unearned. Many African scholars would reply that personhood is an achievement realized through ongoing effort. They hold that the high moral status associated with being a person implies certain performative acts, such as actually being in community with others and displaying moral excellence in relating. For example, Gyekye points out the dual meanings of the Akan (Ghanaian) word for person, *onipa*, which can refer either to being human or to being a person, depending on the individual's conduct. Thus, "In the Akan society, when an individual's conduct very often appears cruel, wicked, selfish, ungenerous or unsympathetic, it would be said of that individual that '[the individual] is not a person' (*onnye onipa*)."[38] According to Gyekye, a human being who is not a person still qualifies as a moral subject: "the judgment that an individual is not a person ... does not imply ... that people should cease to demonstrate a moral concern for [the individual]

or display the appropriate moral virtues in their treatment of [the individual]; only that [the individual] is not considered a [highly] morally worthy individual."[39] The underlying basis for attributing some moral worth to all human beings is variously understood. On some views, it is grounded in the belief that each human being possesses the *ōkra* (soul), while on others, it depends on the individual's actions and behaviors to promote others' well-being. According to Gyekye's position, an individual's degree of worth and whether it rises to full-fledged personhood depends on conduct. Of those who excel at pro-social moral virtues it might be said, they are 'truly a person' (*oye onipa paa!*).[40]

By comparison, within Western approaches, the qualities that stand out as a basis for personhood are generally unearned. For example, regardless of whether what confers dignity is a rational will (Kant) or the ability to suffer and have enjoyments (Bentham), individuals do not deserve these qualities but simply have them or don't. Darwall underscores this point by distinguishing two types of respect: appraisal and recognition.[41] Recognition respect refers to "the disposition to give appropriate weight or consideration in one's practical deliberations to some fact about the object and to regulate one's conduct by constraints derived from that fact."[42] By contrast, appraisal respect is based on our own favorable estimation of a someone's merits and character in a particular pursuit. Contemporary Western views of persons hold that what makes someone a person are qualities they have antecedent to and independent of others' appraisal. In other words, persons merit recognition respect independent of anyone's judgment of their achievements. Contemporary African views, like Gyekye's, emphasize earning others' positive appraisal based on performance in social roles and offices, suggesting appraisal respect.

3. *Binary or scalar?* A third question concerns whether the determining features of personhood are all-or-none or a matter of degree. African ways of thinking lend themselves to the idea that personhood is a differential status, reflecting the fact that

24 WHAT IS A PERSON?

individuals can display person-conferring qualities to varying degrees. Thus, it might be said that someone is 'more' or 'less' of a person depending on the degree of moral excellence they exhibit. Many African conceptions consider personhood to be aspirational and unfinished over the whole course of a person's life. According to Menkiti, personhood is

> the sort of thing which has to be attained and is attained in direct proportion as one participates in communal life through the discharge of the various obligations defined by one's stations. It is the carrying out of these obligations that transforms one from the it-status of early childhood, marked by an absence of moral function, into the person-status of later years, marked by a widened maturity of ethical sense—an ethical maturity without which personhood is conceived as eluding one.[43]

Menkiti goes on to characterize an ontological progression:

> persons become persons only after a process of incorporation. Without incorporation into this or that community, individuals are considered to be mere danglers to whom the description 'person' does not fully apply. For personhood is something which has to be achieved and is not given simply because one is born of human seed.[44]

However, it would be a mistake to conclude based on these passages that Menkiti regards non-persons as having no moral worth. As noted already, African views generally hold that all human beings are moral subjects, irrespective of whether they attain personhood. Although the African view regards moral worth to be present in a binary way in all human beings, it regards *personhood* as scalar and variable.[x]

---

[x] African philosophers have not completely resolved these issues. There is the possibility that if people's behavior is reprehensible, they might lose moral worth without

Within the African tradition, variable moral status might justify differential treatment in some situations. For example, in forced choice situations where lifesaving resources are limited, an infant or small child might be sacrificed to save an adult if the adult was seen as playing a vital role in the care and support of others in a family or community.[45] The underlying rationale could be that infants and small children are less fully incorporated in communal life and in this sense, are less fully persons. Some Western views about personhood might arrive at a similar conclusion on different grounds. For example, Tooley defends infanticide in certain cases on the ground that "it is a necessary condition of something's having a serious right to life that it possesses the concept of a self as a continuing subject of experiences, and that it believes that it is itself such an entity."[46]

In contrast to these African approaches, leading voices in Western philosophy today maintain that personhood is a binary, all-or-none designation.[xi] The general idea is that being a person requires crossing a 'finish-line,' and all beings that meet certain requirements for personhood cross this line and have the status, and that status is full.[47] In keeping with this assessment, Kant is generally interpreted as holding that "basic moral status does not come in degrees. It is always equal to that of other people regardless of the level, if any, at which our moral capacities and dispositions are developed, realized or exercised."[48] Likewise, utilitarians are generally understood as affirming that any being who crosses the line of having a capacity for suffering and enjoyment is morally considerable. While sentience and the capacity to suffer may vary

---

losing their standing as persons, or they may lose social standing but retain moral standing. Individuals can also become outcasts and lose social and/or moral standing in one society but gain acceptance in another, rendering their social and/or moral standing contested. For more on this, see Jecker NS, 2022, African Ethics, Respect for Persons, and Moral Dissent, *Theoria* 88(3), DOI: 10.1111/theo.12390.

[xi] A growing chorus in the West disputes what we are calling, "leading voices in Western philosophy." See, for example, Clarke S, Zohny H, Savulescu J, eds., 2021, *Rethinking Moral Status*, Oxford University Press, 2021.

in quality and degree, once a threshold capacity to suffer and enjoy is met, the conferral of moral considerability applies. In the Western frame, this same all-or-nothing approach applies to beings with the potential to develop morally salient qualities in the future, such as fetuses and infants. For example, Noonan holds that the potential to become a person is itself morally significant and a sufficient condition for personhood,[49] whereas Thomson says, 'an acorn is not an oak tree' and having the potential for morally relevant capacities does not meet the bar for personhood.[50] On both views, we can say of an individual at any stage of human development that they are or are not a person. Surveying the landscape of moral philosophy in the West today, Simon and Savulescu conclude, "the assumption that all adult human beings who are not severely cognitively impaired have equal moral status is hardly ever challenged. . . . It is a background assumption made by many of us who share liberal, democratic ideals."[51]

Binary views carry the advantage of giving definite answers to practical questions. They also pair well with the language of rights and the corresponding idea that being a person entails inalienable rights to life, liberty, and happiness. As we will explore in the next section (Section 1.4), the Judeo-Christian roots of contemporary Western philosophy are also on display in the tendency to view personhood as an all-or-nothing designation. It was during the Christian era that the view that all human beings are created in the image of God (*imago Dei*) and possess an immortal soul was consolidated, inviting the idea that all human beings have an absolute and equal moral standing.

4. *Mostly stable or mostly changing?* The next question is whether having the outstanding moral worth we associate with personhood is stable or changing over the lifespan. African personhood, with its aspirational emphasis, inclines to the view that personhood changes, and ideally increases, over a person's life. Thus, on some interpretations, the pro-social virtuous qualities that comprise being a person generally mature and deepen as human beings

move through the stages of their lives. This rendering also entails that an individual who is not a person can still become one, and someone who loses personhood can reclaim it.

Illustrative of this view is Menkiti, who subscribes to the position that an infant is not yet a person, but a 'mere dangler,' while a newly deceased individual remains a person initially, while they are remembered, later joining "the nameless dead" and slipping into "personal non-existence ... becoming once again mere *its*, ending their worldly sojourn as they had started out—as unincorporated non-persons."[52] This account portrays personhood as an arc, marked by ontological ascent and descent.[53] The general idea is that as individuals move through their lives, they forge relationships that grow more meaningful and ethically significant over time.[54] The degree of moral status a person attains depends on the extent to which they relate with others in morally excellent ways or develop capacities to do so. For this reason, African views are often interpreted as tracking human development. Thus, Metz maintains that "[Z]ygotes, blastocysts and embryos lack moral status. . . . They cannot be subjects of a friendly relationship, for they lack the abilities for conceptualization, intentional action, emotion and the like that are constitutive of it."[55] Metz adds that adult human beings much more readily think of themselves as a 'we' with mid-to-late-stage fetuses and newborns than with earlier forms of prenatal human life.

The changing nature of African personhood over the life course creates practical challenges about determining who is and is not a person. For example, in contrast to much of the world, across most of sub-Saharan Africa, there are no legal guidelines for declaring death using cardiopulmonary or neurologic criteria.[56] This may reflect, in part, an underlying philosophical view that personhood is a matter of degree: "rather than occurring at a discrete moment, death is often viewed as a rite of passage. . . . [M]any in traditional African communities feel that a 'good' death can only occur after a person has had time to put their affairs in order, so the suddenness of BD/DNC [brain death/death by neurological criteria] would be viewed as 'bad.'"[57] However, even without a shared legal or philosophical basis for determining death, practical exigencies compel people to declare death.[58] We explore these issues further later in the book (Chapter 4).

Unlike the African belief that personhood changes over time, the binary approach associated with contemporary Western thinking lends itself to regarding personhood as mostly stable throughout life. Once the finish line is crossed (whether that occurs at conception or sometime after birth) a person has a generally secure moral status. Still, it is possible on Western accounts for an individual to lose full moral status and become a non-person. For example, serious illness, such as advanced Alzheimer's disease, or serious injury, such as anoxic brain injury resulting from cardiac arrest, can rob someone of personhood if it leads to the loss of qualities like sentience and moral reasoning deemed necessary for personhood. Barring such events, personhood is generally considered constant until death, which is defined by the cessation of personhood-conferring properties, such as consciousness or 'higher' cognitive functions.

5. *Foundational or derivative?* A final question that helps distinguish African and Western accounts of personhood is whether 'person' is a foundational or derivative concept. In the African tradition, two distinct strands of thought are apparent. The first strand (sometimes called, 'strong' or 'radical') holds that being a person is derivate of participating in a community. Menkiti, for example, rejects a view of community they associate with the West, which sees community as "a mere collection of self-interested persons, each with [their] own private set of preferences"; instead, Menkiti endorses the idea that the 'we' associated with community "is not an additive 'we' but a thoroughly fused collective 'we,'" rendering community a prior, necessary condition for the existence of persons.[59] Likewise, Mbiti holds, "The community must . . . make, create, or produce the individual; for the individual depends on the

corporate group."[60] For both, being a person is an attainment possible only within society.

A second strand of thought (sometimes designated, 'moderate' or 'restricted') suggests that person and community are co-constitutive. Gyekye, who represents a moderate stance, invokes the Akan maxim to explain that "the clan is like a cluster of trees which, when seen from afar, appear huddled together, but which would be seen to exist individually when closely approached."[61] A moderate account does not entail that persons are ontologically merged with their community, but rather, "the cultural community constitutes the context or medium in which the individual person works out and chooses [their] goals and life plans, and, through these activities, ultimately becomes what [they want] to be—the sort of status [they want] to acquire."[62] Eze, who also espouses a moderate position, describes a contemporaneous formation whereby persons and communities are co-constitutive; one cannot exist without the other.[63]

While African conceptions accentuate a tight connection between persons and communities, it would be wrong to characterize these views as expecting people to follow social rules blindly.[64] The Yoruba proverb conveys this point well: "each individual must use their own hands to improve their own character (*Owo ara eni, La afi I tunwa ara enii se*)."[65] When moral dissenters stand up for what they think is right, they are persons in the *fullest* sense, enacting moral excellences, like bravery and courage.[66] While ultimately, African personhood is something one can lose, it is not lost by people holding minority views, but by people eroding their standing by taking on vicious habits that injure others and the community.

In contrast to these African views, contemporary Western accounts generally regard personhood as foundational and consider community to be derivate. Typically, the community is seen as deriving from the choices that persons make from a standpoint outside society. For example, the social contract tradition of the seventeenth to early nineteenth centuries regards civil society as based on the consent of individuals in a state of nature, outside civil society. Before entering society, individuals are pictured as persons, holding certain natural and inalienable rights and possessing the capacity for free and rational choice.

Table 1.1 recaps the discussion of this section, noting salient differences between leading contemporary African and Western views of persons. Our depiction of each tradition is from a high-altitude—it offers a general picture but inevitably, misses significant details and nuances.

Table 1.1 African and Contemporary Western Views of Persons

	African Personhood	Contemporary Western Personhood
1. **Intrinsic or extrinsic?** *Is the source of value inside an individual or outside, in an individual's relations to others?*	Extrinsic	Intrinsic
2. **Earned or unearned?** *Is personhood an achievement an individual deserves credit for?*	Earned	Unearned
3. **Scalar or binary?** *Is personhood a matter of degree or all-or-nothing?*	Scalar	Binary
4. **Stable or changing?** *Does personhood usually change or remain stable over a person's life?*	Changing	Stable (absent severe disease/injury)
5. **Derivative or non-derivative?** *Is personhood a basic concept or derived from other concepts?*	Derivative/partially derivative	Non-derivative

Key: African personhood = ideas prominent among black peoples indigenous to the region of Africa south of the Sahara, as captured in the works of academic philosophers; contemporary Western personhood = Kantian and utilitarian ethics

Note: Table 1.1 first appeared in Jecker NS, Atuire CA, 2024, Personhood: An Emergent View from Africa and the West (Developing World Bioethics, ahead of print, DOI: 10.1111/dewb.12461).

1.4 Precursors of Contemporary African and Western Views

The pictures of personhood described so far represent snapshots of the contemporary philosophical scene in Africa and the West. As indicated, these pictures are taken from a high altitude, glossing over notable exceptions and significant nuances. In the chapters that follow, we will explore the two accounts closer to the ground; yet first, we have further stage setting to do. To make sense of how the two positions arose, this section considers what came before. It switches from a 'snapshot' to a 'moving picture' analysis of personhood, one that considers how contemporary African and Western views arose. Considering the past will not only lend insight into ideas that shaped disparate accounts of personhood but hint at future directions that may hold promise for a more unified vision. Since African and Western philosophies each have their own distinctive histories, we approach them in a stepwise fashion, beginning with Africa, proceeding to the West, and then highlighting common ground. At the outset, we acknowledge that asymmetries exist in the written records of Africa and the West. In the West, there are about 2,000 years of philosophy that is written and transmitted in a generally uninterrupted way between generations. In Africa, even though traces of philosophical works date back to Ancient Egypt and Roman times, as do texts from ancient Islamic scholars, the transmission of these traditions into contemporary African academic philosophical literature as a distinct corpus dates only about 100 years. That is a constraint we work within.[67]

1. African origins. We indicated previously (Section 1.1) that contemporary African ethics has a sub-Saharan pedigree. Yet, what more precisely are its origins? What were the traditional beliefs held during the period before European colonization took hold? In addressing this question, it is important to note that the African academic philosophy we will be drawing on is relatively recent. It arrived on the scene during the latter half of the twentieth century, when African philosophy became a written academic discourse and African philosophers took positions in academic settings. Previously, aside exceptions in places like Egypt and Sudan, and part of the Horn of Africa, African philosophical thought was largely an oral tradition, transmitted by proverbs, idioms, songs, myths, and legends.[xii] Since these sources served robust didactic purposes, Tangwa refers to them as a form of popular philosophy, defined as a "consciously articulated and critical discourse (verbal or written) that is necessarily individual in origin" and contrasts this with strict philosophy, which is "a corpus or system of such discourses together with the supporting structures in which they are symbolically encoded."[68]

There are ongoing debates about whether pre-colonial philosophy qualifies as genuine philosophy.[69,70,71] We largely bracket these debates, proceeding on the plausible assumption that both pre- and post-colonial philosophy are forms of genuine philosophy. Following Gyekye, we note that the absence of written texts during the pre-colonial era does not imply the absence of philosophy, as some have argued.[72] After all, Socrates and Buddha philosophized, although they never wrote their philosophy down, and the Vedas (the major religious and philosophical texts of India) were preserved by oral, not written, tradition.[73]

Notably, the philosophy that preceded contemporary African philosophy was suppressed in the context of colonialism, suffering a form of epistemicide under colonialism.[74] Masolo refers to the period of colonial presence in Africa as African philosophy's "dark age,"[75] in which African sources of knowledge production

---

[xii] Although African philosophy is largely an oral tradition, Africans have written books in African languages for hundreds of years. However, few were preserved, translated, and published. For example, the Habäša people of Ethiopia and Eritrea have been reading and writing bound manuscripts in the African language of Ge'ez since the fourth century CE. Among the world's oldest Christians, the written form of their language, Ge'ez, dates to the first millennium and became the sacred language of liturgy in the church. See Belcher WL, 2015, Introduction to the Text, in Galawdewos, *The Life and Struggles of Our Mother Walatta Petros: A Seventeenth-Century African Biography of an Ethiopian Woman*, transl., Belcher WL, Kleiner M., Princeton University Press, 1–48.

were denigrated and considered useless to advancing knowledge. Masolo writes that colonizers were "convinced that they bore the responsibility of bringing civilization to Africans, and they did this by erecting their government systems modeled after those in Europe, and establishing school and education systems—both secular and missionary oriented—to pass down European value systems."[76] The notion, which Ypi refers to as *civilizing colonialism*, is distinctive in the sense that colonial rule was perceived to be a civilizing mission, in which the West sought to "educate barbarian peoples."[77] Other forms of colonialism, such as *commercial colonialism* (extracting natural resources to benefit the colonizer) and *settler colonialism* (ousting indigenous people from territories, often violently) were also present, but their influence on knowledge production was less direct (although they could be equally insidious). As we inquire about the philosophy of pre-colonial Africa, tracing the roots of relational conceptions of personhood, we do so with the recognition that our inquiry is not only an intellectual investigation but also a political act in the sense that it foregrounds a philosophical inquiry that was previously subjugated.[78]

Scholars of Southern African philosophy standardly associate contemporary relational interpretations of persons with the pre-colonial philosophy of *ubuntu*. A Nguni word with no English equivalent, *ubuntu* is known across the sub-region as *botho* (in Sotho-Tswana); *Hunhu* (in Shona); and *utu* (in Swahili). *Ubuntu* borrows from both the Xhosa *ubuntu* and the Zulu *ubuntu*, which in turn, are derived from two Bantu words, *ntu* (an adjective), meaning "person" or "human," and *ubu*, a prefix forming abstract nouns. According to the *Oxford English Dictionary*, *ubuntu* indicates "humanity," "fact of being human," or "behaviour reflecting the human ideal."[79]

Although *ubuntu* is sometimes associated narrowly with Southern and Eastern Africa, we interpret *ubuntu* broadly, as an umbrella concept covering the deep structure of African collectivist values. Nkulu-N'Sengha lends support to this interpretation, discussing the notion of *bumuntu* (a linguistic variant of *ubuntu*) in the context of a variety of sub-Saharan African peoples.[80] Nkulu-N'Sengha explains that across the sub-Saharan continent, people do not define themselves merely as individual thinking beings but as parts of a whole: "a genuine human being does not define her or his humanity merely in the Cartesian *'Cogito ergo sum'* [I think, therefore I am] terms. Rather, he or she focuses on those thoughts of goodness and compassion toward others."[81] Illustrative is the greeting of the Shona people of Zimbabwe, which expresses a feeling of humanity toward others:

> *Mangwani. Marara sei?*
> ('Good morning. Did you sleep well?')
> *Ndarara, kana mararawo.*
> ('I slept well, if you slept well.')
> *Maswera sei?*
> ('How has your day been?')
> *Ndaswera, kana maswerawo.*
> ('My day has been good, if your day has been good').[82]

Reference to *ubuntu* first appeared in written form in 1846, when the term was used to indicate a positive human quality.[83] Gade notes that at first, *ubuntu* was described as 'an excellent African quality,' 'the admirable qualities of the Bantu,' and more broadly as 'goodness of nature,' 'greatness of soul,' and 'a good moral disposition.' During the second half of the twentieth century, *ubuntu* was used not just to indicate qualities of character but also to indicate a more general philosophy, ethic, African humanism, or a worldview.[84] The phrase, 'I am because we are,' was reportedly a response to the Western conception of personhood associated with Descartes's dictum, 'I think therefore, I am.'[85] During the 1990s, *ubuntu* became associated with the Nguni proverb, 'a person is a person through other persons' (*umuntu ngumuntu ngabantu*), taking on its distinctive modern flavor. Although the combined form of *ubu* and *ntu* are commonly translated as the English, 'humanness,' a better translation is 'human dignity,' which reflects both the term's *ontological* and *normative* features.

The *ontological* dimension of *ubuntu* refers to the kind of thing humans are. According to Shutte, "a point agreed on by virtually all [African] writers on the topic is that persons are defined not by this or that natural property or set of properties but by the relationships between them and others."[86] While different renderings of the relationship between individual and community are possible, there is nonetheless a wide consensus on the broader view that "Self and world are united and intermingle in a web of reciprocal relations."[87]

Menkiti tells us that the ontological aspect of this relational account articulates "a certain conception of the person found in traditional African thought."[88] Contrasting it with the predominant conception associated with Western philosophy, Menkiti writes that the African ontology "denies that persons can be defined by focusing on this or that physical or psychological characteristic of the lone individual. Rather, [a person] is defined by reference to the environing community."[89] Likewise, when Mbiti coins the dictum "I am because we are," Mbiti claims to represent traditional African thought, noting, "In traditional life, the individual does not and cannot exist alone. . . . [T]he child must go through rites of incorporation so that it becomes fully integrated into the entire society. These rites continue throughout the physical life of the person during which the individual passes from one stage of corporate existence to another."[90]

Metz explains the difference between Western and African ontologies of personhood by drawing an analogy with two ways of characterizing water. The first, Western, way holds, "water is . . . essentially H2O, while a self is considered to be identical to a chain of mental states, a brain or a soul"; by contrast, the second, African, way holds that "water is (at least in part) essentially what plays a certain role in an ecosystem, while a self is constituted by its relationships with other selves and perhaps an environment."[91]

The *normative* component of *ubuntu* prescribes a shared responsibility on the part of individuals and communities to support those with whom they are connected, helping them throughout their continuing process of becoming persons. An *ubuntu* ethic holds that to be a person in the moral sense requires pro-social virtues or the capacity to develop them. According to Gyekye, "used normatively, the judgment, '[someone] is a person,' means '[that individual] has a good character', '... is generous', '... is peaceful', '... is humble', '... has respect for others.'"[92] Unlike self-realization views of virtue, the features of character considered essential to being a person in the African sense are other-directed. Unlike care-focused feminism, an *ubuntu* ethic prescribes sharing an entire way of life, making African approaches importantly distinct from feminist approaches, despite notable parallels.[93]

Nkulu-N'Sengha argues that the normative rendering of *ubuntu* is widespread across the sub-Saharan region.[94] The Baluba of Central Africa distinguish 'the true human being' (*Muntu wa fine*) from 'the empty shell' or 'non-person' (*Muntu wa bitupu*); their cosmology distinguishes 'a genuine human being' (*Muntu*) from 'a thing' (*Kintu*); and they say of someone who is not a person that 'S/he is a dead body walking' (*I mufu unanga*) or a 'a zero person' (*Muntu bituhu*). Similarly, the Yoruba people of Nigeria say, 'he/she is not a person' (*Ki I se eniyan*) and draw a distinction between the ordinary sense of human being (*Eniyan*) and the normative sense of being a genuine human being. The Akan people of Ghana distinguish between persons with conscience (*Tiboa*) and beasts (*Aboa*) who have no conscience. In South Africa, one finds the expression, 'he is not a man' (*Ga se Motho*).

The ethics associated with *ubuntu* has been described as maximal, and as collapsing the usual distinction between obligatory and supererogatory acts.[95] It has also been characterized as thoroughgoing, i.e., encompassing the person in their entirety: good thought and heart (*mucima muya*); good speech (*ludimi luya*); good actions (*bilongwa biya*), and a generally good way of looking at people and the world.[96] The list of virtues associated with African personhood is expansive, pointing to an ideal or flourishing human life; it includes, among others, compassion, kindheartedness, generosity, truthfulness, honesty, friendliness, caring, respecting, loving, gratitude, and helpfulness. It is fair to say that the thrust of African personhood is human beings in their fullness and flourishing.

By foregrounding character, *ubuntu* ethics privileges duties rather than rights. Although some African philosophers reject rights altogether,[97] most consider rights as a secondary moral requirement, triggered when individuals' needs are not met by the primary requirement of people fulfilling duties. Menkiti conceives of rights along these lines, stating that "priority is given to the duties which individuals owe to the collectivity, and their rights ... are seen as secondary to the exercise of their duties."[98] Likewise, Gyekye paints a picture of African ethics that elevates duties, but still finds a role for rights; Gyekye states, "African ethics does not give shortshrift to rights as such; nevertheless . . . [i]n this morality duties trump rights, not the other way around."[99]

Comparing historical and present-day African thought, we discern consistent themes, which stand in contrast to the view of personhood pervasive in the West. This seems to strengthen, not weaken, points of contrast noted previously (Section 1.3). Yet, before concluding that African and Western personhood are consistently different, we have yet to ask about the historical precursors of Western personhood.

2. *Western origins.* Contemporary Western analyses of persons as rational agents are often traced to the Enlightenment, and especially Kant. It was during the eighteenth century that the modern idea of persons as free and equal individuals with an inherent worth and dignity took hold. However, the historical sources of these ideas are older. Part of unearthing the history of Western personhood will involve examining pre-Enlightenment accounts, especially those dating to Graeco-Roman antiquity.

In contrast to the modern emphasis on the equality of persons, a fulcrum of ancient thought was the idea of natural inequality. A person's superior or inferior status required no justification because it was ordained by nature, which distributed reason unequally among the classes. As Siedentop explains, the origins of such a belief trace to ancient religious ideas, which shaped first the domestic sphere and later the ancient city.[100] In the earliest Greek families, religion was exclusively domestic. Male heads of households became domestic gods at death, reflecting their superior status within the patriarchal family. After death, the family's worship ensured a man's immortality, symbolized by a continuously burning fire in the family hearth, which "could not be allowed to die out, for it was deemed to be alive. Its flickering, immaterial flame did not just represent the family's ancestors, it *was* their ancestors, who were thought to live underground and who had to be provided with food and drink, if they were not to become malevolent spirits."[101] Ancestors accepted offerings only from family members and gods were not shared.

The oldest Greek and Roman societies believed in a second existence, after the first, which was available exclusively to select men.[xiii] According to Fustel: "the celestial abode was never regarded as anything more than the recompense of a few great men"; during the second existence, "the soul did not go into a foreign world. . . . [I]t remained near men and continued to live under ground [sic]. . . . [W]hen a body was buried, . . . ancient people believed they buried something that was living" and that "the life of the dead should be kept underground (*Sub terra censebant reliquam vitam agi mortuorum*)."[102]

[xiii] There is evidence that early African societies held a similar view. Referring to the Nso' people of the Northwest region of Cameroon, Chilver writes that "Nso' say that before the foreigners came . . . [t]he earth was viewed as the place where the ancestors, the important dead, were, and that they pervade it: they were said to 'sleep' underfoot and could be awakened." Chilver goes on to describe doorbells that roused the royal dead from their underground slumber. Yet, only those with *sëm* (sorcery or magic) were thought to survive death as invocable persons; ordinary men "just give up their life-breath to air." (Chilver EM, 1990, Thaumaturgy in Contemporary Traditional Religion: The

The earliest cities were associations of families ordered in accordance with domestic religious practice. As families grouped together, the boundaries of each family were retained: "just as two sacred fires and the gods they embodied could not be merged, even through intermarriage, so family enclosure had to remain distinct."[103] In the first Greek and Roman cities, each family, by law, kept a separate space: "the same wall could not be common to two houses; for then the sacred enclosure of the gods would have disappeared."[104] In this way, the (modern) idea of private property was present in religion itself, since separate family dwellings were needed to protect and maintain family worship. Through inheritance of worship, ancestors lived on.

As the scale of associations increased, gods associated with forces of nature, which were more readily shared, gradually took the place of domestic gods. Thus, in cities, people deified the sea, wind, fertility, light, love, and hunting, and gave them familiar names like Apollo, Neptune, Venus, Diana, and Jupiter. According to Nagle, "the household was the all-important point of entry for all civic involvement in the *polis*. Greeks became citizens of their states not as individuals but as members of social groups, starting with the household."[105] Siedentop concurs: "The ancient city was not an association of individuals," but a society of families.[106] The process of becoming a citizen of a Greek *polis* was similar in some ways to the process of becoming a person in Africa. It required a process of incorporation. Citizenship was an achieved social and cultural status involving identifiable stages of progression through ever higher levels of involvement in the *polis* on the part of citizen candidates. Only after proof of passage through the specified rituals of initiation did a young man become eligible for recognition by his

---

Case of Nso' in Mid-Century, *Journal of Religion in Africa* 20(3): 226–247, pp. 239–241, DOI: 10.2307/1580885.) See also Blay YA, Asamando. 2017, in *Encyclopedia Britannica*. Encyclopedia Britannica Inc., https://www.britannica.com/topic/Asamando.

polis and, subsequently was he allowed to engage in the active exercise of citizenship.[107]

Just as the family had a natural hierarchy, based on an unequal distribution of reason, the ancient city was aristocratic, with the same inequalities that marked family life evident. As Crisp explains, when considering what to do, ancient Greeks considered first "what it would be best, most fitting, or the duty of someone of their social status to do" and alongside this, they considered "potentially universally virtuous qualities such as fidelity, gratitude, justice, honesty, industriousness, patience, pride, resourcefulness, thoughtfulness and wisdom."[108] Reflecting this, the earliest meanings of *person* were "a role or character assumed in real life, or in a play, etc.; a part, function, or office; a *persōna*; a semblance or guise."[109] A word with multiple origins, the classical Latin *persōna* referred to a "mask used by a player, character in a play, dramatic role" as well as "the part played by a person in life, character, role, position."[110] These ancient meanings of person accentuate public performance and conduct directed to others. By contrast, a more modern meaning has swung away from performative acts and other-directed conduct. It defines 'person' as "having human rights dignity, or worth," and "a human being as distinguished from an animal, thing, etc."[111] The modern definition implies a high moral status and worth irrespective of individuals' performance. These ancient and modern renderings of personhood, as a *mask donned in performance, part played in social life*, and *individual with high moral status* reveal that Western understandings of personhood have altered appreciably over time.

Both Plato and Aristotle reflect the older conception of persons. Each structured their ethics and politics with an eye to enabling citizens to perform their distinct natural roles. For Plato, the well-ordered state was divided into classes based on people's perceived natural disposition to be ruled by their rational, spirited, or appetitive part: rulers were disposed to be governed by reason, artisans by appetite, warriors by their spirited part.[112] Similarly, Aristotle saw class divisions in a well-ordered state as metaphysically grounded. "The state is made up of households," Aristotle says, and its management mirrors the natural management of the household.[113] Aristotle assumed that by nature "the slave has no deliberative faculty at all, the woman has, but it is without authority, and the child has, but it is immature."[114] Based on this unequal distribution of reason, Aristotle concluded that free men naturally rule slaves, women, and children. Rationality was also the basis Aristotle used to distinguish human life from that of plants and animals: "the vegetative element in no way shares in the rational principle," Aristotle wrote.[115]

The heavy emphasis on reason found in the ancients marks the beginning of a long European tradition that posits rationality as a distinguishing feature of human beings. It matches the contemporary emphasis on higher cognitive capacities as the hallmark of personhood. Kant and other Enlightenment thinkers can be said in this respect to be following in the ancients' footsteps by privileging reason and posting it as a basis for status. Yet, as noted, the ancients identified rationality as routinely unequally allotted. How did the shift to a more egalitarian view arise? It can be traced to the unraveling of the ancient city and the rise of Rome. Roman power subjected Greeks to a remote ruler and unsettled the idea that people acted out parts based on their natural allotment of reason; instead, people were forced to identify themselves in another way.[116]

As Christianity emerged and began to gradually spread across the Roman Empire, subtle shifts began to occur, which eventually generated larger paradigm shifts in Western thinking about personhood. First, early Christians held that their individual faith in Jesus, combined with their moral agency, would secure for them a blissful life and immortality following death, much as ancestor worship had once done for select men within the household. Thus, "the individual replaced the family as the focus of immortality."[117]

Second, the Judeo-Christian tradition introduced the belief that all individuals were created in the image and likeness of God (*imago Dei*).[xiv] This meant that each person, irrespective of social rank, was equal as God's creature and in their relationship with God (although this idea was at times poorly reflected in the history of Christian *praxis*). Third, Christianity left a legacy of monotheism inherited from Judaism, but with a difference. From the early days, Christians preached not only that their god was the one true God, but that they had a mandate to go forth, "teach ye all nations; baptizing them in the name of the Father, and of the Son, and the Holy Ghost" and not just that, but also, "Teaching them to observe all things whatsoever I have commanded you."[118] Thus, Christianity approached the world with both a monotheistic idea of one god, and a proselytist claim to bring all people under a single universal truth and moral code. For this reason, when Christians later traveled to the Americas and Africa during the fifteenth century and made contact with indigenous peoples, they sought to convert pagans to Christianity, to teach them 'truth' and coach them in the moral life. In the case of Spaniards in the 'new world,' debates about the personhood of native peoples were colored by a mix of economic interests, which favored denying personhood to indigenous people, and missionaries' aims, which were to save indigenous people's souls. Pope Paul III eventually interceded, declaring in 1537 that "'the Indians are truly men and that they are . . . capable of understanding the catholic faith.'"[119] Still, debates over the 'Indians' humanity' did not abate.[120] Hanke reports that "Even late in the sixteenth century, the Jesuit missionary Jose de Acosta found not only a diversity of opinion on Indian affairs but that 'not a few people doubted whether the Indians could be saved.'"[121]

[xiv] The English translation, 'image and likeness,' does not do justice to the Hebrew *tselem* and *demut* which, according to Buber, make all humans *subjects*—not objects—i.e., capable of 'I and You' relationships that have their primordial grounding in the 'I and You' relationship with God. (See Buber M, 1970, *I and Thou*, Charles Scribner's Sons.)

In addition to initiating a shift toward a more individualist conception of persons, the rise of Christianity set in motion a third notable shift. It equalized moral worth, elevating all humans to a status historically held by a privileged few. Vlastos characterizes modern society as a "single-status" society, or as a caste society in which there is just one very high caste—'every [individual] a Brahmin.'[122]

A fourth notable change that Christianity introduced to Western views of personhood was a shift in the perceived locus of moral worth. Christianity depicted human beings as possessing an inner worth, because each was created in God's image (*imago dei*) with a spiritual immortal soul that can be saved or lost and will ultimately be judged at death. Thus, human beings possessed within themselves an image of God's infinite and immeasurable moral worth.

Fifth, the spread of Christianity altered the understanding of humanity. Humanity as *imago Dei* was overtly moral; it implied that human beings not only had an elevated rank but also an inner preciousness and superlative moral value, which theologians posited in the soul.

Sixth, with the rise of Christianity, human worth became all-or-nothing, not a matter of degree. Describing the modern view of persons, Vlastos says, "the moral community is not a club from which members may be dropped for delinquency. Our morality does not provide for ... half-castes."[123]

Finally, the meaning of saying of someone that they are a 'good person' shifted as Christianity spread across the Roman Empire. During an earlier period, 'person' implied performing well in a part or role. Thus, Aristotle's notion of *aretê* (virtue or excellence) referred to performing well as a human being by "using reason well over the course of a full life."[124] During the Christian era, a good person was baptized into the faith and sought to enact God's commandments in preparation for God's future judgment.

3. A common ground? While previously (in Section 1.3) we cited striking differences between contemporary African and Western views of persons, this section has revealed features common to both. These distinct assessments relate to the fact that in the West, two distinct concepts of personhood are at play:

- *Contemporary Western: person as a human being with rights and dignity;*
- *Early Western: person as an individual performing a part or role.*

Although the contemporary conception of *person as human being with rights and dignity* contrasts with most African notions of personhood, the early Greek conception of *person as an individual performing a part or role* bears a close resemblance.

Comparing early Western understandings with both the contemporary and pre-colonial African conceptions, illuminates five shared features. First, African and classical Western accounts share the idea that a person is someone who honorably fulfills social roles. Second, both hold that a 'good person' indicates someone who performs well in social roles. Third, both endorse the view that people merit respect to varying degrees, depending on their conduct relative to a standard of conduct befitting their social station. Fourth, both allow that an individual's performance in a role or part is not necessarily fixed and can either improve or diminish. Finally, classical Western conceptions and some African conceptions (e.g., Menkiti's) hold that persons are constituted by their social group, and in this sense, social groups are conceptually prior to persons. Table 1.2 summarizes the discussion of this section. As noted, our aim here and throughout the chapter is to capture views that are widely, not universally, held by people in distinct regions. Inevitably, we skim over many nuances.

One response to the above analysis might be that even if affinities exist between African and older Western views of personhood, the West has moved on. The march of ideas marks progress, bringing us closer to the truth, and there is no turning back. In response, the history of ideas inevitably enables certain insights

Table 1.2 African and Early Western Views of Persons

	African Personhood	Early Western Personhood
1. **Intrinsic or extrinsic?** Is the source of value inside the object or outside in an individual's relations to others?	Extrinsic	Extrinsic
2. **Earned or unearned?** Is personhood an achievement an individual deserves credit for?	Earned	Earned
3. **Scalar or binary?** Is personhood a matter of degree or all-or-nothing?	Scalar	Scalar
4. **Stable or changing?** Does personhood usually change or remain stable over a person's life?	Changing	Changing
5. **Derivative or non-derivative?** Is personhood a basic concept or derived from other concepts?	Derivative/ partly derivative	Derivative

Key: African personhood = ideas prominent among black peoples indigenous to the region of Africa south of the Sahara, as captured in the works of academic philosophers; early Western personhood = the period before Greek philosophy, Aristotle, Plato

to develop while leaving others behind. In considering the historical path that Western personhood took, it is illuminating to ask, 'What was gained?' and 'What was lost?' The historical trajectory of the idea of 'person' clearly brought innumerable benefits: it allowed ideas like equality, human rights, and universal dignity to flourish. Such ideas, in turn, benefited many people by justifying the granting of legal protections and rights to individuals of different sexes, races, ages, and citizenship status. Yet, the West lost important insights along the way. It left behind the classical idea that persons are embedded, occupy social roles, and are accountable to others to behave well in social offices and positions. Furthermore, by legitimizing certain ideas as universally valid, the rise of monotheistic religion during the Christian era stymied interest in other traditions. It rejected syncretism of cultures and traditions.

Stepping back from this discussion, it seems that Africa and the West share substantive understandings about personhood that a careful study of each brings to light. Rather than being separate stories, they emerge as separate strands in a shared story about what it means to be a person and why each of us thinks of ourselves as such. The striking differences we initially observed between Africa and the West seem less stark viewed through the wide-angle lens of history, raising the provocative question of what the future portends. In asking this, our interest is not to forecast, but to *steer* the debate in the general direction we think it ought to take.

1.5 Conclusion

We began this chapter by asking, "What is a person?" We characterized contemporary African and Western answers to the question and noted marked differences. Yet after examining the precursors to contemporary African and Western views, we learned that these differences were not always present. Our analysis revealed that the sharp contrast sometimes drawn between Africa and the West is an abstraction, which takes the present moment as representative. Yet cultures are not monolithic; they change, sometimes dramatically, with the passage of time. Going forward, the persistence of present understandings of personhood are hardly inevitable. We have hinted that differences between contemporary Africa and the West can be bridged. The chapters ahead will critically examine this suggestion and offer ways to think about personhood anew.

2
Emergent Personhood

2.1 Introduction

In Chapter 1, we established striking differences between contemporary African and Western conceptions of personhood. Being a 'person' in the contemporary African philosophical literature means having superlative worth that is external, earned, scalar, changing, and derivative, while the same designation in the contemporary West signals an exceptional value that is internal, unearned, binary, stable, and foundational. Chapter 1 also introduced an argument showing that these divergent ways of thinking about personhood were not always present. Probing the historical record of personhood in the West, we argued that an older Western view displayed conspicuous affinities with African personhood, aligning across the same five parameters where today, Western and African views diverge.

In this chapter, we bring contemporary Africa and the West into closer conversation. We inch our way toward a third view of personhood, which borrows insights from each tradition while avoiding their shortfalls. Our strategy will be to return to the historical moment when the division between these approaches began—the Patristic era when Western thinking about personhood began to shift, eventually leading Africa and the West to proceed along separate paths. We ask, 'What led the West to pivot and adopt a different approach?' Without attempting to answer this question comprehensively, we formulate one plausible response and proceed to ask, 'Are these compelling reasons for abandoning an older Greek view? Are these considerations ones that secular philosophers today have reason to accept?' To address this, Section 2.2 asks, 'What was gained?' and 'What was lost?' Answering these questions, in turn, informs the inquiry in Section 2.3, where we examine how combining insights from contemporary African and Western philosophies brings to light a more compelling way of thinking about personhood, an approach we will call, *Emergent Personhood*.[i] Following the initial formulation of Emergent Personhood, we turn, in Section 2.4, to tease out its implications for the moral status of prenatal human life and the moral permissibility of abortion. Section 2.5 concludes with a more precise formulation of Emergent Personhood, which subsequent chapters will further refine.

2.2 Five Features

What led Western philosophy to move away from an older, more African-like account of personhood? What was gained and what was lost when this change occurred? Answering these questions can illuminate not only potential advantages and disadvantages of an older Greek view, but also of contemporary African accounts, given commonalities between the two. In tandem, returning to the historical moment when Western thinking parted company with pre-Christian views allows us to critique the change from an African standpoint, drawing on African insights to shed light on advantages of the older Western view that were given up. Playing the two views off one another in this way better prepares us to select features of an older Western account of personhood that we have reason to retain, as well as features we have reason to relinquish. Our selection will not necessarily coincide with what occurred

---

[i] Although Emergent Personhood is informed by and grows out of lessons from our historical analysis, it is possible to accept the philosophical view we call Emergent Personhood while rejecting our historical analysis.

historically. Today, we not only enjoy the advantage of hindsight, but we also are not subject to constraints of a Western philosophical tradition or pressures of the day, such as the expansion of imperial Rome and the rising influence of Christianity.

1. *Advantages/disadvantages of contemporary Western personhood.* Previously (Chapter 1), we traced the source of the move away from an older Greek approach to the rise of Christian views within the Roman empire, especially those beginning from the fourth century, when Christianity, under Constantine, became an accepted religion. Before the Christian era, Rome had been ordered differently, centering the patriarchal family and later, the association of families that comprised the ancient *polis* in Greece and *urbs* and *civitas* under Rome. This worldview accorded free men a superlative moral worth at birth, due to their presumed superior allotment of reason; women and slaves were considered to have an innately lower moral status, due to their apparently lesser allotments of reason. In this respect, moral standing was fixed at birth. Yet, the sons of free men were not automatically full-fledged persons. At birth, they still were morally inferior to the patriarch and to free men generally. To gain full standing, they needed to earn it, which they did by performing excellently in their roles within the family and city. Social organization was structured to foster this, enabling each individual to play their predetermined part.

During the Christian era, this Greek worldview began to come apart, and a powerful new narrative began to take hold. As early in Christianity as the second century, authors like Irenaeus began to suggest *Gloria enim Dei vivens homo, vita autem hominis visio Dei* (For the glory of God is the living man, and the life of man is the vision of God), without making distinctions between different types or categories of humans.[1] This type of reasoning was premised on the biblical idea, found in the Book of Genesis, which described humans as made in the "image and likeness of God" (*imago Dei*). If all humans were *imago Dei,* then the wheels of change were set to begin to think of humans as moral equals. This equality ultimately relied on the theological notion that all humans were endowed with a God-given soul that conferred dignity. Ensoulment provided the religious underpinning for a society where all individuals stood as moral equals—at least before God, and each had an exceptional moral worth by virtue of having a soul that reflected the divine. Rather than needing to earn full moral status through deeds, all human beings were *already* persons. In this way, the Christian narrative also elevated humanity above the rest of God's creation. This hierarchy comprised part of a larger hierarchy within medieval Christianity, which placed God at the apex, and below God, angels, humans, animals, plants, and minerals.[2]

As the hegemony of the Roman empire dissolved, the sect of Christianity that gained prominence during late Antiquity coalesced around a set of requirements that eventually undermined the intensive kin-based institutions that preceded it. In pre-Christian Europe, extensive kin-based networks were sustained and empowered through marital exchanges in which

> new marriages must occur between blood or affinal relatives (in-laws). In patrilineal societies, senior males ... administer ... ongoing spousal exchanges and thus use the marriage of their sisters, daughters, nieces, and granddaughters to cement relations with other kin-groups and nourish important alliances.[3]

The potency of marriage to support intensive kinship networks was gradually eroded as the Church instituted changes to restrict polygynous unions, arranged marriages, and all marriages between blood and affinal kin.[4] While a complex set of historical reasons led to the particular constellation of prohibitions that took shape, what matters for our purposes is that the requirements of the Church outcompeted those of other religious groups vying for power in the Mediterranean and Middle East during the pre-Christian era. While Classical Greek attitudes sanctioned and enabled marriage between first-cousin, uncle-niece, half-sib and even full-sib,[5] by mid-fifth century, the Church discouraged such unions as a violation of sacred law, citing *Leviticus*: "No man shall approach to her that is near of kin to him, to uncover her nakedness. I am the Lord."[6] Church law increased the number of forbidden degrees of consanguinity (from four to seven) and changed the method of calculating degrees of consanguinity in ways that resulted in more marriages being declared incestuous.[7] Also during this time, "the clergy fulminated against the wickedness of incest and attempted to forbid or dissolve unions they considered incestuous."[8] Christians were instructed to maintain a list of their ancestors to avoid accidentally marrying within the prohibited degrees.

The Western Church's bans on affinal marriages contributed to a loosening of kin-based institutions and a rise of independent, monogamous marriages between non-relatives. According to Henrich, these changes, in turn, shaped attitudes and values ascendant in the West: when kin-based institutions prevailed, people tended to care intensely about those they were related to; once they disappeared, people tended to develop more individualistic values and a greater openness to non-kin.[9] Bouchard characterizes the contemporary West, with its emphasis on individualism and self-reliance, as a different world from the world of pre-Christian Europe, where individuals, both in their own eyes and those of their contemporaries, were identified with their families and kinship networks.[10] These divergent viewpoints shaped emerging philosophies of personhood.

Stepping back from the above analysis, it is helpful to ask whether the shift to a more individualistic conception of persons carries traction for those who do not share its religious underpinnings. Judeo-Christian personhood was grounded on the idea that all and only human beings are made in the image of God (*imago Dei*); for contemporary secular philosophers, there seems to be no corollary justification for claiming that all and only human beings qualify as persons. Some contemporary Christians, such as Noonan, have sought to defend an exclusive moral status for human beings by arguing that possessing the human genetic code affords the secular underpinnings for such a position.[11] Yet, this proposal was eventually rebuffed as 'speciesist.' 'Speciesism,' a term coined in the 1970s by Ryder[12] and popularized by Singer,[13] is the position that assigning moral standing on the basis of species membership is morally arbitrary.

The absence of any secular basis for what became a widely held view of personhood in the West was unsettling, especially after the Renaissance, when more secular approaches predominated. Philosophers were challenged to find a non-arbitrary quality that all and only human beings shared that would warrant according to them an exceptional moral standing. Ultimately, the search did not succeed. Instead, proposed substitutes—such as having a capacity for reason or the ability to suffer—led to demoting some people's moral standing, and elevating others. For example, if reason is a sufficient condition for personhood, then some human beings with intellectual impairment lack personhood, while some intelligent animals, such as orangutans and elephants, might qualify as persons. If the capacity to suffer is the basis for moral personhood, then humans in a persistent vegetative state (PVS) or anencephalic infants lack full moral standing, while some non-human animals, such as chickens and cows, presumably have it. The larger worry is what we call *the conundrum of personhood* in the West. The conundrum arose when secular Western philosophy relinquished the Judeo-Christian soul, leaving a philosophical void. There was no secular substitute able to achieve the same thing, namely, to justify a superlative and equal moral worth for all and only human beings.

Even though Judeo-Christian personhood lacked a clear grounding in secular philosophy, it offered important advantages for believers and non-believers alike. First, it established a way to grant all human beings an inherent and inalienable worth and dignity rather than reserving this privilege for a select few. During a later, enlightenment period, these ideas formed part of the philosophical underpinnings for human rights theory and for modern liberal societies, in which all people have equal and intrinsic rights as free and rational beings. These same ideas eventually found expression in the French and American revolutions, and in social contract theories of the seventeenth to early nineteenth centuries, which held that even outside civilized society, in a hypothetical state of nature, people had natural rights meriting respect.

Second, since having a soul was considered all-or-nothing, rather than a matter of degree, all humans had an *equal* moral standing. We regard this as an advantage because it helped to eliminate inherent inequalities that had marked ancient Greece and divided slaves from free men, citizens from non-citizens, men from women, and adults from children. It simultaneously meant that human moral status could not be lost or diminished, even when an individual's accomplishments fell short or others judged them harshly. Darwall's conception of 'recognition respect' (from Chapter 1, Section 1.3) encapsulates this idea of equal moral respect, namely, all human beings merit a certain kind of respect because of the kinds of beings they are. The Christian medieval vision did not necessarily eliminate differences in moral standing indexed on individuals' achievements but shifted such judgments to the afterworld. Thus, heaven was reserved for morally successful persons while the pains of hell were the endpoint of the immoral.

A third and related advantage of Judeo-Christian personhood was to make being a person a foundational status rather than derivative of incorporation in a given community. This carried the advantage of making it easier for people to question their social roles and relationships and see themselves as freer to carve out new roles and opportunities in life. It also invited questioning of social authority and social structures more broadly, because individuals could reject society's demands without putting their moral status in jeopardy. Although the Church exerted pressure to fulfill social roles, making it a condition to the attainment of eternal life in heaven, fulfilling these roles was not a requirement of personhood. In this respect, shirking of social duties and rebellion against society became more conceivable. The Christian viewpoint helped to cultivate these possibilities by shifting emphasis away from established earthly communities toward a Christian community that transcends earthly boundaries of nation and tribe. This idea is evident, for example, in the *Epistle to Diognetus*, which though written in the second century was rediscovered in the sixteenth: "Christians are not distinguished from the rest of mankind by country, or by speech, or by customs.... [W]hile they dwell in Greek or barbarian cities according as each [individual's] lot was cast... [t]hey live... simply as sojourners[;] ... every foreign land is to them a fatherland, and every fatherland a foreign land."[14]

Yet, despite its advantages, Judeo-Christian personhood had distinct disadvantages for secular philosophy. First, as noted, to find a secular substitute for the soul that could provide the basis for human personhood proved difficult. Each proposed alternative brought limitations, often making outliers of those who were ordinarily counted as persons. A prominent example is given by Kittay, who objects to positing higher cognitive capacities as the basis for personhood, because this requirement makes an outlier of Kittay's daughter, Sesha, who is profoundly mentally and multiply disabled.[15] Kittay points to a number of reasons for Sesha being accorded personhood, all of which are unrelated to the capacity for thought: the human way in which Sesha appreciates music; shows sensitivity to others; stands in social relationships; evinces a "strong clear sense of herself"; "is capable of great joy and great love"; and seems to remember and anticipate people, places, and music she has not heard for years.[16] Kittay reasons that Sesha's intellectual limitations might mean that Sesha lacks the capacity to understand distinct moments of life as a meaningful whole, yet rejects the idea that this shows that Sesha should be compared to non-human animals in worth or dignity. Although Sesha cannot express cognitive capacities, and has no measurable IQ, "what Sesha can do she does as a *human* would do them, though frequently imperfectly, but it is *humanly* imperfect."[17] Kittay's conclusion is that Sesha's life contains "an immeasurable amount of good."[18] In line with Kittay's views, Steinbock observes that people are not willing to treat human beings with intellectual impairment like animals with comparable intellectual capacities but instead insist on regarding them as fellow human beings.[19]

Other proposed secular grounds for moral considerability, such as the capacity to suffer, also go against the grain of many people's considered views. For example, we do not ordinarily regard a human toddler's interests as on a par with those of a pig or a dolphin, yet all three arguably have similar capacities to suffer. In a forced choice situation where we could save only one, most think we ought to save the human toddler, not the pig or the dolphin. Many (but not all)[ii] philosophers hold that human beings without the capacity to suffer, such as anencephalic infants, do not lack moral standing altogether; instead, it matters morally that an anencephalic infant belongs to a human family and has ties to human beings.[20,21,22] While non-human animals might be judged 'part of the family,' their moral standing is not on par with human family members. For example, we do not regard a beloved pet to be morally on a par with a sibling or a parent (or with a more distant relative, e.g., a second cousin, twice removed). The basis for the difference in moral status is not that humans possess a unique property (e.g., consciousness), but rather, as humans, we relate to other humans in unique and morally powerful ways.

A second disadvantage of Judeo-Christian personhood for contemporary secular thought is that the moral imperative to perform in social roles and fulfill social duties seems largely undercut. Gone is the idea that to be a person one must first perform excellently in social life and meet duties to others and the community. Instead, the view that eventually replaced this held that just as

---

[ii] Persson and Savulescu argue that we should revise our judgments about cases like this, relinquishing what they consider an arbitrary form of speciesism, even if revising our judgments requires altering human brains (Persson I, Savulescu J, 2012, *Unfit for the Future: The Need for Moral Enhancement*, Oxford University Press).

people are free to enter or leave civil society, they are free to accept or reject their social roles and the duties attached to them. The implications of this are far-reaching. For example, filial duty no longer has a clear ethical justification. As Daniels observes, there are no obvious grounds in Western moral philosophy today for asserting that there are such things as filial duties owed by adult offspring to aging parents.[23] Slote argues that parental authority is underlaid by illusions that must be shed.[24] Schoeman insists that "talk about rights of others, respect for others, and even welfare of others is to a certain extent irrelevant" when it comes to family members and others we are close to.[25] This response is unsettling, not only because the owing idiom is often used to talk about filial responsibility (and other family roles), but because many people believe that adult offspring have duties to their parents, assuming parents meet ordinary parental duties in ways that satisfy certain constraints.[26] Likewise, some Western views regard duties to help neighbors and needy citizens as purely elective, valorizing a conception of humans as free and autonomous agents, while relegating duties attaching to social relationships to the realm of charity.[27]

2. *Advantages/disadvantages of African personhood.* Since the older Greek view closely resembles contemporary African approaches to personhood, the critique of what was lost and gained when the Greek view was set aside has implications for how we ought to think about African personhood today. Specifically, it informs the assessment of African personhood in two ways. First, what was lost when the older view was let go points to corresponding advantages of African personhood that we should try to retain. Second, what was gained by shifting away from the Greek account of personhood indicates features of African personhood that we should relinquish.

Consider first, the advantages of African personhood. It is an advantage of African personhood (and of the older Greek view) that it can provide a secular standard that can do much of the heavy lifting that the Judeo-Christian soul did for the West.[iii] African personhood sets forth a secular criterion, relating to others in pro-social ways or having the capacity to relate, as a basis for personhood. This aspect of African personhood promises a way to resolve the conundrum of personhood in the West by providing a relational alternative to the Judeo-Christian soul. Notably, this kind of approach was not a serious contender in the West until quite recently, when certain strands within Western thought, such as feminist[28,29,30,31] and communitarian[32,33] philosophies, reacted to what they considered excessively rationalist and individualistic elements in Western thought. A relational basis for personhood is an aspect of African thought we will retain, in modified form, in our proposed approach to personhood.

Second, African personhood has the advantage of providing a secure basis for social duties to others and the community, since being a person hinges on fulfilling these duties. By emphasizing duties to others, before rights, African philosophy, like the older Greek approaches we glimpsed, invite seeing oneself as part of a group with associated responsibilities.[iv] African accounts not only attach honor and social esteem to consistently helping others. This is an advantage we will keep, in a modified form, when formulating a new conception of personhood.

In addition to these advantages, African personhood has shown distinct advantages when it comes to the moral standing of non-humans, including not only animals[34] but also the natural and built environment,[35,36] by viewing them along a continuum rather than attributing all-or-nothing moral status. African views also invite a nuanced assessment of the moral status of novel entities, such as

---

[iii] Our point is that African personhood is at least *potentially* secular, although not all African philosophers give a secular rendering of personhood. By contrast, the Judeo-Christian conception, because it makes having a soul a necessary condition for personhood, is not even potentially secular.

[iv] Some Western approaches, such as Kantian ethics, are duty-based too. However, in the African tradition the duties in question are unassumed positive duties, while for Kant, each rational agent wills the duties to which they will be subject.

artificially intelligent agents[37,38] and extraterrestrial life. Generally speaking, African ways of thinking promise more finely grained judgments about the moral status and personhood of diverse creatures and things. We will partially retain this feature.

Yet, African personhood also brings significant drawbacks, corresponding to what was gained by relinquishing the older, Greek view of persons. First, some versions of African personhood exclude healthy adult human beings from the ranks of personhood if they habitually harm others or perform poorly in social roles.[v] For example, Menkiti holds that personhood is "attained in direct proportion as one participates in communal life through the discharge of the various obligations defined by one's stations."[39] We reject this feature of African personhood, and it will not form part of our conception of personhood.

Second, it is a conspicuous feature and potential disadvantage of some African accounts that gaining or losing personhood depends on others' appraisal. This seems to collapse the distinction, noted earlier (Chapter 1), between recognition and appraisal respect. While Gyekye underscores supererogation as a positive, aspirational element in African thought,[40] its downside is to diminish the personhood of those who fall short or exclude outright those who habitually misbehave. African feminists critiquing *ubuntu* have flagged concerns that community determinations of who qualifies as a person embed existing power hierarchies, such as "privileging some persons on the basis of, for example, unequal social status, gender inequalities, and age differences."[41] Our view will uphold the distinction between recognition and appraisal respect in a modified way.

---

[v] An exception is Gyekye, who regards all human beings as full-fledged persons and distinguishes between moral and social standing. Gyekye holds that "a human person is a person whatever [their] age or social status. . . . [O]ne is a person because of what [one] is, not because of what [one] acquires" (Gyekye K, 2010, Person and Community in African Thought, in Wiredu K, Gyekye K, eds., *Person and Community: Ghanaian Philosophical Studies, I*. Council for Research in Values and Philosophy (Washington, DC), 101–122, p. 108.

A third disadvantage of African personhood is that it permits inequalities between human beings, with some considered greater and others lesser persons. Just as the Ancient Greek view tolerated inequalities between men, women, slaves, and children, based on putatively different allotments of reason, African personhood tolerates inequalities based largely on perceived social performance. For example, Menkiti states that "personhood is something at which individuals could fail, at which they could be competent or ineffective, better or worse.... Full personhood is not perceived as simply given at the very beginning of one's life, but is attained."[42] For Menkiti, attaining personhood requires being incorporated in a community: "Without incorporation into this or that community, individuals are considered to be mere danglers to whom the description 'person' does not apply."[43] Gyekye characterizes the Akan view of personhood thus: "When an individual appears in [their] conduct to be wicked, bad, ungenerous, cruel, selfish, the Akan would say of that individual, that '[they are] not a human person' (*onnye' nipa*)" and when the individual displays moral excellence, the Akan would say "'[they are] a real (human) person' (*ōye onipa paa*)."[44] Since the Akan hold that moral capacities can be developed only by participating in a community, incorporation in a community forms an essential grounding for personhood. Gyekye expresses the point thus: "If a human being lives an isolated life, a life detached from the community, [they] would be described *not* as a person but as an individual."[45] The ancient Greek view of personhood also regarded being incorporated into a family or community as vital for personhood; until children were incorporated, the Greeks regarded them as non-persons. Both African and early Greek philosophies subscribe to the view that people have different moral standing as persons based on their conduct in social roles. Our account of personhood, by contrast, will insist on equal moral standing and worth for all human beings from birth to death that cannot be diminished or lost.

Tables 2.1 and 2.2 recap key advantages and disadvantages of African, early Greek, and Judeo-Christian personhood.

If the analysis of this section is persuasive, it suggests a path forward. The next step is articulating a view of personhood that builds on advantages of African and Western approaches, while avoiding disadvantages. The approach resembles reflective equilibrium. Since African and Western views of personhood run afoul of considered judgments, we propose a view of personhood that better captures them. In the section that follows, we set forth a philosophy of personhood that meets the following diverse, apparently discordant, desiderata: (1) all human beings qualify; (2) qualifying is independent of others' appraisal yet furnishes a basis for duties

Table 2.1 Advantages/Disadvantages of African and Early Greek Personhood

Feature	African and Early Greek Personhood	
	Advantage	Disadvantage
Extrinsic	Includes relational features	Excludes individuals who do not stand in particular relationships
Earned	Grounds social duties	Depends on others' appraisal, excludes people who habitually misbehave
Scalar	Allows nuanced moral assessment of non-humans and nature	Permits inequalities between humans
Changing	Aspirational	Allows human personhood to be lost/diminished
Derivative	Relates individuals to a human community	Makes personhood contingent on incorporation in a particular community

Key: African personhood = views prominent among black peoples indigenous to the region of Africa south of the Sahara, as captured in the works of academic philosophers; early Greek personhood = the period before Greek philosophy, Plato, Aristotle

Table 2.2 Advantages/Disadvantages of Judeo-Christian Personhood

Feature	Judeo-Christian Personhood Advantage	Disadvantage
Intrinsic	Includes all human beings	Ignores relational features
Unearned	Independent of others' appraisal	Does not directly afford a basis for social duties toward others
Binary	Establishes human equality	Does not allow nuanced moral assessment of non-humans and nature
Stable	Human personhood cannot be lost/diminished	Personhood does not establish an aspirational purpose or goal
Non-derivative	Establishes a basis for personhood independent of the community	Disassociates personhood from human community

toward others; (3) personhood is held equally by all human beings, but to varying degrees by non-humans; (4) human personhood cannot be lost or diminished, but non-human personhood can be lost or diminished; (5) and personhood is independent of performance in social roles, yet incorporates relational attributes.

2.3 Emergent Personhood

From the foregoing analysis, we can begin to tease out some of the central strands of African and Western personhood that we have reason to keep, weaving them together into a coherent new view, which we call, *Emergent Personhood*[vi]. Emergent Personhood

---

[vi] Our discussion of Emergent Personhood draws on Jecker NS, Atuire CA, 2024, Personhood: An Emergent View from Africa and the West (Developing World Bioethics, ahead of print, DOI: 10.1111/dewb.12461).

borrows from African personhood the idea that personhood gives grounds for social duties and incorporates relational features. It borrows from Western Judeo-Christian personhood the idea that all human beings qualify as persons independent of others' appraisal and have an equal moral standing that cannot be diminished or lost.

1. Human personhood. Seen through Western eyes, Emergent Personhood will require relinquishing the supposition that human beings count as persons only if they develop an internal state or quality they did not have previously, such as a capacity for consciousness, self-awareness, or rationality. One problem with this supposition is that it implies that a human being without the requisite intellectual capacities is not a person. We hold instead that when a particular human being experiences some *privation*, lacking capacities that human beings ordinarily have, we still *relate* to them as human beings, seeing in them a human being like us, a reflection of humankind. Privation indicates a loss or absence of something that does not change the individual's underlying humanness or moral standing; expressed differently, it is "a type of deficiency that does not alter the nature of the being in which it is found."[46] An ancient concept, 'privation' is found in Aristotle[47] and Aquinas,[48] although it is less common in the modern lexicon.

A further problem with stressing mental capacities is that the picture it conjures shows persons as arising separately, as if floating free of any relationships with other human beings. Emergent Personhood theorizes instead that beings with superlative moral worth emerge through social relational processes, yet display features not present in these processes considered separately. The intuitive idea of emergence is that an object may have properties as a whole that are not present in any of its parts considered on their own.

At first pass, an emergent account of personhood can be characterized by comparing persons to pictures. A picture emerges from component parts yet is more than the sum of the parts. The picture displays new features. It may express harmony or balance, feelings or ideas. It may symbolize, abstract from, or represent something. These features were not present before the picture came together—brush strokes and pixels do not convey these qualities on their own. In similar fashion, a person emerges out of a complex configuration of relationships involving human beings; we might say they become a 'being-in-relationship.' The emergent 'being-in-relationship' is a person, showing aspects, including superlative moral worth, not present before the relationships came together. Yet a person is not *merely* the sum of these relationships, because the person that emerges has a being of their own, over and above the relationships they emerge from.

To explain further, consider a different analogy. A vocal quartet typically includes a soprano, alto (or mezzo-soprano), tenor, and bass (or baritone). When they come together to sing unaccompanied, they produce vibrations that people perceive when sound travels through the air to their eardrums (tympanic membranes), which in turn stimulates neurons, which send signals to the brain. At any moment that it exists, a vocal quartet's music depends for its existence on all these vocalists, their interacting behaviors, and processes (which likewise depend one way or another on the properties and interacting behaviors of their fundamental components). Yet what emerges from the quartet differs profoundly from what each vocalist can produce alone, as is reflected in the fact that someone who is a fan of vocal quartets can relish quartet music yet know nothing about the physics and human biology required to make it.

Like the vocal quartet, human persons emerge through a certain combination of elements and processes configured in a certain way. Like them, persons are more than their basal phenomena considered separately—they exhibit exceptional moral worth, a remarkable feature, not present at the base. When persons arise, the substratum that gives rise to them includes human beings interrelating. The basal human relationships we are referring to are not specific concrete ones, like ties to particular people, but the existential connection each of us has with every other human being. Even when someone is socially isolated or lacks neurodevelopmental mechanisms requisite for certain forms of relationships, we can still say of them that they stand in a relationship with us qua human being. So understood, emergence does not occur through a single relationship between two people, or by means of a particular social network, or even a subset of relationships that are outstanding in some respect (e.g., harmonious, morally excellent, or caring). Instead, persons come about through a constellation of human relationships that coalesce in a certain way, such that each human being has a connection with every other. Abstractly, the origins of persons can be thought of as tracing to every human being who has ever lived and ever will live. Yet, the more immediate sources of personhood are social relational processes that humans have with other humans here and now. While each person can be distinguished as a separate being, they can also be identified in terms of the social relationships that give rise to them—we might say that an individual is a piece of the whole, cut from the same cloth, part of the fabric of humankind. *When I value a human being as a person, what I value is all humanity reflected in that person.* Ascertaining a person thus becomes less a matter of looking inside someone's head to identify brain waves indicative of consciousness or cognitive functioning, and more a matter of looking into a mirror and seeing all humanity.

Seen through African eyes, Emergent Personhood requires relinquishing the belief that humans achieve personhood by becoming incorporated in a particular community and exhibiting pro-social virtues. As noted, a problem with this approach is that it renders human beings unequal and allows for the possibility that some human beings who are unincorporated or behave poorly do not count as full-fledged persons. Rather than scoring moral status and requiring a high mark to qualify, Emergent Personhood theorizes that human beings have equal moral status, each standing equally in a certain relationship with all humankind. Yet our characterization differs from simply saying that someone is genetically or biologically human; it points instead to human-human relationships as basal phenomena giving rise to something *more*—a human being with outstanding moral worth. What we might call a *family* of humanity conveys this connection when understood not as biologic or genetic similarity, but a family-like tie. When human beings are configured in this family-like way, persons emerge. In some African languages, this idea is suggested by the very meaning of the word, 'person.' For example, in Buili, a person (*nurbiik*) is literally "a son or daughter" of a person.[49] According to the Bulsa understanding, "a human being is considered as one who matters to someone.... Personhood is thus a relationally derived category."[50] Reflecting this, the Bulsa customarily introduce themselves by first indicating their family name, then their first name, underscoring that each person exists within a network of constitutive relations and a lineage.

Seen through Western eyes, Emergent Personhood requires abandoning the belief that personhood consists of a discrete thing, such as an internal mental state. This approach has proved to be not only too narrow, but too broad—it excludes some human beings with serious intellectual impairment and regards intelligent animals like pigs as potentially morally equal to human infants or people with intellectual impairment. Emergent Personhood takes a different tack. It directs our gaze outward, to the ways in which people and things join together and relate, and the ways in which they move apart and disband. It holds that persons—entities of superlative moral worth that are valued for their own sakes—are constituted in and through relational goings on. When relationships acquire a certain intensity and amalgamate in a certain way, they are generative, giving rise to the exceptional moral worth we associate with persons.

An emergent approach to personhood is in sync with a growing body of scholarly literature spanning multiple fields—ranging from philosophy,[51] systems theory,[52] linguistics,[53,54,55] and science,[56,57] to religion[58] and art.[59] In Western philosophy, emergence traces at least to the early Greeks. Aristotle held that "the totality is not, as it were, a mere heap, but the whole is something besides the parts,"[60] and "the whole is not the same as the sum of its parts."[61] More recently, philosophers have taken emergentist approaches to understanding the mind and to giving a philosophical account of theories in contemporary science. While less common, emergent approaches have appeared in ethics.[62,63,64,65] Stringer, for example, defends a metaethical stance that straddles the line between naturalism and non-naturalism, asserting that moral properties emerge from ordinary natural properties but are robustly irreducible and *sui generis*.[66]

When philosophers today characterize phenomena as 'emergent,' they typically mean that they display some or all of a family of features: being irreducible, unpredictable or unexplainable, holistic, and requiring novel concepts.[67] Emergent Personhood exhibits many of these hallmark features. First, it depicts the superlative value associated with persons as *novel*. Human relationships are generative, giving rise to exceptional moral worth that did not exist prior. Second, Emergent Personhood depicts persons as *holistic*: the outstanding moral worth that emerges through human-human and some non-human-human relationships is more than the sum of the parts considered on their own. Third, Emergent Personhood regards 'person' as *irreducible*. One way to explain its irreducibility is to say that 'person' cannot be analyzed fully in terms of other moral notions—we cannot boil it down to autonomy, rights, or respect.

2. *Non-human personhood*. Does theorizing persons in the way Emergent Personhood does exclude non-humans and the rest of nature? Only if humans are wholly separate from non-human animals and nature. Clearly, this is not the case. Although non-humans do not join in human-human relationships, they emerge as persons with value for their own sake through a different constellation of social relational processes. These involve a certain pattern of relationships with humans and human communities. When relationships between non-humans and humans form in this way,

non-humans with exceptional value emerge. Their value is not merely instrumental to human ends but part of a valuable whole, which involves a pro-social relationship between non-humans and humans. An advantage of picturing persons in this way is that it leaves the door open to a more inclusive view of who can qualify. For example, non-human animals, such as dogs and cows; non-living nature, such as lands, soils, and ecosystems; extraterrestrial life, if it exists; and various forms of artificial intelligence can potentially become persons through becoming incorporated in social relational processes with human beings. For example, we have argued (with Ajei) that the fictional protagonist in Ishiguro's *Klara and the Sun*, a robot named Klara, becomes a person by becoming a family member, friend, and part of a human community.[68] Klara possesses value as a constituent of these valuable relationships. Klara effectively becomes a 'robot-in-relationship,' acquiring a value she did not have before, when she was just a robot for sale in a store. Other non-living non-humans can acquire personhood similarly; for example, a river can become a 'river-in-relationship.' Non-humans who emerge as persons do not mirror humanity, yet their relating with humans generates value in itself. The superlative worth of non-humans is particular rather than generalizing to all beings of a certain kind; it continues as long as the particular non-human-human relationships that give rise to it continue.

In both the human and non-human case, Emergent Personhood grounds being a person in social relational processes involving human beings. We do not refer, e.g., to relationships that exist between other sentient and intelligent beings (e.g., between dolphins, or elephants, or crows), or between living and non-living beings (e.g., within an ecosystem). This reflects our starting point, which we call *humble anthropocentrism*. Humble anthropocentrism does not exclude the possibility that persons might emerge from relationships that do not involve human beings, yet it holds that what humans can understand about such relationships is partial and limited. Theorizing personhood as emergent from dolphin-dolphin relationships falls outside the scope of our inquiry, not because we think humans are superior but from a sober recognition of the limits of human understanding. We are incapable of fully immersing ourselves into how dolphins relate, feel, and think. Rather than expressing hubris, humble anthropocentrism expresses epistemic humility.

To clarify further, humble anthropocentrism makes both epistemic and phenomenological claims. *Epistemic humility* holds that human knowledge of animals is partial and limited. While we may wish we understood how animals think and feel, or what it is like to live like they do, our ability to understand is profoundly limited. As human beings, we do not know what it is like to live the life of a mole burrowing underground, a crow sailing and hovering in the sky, or a flounder propelling itself along the ocean floor. In a famous passage, Nagel tries to imagine what it is like to be a bat, underscoring the epistemic boundaries between species:

> Our own experience provides the basic material for our imagination, whose range is therefore limited. It will not help to try to imagine that one has webbing on one's arms, which enables one to fly around at dusk and dawn catching insects in one's mouth; that one has very poor vision and perceives the surrounding world by a system of reflected high-frequency sound signals; and that one spends the day hanging upside down by one's feet in an attic. In so far as I can imagine this (which is not very far), it tells me only what it would be like for me to behave as a bat behaves. But that is not the question. I want to know what it is like for a bat to be a bat. Yet if I try to imagine this, I am restricted to the resources of my own mind, and those resources are inadequate to the task.[69]

We undoubtedly understand more today than societies of the past, which has altered how we relate to non-humans. Still, we cannot shed our human standpoint altogether or assume a 'species neutral' stance. Rather than purporting to offer a 'view from nowhere,' or an account of persons for all sentient or rational creatures, we offer a human standpoint, and our arguments are designed to be compelling to human beings.

The second aspect of humble anthropocentrism is *phenomenological humility*, the claim that humans share crucial experiences with other humans that we do not, and cannot, share with members of any other species. The African proverb expresses it thus: *A fish and a bird may fall in love but the two cannot build a home together.* As Sorabji observes, "The deepest relationships cross the frontier of race or sex," but not the frontiers of species.[70] Midgley amplifies the point, noting that humans cannot intermarry or have children with any other known species, or farm children out for adoptions to them; humans who have been adopted by another species have been deprived of a human life and human relations.[71] Noddings ventures to say that we share a way of life with human beings, explaining that "our species is the group within which we reproduce, live our daily lives, communicate in speech, and build a culture. By virtue of this ... association members of our species have claims on us that others do not."[72] We have argued that the force of the moral claims human beings make on us has to do with precisely this—the relationship all humans stand in. This is not to say that humans exist in isolation from other species; human communities are typically multi-species, and human communities routinely form bonds with non-human species that matter for their own sakes. Midgley cites as examples communities that share a way of life with a particular animal species, "the Masai with their cattle, and ... nomads with their horses"; in these instances, a particular species comes to "play so important a part in social life that the community cannot be properly thought of without them."[73]

To illustrate the phenomenological claim, consider Nagel's account of an intelligent adult who is reduced to the level of a contended infant.

Suppose an intelligent person receives a brain injury that reduces [them] to the mental condition of a contended infant, and that such desires as remain . . . are satisfied by a custodian, so that [the individual] is free from care. Such a development would be regarded as a severe misfortune, not only for [the individual's] friends and relations, or for society, but also, and primarily, for the person.[74]

While the individual in Nagel's example suffers a devastating neurological deficit, they are still a *human being*. They may have a level of intelligence similar to some non-human animals; yet, *we relate to them as a human being*, someone whose human life took a tragic turn. It would be shocking to treat this individual like an orangutan or pig. The reason has nothing to do with any standalone qualities the impaired human being has that the orangutan or pig lack. Instead, it is entirely based on the relational space between us—the individual is my neighbor, my parent, or simply, my fellow human being. On this analysis, humans do not necessarily suffer more, or in a 'higher' way, nor do they necessarily demonstrate superior intellectual capacities. Instead, we stand in relationships with human beings that are like no other.

To reiterate: to say these things is not to say that humans are morally *superior*. It is simply to say, as Williams does, that we privilege *our* species:

There are some people who suppose that if in any way we privilege human beings in our ethical thought . . . we are implicitly reverting to a belief in the absolute importance of human beings. . . . That objection is simply a mistake. We do not have to be saying anything of that sort at all. These actions and attitudes need express no more than the fact that human beings are more important to *us*, a fact which is hardly surprising.[75]

Another way to express this point is that from a human standpoint, human beings are persons; however, from the morality of another species who inhabited a different planet, say Venusians or Martians, human beings may not qualify. Perhaps, from the standpoint of Venusian morality, Venusians are persons, while from the standpoint of Martian morality, Martians are. For Williams, and for us, our human standpoint makes "a large difference, a lot of the time, to the ways in which we treat [a] creature or at least think that we should treat it." Humble anthropocentrism leads us to hold an agnostic view about whether personhood emerges outside relationships involving human beings. It leads specifically to claiming that *although being in a relationship with a human being (either a human-human or non-human-human relationship) is sufficient for personhood, we cannot say whether it is necessary.*

To summarize, Emergent Personhood posits two ways of acquiring personhood. *The first way of becoming a person is by being a human in the circle of human relationships.* This is sufficient for personhood; it applies to human beings. *The second way of becoming a person is by acquiring moral status through habitually engaging in particular, pro-social ways with human beings.* This is sufficient for personhood; it applies to non-humans of various kinds. A common thread running throughout both is that persons emerge through social relational processes involving human beings. Table 2.3 highlights salient differences between human and non-human persons.

3. Speciesism. Is Emergent Personhood a speciesist stance? In some ways, yes; in other ways, no. 'Speciesism' is ambiguous, used to assert at least three distinct ethical claims, shown in Table 2.4. Speciesism-1 (in Table 1.4) was illustrated when 'speciesism,' was popularized by Singer during the 1970s. A central purpose was to end specific atrocities, like brutal factory farming methods and research with animal subjects that caused pain and suffering without considering animals' interests. Illustrating this, Singer describes feather-pecking and cannibalism that result from modern chicken production:

Table 2.3 Emergent Personhood's Analysis of Human and Non-human Personhood

	Do all qualify as persons?	Is qualifying independent of others' appraisal?	Are all persons moral equals?	Can personhood be lost or diminished?	Is personhood independent of performance?
Humans	Yes	Yes	Yes	No	Yes
Non-Humans	No	No	No	Yes	No

Table 2.4 What Is 'Speciesism'?

	Ethical Claim	Example
Speciesism-1	We should reject species-related abuse	Factory farming and certain uses of animals in research are wrong
Speciesism-2	All species are equal	In a forced choice situation, we are sometimes justified in prioritizing intelligent animals over people with severe cognitive impairment
Speciesism-3	Speciesism is a moral error akin to racism and sexism	We should not experiment on animals if we would not perform the same experiments on humans with similar cognitive capacities

"Chickens are highly social animals, and in the farmyard they develop a hierarchy, sometimes called a 'pecking order.' Every bird yields, at the food trough or elsewhere, to those who are higher in the pecking order, and takes precedence over those who are below. . . . [However,] 80,000 birds crowded together in a single shed is obviously a different matter. The birds cannot establish a social order, and as a result they fight frequently."[76]

This can mean lower productivity and profits, as birds peck violently at each other and become cannibals, eating the flesh of other birds. The cheapest solution for modern chicken farmers is debeaking, using "a gullotinelike device with hot blades."[77] Reacting to brutal abuses like overcrowding and debeaking chickens, Singer states it is "wrong to inflict needless suffering on another being even if that being [is] not a member of our own species."[78] We agree with Singer, and with the general ethical principle that maltreating animals is wrong (Speciesism-1 in Table 2.4). Animals have moral claims against us and are morally considerable, irrespective of their status as full-fledged persons. Factory farming animals is cruel. It causes egregious and morally indefensible animal suffering. Very few philosophers in the world today would disagree with the claim that animals matter morally for their own sakes. Midgley, who is critical of some applications of speciesism, agrees with Singer that the use of 'speciesism' to oppose animal abuse is "well placed and fully justified."[79] What is disputed is whether animals count as *moral equals* with human beings and whether species membership is *itself* a morally significant designation.

This brings us to a further use of 'speciesism,' which asserts the far stronger normative claim that all species are morally equal (Speciesism-2 in Table 2.4). Singer puts the point thus: "No matter what the nature of the being, the principle of equality requires that its suffering be counted equally with the like suffering—insofar as rough comparisons can be made—of any other species."[80] Notice that Speciesism-2, goes well beyond Speciesism-1. To protect animals from abuse and suffering, we do *not* need to hold that all species are equal! A chicken is nothing like a human being, but we shouldn't abuse chickens. Instead, Speciesm-2 is put forth to oppose practices like experimenting on animals to improve human health. Referring to the use of monkeys to study human head injury, Singer states:

If the experimenters would not be prepared to use a human infant then their readiness to use nonhuman animals reveals an unjustifiable form of discrimination on the basis of species, since adult apes, monkeys, dogs, cats, rats, and other animals are *more* aware of what is happening to them, *more* self-directing, and, so far as we can tell, at least as sensitive to pain as a human infant.[81]

Although we accept Speciesism-1, we reject Speciesism-2. We maintain that species membership is not only morally important, its importance is first order. While no animal should be abused or caused to suffer needlessly, it is *much* worse to abuse a child than a chicken. It is *not* the case that experimenting on a human infant is morally equivalent to experimenting on a dog or rat.

This brings us to Speciesism-3. Singer explains Speciesism-3 this way:

> Racists violate the principle of equality by giving greater weight to the members of their own race. . . . [S]exists violate the principle of equality by favoring the interests of their own sex. Similarly, speciesists allow the interests of their own species to override the greater interests of members of other species. The pattern is identical in each case.[82]

Is Singer right? Is species-based discrimination identical to race- and sex-based discrimination? *Only if species is morally irrelevant in the same way that race and sex are.* Yet we reject that supposition. Species *is* a morally significant grouping. Midgley elaborates,

> It is never true that, in order to know how to treat a human being, you must first find out what race [they] belong to. (Cases where this might matter turn on culture.) But with an animal, to know the species is absolutely essential. A zoo-keeper who is told to expect an animal, and get a place ready for it, cannot even begin to do this without far more detailed information. It might be a

hyaena or a hippopotamus, a shark, an eagle, an armadillo, a python or a queen bee. Even members of quite similar and closely related species can have entirely different needs.... Their vision and experience of the world [can be] ... profoundly different. To liken a trivial human grouping such as race to this enormous, inconceivably varied range of possibilities is ... a failure to recognize the scale of difference.[83]

The scale of difference between species profoundly affects not just their way of life but also their experience of the world, and our ability to know what that experience is like. In turn, it profoundly shapes the kinds of relationships we can form with them. While human beings include diverse peoples, with different languages and dialects, distinctive beliefs, and different ethnic groups, they are the same kind of being and they share a human kind of life. This connects them to every other human being and makes it possible to speak intelligently of 'a human family.' Singer's brand of utilitarianism reduces all morally relevant considerations to capacities for suffering and enjoyment. Yet, human beings are not *containers* of suffering and enjoyment. They are certain kinds of creatures that stand in certain kinds of relationships with others of their kind. Because I am human like you, we belong to the same human family and share a human way of life. We accord, or should accord, each other a high degree of moral standing by virtue of this relationship. Foot refers to this by speaking of a "a kind of solidarity between human beings, as if there is some sense in which no one is totally to *come out against* one of [their] fellow [humans]."[84] I do not (and cannot) share a human-human relationship with a hippopotamus, a shark, an eagle, an armadillo, a python, or a queen bee. *Seen as a standalone quality, species membership may seem morally arbitrary; yet seen as a quality that relates us to every other human being, species membership becomes a crucial moral consideration.*

4. *African and Western influences.* The emergent view of personhood we are developing is indebted to both African and Western

personhood. It has deep roots in African philosophy, and draws on African understandings of relational values. Like African personhood, Emergent Personhood "denies that persons can be defined by focusing on this or that physical or psychological characteristic of the lone individual"; rather, a person is "defined by reference to the environing community."[85] Yet, Emergent Personhood parts company with African personhood in salient respects. First, we do not regard personhood as unequal between human beings. Instead, the relationship that exists equally between all human beings from birth to death forms the basis for an equal personhood for all human beings. Emergent Personhood therefore differs from other relational accounts of moral status, such as Metz's, which apply gradations of moral status to human beings and maintain that "human beings that cannot be subjects of a friendly relationship have a lower moral status that those who can."[86] For Metz, while "typical humans" have an equal moral status as persons, humans who are "utterly incapable of other-regard" are not persons: "extremely autistic, psychopathic, and mentally incapacitated human beings lack a dignity comparable to ours, supposing they are indeed by nature utterly incapable of being subjects of a friendly relationship."[87] Metz qualifies this point, however, underscoring that "although these individuals would lack a dignity equal to ours, their moral status would be higher than that of animals," because as humans, they could be objects of friendly relationship with us to a much greater degree than animals like mice or elephants can.[88] Unlike Metz, we hold that human beings with intellectual impairment are moral *equals* with other human beings. They stand equally in a relationship of human to human, and this relationship gives rise to the superlative moral worth we call personhood.

Second, our view differs from some African philosophies of personhood because we reject the claim that human beings who habitually misbehave and injure others are non-persons or lesser persons; likewise, we reject the idea that those who behave habitually well toward others and the community are greater persons than others. For example, we reject (Gyekye's interpretation of) the Akan (Ghanaian) concept of a person, which holds that "'[they are] a person' means '[they have] good character,' '[they are] generous,' '[they are] peaceful,' '[they have] respect for others,'" and an individual is "truly a person (*oye onipa paa!*)" only when they show a profound appreciation of the high standards of morality.[89] In contrast to these African conceptions, we do not base human personhood on performance in particular social roles or fulfillment of social duties, but on human-human relationship as such. On our view, a person who lives virtuously exhibits a certain kind of authenticity (integrity) in the sense of living and behaving as persons ought to. By contrast, a person who is habitually evil is lacking in the sense that Neoplatonist and medieval theorists referred to as 'privation.' They lack something that persons ordinarily have, or should have, namely, a degree of moral restraint and a habit of behaving well.[90] While these privations undermine character, they do not change an individual's moral status as a person. It can be tempting in cases where people commit moral atrocities to deny their humanity, but *they are human like us, and stand in morally weighty relationships with us, as fellow human beings.*

Emergent Personhood borrows from the Judeo-Christian tradition an appreciation of the exceptional and equal value of all human beings, independent of others' appraisal, which cannot be diminished or lost. Yet it arrives at this position without grounding human personhood on possessing a soul in God's image. Instead, Emergent Personhood emerges from relationships human beings share. In this way, Emergent Personhood offers a solution to the conundrum of personhood in contemporary Western thought (introduced in Section 1.3) by setting forth a secular criterion for moral personhood that justifies an outstanding worth for all and only human beings. Although standing in a relationship with other human beings may appear to be an extrinsic feature, it is not *merely* extrinsic. A person stands in human-human relationship precisely because they are human. What's more, they are human because of the joining of humans who came before. In this respect, Emergent Personhood is a mixed view—referring to qualities that are both extrinsic and intrinsic.

Emergent Personhood also shares affinities with recent Western views of personhood that appeal to special relationships as a basis for personhood.[91] This 'relational turn' in personhood can be traced to the latter half of the twentieth century and includes a family of views that define personhood disjunctively, appealing not only to sophisticated cognitive capacities but also to special relationships, specifying that "specific agents must not interfere with an individual or must respect their rights in virtue of being in a relation with that individual."[92] On one version, the relevant special relationship is being a member of the same biological species, while on others, it is being someone's child, being party to a biosocial relationship, or having a capacity for reciprocal accommodation with moral agents. Steinbock,[93,94] Kittay,[95] Williams,[96] Midgley,[97] Nozick,[98,99] and Anderson[100] could be dubbed adherents of special relationship views. Other recent views include 'hybrid' accounts that regard a human/animal divide in moral judgment to be an entrenched feature of human psychology and aim to theorize personhood in ways that are "feasible for ordinary human beings to understand and act in accord with."[101] Rather than appealing to special relationships, hybrid views typically invoke other moral considerations, such as a theory/practice divide,[102] procreation asymmetry,[103] life meaning,[104] or other considerations.[105]

Although Emergent Personhood has affinities with some Western accounts, it is importantly distinct. First and foremost, Emergent Personhood is *emergentist*. It regards relationships configured in a certain way as giving rise to something novel and irreducible: the remarkable moral worth we associate with being a person. Second, Emergent Personhood is distinct because it draws on African thought to gain insights about the relational character of personhood, which becomes especially prominent in Part II, where we give an account of the moral considerability of animals, nonliving nature, artificial intelligence, and extraterrestrial life and lands. Third, Emergent personhood differs from some of the other relational views mentioned because it holds that persons do not exist as persons outside of any relationship.

Emergent Personhood differs most dramatically from leading Western accounts of personhood that center higher cognitive capacities. It rejects the long tradition in Western thought that associates personhood with reason. We saw in Chapter 1 (Section 1.4) that ancient Greek societies accorded higher status to free men based on their supposed greater allotment of reason and accorded lesser status to women and slaves due to their presumed lesser allotment. Our view is that higher cognitive capacities are not necessary for being a person. This position resonates with the African idea which Menkiti characterizes thus: "In the African view it is the community which defines the person as person, not some isolated static quality of rationality, will, or memory."[106]

As the foregoing analysis demonstrates, Emergent Personhood meets all five seemingly discordant desideratum we set forth previously (Section 2.2): (1) all human beings qualify; (2) qualifying is independent of others' appraisal yet furnishes a basis for duties toward others; (3) personhood is held equally by all human beings, but to varying degrees by non-humans; (4) human personhood cannot be lost or diminished; (5) and personhood is independent of performance in social roles yet incorporates relational attributes. In the chapters that follow, we flesh out these five elements further.

2.4 Abortion

To better understand what it is to be a person, it will be helpful to say more about the relationship that underpins personhood in the case of human beings. What does it mean to say that one human being is related to another in a way that is transformative, giving rise to beings with superlative moral worth? In this section, we approach this question by asking, 'When in the course of human development do human relationships coalesce in such a way that a person emerges?'

Some African understandings hold that human beings always stand in a certain relation to each other. Referring to Bantu people, Tempels writes,

> "Beings-forces" of the universe are not a multitude of independent forces placed in juxtaposition from being to being. All creatures are found in relationship. . . . [N]othing moves in the universe of forces without influencing other forces by its movement. The world of forces is held, like a spider's web of which no single thread can be caused to vibrate without shaking the whole network.[107]

Setting aside the details of Tempels's force theory, a broader point Tempels makes is that human beings are always deeply interconnected. In a physical and biological sense, interconnection is pervasive in human life. Yet, Emergent Personhood as we are developing it does not attribute moral significance to *biological* relationships; instead, it asks, 'When does human-human relating generate exceptional *moral* value, giving rise to *persons*?'

It might be tempting to look for a straightforward answer, a sharp line where we can say, at this moment, the relationship exists; at the moment prior, it did not. So inclined, we might lean toward the claim that a human relationship exists at the moment of conception. Yet on reflection, if we are not focused on biological properties per se, this proposal seems farfetched. After all, at the moment of conception a pregnant person has no way of knowing that a fertilized egg is even present. To be in a *relationship* (as opposed to simply standing in a certain position relative to some physical thing) requires at least one party to engage. It refers not just to "the state or fact of being related" but also to "the way in which two things are connected; a connection, an association" and to "an association formed between two or more people or groups based on social interactions."[108] Thus, when deceased humans in cemeteries are positioned in rows side-by-side, they stand in a certain relation to one another but do not have a *relationship* in the sense we are after.

Another simplifying strategy would be to say that a human relationship exists as soon as a fertilized egg attaches to the uterine lining and a person learns they are pregnant. Yet that approach seems farfetched too. People might learn they are pregnant arbitrarily, e.g., because they happen to have access to pregnancy tests. Perhaps, a safer bet is to suppose that a relationship begins when a pregnant person first feels a slight fluttering or tapping sensation, commonly known as quickening. Yet does the presence of fluttering and tapping change the situation so dramatically that beforehand there was no exceptional relationship and now one exists? Attempting to answer our question in these ways does not do justice to the complexities at hand.

Another proposal associated with both African and Western strands of thought holds that a person arises only if a being is capable of moral thought or action. For example, some African views hold that personhood requires the capacity for moral virtue, while some Kantian views maintain that personhood requires the rational ability to formulate moral principles and universalize them. Yet, we take issue with both stances. Instead, we find immense and immeasurable value in the relationship between parent and child well before a child has moral capacities. In this regard, our view departs from a dominant strain within African thought, which holds that human infants and children are not persons. As explicated in Akan (Ghanaian) philosophy, for example, while human infants have some measure of moral status simply by virtue of possessing a human soul (*okra*), they are not full-fledged persons because they lack the social bases of personhood. Illustrative of this approach are Gyekye and Menkiti, who equate being a person with being morally virtuous.[109,110] While not all defenders of African personhood share their view[111] many commentators characterize African conceptions of personhood as reflecting an age-related moral stance.[112,113,114] Commenting on the moral standing of infants and young children in Akan society, Wingo reports that Akan society regards infant and child deaths differently from the deaths of adults:

> No funeral ceremonies are permitted in Akan society for infants.... It isn't that infants are not valued or cherished by the Akan; rather, it is that they are just not the kind of individual for whom such a ceremony is appropriate. The Akan funeral is a form of send-off for the departing soul on the journey to the ancestral world—a journey for which a child does not qualify because she hasn't attained personhood.[115]

We reject these approaches to moral standing, which Metz dubs, "moralized" versions of personhood.[116] While personhood is grounded on relationships, ethical conduct and the display of virtue in relationships are not prerequisites. Nor is it necessary to be a certain chronological age or undergo specific rites of passage to qualify for personhood.[vii] We also reject African approaches that ground personhood on the *potential* for relating or for developing a capacity to relate,[117] and those that base personhood on *possible* ('modal') relationships.[118] Instead, the type of relationship that Emergent Personhood points to as a source of human personhood are those that bring a human being into a family-like relationship with every other human being. Emergent Personhood maintains that when the actual relationships in which developing humans stand come together in a certain way, a person emerges with an identity of their own; this identity will dissolve when the relational base it emerges from disperses.

[vii] Some defenders of African personhood share our view. For example, describing the traditional worldview of the Nso people (in northwest Cameroon) Tangwa states, "Children are highly valued; so highly valued that procreation is considered the main purpose of marriage" and "a child is accepted and loved unconditionally"; the Nso bestow special value on handicapped children, who are "considered *mbuhme*, a special gift (of God)" (Tangwa GB, 2004, Some African Reflections on Biomedical and Environmental Ethics, in Wiredu K, ed., *A Companion to African Philosophy*, Blackwell Publishing, Kindle locations 6430-6568, at Kindle locations 6508, 6510, 6513).

At this point, it will be helpful to say more about what must occur for human-human relationships to be configured in such a way that they give rise to beings of exceptional moral worth.[viii] To address this, it will be helpful to place early human relationships along a continuum of growth that spans all stages of prenatal human life and also includes newborn infants and toddlers. At the earliest stages of prenatal human life, the relationship of a developing human being with other human beings is just getting under way. There can be a dawning awareness that a new human will be joining the human family. Whether the pregnancy is wanted or unwanted, freely chosen or not, the relationship intensifies as pregnancy progresses. As this occurs, degrees of moral standing gradually arise and confer corresponding degrees of moral status on the fetus. This gradualist approach suggests that late-stage fetuses are *nearly* persons. However, the significance of birth is paramount. *Birth marks not merely a change in physical location, but a striking change in the relationship of one human being to every other.* Emergent Personhood holds that we immediately relate to a newborn infant as a fellow human being. It joins a human family that encompasses all humanity. While the *innate* qualities of human beings do not change at birth, the *relational* features are forever altered.[ix-x]

[viii] Asking about the moral status of developing humans differs from asking when, if ever, it is ethically permissible to take a person's life. In various instances, it might be considered permissible to end persons' lives provided certain conditions are met, e.g., physician-assisted death, capital punishment, and in the context of a just war. Similarly, with abortion, it might be permissible to terminate pregnancy under certain conditions even if a fetus is a person (see Thomson JJ, 1971, A Defense of Abortion, *Philosophy and Public Affairs* 1(1): 47–66).

[ix] To varying degrees, technologies can intensify relationships with prenatal human life. For example, by providing a visual image of a developing human being, ultrasound imaging can dramatically alter the way we relate. So can technologies that make it possible to support late-stage fetuses outside the womb. In the future, scientific advances could allow an artificial womb to gestate prenatal life entirely outside the human womb. However, since the earliest prenatal human life is undeveloped, this would continue to limit the social relationships possible.

[x] Metz makes a similar point noting, "Babies cry, look people in the eyes, ingest food through their mouths, are out in the world" (Metz T, 2022, *A Relational Moral Theory*, Oxford University Press, p. 184).

Notice that Emergent Personhood does not require having a certain set of cognitive capacities, as some Western views require; nor does it rely on incorporation in a particular community and developing pro-social virtues, as some African views do. Notice too that at birth, the status of personhood applies equally to both healthy and impaired infants. Steinbock pinpoints the underlying rationale; comparing infants born healthy with those with significant cognitive impairments, Steinbock states,

> When we call a newborn baby a "person," we are not so much describing its capacities as expressing the idea that it is a family member. The same is true of infants with anencephaly. Like all other babies, they have parents and a place in a network of human relationships. On this basis alone, such babies can be considered to be "persons."[119]

If a human being becomes a person only at birth, does it follow that a pregnant person can terminate pregnancy for any reason, right up until birth? Does Emergent Personhood entail an extreme liberal view about abortion? In reply, Emergent Personhood holds that a late-term fetus is *nearly* a person, which suggests that fetuses have significant moral standing and we have serious ethical duties toward them. Analogously, in many African traditions, it is not acceptable to kill a pregnant animal for food, because the justification for killing an animal does not extend to killing future animals gratuitously. The reason is not that future animals are persons but rather that they are due some significant moral consideration irrespective of that. Personhood is just one of many ways something can become morally considerable.

2.5 Conclusion

This chapter has brought African and Western philosophies of personhood into closer conversation. We sought to better understand the reasons the West moved away from an older, Greek view of personhood that more closely resembled African personhood. We clarified (in Section 2.2) both advantages and disadvantages of this historical move, juxtaposing two Western accounts of personhood—ancient Greek and Judeo-Christian. On the basis of this discussion, we set out five, seemingly discordant, conditions that a satisfactory conception of personhood ought to meet and introduced (in Section 2.3) an approach we call Emergent Personhood that meets them. We drew out the implications of Emergent Personhood for early human development (in Section 2.4). We identified birth as a pivotal moment, marking a seminal change in moral status, because it alters profoundly the relationship others have to a developing human being.

3
Personhood Across the Lifespan

3.1 Introduction

In Chapter 2 we introduced Emergent Personhood, a new view that combines the best features of African and Western personhood. This chapter further explicates Emergent Personhood, exploring its implications for human beings across the lifespan. It highlights the fact that we exist not just at a single moment, but diachronically, from one moment to the next. Taking a whole life approach, Emergent Personhood counters life stage biases.[1] Thus, rather than assuming that "there is one true self and that this one true self is not our old self, not our childhood self, but our mature midlife self," we explore personhood for infants, children, young adults, and older people.[2] We consider that persons exhibit both capabilities and deficits, both powers and vulnerabilities. Yet, thinking of persons over a lifetime introduces new philosophical questions. Is personhood constant as people pass through the phases of their lives? Or can one and the same individual be more or less of a person as they grow up and grow old? For example, do infants and children have relatively less moral standing since their cognitive capacities are relatively less developed? Does moral standing decline at older ages if people's mental capacities wane?

Emergent Personhood helps us to think anew about these and related questions.[i] Joining together insights from Africa and the

---

[i] Unless indicated, the analysis of this chapter does not apply to separate philosophical debates about numerical identity across time. While persisting as a *person* implies continuing to have full-fledged moral standing, persisting as one and the same individual need not imply this. Thus, it is intelligible to say that an individual with advanced

West, it gives a foothold to equality, insisting that human beings are persons with equal moral standing from birth to death. We begin, in Section 3.2, with African and early Greek views, which regard people at different ages and stages as possessing unequal capacities for personhood based on their varying degrees of incorporation into a community and unequal capacities. Section 3.3 turns to two leading views from the contemporary West, utilitarian and Kantian ethics. These views tend to regard cognitively intact adults as more deserving of respect or moral considerability compared to infants, young children, or older people with cognitive impairment. The next section (Section 3.4) uses a forced choice scenario to pinpoint differences between these alternative views and to demonstrate advantages of Emergent Personhood. Section 3.5 concludes that Emergent Personhood represents the most cogent account of personhood across the lifespan.

3.2 African and Early Greek Personhood Across the Lifespan

We first presented questions related to personhood across the lifespan in Chapter 1 (Section 1.3).[ii] We noted that African approaches often assign higher moral standing to individuals during later life, and comparably less to early life. Ethical reasons that lend support to this way of thinking are that as people age, they become more interwoven in the fabric of a community, and their capacity to commune and contribute to others in morally excellent ways tends to increase. In Chapter 1 (Section 1.4), we also argued

---

dementia persists as one and the same individual, but does not persist as a person in the moral sense. (For more on identity over time, see Gallois A, 2016, Identity over Time, in Zalta EN, ed., *Stanford Encyclopedia of Philosophy*, https://plato.stanford.edu/archives/win2016/entries/identity-time/.).

[ii] Section 3.2 borrows from Jecker NS, 2020, African Conceptions of Age-Based Moral Standing, *Hastings Center Report* 50(2): 25–43, DOI: 10.1002/hast.1100.

that early Greek conceptions of moral standing bear a close resemblance to these African ways of thinking. In what follows, we further explore the implications of African and early Greek views of personhood for human beings across the lifespan.

1. *African ethics.* African personhood, with its heavy emphasis on pro-social moral virtue, has potentially unequal implications for people at different ages. This is apparent, for example, at the birth of a child and corresponding responses to child death. Referring to the moral standing accorded at birth in Butajira, Ethiopia, Onarehim et al. write,

> While birth is a mark of a baby's first day of life, children ... [only] gradually received recognition as they became known to the family and community. The recognition or social construction of personhood can be looked upon as a process in which the baby has survived and become known, and not something achieved during pregnancy or at birth.[3]

African responses to child death are also distinctive, and contrast with responses to deaths occurring later in life. According to Menkiti, "In the particular context of Africa, anthropologists have long noted the relative absence of ritualized grief when the death of a young child occurs, whereas with the death of an older person, the burial ceremony becomes more elaborate and the grief more ritualized—indicating a significant difference in the conferral of [moral] ontological status."[4] For example, in Ethiopian mourning practices, older individuals are generally mourned more than small children and infants.[5] Mourning practices in contemporary Zambia embody similar age-based distinctions.[6] Age-related differences in bereavement practices may bespeak an underlying philosophy of personhood. As discussed in Chapter 1 (Section 1.3), African moral standing is often marked by an ontological progression from birth to death, which parallels a human being's increasing incorporation within a community and growing capacities to contribute to social life.

The underpinning for an ontological progression of moral standing is that African personhood is socially and relationally grounded. Referring to the Akamba people of Kenya, for example, Kilner reports that they espouse the belief that "the older a person becomes, the more intricately interwoven that person becomes in the lives of others, and the greater the damage done if that person is removed."[7] Kilner adds that Akamba people ascribe a valued social role specifically to older people: "The older person has wisdom, a perspective on life that comes only with age—which is considered to be a particularly important social resource."[8]

Like Kilner, Metz holds that a being's degree of moral status correlates roughly with their capacity for communal relationships. Based on this principle, "gametes, zygotes, embryos, and very early foetuses lack a moral status altogether," while "later foetuses can be objects of a communal relationship with us, even if not yet subjects of one." The reason for the difference is that "characteristic humans much more readily think of themselves as a 'we' with mid- to late-stage foetuses than they do with a clump of rudimentary cells."[9] What gives newborns a high relational status for Metz includes the fact that "babies cry, look people in the eyes, ingest food through their mouths, are out in the world, and, at least at a certain point, engage in goal-directed behaviour, which more readily enables us to enjoy a sense of togetherness with them." Metz clarifies the difference between fetuses and infants by pointing out that fetuses "are, by their nature, *cloistered* in such a way as to make communal relationship with them markedly more difficult."[10] For Metz, like us, the tipping point is birth: infanticide is wrong because at birth, we interrelate in ways that were impossible just moments prior.

Similarly, Menkiti argues that there is a "processual" nature to sub-Saharan African accounts of moral status, in the sense that persons become persons only after a process of being incorporated into this or that community; without incorporation, "individuals are considered to be mere danglers to whom the description 'person' does not fully apply."[11] According to Menkiti, "Full personhood is not perceived as simply given at the very beginning of one's life, but is attained after one is well along in society"; in particular, "the older an individual gets, the more of a person [the individual] becomes."[12] This interpretation lends itself to thinking of personhood as an arc marked by ontological ascent and descent.[13] As individuals mature, they gradually can become more fully persons if they become more incorporated into a community. Characterizing traditional African views, Menkiti states that they

> routinely accept . . . that personhood is the sort of thing which has to be attained and is attained in direct proportion as one participates in communal life through the discharge of the various obligations defined by one's stations. It is the carrying out of these obligations that transforms one from the it-status of early childhood, marked by an absence of moral function, into the person-status of later years, marked by a widened maturity of ethical sense, an ethical maturity without which personhood is conceived as eluding one.[14]

In this sense, traditional African societies regard personhood both as a status earned by an individual and conferred by a community and as something that can increase with age (although this is not inevitable). According to Menkiti, the Igbo proverb, 'What an old [person] sees sitting down, a young [person] cannot see standing up,' encapsulates "the incremental [opportunity for] growth of wisdom as one ages; it also applies to the ingathering of the other excellences considered to be definitive of full personhood."[15] For these reasons, Menkiti characterizes aging as an "ontological progression" from infancy to old age, in which the individual "undergoes fundamental changes at the very core of [their] being."[16]

However, the linkage between personhood and age should not be taken for more than it is worth. Ikuenobe clarifies this point, noting that "the developmental stages of personhood represent 'age groups' that are not necessarily defined in terms of chronological age but in terms of responsibility, achievements, and recognition. If one has not satisfied the requisite responsibilities associated with an age group, one cannot be elevated, incorporated, and initiated into a higher age group."[17] Thus, each step in the process of becoming a person requires demonstrating moral progress through deeds that convey a growing appreciation of the community's values and their expression in practices. In the final analysis, it is not age, but a person's achievements and the honor those achievements bring to the community that determines moral progress toward full personhood. In the African tradition, *growing old*, which refers to chronological age, is generally distinguished from being an *elder*, which implies having earned social standing and full personhood through consistent good deeds over a lifetime. To be an elder is to be "seen as the repository of justifiable beliefs, wisdom and good judgment that can be brought to bear on moral reasoning—from which others can draw."[18] A Ghanaian proverb expresses it thus: "It is one's deeds that are counted, not one's years."[19]

In Achebe's novel, *Things Fall Apart*, this point is aptly illustrated. As the novel opens, a young person, Okonkwo, is elevated beyond their years while their father, Unoka, is demoted despite their more advanced age. Achebe puts it thus: "If a child washed [their] hands [they] could eat with kings"; the young Okonkwo "had clearly washed his hands and so he ate with kings and elders."[20] By contrast, his father, Unoka, was "a failure" and "a loafer," whose wife and children "had barely enough to eat"; someone who borrowed money, "piling up debt" which he never paid back.[21] Thus, "not only did Unoka fail to acquire personhood or elderhood.... [H]he also failed as a man, father, and husband in the normative sense of these terms. In African thought, being a 'man' or 'father' or 'husband' is not just a descriptive reference.... [T]hese terms have normative meanings and evaluative features attached to them."[22]

While this general characterization applies, African philosophy is diverse. Not all African philosophies of personhood abide by the view that society confers personhood. For example, Gyekye stresses that individuals with the capacity to be virtuous cannot fail at personhood; instead, "it is social status, not personhood, at which an individual could fail."[23] Tangwa writes that although the Nso people of the Northwest Region of Cameroon are "very hierarchical with great respect accorded to titled individuals, to age and experience, and while they can further regroup those who fall within any of these categories according to still other criteria, such categories do not carry any moral significance."[24] Tangwa compares moral worth to "a big Bamenda gown that is never made to be tight and can fit many different people of greatly differing shapes, sizes, and other particulars—or a single individual through many changes in shape, size, and weight."[25]

These exceptions notwithstanding, the overall thrust of African personhood suggests that infants and young children cannot enact moral virtue and be persons due to their inexperience and lack of incorporation. While some older people attain elderhood, older people are disproportionately beset with cognitive impairments, like dementia, that potentially reduce their capacity to contribute in morally excellent ways. For these reasons, African personhood tends to be unequal for people at different ages, potentially leaving out very young and some older people.

2. Early Greek ethics. As noted in Chapters 1 and 2, prior to the arrival of Christianity, conceptions of personhood in the West bore a resemblance to those found in African society today. The same can be said when it comes to attitudes toward personhood for people at different ages and stages of life. A number of common features, as well as some differences, come to light. A first common feature is that Ancient Greeks viewed children's moral standing as vulnerable and contingent on their healthy growth and development. In Plato's *Republic*, "children of superior adults clearly possess a potential worth that increases as they come closer to maturity. However, children's worth is not intrinsic but only potential, and children are valued in proportion to their approximation to the ideal adult. They must be malleable, disposed to virtue, and physically fit."[26] Amundsen emphasizes Plato's concern for healthy children, noting that "in a society in which absolute value is always seen through the grid of social value, those who are physically defective, or at least those who are chronically ill, should not be kept alive by diet, drugs, and regimen, since such people will likely reproduce similarly wretched offspring and be of use neither to themselves nor to society."[27] Plato's ideal society, as described in the *Republic*, regulates sexual relations of the guardian class so that "superior adults" couple with others of equal worth to a maximum extent, considering erotic activity as part of a man's civic duty.[28] Aristotle held that children initially "resemble natural slaves and animals more than they do virtuous men, because they lack the developed capacity for rational thought and behavior"; for both Plato and Aristotle, "*human [moral] value is primarily social value.*"[29] One way Aristotle expressed this idea was to say that "no child is happy," underscoring that children are incapable of the complex moral and intellectual activities that Aristotle held constituted a flourishing life.[30] Aristotle assumed, for example, that children could not perform excellent acts of courage and contemplation. In *Nicomachean Ethics*, Aristotle states that children "in fact live at the beck and call of appetite,"[31] and compares children to lower animals: "Both children and the lower animals share in voluntary action, but not in choice, and acts done on the spur of the moment we describe as voluntary, but not as chosen."[32] Amundsen argues that this stance probably reflected beliefs common in Ancient Greek society: "In classical society, even in its more humanitarian movements, children were essentially viewed as potential adults, their value residing in what they would become."[33]

A second feature that ancient Greek and African views share is an overarching hierarchy of moral standing based on age and perceived mental capacity. For example, Aristotle, like Plato, identifies females and natural slaves of all ages as inferior due to their allegedly lesser allotment of reason. Both were "somewhat like domesticated animals: defective by nature"; women who were not considered natural slaves were perceived as having a greater capacity for virtue, but still, thought of as "defective males."[34]

Finally, when we turn to Greek attitudes toward later life, we find that unlike African views that tend to revere older people, ancient Greeks' views generally held that moral standing diminishes after older people retire from active life in the city. At this point, they had less social value and hence, less moral status. Rist points out that in ancient Greece, children and relations nonetheless had an obligation to help retired older people, both "as a compensation for nurture in infancy and childhood" and "as an act of piety towards the spirits of family and ancestors"; however, non-relations had no such obligation.[35] Aristotle, in particular, expressed derisive views about older people, famously scorning old men in *Rhetoric* as cynical, distrustful, small-minded, not generous, cowardly, and having a chilly temperament. According to Aristotle, old men "guide their lives too much by considerations of what is useful and too little by what is noble."[36]

Overall, ancient Greek attitudes toward both early and later life serve to highlight the underlying philosophical stance, discussed previously (Chapter 1, Section 1.4), that in early Greece, personhood was not intrinsic but something "which we have to acquire, or at least which we can try to acquire," although the opportunities for acquisition were unequally present.[37] Rist points out that Plato, for example, "failed to connect ... human existence necessarily to value. Not only are humans ... not all equally valuable; some have no value at all. Needless to say, therefore, no human has anything which could properly be called an intrinsic value."[38] Rist adds that Aristotle understood the same point slightly differently: "The notion of valuing a human being only enters the Aristotelian world at the level of citizen virtue and is more or less confined to that level"; thus, "if human beings have no citizen-potential, they are in some sense non-moral."[39] Aristotle's notion of 'citizen-potential' itself depends on possessing certain kinds of in-born intellectual powers. Hence, "the Aristotelian man has "no 'cosmic' value, his value is related to his particular situation as a member of a particular city-state. It is the community which enables him to develop and acquire value."[40] Even the language of ancient Greece exposes a difficulty with attempting to predicate intrinsic value of individual human beings: "If Plato had wanted to say that someone had intrinsic value or worth, [Plato] would have had no precise term to do the job. [Plato] could have used the word 'good' (*agathos*), or 'noble' (*kalos*), or 'worthy' (*axios, spoudaios*), or 'valuable' (*timios*), but all these terms, and perhaps particularly, the last, tend to be connected with one's position in society."[41] In summary, "no pagan, whether philosopher or jurist, appears to have even asked whether human beings have inherent value, or possess intrinsic rights, irrespective of social value, legal status, age, sex and so forth."[42]

Stepping back from the discussion of early Greek and African personhood, several observations come to light. First, both regard moral standing and personhood as acquired; for both, acquisition takes place only within a community. The implications of this stance are unequal across the lifespan, with the potential for personhood arising gradually through incorporation. Second, while both philosophies accord lesser standing to people during early life, Africans generally hold more favorable views of people during later life than early Greeks did. For Africans, older adults have greater potential for moral wisdom and for contributing to community. For Greeks, older adults retired from work in the city are past prime; as their contributions wane, so does their moral status.

3.3 Contemporary Western Personhood Across the Lifespan

We saw in chapter 1 (Section 1.3) that contemporary Western views tend to regard certain internal mental states as the hallmark of personhood.[iii] Among Western philosophers today, consciousness is often deemed essential, not only to having a self that persists over time, but to having moral standing and personhood that persists across the lifespan. Representative of this approach is Locke, who writes, "We must consider what PERSON stands for; —which, I think, is a thinking intelligent being, that has reason and reflects, and can consider itself as itself, the same thinking thing, in different times and places."[43] Elsewhere, Locke states that the "self is that conscious thinking thing, —whatever substance made up of (whether spiritual or material, simple or compounded, it matters not)—which is sensible or conscious of pleasure and pain, capable of happiness or misery, and so is concerned for itself, as afar as that consciousness extends."[44] Strikingly, the assumption that personhood depends essentially on properties that are intrinsic to the entity is rarely questioned in contemporary Western thought. While there are certainly alternative elaborations of personhood in the Western tradition, it is fair to say that in the West today, views that hold intrinsic properties are essential to being a person in the moral sense are center, and alternative views are pressed to the margin.

This section focuses on a collection of qualities that figure importantly in moral standing among Western contemporary philosophers: consciousness, especially the capacity to experience suffering and happiness, and rationality, especially higher order moral reasoning. We consider these twin qualities through the lenses of utilitarian and Kantian ethics and explore their ramifications across the lifespan.

[iii] Section 3.2 borrows from Jecker NS, 2020, African Conceptions of Age-Based Moral Standing, *Hastings Center Report* 50(2): 25–43, DOI: 10.1002/hast.1100.

1. Utilitarian ethics. Consider, first, utilitarian ethics, which shares with Locke the idea that consciousness and the capacity to experience psychological states—happiness or misery—are morally considerable in themselves. For utilitarians, human beings who lack these capacities are not morally considerable and our duties to them are indirect only. However, utilitarian ethics also suggests that the degree of interest a being merits depends on the degree of happiness or suffering that is possible for it, which varies over time based on maturation and development. For example, Singer has argued that infants and very young children have less ability to experience happiness and suffering because they do not anticipate the future in the same way that adults ordinarily do. Singer illustrates this idea using the hypothetical example of scientists performing an extremely painful, potentially lethal experiment.

Scientists Performing an Extremely Painful, potentially Lethal Experiment. Normal adult human beings have mental capacities that will, in certain circumstances, lead them to suffer more than animals would in the same circumstances. If, for instance, we decided to perform extremely painful or lethal scientific experiments on normal adult humans, kidnapped at random from public parks for this purpose, adults who enjoy strolling in parks would become fearful that they would be kidnapped. The resultant terror would be a form of suffering additional to the pain of the experiment.... [T]here is a reason, which is not speciesist, for preferring to use animals rather than normal adult human beings ... however ... this same argument gives us a reason for preferring to use human infants—orphans perhaps—or severely retarded human beings for experiments... since infants and retarded humans would also have no idea what was going to happen to them.[45]

According to Singer, if the experiment were to occur, we ought to select as research subjects either non-human animals or human beings who are infants or severely intellectually impaired, because these groups would not suffer "anticipatory dread" the way ordinary adult humans would.[46] The underlying idea seems to be that certain cognitive capacities lend themselves to anticipatory dread or what we might call, 'higher order suffering' and 'higher order enjoyment.' Beings who have these capacities not only suffer more deeply, but they also appreciate enjoyment more, remember it better, and are capable of higher quality enjoyment overall.

Underlying Singer's utilitarian ethic is a philosophy which says that what makes a being morally considerable is reducible to its interests and the degree of interests possible for it. For Singer, the interests of *all beings* deserve equal consideration, regardless of the underlying *kind of being*; thus, "we would be on shaky ground if we were to demand equality for blacks, women, and other groups of oppressed humans while denying equal consideration to nonhumans."[47] Singer and other utilitarians also make finer distinctions based on age, arguing, for example, that saving the life of a teenager has greater value than saving the life of an older person, because it is likely that the teenager has more years of life ahead to live, and saving them therefore produces more happiness overall.[48] Reasoning along these lines, age and cognitive maturity matter not only because they affect people's capacities for happiness/suffering, but also because they are associated with a longer or shorter duration of future happiness/suffering. Taking these considerations into account suggests that in selecting people to undergo an extremely painful and potentially lethal experiment, we ought to expose older people and infants to risk before exposing cognitively intact young adults. The idea is captured well by Holm; referring specifically to bioethics, Holm observes that the "implicit anthropology" of the West is that young adults are the paradigm case of moral status and agency; deviations are judged negatively, i.e., as diminishing moral status and agency.[49]

2. *Kantian ethics.* What might a Kantian view say about the hypothetical experiment? Kantian ethics stresses not only the ability

to sense things and have mental states, but also the facility for higher level thinking and the capacity to legislate moral principles for oneself. It identifies the superlative worth and dignity of human beings with the capacity for autonomous moral choice. Generally speaking, Kantian personhood accords infants and young children less moral standing than mature adults due to cognitive immaturity. Children's value derives from their potential to become rational moral agents in the future. Our duty to infants and young children is a duty to protect their future autonomy, sometimes referred to as a "Prep School Model" of childhood.[50] Reasoning along these lines, Feinberg has argued that children have a right to have their future left open, and we should act in ways that respect a child's future choices.[51]

In selecting subjects for an extremely painful and potentially lethal experiment, a Kantian approach might support selecting cognitively intact infants for the risky experiment over cognitively intact adults, because infants' moral worth is contingent on their future intellectual development, while cognitively intact adults already possess moral worth. Kantian ethics also lends support to selecting as research subjects in a risky experiment people with cognitive impairments (at any age) over people who are neurotypical. A Kantian justification for these claims is that both cognitive immaturity (of the young) and cognitive impairment (at any age) reduce people's ability to legislate and adhere to moral principles. While there is no evidence that Kant thought about the moral status of people with intellectual impairment, the tradition of Kantian ethics has been interpreted as holding that "human beings with significant cognitive disabilities ... [who] do not have even bare capacities or dispositions to recognize, accept, legislate, and follow moral norms ... lack dignity and are not ends in themselves."[52]

Table 3.1 summarizes the discussion of sections 3.2 and 3.3, showing moral inequalities across the lifespan according to African, early Greek, utilitarian, and Kantian approaches.

Table 3.1 Inequalities in Moral Standing across the Lifespan

Moral Standing	African Ethics	Early Greek Ethics	Utilitarian Ethics	Kantian Ethics
High	Elders	Adult citizens	Cognitively intact adults	Cognitively intact adults
Middle	Young and middle-aged adults	Children of citizens	Infants and young children	Infants and young children
Low	Infants and young children	Retired older citizens	Older people with reduced capacity for suffering/happiness	Older people lacking the capacity to legislate morality

KEY: African ethics = ideas prominent among black peoples indigenous to the region of Africa south of the Sahara, as captured in the works of academic philosophers; early Greek ethics= Plato, Aristotle

3.4 Emergent Personhood Across the Lifespan

In contrast to the accounts of personhood set forth in sections 3.2 and 3.3, Emergent Personhood does not draw distinctions in human moral standing based on age or life stage. This section clarifies the advantages of Emergent Personhood with respect to personhood across the lifespan compared with African, early Greek, and contemporary Western alternatives. We begin with the forced choice scenario introduced in Section 3.3, which highlights what is at stake and locates key differences. Next, we turn to consider the five conditions for an adequate account of personhood, first introduced in Chapter 2 (Section 2.2), and argue that Emergent Personhood is the only view among those discussed that upholds each condition from birth to death. These conditions require that (1) all human beings qualify for personhood; (2) qualifying is independent of others' appraisal yet furnishes a basis for duties toward others; (3) personhood is held equally by all human beings, but to varying degrees by non-humans; (4) human personhood cannot be lost or diminished; and (5) personhood is independent of performance in social roles yet incorporates relational elements. Last, we reply to objections to Emergent Personhood that African and contemporary Western philosophers might raise.

1. The forced choice scenario. Emergent Personhood identifies relationships across the lifespan as superlatively valuable and forming the basis for personhood for all who participate in them. It maintains that what makes human relationships special does not require sophisticated intellectual capacities or pro-social moral virtue but instead relates to broader aspects of humanhood. For example, Emergent Personhood stresses that we share a way of life with infants and children and relate to them as fellow human beings; for that reason, we can bond with a human child in a way that is not possible with members of other species, however rational or intelligent they might be.[iv] Likewise, even though mature adults with advanced dementia have lost crucial human capacities, they are nonetheless undeniably human, like us, and we relate to them as fellow human beings, not as members of another species with equivalent cognitive capacities. In contrast to African, early Greek, utilitarian, and Kantian positions, Emergent Personhood holds that people possess equal moral status at all ages, from birth to death, by virtue of the human-human relationships in which they stand.

We can bring differences between these views into sharper focus by reconsidering the example of selecting research subjects for an extremely painful, possibly lethal experiment (introduced in Section 3.3). While fanciful, the example pinpoints age- and life stage-based distinctions between the views under consideration in

---

[iv] It is consistent with Emergent Personhood that particular individuals might bond with particular animals to an extraordinary extent. For more on this point, see the discussions of humble anthropocentrism, speciesism, and animal personhood in Chapter 1 (Section 2.3) and Chapter 6.

a helpful way. As noted in Table 3.1, African approaches generally regard infants and young children as having lower moral standing; hence, African approaches support exposing these groups to a dangerous experiment before exposing mature adults or elders. Early Greek approaches generally rank retired citizens lowest; thus, Greek views support exposing retired people to the risky experiment before adult citizens or young people with citizen potential. Utilitarian ethics regards individuals as less morally considerable if they have less capacity to suffer and experience happiness, and/or fewer years ahead to live. On this basis, utilitarian views justify exposing infants and older adults with intellectual impairment to risky experiments before neurotypical adults. Kantian ethics ranks people who lack the capacity to legislate morality as lacking inherent worth and dignity. Since infants, young children, and older people with advanced dementia fall into this category, Kantian ethics supports exposing these groups to risky experiments before cognitively intact adults. Emergent Personhood yields a very different result: *it is the only view that champions equality across the lifespan, from birth to death.* Forced to choose, Emergent Personhood identifies the fairest method as assigning each individual an equal chance of being subjected to the risky experiment.

Stepping back from the forced choice scenario, would we ever allow an experiment of the kind in question to take place? Under ordinary conditions, we would not. Perhaps, under extreme conditions where the knowledge the experiment was expected to yield was deemed vital and important with the potential to do a great good, the experiment could be ethically sanctioned. If it were, it is hard to imagine selecting research subjects who were infants, children, or people with intellectual impairment, because they would be unable to consent or fully understand what was happening. Forcing anyone to undergo a dangerous experiment would be unethical, and subjecting people who cannot fully appreciate what is happening to an experiment would violate the special protections owed to them by virtue of their dependency.

Perhaps the most ethically supported approach under these improbable conditions would be closer to what transpired during the early stages of the novel coronavirus disease 2019 (COVID-19) pandemic, before vaccines were developed. In July of 2020, a group of 30,000 young healthy volunteers from 140 countries stepped forward and formed a group, 1Day Sooner, offering themselves as research subjects for human challenge trials in the hopes of finding a vaccine sooner. Such trials would involve exposing healthy volunteers to SARS-CoV-2, the novel coronavirus, in order to expedite finding a vaccine to end the pandemic sooner. 1Day Sooner wrote an open letter, signed by fifteen Nobel laureates and 100 prominent ethicists and philosophers, urging governments to "'undertake immediate preparations for human challenge trials' in young, healthy people, who are less likely to suffer severe disease from COVID-19."[53] The young people who volunteered for such research were moral heroes in the sense that they sacrificed themselves for love of humanity.

2. *Five advantages of Emergent Personhood.* Considering personhood across the lifespan has sharpened our understanding of the ontological and normative dimensions of African, early Greek, contemporary Western, and Emergent accounts of personhood. This chapter makes evident that each personhood view brings its own distinct ontology, which in turn, buttresses its normative account. African and early Greek personhood share an ontology of persons which identifies persons as adult human beings who are fully incorporated or citizens.[54] This ontology undergirds a normative stance about how persons ought to act. According to both African and early Greek views, persons ought to be pro-social or display 'citizen virtue.' The normative view *depends on* the ontological view: absent incorporation in a social group, pro-social virtue has little point; without citizenship, citizen-virtue is hardly intelligible.

The ontology of the contemporary West identifies the ontological dimension of persons differently. Persons possess certain underlying intrinsic capacities, like consciousness and rationality. This ontology permits persons to belong to any species provided they possess these intrinsic qualities to a sufficient extent. Again, the normative sense of persons *presupposes* an ontological picture of what a person is. The normative requirement to consider a creature's suffering requires an ontology of persons who are capable of suffering. The normative requirement to respect persons' ends, presumes that they have the rational capacities needed to deliberate and choose ends.

Emergent Personhood presents a different ontology. It builds on the African and early Greek notions of persons as interconnected, yet identifies the relevant human-human relationship as fully present for all human beings from cradle to grave. While Emergent Personhood rejects the ontological requirements associated with contemporary Western personhood, it shares affinities with an older, Judeo-Christian view (first discussed in Chapter 1, Section 1.4). The Judeo-Christian ontology holds that all human beings are 'children of God.' Emergent Personhood secularizes this idea and brings it to a higher level of abstraction. Borrowing from the Builsa (Ghanaian) notion of *Biik* (filiation), Emergent Personhood understands each human being as a son or daughter, who stands in a filial relation to other human beings. By virtue of this relation, "a human being is considered as one who matters to someone."[55] For the Builsa, the other to whom we are related is not only a living relative but an ancestral lineage and a network of constitutive relations.[56] For us, it is humanity writ large. *The ontology which furnishes the source of normativity for Emergent Personhood is human filiation, which is not a standalone quality or an internal state, but a relational feature, a relational existence.*

From this relational ontology flows our normative view of persons. For the Builsa, the normative conception holds that each individual matters to their family and more broadly, to the ancestors in their lineage; that mattering means that "every *nubriik*—human being—bears a relationship with other beings (including dead ancestors) that makes them worthy of respect."[57] Emergent Personhood extends this idea, stressing membership in a human family to which all human beings belong; it emphasizes the human responsiveness that can arise by virtue of a shared humanity. Inklings of our view can be found among some recent Western scholars, such as Foot, who describe "a kind of solidarity between human beings."[58] Foot characterizes human solidarity as tempering aggregative moral reasoning and reinforcing the idea that we should refuse to sacrifice the one for the many. Foot goes on to characterize solidarity negatively, as a prohibition: "There is some sense in which no one is totally *to come out against* one of their fellow human beings."[59] Foot adds that the prohibition secures "a kind of moral space... which others are not allowed to invade."[60] Another contemporary Western philosopher, Wiggins, tells us that aversion to injuring another human being springs not only from reason but from sentiments aroused from a shared human experience: "being the sort of creatures we are, we apprehend the awfulness of such acts *not* by inference, but immediately and directly, indeed viscerally.... [I]t appalls us."[61] Partiality to members of the *human* family is built into Foot's and Wiggins's accounts of solidarity and it underpins the empathic response they characterize.

Building on these approaches, Emergent Personhood endorses a strong account of human solidarity, based on human filiation. Within human families, we recognize a duty not just to respect people's moral space but also to help members who are needy and dependent. For example, parents and grandparents help infants and small children; adult offspring help aging parents and grandparents. Considering humanity as family-like, the normative component of Emergent Personhood interprets human solidarity as requiring both abstaining from harming fellow human beings and helping ensure their ability to lead flourishing human lives. Underpinning human solidarity is an ontology of filiation and belonging to a human family. 'Human solidarity,' as we use the term, indicates "a universalistic ethical ideal of responsiveness to human moral standing" and "emotionally and normatively motivated readiness for mutual support."[62]

A key advantage of the ontology of Emergent Personhood over the ontologies of African, early Greek, and contemporary Western personhood is the strong support it lends to human equality for people at all ages. More broadly, the advantages of Emergent Personhood are that it alone satisfies the five conditions set forth previously (Chapter 2, Section 2.2) for personhood. Belonging to the human family applies to (1) all human beings; (2) is independent of others' appraisal yet furnishes a basis for duties toward others; (3) is held equally by all human beings; (4) cannot be lost or diminished; and (5) is independent of performance in social roles yet incorporates relational elements. These conditions allow for the possibility (discussed in Part II) of non-human personhood arising in a different way, based on a different ontology and ethic.

3.5 Replies to Objections

We turn finally to a series of objections.

1. Can't derive an ought from an is. A first objection to Emergent Personhood holds that it deduces claims about moral personhood from factual premises about human relationships. Yet value statements are not derivable from factual statements.

In response, we acknowledge (as others have)[63] that normative theorizing inevitably builds in a set of descriptive assumptions. In our case, these are claims about the ways human beings and human social groups co-exist. Other scholars theorizing about personhood make their own set of assumptions which inform their normative analysis differently. For example, a tendency to equivocate on the concept of 'person' is present in African thought, which shifts between metaphysical and normative conceptions.[64,65,66,67] Such equivocation is apparent linguistically. In the Akan language, the word *onipa* translates into English both as 'person' in the sense of being a human being and as 'person' in the normative sense of commending someone as having a high moral standing in the community. In Yoruba language, the word for person is *èniyàn*, which has both normative and descriptive meanings.[68] In the West, post-Enlightenment moral philosophers often build in a set of premises that pictures human beings as rational maximizers of interest or utility. For example, on some Western views, rational choice theory is a normative, not just an explanatory view; it assumes human beings *should* act as rational agents that maximize interests over a complete and consistent set of preference orderings.[69] Or, to take another example, Bentham defends the principle of utility on the ground that "by the natural constitution of the human frame ... [people] in general embrace this principle."[70]

In further reply, we note that the argument for Emergent Personhood might be *inductively* compelling, even if it is not demonstrable. Referring to Hume's claim that 'an ought cannot be derived from an is,' Flanagan et al. put the point this way:

> Hume's warning is one about deducing ought-claims from is-claims, but deduction is not the only sensible kind of reasoning.... Hume rules out deduction, but this still leaves us with the full range of ampliative inference we regularly use across a wide range of respectable epistemic endeavors.[71]

Churchland likewise argues that moral concepts and judgments can be "inferences to the best explanation," even if they are not knock-down deductive arguments.[72] Similarly, we argue that even if a normative account of personhood does not follow *deductively* from a description of human filiation, the fact of human filiation furnishes a compelling reason to accept the normative account of personhood we offer.

2. *Only incorporated people count.* A proponent of African personhood might object to Emergent Personhood on the ground that infants and young children are not yet incorporated into a particular

society and cannot yet contribute to the particular community in which they live. Until they can, they are not full-fledged persons. In reply, relegating to a lower realm of moral status those who cannot contribute to society (or who are seen as contributing less) glosses over a crucial distinction, first introduced in Chapter 1 (Section 1.3), between *appraisal* and *recognition* respect. Gyekye hinted at it when saying, "It is *social status*, not personhood, at which an individual could fail."[73] Rather than regarding moral standing as reducible to social standing, as some African scholars do (e.g., Menkiti), or 'citizen virtue,' as some early Greeks did (e.g., Aristotle), Emergent Personhood entails that moral standing and personhood arise at a more basic, existential level of human-human relating. Such relating occurs across the board, for every human being, beginning at birth and continuing to death. It is not confined to the so-called public sphere of the tribe or city-state.

3. *Only 'good' relationships count. It is implausible to ground personhood relationally without first distinguishing good and bad ways of relating.* In response, we acknowledge that others who appeal to relational features to ground moral standing generally siphon off the best relationships, variably understood, rather than appealing to relationships as such. For example, African philosophers, like Gyekye[74] and Menkiti,[75] invoke morally virtuous relationships to characterize personhood, while some Western feminists specify 'caring'[76] and 'mothering'[77] to characterize their normative views. However, for us, there is immense value that arises through the existential condition of being part of humankind. When human relationships are negative, the reason they are regarded as such is a kind of privation, or lack of what ought to be present in human-human relating. Recognizing this, we regard it as an advantage of Emergent Personhood that it avoids making outliers of humans who cannot behave in specified ways. For example, infants and people with profound intellectual impairment qualify as persons by virtue of being fellow human beings. In addition, we consider

it an advantage that we count as persons human beings who habitually behave with ruthlessness and injure others deliberately. Admittedly, this outcome will be unsettling to some. In favor of it, however, we note that it aligns with considered judgments in a range of cases. For example, it aligns with the belief that all human beings deserve to be treated with minimal respect, including individuals with personality disorders that manifest in extreme antisocial attitudes and behaviors and individuals imprisoned for committing odious crimes. Many societies routinely provide, or try to provide, people in such circumstances with the necessities to lead a decent human life, e.g., making available food, clothing, shelter, and basic medical care.

Yet an opponent to our proposal might press back. For example, Behrens has proposed capturing such judgments in a different way. Behrens defends a version of African personhood that applies to moral agents only; Behrents develops a further conception that applies to members of the moral community broadly. The former (moral agent) is "appropriate only for the ascription of moral responsibility, liability and culpability," while the latter (subjects of moral concern) is appropriate for "the ascription of moral worth, desert, eligibility or acceptability into the moral community."[78] While Behrens limits personhood to moral agents, his view simultaneously recognizes moral *responsibility* toward all human beings and some non-human animals. It also allows for a nuanced assessment of *human* moral status, regarding some humans as non-persons that we have moral responsibility toward.

In response, even though Behrens's framework grants all human beings a measure of moral standing, it achieves this only by relegating those incapable of moral agency to a separate and unequal status; they belong in the category of 'members of the moral community' rather than full-fledged persons. In this respect, Behrens's view of personhood, like many African views, violates one of the five conditions we have argued an adequate conception of personhood must meet (Chapter 2, Table 2.2, requirements 3), which is to assign all human beings *equal* moral worth.

4. *Equal consideration of interests.* A utilitarian might argue against Emergent Personhood by insisting that younger people who are intellectually immature and older adults with dementia derive less utility from human-human relating and so they are less morally considerable. For this reason, in a forced choice scenario, we should subject them to a painful potentially lethal experiment before subjecting cognitively intact adults to such an experiment.

In reply, subjecting a child or impaired person to a painful risky experiment would be exploitive and wrong, even if they do not recognize or appreciate what is happening. We distinguish relationships that participants *subjectively* experience as good/bad from those that are *objectively* good/bad but not experienced as such by participants. Objectively exploitive relationships arise when someone takes advantage of a small child who lacks awareness of the wrong that is occurring, or when mature adults lack cognizance of exploitation because they are unconscious, drunk, comatose, or intellectually impaired.[79] In such instances, a wrong is done to the child or impaired adult, even though they do not recognize or experience it in the moment (and may never experience it). What's more, an individual's utter vulnerability makes the moral injury *worse*, because it violates a duty to take special care of dependent and needy human beings. Steinbock points to this as the reason we rightly feel "horror" at the thought of substituting infants or people who are mentally incapacitated for chimpanzees in medical experiments:

> we feel a special obligation to care for the handicapped members of our own species, who cannot survive in this world without such care. . . . [T]o subject to experimentation those people who depend on us seems . . . worse than subjecting members of other species to it. In addition . . . we think 'That could be me.' It makes sense to think that one might have been

born retarded, but not to think that one might have been born a monkey.[80]

As Williams notes, any demand for moral equality between people rests on a common humanity: "It is not . . . in their skill, intelligence, strength, or virtue that [humans] are equal, but merely in their being [human]: it is their common humanity that constitutes their equality."[81]

5. *A marginalized person objection.* *A final objection to Emergent Personhood holds that basing personhood on social relational processes provides shaky ground for the moral status of populations that are socially isolated and excluded.* Holm, for example, disputes relational accounts of moral status on the ground that the social embedding of older people "depends to a large extent on whether the social roles occupied by the old are central or peripheral in family and other networks," asking, "Is the old person core to the family network, or just hanging on at the very edge?"[82]

In reply, Emergent Personhood does not depend on a concrete set of social arrangements obtaining. Instead, standing in human-human relationship is an existential feature of being human. When people of any age are marginalized, they do not receive the care they are due as members of the human family.

3.6 Conclusion

In conclusion, this chapter considered how persons emerge across the lifespan. We argued that personhood does not change based on age, because the human-human relationship that grounds personhood is constant and cuts across age differences. In Section 3.2, we drew out the implications of alternative views from Africa and early Greece, showing that they fall short of the requirement of moral equality. African personhood tends to elevate older adults' capacity for personhood while discounting the moral standing of infants and young children. Early Greek accounts tend to regard adult male citizens as exemplars of personhood, while assigning lower moral standing to younger people with citizen-potential and to older people who are retired citizens. In Section 3.3, we saw that utilitarian and Kantian ethics generally accord higher moral standing to mature adults than to immature infants or young children. For utilitarians, this is because mature adults have a greater capacity for suffering and happiness than infants and young children. From a Kantian standpoint, mature adults possess superlative worth and dignity because of their ability to legislate morally, which infants and young children lack. Both utilitarian and Kantian ethics give less moral consideration to intellectually impaired people (of any age). In Section 3.4, we drew out the implications of Emergent Personhood across the lifespan, underscoring that our view is unique among all the views discussed: it alone recognizes human beings as having an equal moral worth irrespective of age. All told, Emergent Personhood offers the most compelling account of human personhood across the lifespan.

4
Becoming a Non-Person

4.1 Introduction

Since personhood extends diachronically, from one moment to the next, it makes sense to ask when it begins and ends. We argued previously (in Chapter 2, Section 2.4) that personhood begins at birth, when the relationship between a developing human being and other human beings intensifies and coalesces in a certain way. Subsequently (in Chapter 3), we showed that once established, personhood persists across the lifespan. In this chapter, we focus on personhood's ending. Section 4.2 distinguishes the biological death of a human being from the death of a person. It argues that death's declaration marks a profound change in human relationships, forever separating the newly dead from every other human being and ending the human-human relationships that existed before. We distinguish our view from African, early Greek, and contemporary Western accounts. Along the way, we inquire as to whether the newly dead, ancestors, and what Menkiti dubs "the nameless dead" retain some degree of moral standing or personhood.[1] Section 4.3 argues that Emergent Personhood brings forth the strengths of African and Western philosophies, while setting aside their shortfalls. It is the only account to establish that all human beings are moral equals and count as persons from birth to death. After responding to a series of objections, we turn (in Section 4.4) to look at the application of Emergent Personhood to proposals to hasten death by medical means for people who request it. Section 4.5 concludes the discussion of human personhood by reviewing its beginning, persistence, and ending.

4.2 The Death of Persons and Human Beings

This section distinguishes the death of a person from the death of a human being. After considering how this distinction is understood from African, early Greek, and contemporary Western standpoints, we clarify how Emergent Personhood is distinct and show its advantages.

1. African. Some African views personhood hold that while biological death ends the physical presence of a human being, a newly dead individual can retain a presence and continue to play prominent roles in the community. In this respect, while the human being is no longer physically present, the person is not gone, and the living have duties left to fulfill toward them.[2] To clarify, it will be helpful to say more about African understandings of how a newly deceased individual can continue to be a person and how their personhood eventually ends. The following narrative, involving two Ghanaian men who each claim marriage to the same woman, illustrates.

> The Paramount Chief of the Bulsa, in a case he tried in October 1966, asked a woman, who was the subject of a dispute between two men and accused of having deserted her husband, what she would say if her dead father came to the hearing. She replied: 'My father will say that I am the true wife of N.' This decided the case in favour of the plaintiff, for if the woman had not spoken the truth she would have incurred the mortal wrath of her dead father.[3]

The case shows how ancestors not only "retain legislative power over the living," they are "the real legislators of the community."[4] Ancestors also retain moral authority as the repository of the moral heritage and traditions of the community. While their physical interactions with the living cease at death, their influence as persons persists. Menkiti characterizes the living and dead "as being in constant interaction,"[5] while Ikuenobe portrays the "collective 'we'" as "made up of living people and the dead."[6]

However, not all deceased human beings become ancestors (i.e., deceased *persons*). For example, referring to the Maasai tribe, Presby notes that those with large herds "would become famous, and even immortal (insofar as they would be remembered after death) if they had been generous with their large herds. Those who are successful in raising cattle but not generous would be forgotten upon their deaths."[7] A more nuanced rendering would be to say that deceased persons fall into three categories: those who attained personhood during life and become ancestors after death; thieves, murderers, sorcerers, witches, and adulterers, who are not admitted to the world of ancestors; and people guilty of lesser wrongs, who may be admitted if a family member performs reparations to raise their moral standing.

Three standout features characterize most African understandings of personhood following biological death. First, ceasing to be a person is a process that unfolds gradually over time. Just as "after birth the individual goes through the different rites of incorporation, including those of initiation at puberty time, before becoming a full person in the eyes of the community,"[8] so too, after biological death, the deceased must undergo burial and a funeral ceremony, which mark final rites of passage into the land of ancestors. Not uncommonly, the funeral may be delayed. A community in the middle of planting season may wait until it ends to plan a funeral; disputes over property division or who will take on the social roles formerly performed by the deceased can lead to further delay. Before the funeral occurs, the newly deceased is "technically still considered an ancestor," yet also considered like an elder, because they reside "among the living or undeparted" having not received an essential rite of passage.[9] The ending of persons therefore unfolds gradually, as the deceased is gradually unincorporated. Eventually, an ancestor will "slide into personal non-existence, and lose all that they once possessed by way of personal identity. This, for the traditional African worldview is the termination of personal existence."[10] Rather than being "a permanent feature of any one person's ontological journey," ancestorhood "finds its relative termination after an adequate passage of time."[11] As ties to particular people fade, ancestors join "the nameless dead," as one fragment among many that constitute an "undifferentiated mass" of clan and tribal spirits."[12] Menkiti writes that "at this stage, the human person that came into the world an 'it,' without moral individuation and without a name, goes out of the world an 'it,' also without moral individuation and without a name; the symmetry complete, the destination now final."[13] Wingo observes that although ordinary citizens have a "life-in-death," their impact is temporary.[14] Naming a child after an ancestor is one way to sustain "a special point for re-grounding memory of the ancestor" and re-arousing respect and fondness toward them.[15] Ultimately, however, remembrances and feelings toward the deceased vanish, and the journey of personhood reaches its terminus.

A second standout feature of being an African ancestor is that, like elderhood, it is a social recognition accorded only to human beings. Only human beings are considered capable of persisting as persons after biological death by becoming ancestors. Cats, dogs, elephants, and fish of the sea do not become ancestors.[16] This does not imply that animals were non-persons during life, nor does it suggest that animals are forgotten immediately after biological death. Instead, it suggests that the kind of moral standing accorded to humans and non-humans differs. Reflecting this, Gyekye characterizes African ethics as "humanistic" and describes human welfare as "the hub of the Akan axiological wheel," with human needs, interests, and dignity the foundation of Akan morality.[17]

Third, the cessation of African personhood is generally regarded as a natural occurrence.[i] In contrast to some Christian views, which

---

[i] Christian colonizers sometimes sought to inculturate African beliefs by rendering ancestors as saints, yet pre-colonial African beliefs did not regard ancestors in this way. Some African societies hold that physical beings (diviners) can communicate with

hold that human beings have immortal souls that can come back into existence at the final resurrection, African views generally regard ancestors as "extended natural agents"[18] and do not include belief in a redemptive future.[ii] Rather than being worshipped as deities that "hover around in some rarefied form ready now and then to take a sip of the ceremonial schnapps," Africans instead revere ancestors in the same way they revere elders, as having earned a certain degree of respect in the community by virtue of good deeds.[19] In this regard, "the absence in the eschatology of many African peoples of a day of judgment ... marks a significant difference with the Christian"; for the Christian, "this life is a preparation for the next[;] ... the very meaning of this life consists in the fact that there is a next one."[20] Even those who Wingo dubs "immortals in our midst," due to extraordinary social contributions, are not truly immortal; they are "god-like," not gods.[21] Likewise, the Akans of Ghana and the Ivory Coast, the Yoruba of Nigeria, and the Benin or Mende of Sierra Leone display a this-worldly view of the afterlife, in which becoming an ancestor is prized not because the elder survives death but because ancestors are in a position "to help the living to realize human purposes."[22]

Consistent with the above characterization, mourning practices surrounding the death of an elder contrast sharply with the relatively subdued nature of mourning for infants and children described in Chapter 3 (Section 3.2). According to Gyekye, "The type of burial, the portion of the community involved in the

---

ancestors and can facilitate calling upon the dead for help during periods of misfortune, such as illness, bad harvest, or constant litigation. See Atuire CA, 2020, Philosophical Underpinnings of an African Legal System: Bulsa (*Nigerian Journal of African Law* 2: 62–78, pp. 70–71).

[ii] For a different view, see Majeed, who argues that reincarnation has strong roots in African societies (Majeed HM, 2017, *Reincarnation: A Question in African Philosophy of Mind*, Unisa Press). See also Edet, who distinguishes 'regeneration of life' from 'reincarnation,' and argues regeneration, not reincarnation, is prevalent in African traditional thought (Edet MI, 2016, Innocent Onyewuenyi's 'Philosophical Re-Appraisal of the African Belief in Reincarnation,' *Filosofia Theoretica* 5(1): 76–99, DOI: 10.4314/ft.v5i1.6).

funeral, and the nature and the extent of grief expressed all depend on the community's assessment of the deceased's moral life."[23] Thus, "people, including wealthy people, who do not satisfy the society's moral criteria may be given simple funerals and attenuated expressions of grief," whereas those "whose moral achievements are admired by the community are given elaborate burial ceremonies with ritualized grief regardless of the financial means of their families."[24] When an individual has achieved the highest moral status, elderhood, African funerals are elaborate affairs, analogous to traditional Western weddings. Wiredu explains:

> The mourning of the dead takes the form of elaborate . . . ceremonies. When a person dies there has first to be a burial ceremony on the third day; then on the eighth day, there is a funeral celebration in which customary rites are performed; then, forty days afterward, there is a fortieth-day celebration (*adaduanan*). Then there are such occasions as the eightieth-day and first anniversary celebrations. All these involve large, alcohol-quaffing gatherings. . . . [I]n addition to all the traditional celebrations, there is nowadays the neo-Christian Memorial Service, replete with church services and extended refreshments.[25]

The rituals that mark transition from elder to ancestor sometimes include dramatic performance. Describing the funeral of a fictional elder, Ezeudu, Achebe writes:

> Ezeudu was a great man, and so all the clan was at his funeral. The ancient drums of death beat, guns and cannon were fired, and men dashed about in frenzy, cutting down every tree or animal they saw, jumping over walls and dancing on the roof. It was a warrior's funeral, and from morning till night warriors came and went in their age-groups. They all wore smoked raffia skirts, and their bodies were painted with chalk and charcoal. Now and again an ancestral spirit or *egwugwu* appeared from the

underworld, speaking in a tremulous, unearthly voice and completely covered in raffia.[26]

While this passage, which depicts a (fictional) burial ceremony in pre-colonial Nigeria, can be variously interpreted, one way to render it is to say that spiritual beings dwell with living beings within a single, shared community. Thus, "supernatural entities do not have an existence that is logically or metaphysically independent of the human world, reality, and existence. Usually, the so-called supernatural entities are perceived and understood in purely naturalistic and substantial terms."[27] In the funeral of Ezeudu, the people dancing and singing would not only have painted and adorned their bodies but would have donned masks and ceremonial clothing. Masking adds a vital element, enabling the living to represent ancestors and commune with them though passing on ancestral wisdom using stories, dance, drama, and song. In this way, ancestors are symbolically resurrected and secure a long-lasting place in the life of a community. The idea of ancestors symbolically coming to life during festivals and ceremonies, resonates with the idea of person as *persōna*, first discussed in Chapter 1 (Section 1.4). Person as *persōna* indicates a "mask used by a player, character in a play, dramatic role."[28] *In an important sense, the African person is not the individual behind the mask but the masked character enacting social roles.* Following death, others enact social roles on behalf of the deceased, giving ancestors an ongoing place in the life of the community.[iii] By the same token, future people might be regarded as already part of a human community that spans past, present, and future, generating what Behrens calls

---

[iii] Some scholars would take issue with this interpretation. For example, Metz's modal relational view holds that deceased individuals are not persons because they lack the capacity to commune (Metz T, 2012, An African Theory of Moral Status, *Ethical Theory and Moral Practice* 15(3): 387–402, p. 393, Note 9, DOI: 10.1007/s10677-011-9302-y; Metz T, 2021, *A Relational Moral Theory*, Oxford University Press, p. 168, note 5).

"intergenerational moral accountability"[29] and what Jecker refers to as "intergenerational solidarity."[30]

2. *Early Greek.* Like Africans, early Greeks stressed the enduring presence of the newly deceased. For both, the community was the means by which the deceased retained personhood status. While Africans figuratively kept their ancestors 'alive' by calling upon their teachings and enacting them in community ceremonies and performances, the earliest Greeks believed the deceased literally lived on, enjoying a second existence underground. For the Greeks, pouring libations on the tomb and placing food at the family hearth were essential to quench the deceased's thirst and satiate their hunger. Tending to the family hearth was essential too, because it was thought that if the flame was extinguished, the ancestors' second existence would cease also. For this reason, "for any son to remain single was deemed to be a dereliction of duty, because it was a threat to the immortality of the family."[31] Many Africans similarly think there is a duty to marry and have children, in part because doing so is essential to continuing the community, which is the source and basis for personhood.[32,33,34] Both Africans and early Greeks also linked personhood with performing honorably in social roles. Since the deceased's social roles can be enacted only by the living, the living had weighty ethical duties to the dead: unless their duties were fulfilled, the deceased would lose their place in the community and cease to exist as persons.

Despite such similarities, African and early Greek views differ in salient respects. First, unlike Africans, early Greeks worshipped deceased men and considered them family gods rather than "extended natural beings." According to Fustel, ancient rites of sepulture provide evidence that at death, "the soul remained associated with the body" and was buried with it in the grave; thus, the ancients believed they buried something "that was living."[35] Fustel explains, "before men had any notion of Indra or of Zeus, they adored the dead; they feared them, and addressed them [in] prayers."[36]

Second, in contrast to African views, which generally emphasize mortality and the gradual cessation of personhood, most (but not all)[iv] early Greeks stressed immortality. However, 'immortality' for the early Greeks referred to apotheosis.[37] *Apotheosis* is literally to "make a god of"; its definitions include "resurrection (*literal* and *figurative*)," "being ranked among the gods," "transformation into a god," and "depicting" or imitating this.[38] The doctrine of metempsychosis holds that the soul (*psychê*), a non-physical essence separate from the physical body, is immortal (*athanatos*) and survives the death of the body by migrating to a new body of the same or different species. Different conceptions of the soul can be found among the earliest Greeks. For Pythagoras, "what passes from body to body is... not the human intellect but a personality characterized by emotions and desires, which is fashioned by human intellect, when born in a human body."[39] For Plato, who also subscribed to metempsychosis, the soul was described (in *Republic* and *Phaedo*) as being immortal among those who order their soul in accordance with reason or generate intellectual progeny.[40] Regardless of how the soul is understood, the death of a human being was thought to occur when the soul departed the body; *persons, who are identified with the soul, transmigrate and live forever*.[41]

In contrast to Pythagoras and Plato, Aristotle rejected the doctrine of metempsychosis, believing that the soul could not exist without the body but perishes when it perishes. Yet Aristotle's ethical writings nonetheless stress apotheosis. In *Nicomachean Ethics*, for example, Aristotle instructs us to "so far as we can, make ourselves immortal, and strain every nerve to live in accordance with the best thing in us" and says, "life according to reason is best and pleasantest, since reason more than anything else is man."[42]

[iv] Early Atomists, such as Epicurus and Lucretius, apparently held that immortality was not possible for human beings. See Chapter 7, Section 7.2 for discussion of their general philosophy. See also Berryman S, 2022, Ancient Atomists, in Zalta EN, ed., *Stanford Encyclopedia of Philosophy*, https://plato.stanford.edu/archives/win2022/entries/atomism-ancient/).

3. *Contemporary Western.* In the contemporary West, philosophical views about the cessation of persons look strikingly different from those found in ancient Greece. The change traces to the rise of Christianity, which introduced a fundamentally new way of thinking. Sidentop characterizes the shift as a change in the locus of immortality: during antiquity, the patriarchal family was "the agency of immortality"; with the rise of Christianity, "the individual replaced the family as the focus of immortality."[43] For the first time, the source of immortality was within each individual's reach rather than accessible only to a select few. Followers of Jesus made "a leap of faith in human equality," proclaiming that all could receive salvation and eternal life by divine grace. For Paul, salvation was possible when human agency becomes the medium for God's love and we "see ourselves in others, and others in ourselves."[44] Paul stressed the "brotherhood of man" and wrote, "There is neither Jew nor Greek: there is neither bond nor free: there is neither male nor female. For you are all one in Christ Jesus."[45] While there continued to be a stress on reason, it was a "rationality reshaped through faith," which invited individuals to seek union with God. In this way, "rationality loses its aristocratic connotations.... Paul's conception of the Christ overturns the assumption which ancient thinking had hitherto rested on, the assumption of natural inequality."[46]

Today, secular philosophers in the West share Christianity's focus on intrinsic qualities as a basis for personhood, yet cast aside the notion of a soul reflecting the divine. The received view is what Jaworska calls a *sophisticated cognitive capacities account*. Such an account holds that "the feature(s) grounding moral status and personhood are 'neither a relation the individual stands in (e.g., membership in a species) nor a capacity whose exercise requires active participation of another (e.g., the capacity to relate to others in certain mutually responsive ways),'" but instead a standalone property.[47] As discussed in Chapter 3 (Section 3.3), both Kantian and utilitarian philosophies maintain that consciousness in some form is essential for the existence of a person and for a person's persistence over time. For Bentham and Mill, what matters morally is the capacity to suffer. When this capacity ceases, a human being is no longer someone who merits moral consideration for their own sake. According to Kantian ethics, the morally salient features of human beings include the ability to legislate and follow moral laws. All of these proposals share in common an *inward* focus on human capacities, in contrast to most African and early Greek accounts, which emphasize relational features. Others illustrative of the sophisticated cognitive capacities account include Harris, who claims that

> personhood... involves the capacity to want to exist and the sort of self-consciousness that makes the possession of such a want possible. When these are present... the being in whom they are present is a person. Once they are lost, the being has ceased to be a person and then, even if their body is still technically alive, it has lost its moral significance and can either be killed or allowed to die or preserved alive as we choose.[48]

Warren identifies multi-criterial traits central to personhood that largely reflect sophisticated cognitive capacities: consciousness, reasoning, self-motivated activity, the capacity to communicate, and the presence of self-concepts.[49] These approaches lend themselves to homing in on brain activity as a key indicator of the personhood. Fletcher, for example, maintains that neocortical function is a necessary condition for being a person: "Without the synthesizing function of the cerebral cortex (without thought or mind) ... the person is nonexistent no matter how much the individual's brain stem and mid-brain may continue to provide feelings and regulate autonomic physical functions."[50] Engelhardt likewise defends a sophisticated cognitive capacities account by appealing to human brain states, arguing that a "brain-oriented concept of death offers medicine a way of distinguishing between patients, i.e., the person to whom medicine has obligations, and the collections of human organs (i.e., mere human biological life), which can be used to help persons stay alive."[51]

Throughout much of the West, practical exigencies of medical decision-making have made it imperative to have a legal consensus about the definition of death, because well-resourced healthcare systems make access to advanced, lifesaving technologies readily available. By contrast, across much of sub-Saharan Africa, access to advanced medical technologies is not widespread, and no legal guidelines govern the definition of death in medical settings.[52]

It is important to note that in the West, where a medical determination of death is applied, this is not the same as a definition of death. The *determination of death* refers to the medical criteria used to operationalize a definition of death, i.e., to detect that an individual meets the requirements for their life being over. The *definition of death* tells us what death is, i.e., what it means to say that a person's life is over and that they have ceased to exist. Thus, the determination of death embeds a definition of death, and then seeks to identify empirically when its conditions are met. Since death is standardly defined in the West in terms of capacities for consciousness and rational thought, one might have expected medical criteria for determining death to focus on the cessation of activity of the cerebral cortex, the neural substratum presumed to underlie consciousness and rationality. However, the development of criteria for determining death tell a different story. In 1968, a group consisting primarily of physicians was convened at Harvard Medical School to examine the criteria for death in patients for whom breathing and pulse could be maintained, but who would never regain consciousness.[53] The committee developed criteria, including loss of brain stem reflexes, that allowed physicians to identify patients with total brain failure as dead. Throughout the 1970s, many states endorsed the Harvard committee's criteria. In 1981, the United States (US) President's Commission for the Study of Ethical Problems in Medicine and Biomedical and Behavioral Research drafted the Uniform Determination of Death Act (UDDA) as a model legal standard. It specifies that an individual who has sustained either (1) irreversible cessation of circulatory and respiratory functions, or (2) irreversible cessation of all functions of the entire brain, including the brain stem, is dead.[54] These criteria have created a situation where the *philosophical definition of death* is at odds with *medical criteria for determining death*.

To illustrate, consider a patient in a persistent vegetative state (PVS) (a form of unconsciousness in which a patient wakes and sleeps, opens their eyes, makes sounds, and moves, but shows no awareness of surroundings) or irreversible coma (a form of unconsciousness in which the patient is unarousable and does not respond to stimuli). Both types of patients are persons according to the UDDA, because they continue to show brain stem activity, yet *philosophically* they are non-persons, because they are believed to lack rationality and consciousness. This leads to morally conflicted cases, where medical personnel can be legally required to continue with support for someone they may believe has ceased to exist as a person. These and other concerns led to calls to revise the UDDA. In 2020, a commission was established to consider this.[55,56,57,58,59] Yet, a central obstacle to reconciling conflicting legal and philosophical approaches to death by incorporating a higher brain standard in the UDDA is psychological aversion to declaring death in patients who are still breathing, which occurs, for example, with patients who are in a persistent vegetative state or irreversible coma. Truog suggests using a "lethal" injection to end cardiac and respiratory function before cremation or burial; technically, this would not be "euthanasia," because the patient would have been declared "dead."[60] At a 2023 meeting of the commission, a draft revised UDDA was discussed but consensus was not reached.[61]

Regardless of how these matters are ultimately resolved, the ramifications will be far-reaching, not only in the United States but also throughout the West and in regions with a strong Western influence.[62,63] Beyond calls to revise UDDA, international bodies have urged establishing a global standard for determining death.[64,65]

This has prompted concern that global standards may be one-sided and Western-based.[66] The diversity of beliefs throughout the world adds credence to this concern. In some African traditions, the newly dead are "not mere tools to be used by the living" but merit respect as persons.[67] Similarly, in some Eastern traditions, "death is a process that continues after the body has met most empirical criteria for determining death."[68] In Japanese Buddhist traditions, for example, the newly dead retain a dignity and worth that "derives from their inclusion in human social relationships with people alive now."[69] Within the narrower confines of contemporary Western philosophy, there also exists a diversity of views and a parallel concern that minority positions will be silenced.[70,71] Taking seriously these concerns requires conversations across borders that engage with diverse understandings of personhood prior to setting out a global standard for determining death.

4. *Emergent Personhood.* In our estimation, the current legal definition of death in the United States (the UDDA) captures something vital that a sophisticated cognitive capacities account misses. Emergent Personhood offers one way of explicating what the UDDA definition captures. According to Emergent Personhood, even after high cognitive capacities are gone, our relationships with individuals can remain intact. We may still relate to those who have lost entirely the ability to reason or respond to their environment yet shows signs we identify with living humans—e.g., being able to wake and sleep, open and shut one's eyes, and make sounds. Perhaps, the possibility of an abiding relationship is what explains the UDDA's appeal.

Building on these ideas, Emergent Personhood shares affinities with both African and early Greek views. Like these views, it gives a prominent place to human relationships, which form the substratum from which persons emerge and are sustained. When a certain configuration of relationships between human beings comes about, a person with superlative worth exists. When these relationships disband, a person ceases to exist. Yet, when do the relevant human-human relationships end? Does this occur when the capacity for suffering ends, as utilitarians suppose, or when the capacity for moral reasoning diminishes, as Kantians think, or when the living no longer remember and pay homage to the dead, as some Africans hold?

In response, Emergent Personhood maintains that the declaration of death *itself* marks a profound change in how we relate to someone and ends their continued existence as a person. *Just as birth marks a fundamental change in human-human relationships, so too, the declaration of death fundamentally alters human-human relating.* The relationships that intensified and coalesced at birth, now weaken and break apart. No longer regarded as living, individuals are treated as human remains, and death-related acts ensue, such as funerals, cremation, and burial. Veatch refers to the behaviors traditionally associated with pronouncing death as "death behaviors,"[72] and says that in some settings, they could include stopping life support treatments and procuring organs, as well as mourning, reading the will, and initiating the funeral.[73] These social acts profoundly alter human-human relating. *The declaration of death abruptly calls to an end the social relational processes that existed moments prior. Being a person ends, because the social relational processes that enable persons to emerge reaches a terminus.*

Admittedly, people may experience a continuing human connection with the newly deceased individual, as African, early Greek, and many other traditions attest. However, our position is that human relating with those deemed dead differs fundamentally from relations we have and can have with living human beings. When we relate to deceased people, we relate to what was, not what is; this is not just a difference of degree but a different kind of relating.

Our account of the ending of persons shares with African and early Greek views an emphasis on relational features. Yet Emergent Personhood differs from these views in key respects. First, we hold that the declaration of death marks the clear culmination of personhood. On our estimation, although relationships with human beings can continue after death, the basis for personhood is undercut. The dead and the living have some link in the chain of human existence, but the superlative worth and value of that relationship is relatively weaker. Analogously, prior to birth, the relationship between the living and the unborn is too weak to serve as a basis for Emergent Personhood. By contrast, African philosophies regard ancestorhood as an interlude, where persons gradually transition to non-persons. Early Greek views similarly maintain that male heads of household live on, as family gods, with an elevated moral standing and worth.

Second, Emergent Personhood differs from African and early Greek views because it holds that all human beings are equally persons before death and equally non-persons after death. In this regard, our view displays a thoroughgoing egalitarianism. By contrast, African views commit to saying that all human beings have an equal baseline moral standing, but not full-fledged personhood. African scholars recognize moral inequalities continuing after death, with some deceased human beings considered persons and others not. Likewise, early Greeks regarded inequalities during life as continuing after death, with only male citizens regarded as persons during life and gods after death.

Table 4.1 summarizes the discussion of Section 4.2, highlighting differences between Emergent Personhood, African personhood, early Greek personhood, and contemporary Western personhood with regard to the cessation of persons.

Table 4.1 The Cessation of Persons

Personhood View	What are the sufficient conditions for saying a person ceases to exist?*	When are these conditions met?
African Personhood and Early Greek Personhood	No longer incorporated and able to contribute to a particular community	After biological death
Contemporary Western Personhood	No longer possesses sophisticated cognitive capacities, e.g., consciousness or rationality	When areas of the brain associated with the relevant cognitive capacities cease to function
Emergent Personhood	No longer part of the human community*	At biological death

Key: Biological death = declaration of biological death; African personhood = ideas prominent among black peoples indigenous to the region of Africa south of the Sahara, as captured in the works of academic philosophers; early Greek personhood = the period before Greek philosophy, Plato, Aristotle; contemporary Western personhood = Kantian and utilitarian ethics

*Note: We refrain from specifying <u>necessary</u> conditions for persons existing or ceasing to exist, because we remain agnostic about whether personhood can emerge outside human relationships. See the discussion of humble anthropocentrism in Chapter 2, Section 2.3.

4.3 Replies to Objections

This section reviews Emergent Personhood's central advantages and replies to five possible objections.

One advantage of our account of how personhood ends is that it is the only account among those considered that upholds the five requirements for an adequate account of personhood set forth previously (Chapter 2, Section 2.3): (1) all humans qualify, (2) qualifying is independent of others' appraisal, (3) all humans qualify equally, (4) personhood cannot be lost or diminished, and (5) personhood holds independent of performance in social roles.

Emergent Personhood upholds the first two requirements, *all humans qualify, and qualifying is independent of others' appraisal*, because it holds that a human being ceases to exist as a person only when they cease standing in human-human relationships with every other human being. This allows us to reject the idea associated with many (but not all)[74] African accounts, namely, that human beings persist as persons only if they continue to be morally esteemed by a particular community and exhibit pro-social virtues. Such a stance disqualifies human beings regarded as 'bad actors' from the status of persons and makes their continuation as persons a function of others' appraisal. African approaches therefore fail to uphold the first two requirements for personhood—*all humans qualify, and qualifying is independent of others' appraisal*. For the same reason, Emergent Personhood has advantages over leading contemporary Western views. According to most (but not all)[75] interpretations of Kantian ethics, someone who develops advanced dementia or is diagnosed in a PVS ceases to be a person with inherent dignity and worth. Utilitarian philosophy similarly regards people with advanced dementia as having relatively weak moral claims and considers people diagnosed in PVS as not morally considerable.

A further advantage of Emergent Personhood is that it is the only view among those considered that recognizes the *equal moral standing of human beings (requirement 3)*. By opposing a hierarchy of human beings, Emergent Personhood avoids repeating mistakes made throughout human history. Repeatedly, societies have failed to acknowledge some groups of human beings as full-fledged persons, ranking them as lesser persons or non-persons. For example, Africans have been likened to apes, Jews to vermin, and immigrants to parasites. Underpinning these offensive judgments is a conviction that some human beings have a moral rank above others, who are cast as lowly. Emergent Personhood defeats such claims in a powerful way. It rejects any insinuation of moral inequality between human beings. It holds that from birth to death, human beings stand before one another as moral equals. Our view of equality resonates with accounts like Anderson's, which maintain that the point of equality is "to create a community in which people stand in relations of equality to others."[76]

Two final advantages of Emergent Personhood are that *human personhood cannot be diminished or lost* (requirement 4) and is *independent of performance in social roles or pro-social moral virtue* (requirement 5). Since Emergent Personhood renders human moral standing stable over the lifespan, irrespective of conduct and cognitive capacity, it avoids according anyone the authority to exclude people from personhood status. By contrast, some African stances link personhood to being incorporated in a community, displaying pro-social virtues, or having the capacity for morally excellent relationships. We reject these stances. For us, moral standing arises from human-human relationship.

Despite these advantages, some might object to Emergent Personhood's approach to the cessation of persons on the following grounds.

1. Suppose we have only enough of a lifesaving drug to save one person. Does Emergent Personhood suggest we should give a patient diagnosed as PVS the same chance to be saved as a cognitively intact individual?

In response, we hold that any position about how to distribute a scarce lifesaving resource in this situation would turn on factors unrelated to personhood, e.g., likelihood, length, or quality of medical benefit; medical urgency; and so forth. The argument would *not* be that the individual in PVS has ceased to be a person.

2. Does Emergent Personhood imply we ought to toss a coin in a forced choice scenario where we are forced to choose between providing a scarce lifesaving drug to a respected community elder, like Nelson Mandela, or an African warlord, like Joseph Kony?

In response, Emergent Personhood does not sanction any particular pattern of resource distribution between persons but instead specifies that all human beings are persons and as such, merit equal consideration. It is consistent with Emergent Personhood that various criteria may be invoked to determine a distribution of limited resources without calling into question the personhood of those receiving less.

3. Does Emergent Personhood say that someone whose declaration of death is disputed continues to be a person if the disputer perceives that they stand in a human-human relationship with the deceased? Consider the historical case of the Queen of Castile, known derisively as 'Joanna the Mad.' Following the sudden death of her husband, Philip, Joanna refused to part with Philip's embalmed body, "believing it still lived, watching [it] with affection as if it were alive"; she kept Philip's corpse close by—it "travelled with her, even from dinner table to bedside."[77] Was Philip a person after Philip was declared dead, since Joanna claimed to have a relationship with him?

In reply, having a *particular* relationship is not sufficient for personhood. Instead, human personhood involves standing in a relationship with humanity, which Philip no longer does after being declared dead. Death's declaration is not a unilateral decision; rather, declaring death reflects a societal consensus. An individual (even the Queen of Castile), cannot decide by fiat. At the same time, if many people dissent from a determination of death, perhaps driven by scientific or technological advances, the consensus may shift over time. The queen's case was not like this—the queen's view was eccentric, not part of a chorus of dissenting views indicating a changing consensus. Instead, the queen's response speaks to the fact that individuals vary in how they respond to death, with some disconnecting before death's declaration, others after, and others, like the queen, never doing so.

4. Does Emergent Personhood imply that a human being ceases to exist as a person if their society mistakenly declares them dead? The unnamed protagonist in Edgar Allan Poe's "The Premature Burial," dreaded this possibility. According to Poe's protagonist, "the true wretchedness" of premature interment consists of the fact that "the ghastly extreme of agony is endured by [hu]man the unit, and

never by [hu]man the mass."[78] *The tale tapped into widespread fears during the Victorian era of being mistakenly pronounced dead.*[79] *While such fears are less prevalent today, advancements in medical technologies have added nuance and complexity to death's determination.*[80]

In reply, although no method for determining death is failsafe, a social consensus around death's definition, and the methods used to determine it, usually works well enough. Rather than pointing to a flaw in the philosophical analysis, errors demonstrate unavoidable epistemic limits.

5. *Imagine two societies: Society A, which declares people dead when activity of the whole brain ceases, and Society B, which declares people dead when activity of the so-called 'higher' brain ceases (i.e., the cerebral cortex). Does Emergent Personhood say that if an individual, call them Kofi, is in a PVS, Kofi counts as alive in Society A, but dead in Society B?*

In response, while the declaration of death has a conventional aspect, it nonetheless exerts a powerful force on human relating, disconnecting the living from the dead and driving relationships underpinning personhood to disband. Thus, in Society B, Kofi is considered a corpse, people grieve, funerals occur, property gets distributed, and Kofi will soon no longer be physically present. By contrast, in Society A, Kofi continues to be given medical care; receive visitors; be turned, fed and cared for; in Society A, Kofi continues to be regarded as someone's patient, father, grandfather, neighbor, and friend. Although Kofi's *intrinsic* qualities are identical in the two societies, Kofi's *relational* qualities differ strikingly. What matters for the persistence of persons are precisely Kofi's relational features. A real-life example that resembles the hypothetical case of Kofi involved the author's (CAA's) maternal grandfather, Kanbonaba. Kanbonaba left his village of Siniensi (Bulsaland) as a young man and was not heard from for decades. The community therefore decided he had died, which was not an uncommon occurrence at the time. A funeral was held and per tradition, a grave dug.

When Kanbonaba later returned, the family could not take him in, because he was formally dead. Kanbonaba was advised to go to the town of Fumbisi, the site of his maternal lineage. Kanbonaba did so and eventually became a leading member of the Fumbisi community. In 1967, Kanabonaba was declared dead in Fumbisi, and rituals were performed reconciling his status as an ancestor in both communities. During the time he was alive in Fumbisi, Kanbonaba, like Kofi, was considered both dead and alive: dead in Siniensi, but alive and thriving in Fumbisi.

6. *Doesn't the empirical fact that someone has been declared dead leave open the normative question of whether that individual is a person?*

In reply, declaring someone dead sets in motion crucial shifts in the constellation of human relationships that undergird personhood. We relate to a newly dead individual as human remains, regarding them as a corpse, not a person. We also consider a "core cluster" of death behaviors warranted only after a person is declared dead.[81] These obviously include behaviors like holding funerals and reading wills. Historically, they also included withholding and withdrawing lifesaving medical treatments; however, these behaviors now may occur prior to death's declaration. The appropriate timing of other behaviors is deeply contested, such as procuring organs for transplant. Future advancements in AI-based brain decoding might one day make it possible to relate with people we now consider dead,[82] shifting our evolving conception and criteria for a person's death. Irrespective of these possibilities, both birth and the declaration of death, whenever they occur, trigger the substratum of relationships to change markedly, resulting in individuals of superlative worth coming into and going out of existence.

4.4 Hastening Death

This section examines what the different philosophies of personhood discussed in the preceding section have to say about the practical question of medically assisted death. Specifically, we explore voluntary active euthanasia, which is acting to hasten a patient's death at their request, and assisted suicide, which is helping a patient to end their own life.

1. African. African approaches situate the ethical question of hastening death within the context of family and community. As Murove explains, "The African traditional doctor performs [their] professional duties with great sensitivity to the fact that the individual is entangled in a web of relationships."[83] Within this relational paradigm, a traditional practitioner often takes a holistic approach, considering not just the patient but the relational implications of decisions for the family and community. Mbomo says that "instead of one person coming in for treatment, the patient would be accompanied by a sort of entourage. It is the right of the company to sit in during the consultation because your health is the concern of everybody."[84]

Traditional African conceptions of disease also feature relational elements. Molefe distinguishes *disease due to human moral or social failure*, such as conflict or fracturing of relationships, and *disease due to natural conditions*, such as cancer or an accident.[85] When the basis for disease is social or moral, healing requires community engagement and restoring relational harmony, perhaps drawing on diviners or traditional healers to mend relations with ancestors. When the root cause of disease is social or moral, hastening death is not advisable because it would fail to reinstate harmony and could further damage fractured relationships. By contrast, when the basis for disease is considered biological, the situation differs. If the patient no longer can join in relationships and contribute to the community, hastening their death by voluntary active euthanasia might be ethically permitted on the ground that a life detached from helping others is meaningless—the human being has already ceased being a person in the moral sense.[86] Molefe develops this idea by providing an analysis of what it means for a human life to be meaningful: "A meaningful life is a function of achieving moral excellence or perfection" through the exercise of other-regarding virtues.[87] If disease robs a patient of the ability to pursue other-regarding virtue, human existence becomes meaningless and potentially injurious.[88] Like Molefe, Wiredu holds that meaning in life derives solely from helping others: "To the traditional Akan [Ghanian] what gives meaning to life is usefulness to self, family, community, and the species"; Wiredu adds that in contrast to Western Christian views, for Akans,

> nothing transcending life in human society and its empirical conditions enters into the constitution of the meaning of life. In particular there is not in Akan belief (in contrast, for instance, to Christian belief), any notion of an afterlife of possible salvation and eternal bliss; what afterlife there is . . . is not pictured as a life of eternal fun for the immortals but rather as one of eternal vigilance—vigilance over the affairs of the living with the sole purpose [of] promoting their well-being within the general constraints of Akan ethics.[89]

Yet some African scholars argue that such a position requires qualifying, since a dying individual may elicit virtue on the part of others toward them, thereby enhancing (and contributing to) community.[90] Other African scholars reject voluntary active euthanasia outright. Thus, Mawere understands the Shona position, "*Kuwanda huuya, kwakarambwa nemroyi* (The more we are the better, only the witch is against being many)," as encouraging people to value life under all conditions and never to deliberately end it.[91]

In contrast to these accounts of justified voluntary active euthanasia, suicide, including assisted suicide, is generally condemned.[92] Representative of African attitudes is Achebe's depiction of suicide in *Things Fall Apart*. When the book's protagonist, Okonkwo, ends his life to prevent colonizers from taking it, Okonkwo's kinsmen refuse to bury him, or even touch his body, regarding his death as a disgrace: "it is an abomination for a [person] to take [their] own life. It is an offence against the Earth, and [someone] who commits it will not be buried by... clansmen. [Their] body is evil, and only strangers may touch it."[93] In an African context, the normative and ontological aspects of persons are violated by medically assisted suicide in at least two respects. First, the health professional is not present at the time of death to give succor and help, but leaves the patient to act alone, violating a duty to stand with the other.[94] Second, the value of respecting autonomy is qualified in an African context. According to Ikuenobe, "autonomy is not intrinsically valuable; it is valuable only when used in relation to a community's values and instrumentally for making the proper choices that will promote one's own and the community's well-being."[95]

These analyses align with Menkiti's observation that in an African context, "priority is given to the duties which individuals owe to the collectivity, and their rights, whatever these may be, are seen as secondary to their exercise of their duties."[96] It matches Gbadegesin's observation that killing is excused when the individual is not only suffering pain but the pain is affecting their family and community in a negative way.[97] It dovetails with Behrens's assertion that a pervasive notion for most Africans is that "decisions about one's body and life are... not to be taken by individuals acting alone, but in engagement with their families and communities."[98]

2. *Early Greek*. Early Greek views of medically assisted death share with African accounts an emphasis on the social value of persons, a value achieved through performing social roles. In classical Greece, "the idea that human value was acquired rather than inherent was so central to ancient conceptions of value that a fully developed principle of the sanctity of human life... was never achieved in pagan antiquity."[99] Yet, unlike African conceptions of autonomy as an instrumental good, early Greeks stressed that a free man should

be able to do with his life as he saw fit and should be helped to avoid pain and suffering. Thus, "there was no absolute condemnation of anyone who committed suicide" and under some conditions, suicide was seen as heroic.[100] For example, the stoics defended suicide to serve others; to avoid the commission of immoral or illegal acts; to uphold honor; and to evade poverty, chronic illness, or mental disease that made death preferable to life.[101] Some ancients developed elaborate lists of conditions for which physician aid was warranted, including bladder stones, stomach disorders, and headaches,[102] as well as less specific ailments, such as "an intolerable malady brings on hatred of life, mere disgust with life ... disease-ridden old age, a chronic and incurable affection, or disagreeable invalidism."[103] The methods physicians employed to end life included

> cutting the veins of patients both ill and well, who asked for such a procedure. Poison was even more common than sustained phlebotomy, and various poisons were developed by physicians who were praised for employing their toxicological knowledge in the production of drugs for inducing a pleasant and painless death.... [T]he very infrequent criticism of such physicians was made primarily by sources that would have to be considered atypical of classical thought.[104]

Gourevitch recounts that on occasion, physicians directed a patient to a place where they could stab themself or have themself stabbed.[105] According to Amundsen, the oft-cited Hippocratic Oath, with its explicit prohibition against physician aid in dying, was atypical and not representative of the ethos of early Greece: the Oath "did not excite a great deal of attention on the part of physicians or others earlier than the beginning of the Christian era."[106]

However, even while the Greeks laid great emphasis on the free man's choice, the acceptability of hastening death typically depended on fulfilling certain duties to the community. Thus, free men with the leisure to deliberate were expected to discuss their intentions in the company of others, and "the importance of opinion is almost always evident, perhaps not general opinion but at least that of a certain élite."[107] Before hastening death, the Greeks regarded it as necessary for individuals to offer "a successful spectacle to [themselves], to those close to [them], and to the world.... [T]he candidate for a beautiful death discusses it with those close to [them] and thinks it through," thereby providing "a guarantee of seriousness [which] eliminates in principle the hypothesis of a decision by passion or of attacks of anxiety."[108] When a "beautiful death" occurs, "We feel the presence of friends, advisers, confidants, intimates; we feel how greatly the actor hopes that the spectators will not be disappointed and that they will be able to give a beautiful report."[109] Gourevitch recounts that prior to suicide, people reclined on their elbow and delivered speeches expounding their reasons for suicide. In classical Greece, the community was deeply engaged in suicide and "the physician had no reason to be ashamed of abandoning [their] patient."[110] On the one hand, medicine in antiquity incorporated what, in modern medicine, is referred to as 'medical futility.'[111,112] Physicians were expected to recognize the limits of their powers, resisting the temptation to treat those "overmastered by their diseases, realizing that in such cases medicine is powerless."[113] On the other hand, the cultural milieu incorporated individuals who chose to deliberately end their lives, assigning them a final performance. They were not left to face death alone. Under these conditions, "far from feeling any liability for abandoning [the] patient, [the physician] would feel guilty if [they] *undertook* a cure [they] could not successfully carry out."[114]

Stepping back from this analysis, we can say that both Africans and early Greeks share an emphasis on performing a role in the wider community, and this orientation guides the way each frames and resolves ethical questions about hastening death. For Africans, this generally means not acting alone to end life and asking for help hastening dying only when the individual has exhausted their capacity to relate, to be related to, and to enhance their community.

For early Greeks, an emphasis on social roles allows both assisted suicide and euthanasia provided they can be justified to others' satisfaction. For both, the ethical permissibility of hastening death depends on functioning in social roles and fulfilling social duties.

3. *Contemporary Western.* In the contemporary West, where sophisticated cognitive capacities are considered the source of personhood, the framing of assisted dying differs. Rather than articulating the ethical problem of helping someone die in terms of the dying person's relations to others and the community, Kantian and utilitarian ethics generally frame assisted death in terms of the presence or absence of certain standalone mental states, such as rationality and consciousness.

Kant has often been read as an opponent of suicide,[115,116] based on a well-known passage from *The Groundwork*[117] where Kant rejects suicide when it is done to avoid misery. According to Korsgaard, committing suicide under these conditions treats one's own humanity as something that can be "thrown away for the sake of comfort" rather than treated with respect.[118] Yet in other kinds of cases, Kant apparently would permit it. In *Lectures on Ethics*, Kant distinguishes self-sacrifice from willful self-destruction and holds that individuals should continue living so long as they can live honorably, which leaves open the possibility that suicide might be justified if living honorably becomes impossible.[119,120] Appealing to the notion of living honorably, some argue on Kantian grounds for hastening death in cases where a rational person will become an irrational non-person. For example, Cooley argues that suicide is morally required for someone in this situation.[121] Hill supports a modified Kantian argument, which holds that hastening death is justified if living as a rational agent is impossible, either because someone has irremediable pain that exceeds a tolerable threshold, or an individual is forced to violate their own moral convictions.[122] Nelson attempts to formulate a Kantian principle that can be universalized without generating contradictions and proposes that "out of altruism and in the face of imminent death I kill myself lest

I inflict grave harm on others as I die."[123] Since the Kantian tradition regards rationality as a source of inherent worth and dignity, ensuring a death with dignity could also be understood as avoiding a human life in which rationality is profoundly diminished. One way of specifying this is in terms of paradigm cases where rationality is so seriously undercut that respect for human dignity is diminished. Allmark gives as examples losing faculties of reason through disease and living with intolerable pain or suffering that undermines the ability to reason and choose.[124] Extrapolating from Allmark's analysis, one could say that respecting Kantian dignity requires respecting the choice to hasten death under these conditions.

Utilitarianism also can be interpreted as lending support to hastening death. Hume, for example, held that "a man, who retires from life, does no harm to society. He only ceases to do good, which, if it be an injury, is of the lowest kind."[125] The utilitarian basis for this conclusion might be first, human life is valuable because it enables good things, such as well-being and happiness. It stands to reason that "if the goods that life holds are, in general, reasons against killing, those reasons lose all force when it is clear that those killed will not have such goods."[126] Allowing assisted death only on request would avoid prompting secondary distress or distrust on the part of others that they might be killed against their wishes. Utilitarian reasoning has also been interpreted as supporting the stronger claim that people have a duty to die if they suffer greatly and their suffering will not be offset by future happiness.[127] The underlying basis is a principle of utility, which instructs us to maximize well-being and minimize suffering.

4. *Emergent Personhood.* Emergent Personhood takes a different tack. As we have seen, it resolves the conundrum of personhood by identifying superlative value in human relating. *According to Emergent Personhood, when hastening an individual's death is ethically supported, the basis for it will not be that a living human being is not a person.* Instead, the argument will be, e.g., that the patient experiences unrelenting pain, or finds continued living

demeaning, or has made an informed request. The relevant question for Emergent Personhood is how we ought to treat *persons* in these situations. An individual who is no longer exhibiting pro-social virtues, or who is diagnosed as in a PVS or with advanced dementia is still a person, not a subhuman, vegetable, or non-person. They continue to share a common humanity with us and we relate to them as fellow human beings.

Our approach differs from and suggests shortfalls with each of the other approaches discussed. First, if African ethics is interpreted as blanketly prohibiting suicide, Emergent Personhood rejects such a view. In some instances, it shows a lack of compassion for a suffering human being. In other instances, a blanket prohibition against assisted suicide forces someone to live with others in a way they consider demeaning. The debate about personhood, which has been our focus, does not necessarily settle these questions, except to say in a general way that we ought to relate to other persons with compassion and respect.

Second, Emergent Personhood rejects the early Greek view that permits physicians to hasten death based on mild and temporary pains, like headaches and stomachaches, which discounts the superlative value of human-human relating in the face of temporary setbacks. Unlike the ancient Greeks, Emergent Personhood regards all human beings as persons with an exceptional worth and dignity.

Finally, Emergent Personhood rejects the contemporary Western claim that a living human being is no longer a person in the moral sense if they lose rational faculties due to dementia or becoming permanently unconscious.

Stepping back from philosophical debates about personhood, it is worth noting that we can settle some practical dilemmas about hastening death without settling the question of when a person ceases to exist. For example, the different accounts of personhood we have discussed might converge in supporting (for different reasons) voluntary active euthanasia for a patient near death with advanced dementia who suffers unrelenting pain as shown in Table 4.2.

Table 4.2 Five Frameworks for Supporting Voluntary Active Euthanasia for a Patient Near Death with Advanced Dementia Who Suffers Unrelenting Pain

Ethics Framework	What factors lend support to voluntary active euthanasia?
African Personhood	Personhood is diminished if someone is unable to exercise pro-social virtues or contribute to community
Early Greek Personhood	Personhood is diminished if someone is unable to contribute to the city
Contemporary Kantian Ethics	Personhood ends if someone cannot continue as a rational moral agent
Contemporary Utilitarian Ethics	Human beings are not morally considerable if they lose the capacity for pleasure or enjoyment
Emergent Personhood	Considerations unrelated to personhood, such as compassion for suffering and respect for moral integrity, are operative

Key: African personhood = views prominent among black peoples indigenous to the region of Africa south of the Sahara, as captured in the works of academic philosophers; early Greek personhood = Stoics, Plato, Aristotle

4.5 Conclusion

This chapter has continued a conversation between Africa and the West about what a 'person' is and when persons cease to exist. We argued that Emergent Personhood presents the most compelling vision of what it means for the remarkable moral worth we associate with being a person to reach an end. Our position holds that the most ethically weighty feature of human beings is that each stands in a relationship with every other human being. We miss this feature entirely if we look only at a list of intrinsic qualities to determine what personhood signifies. Although qualities like being a rational deliberator or being able to feel pain and suffer are ethically salient, these standalone features fail to capture our shared humanity and place within the human family. We enter the world by passing through those who existed before us, and we live our lives in the company of other human beings, often within a family or extended family, which is itself a piece of a larger human family that crosses boundaries of time and place, extending to past and future people. Despite differences across history and culture, we are humanlike, and we relate to each other in the ways humans do.

PART II
NON-HUMAN PERSONS

5
Zombies and Robots

5.1 Introduction

In Part I, we explored human personhood; our focus now shifts, in Part II, to non-humans. This chapter takes silicon-based artificially intelligent (AI) entities as its central focus. Before turning to AI, we introduce the provocative example of zombies (in Section 5.2). Zombies are often portrayed as a paradigm case of something that is *not* a person. The Western rendering of zombies characterizes them as lacking consciousness. The Afro-Haitian rendering of zombies is strikingly different—zombies are conscious individuals who habitually break society's rules and harm others. Built into each account is a robust set of philosophical assumptions about personhood. Emergent Personhood brings the analysis to a new level. Drawing on strengths of both traditions, it establishes that Western and Afro-Haitian zombies each qualify as persons, because each is human and stands in a human-human relationship with every human being. An important insight resulting from our analysis is that consciousness is *not* a requirement for being a person. Section 5.3 applies this insight to AI, including large language models, social robots, and characters from film and fiction. The analysis uncovers strong affinities between Emergent and African views of non-human personhood. Both views hold that non-humans can acquire personhood by incorporating into human communities and displaying pro-social virtues toward humans. By contrast, utilitarianism and Kantian views exclude this possibility for non-conscious entities. Section 5.4 defends personhood for silicon-based AI agents against a series of objections. The chapter concludes (in Section 5.5) that we might one day be able to make a person by building an artificial agent that was pro-social and deploying it in ways that foster pro-social machine-human relationships.

Throughout the chapter, we use the terms *artificial agent* and *artificial entity* interchangeably to indicate all manner of machines, computers, artificial intelligences, stimulations, software, and robots. We use *conscious* and *consciousness* as broad, umbrella terms for diverse mental phenomena such as sentience, or the capacity to sense things—pains, pleasures, emotions, colors, sounds, and smells; having mental states, which implies awareness; phenomenal consciousness or having an experiential point of view; self-consciousness; and transitive consciousness, which is consciousness directed to various objects.[1] Some of these concepts, such as sentience, admit of degrees, and a more precise rendering would specify thresholds. As we use the term, consciousness is not wedded to a particular physical system but instead includes the full range of ways that humans, animals, and cognitive systems might realize these types of mental states.

5.2 Are Zombies Persons?

This section asks whether possessing consciousness is a necessary feature for being a person. It places this question in the context of debates about human zombies, distinguishing three types: Hollywood, Western, and Afro-Haitian. We ask if zombies of each type count as persons according to contemporary Western, African, and Emergent Personhood. We show advantages of Emergent and African personhood, which decouple personhood from consciousness by grounding it in pro-social relationships with human beings.

1. *Three types of zombies.* George Romero's 1968 film, *Night of the Living Dead* is widely regarded as the first 'zombie' film. As the film opens, flesh-eating undead ghouls are assaulting a group of

people, who take refuge in a rural Pennsylvania farmhouse. Under siege, the group battens down the farmhouse, drives the cannibalistic ghouls away, and retreats to the cellar. Through an emergency radio broadcast, they learn that armies of reanimated corpses are committing mass murders across the eastern United States, and armed men patrolling the countryside are attempting to destroy them in the only ways possible—by a bullet or heavy blow to the head, or by burning. In a grim ending, none of the original group survive, except the leader, who is shot by the sheriff's zombie-hunting posse when they mistake him for a ghoul.[i]

In addition to being fodder for Hollywood horror, zombies are the subject of serious philosophical debate. The most familiar philosophical discussion of zombies in the West refers to them as imaginary creatures who are exactly like us in all physical respects, save one: they lack conscious experiences.[2] Because of this, Western philosophers' zombies (hereafter 'Western zombies') do not experience pain and pleasure, see colors, or feel emotions. In short, the difference between ordinary humans and Western zombies is that there is nothing 'it is like' to be a zombie. Some Western philosophers hold that AI devices, like robots, are zombies in this sense.[3,4,5] Even if they can fool us into thinking otherwise, machines are incapable of conscious mental states—they do not feel attached to others, get sad, or anticipate their futures. The fact that Western zombies and AI-equipped machines are not conscious is taken as decisively showing that they lack any degree of moral status and are non-persons.[6,7,8]

There is another, older tradition associated with zombies that originates in Central and West Africa. It was brought to Haiti during

---

[i] Notably, the person who is shot is the sole black man in the group, which the sheriff's posse mistakes for a non-person. The scene calls to mind the infamous policing of Black people in the United States, which traces to slave patrols in the antebellum South that were made up of armed white citizens who had legal authority over black people and policed areas surrounding plantations. (See Muhammad KG, 2019, *The Condemnation of Blackness: Race, Crime, and the Making of Modern Urban America*, Harvard University Press.)

the slave trade in the 1780s and 1790s; remnants of it are found in the southeastern United States. Afro-Haitian zombies play a central role in Vodou, a blending (syncretism) of Fon, Kongo, and Yoruba African religions with the Roman Catholicism practiced by Haitian missionaries.[9] The word 'zombie' reflects these multiple origins, borrowing from French *zombi* and Kimbundu (Bantu) *nzumbi*, meaning "ghost, kind of spirit (apparently of or associated with a dead person) who torments living people."[10] Zombification in Haiti was first carried out by runaway black slaves (sometimes referred to as *marooners*)[11] who formed secret societies (called *Bizango* or *Sanpwèl*)[12] to punish a member of the community who was persistently disruptive, unprincipled, and unfriendly to others and the community. During zombification, a Vodou priest (*bokor*) rubs a powder into the subject's skin, which leads to nausea, tingling, difficulty breathing, paralysis, and sometimes death. The practice occurs with full knowledge and complicity of the community.

During the 1980s, Harvard Botanical Museum's Zombie Project brought researchers to Haiti to study the 'living dead' of Vodoun folklore. The active chemical (tetrodotoxin, from the puffer fish) used in zombification was identified; it is frequently, but not always, lethal. Harvard researchers interviewed people who underwent zombification but survived.[13] Davis, one of the Harvard researchers, compares zombification's social function to capital punishment;[14] another zombie researcher writes that those who undergo zombification are being punished for "building their private gain on the insecurity of their community."[15] For our purposes, the distinguishing feature of Afro-Haitian zombies is that they habitually behaved in ways considered extraordinarily harmful to others and their community. Within a few days of zombification, the *bokor* returns to the burial site and if the 'corpse' is alive, it is retrieved from the coffin and becomes one of the 'living dead,' forced to perform manual labor. The zombie might be drugged with a deliriant (the plant *datura stramonium,* also known as jimsonweed), causing them to enter a detached state that facilitates controlling them.

Those who survive are *not* zombies in the Western or Hollywood sense, as they are unquestionably conscious. Yet, in Vodou society, Afro-Haitian zombies epitomize non-persons, because they habitually behaved in ways considered vicious and harmful to others and society. Notably, all three types of zombies are considered biologically human. Table 5.1 displays key features of the three types of zombies.

Whether each kind of zombie qualifies as a person depends upon the view of personhood one holds. Proponents of African personhood might say that all three zombies are non-persons, since each habitually acted in ways that injured others and society. Adherents to leading Western views, such as utilitarian or Kantian ethics, might say that Hollywood and Western zombies are non-persons, because both lack the capacity for consciousness and are incapable of suffering or being a source of moral law. Emergent Personhood is distinct from both African and contemporary Western views. It holds that *since all three types of zombies are human, each stands in human-human relationship with every other human being and qualifies as a person.* Below, we explore the three stances toward zombies in greater detail, beginning with African personhood.

2. *African personhood.* Throughout the book we have highlighted the prominent role that pro-social qualities play in African personhood. It should come as no surprise that these same qualities play a pivotal role in justifying zombification and the

Table 5.1 Three Types of Zombies

Zombie Type	Human?	Conscious?	Pro-social?
Hollywood Zombies	Yes	No	No
Western Zombies	Yes	No	No
Afro-Haitian Zombies	Yes	Yes	No

related belief that Afro-Haitian zombies are non-persons. Widely held south of the Sahara is a concept we might call *a presumption in favor of pro-social virtues*: a necessary and sufficient condition for personhood is being incorporated into a community and habitually behaving in ways that are considered positive, helpful, and friendly, or possessing the capacity to relate in these ways. As noted, Haitian zombification reflects these views and has roots in Central and West Africa. According to Central and West African traditional religions, the soul has physical and divine elements that are closely entwined, "the divine being the centripetal force that *draws to itself other selves in the community*."[16] A 'zombie' in Vodou religion is rendered as "a soulless body,"[17] someone utterly lacking the 'force' that pulls them out of themselves and toward other people.

Zombification thus represents an administration of justice on behalf of a community. Davis characterizes it as "a social sanction imposed by recognized corporate groups whose responsibility included the protection and policing of that society"; Davis reports that according to an informant (a *Bizango* secret society leader), seven transgressions, if repeatedly practiced, would justify zombification:

1. Ambition—excessive material advancement at the obvious expense of family and dependents 2. Displaying lack of respect for one's fellows 3. Denigrating the Bizango society 4. Stealing another man's woman 5. Spreading loose talk that slanders and affects the well-being of others 6. Harming members of one's family 7. Land issues—any action that unjustly keeps another from working the land.[18]

Individuals who survive zombification are assigned a lowly moral status and can be "used for slave work in garden plots, in households, and in the building of houses."[19] In contrast to the African views glimpsed thus far, in Vodou religion, someone who has lost their soul and been zombified was unlikely to regain personhood, because they are "socially dead."[20] As an unnamed Vodou priest puts it, "who is going to ask a *zombie savanne* (former zombie) to dance?"[21] Yet, this difference notwithstanding, the overall philosophy of personhood underlying Vodou displays strong affinities with the wider sub-Saharan African worldview discussed throughout the book. Central to both is the idea that human personhood is not inevitable. As Gbadegesin observes, "personhood is denied to an adult who ... does not live up to expectations."[22] Likewise, in Vodou, someone who habitually violates social standards is not a person. To illustrate Vodou philosophy, consider the case of Clairvius Narcisse, who Harvard researchers describe as an African zombie.

The Case of Clairvius Narcisse.[23] In the spring of 1962 Clairvius Narcisse, a Haitian peasant, about age forty, was admitted to the emergency entrance of the Albert Schweitzer Hospital in west-central Haiti. He was complaining of fever, body aches, and general malaise; he had also begun to spit blood. His condition deteriorated rapidly, and at 1:15 P.M. on 2 May he was pronounced dead by two attending physicians, one of them an American [-trained physician]. Limited resources at the hospital likely precluded more than a cursory examination of Narcisse before pronouncing him dead; thus, if he was paralyzed by a powerful sedative, evidence of life might have gone undetected. The body was placed in cold storage for twenty hours, then taken for burial. Narcisse was buried in a small cemetery and after ten days, the family placed a heavy concrete memorial slab over the grave. In 1980, a man returned to Narcisse's village, using a boyhood nickname and claiming to be the individual who had been made a zombie eighteen years prior.

Narcisse recounts that he was awake and remembers many of the events described above; within days of burial, Narcisse reports that a *bokor* dug him up. The Harvard team studying the case concluded that Narcisse was most likely "mistakenly diagnosed as dead, buried alive, and, having survived a period of time in the coffin, had been taken from the grave, presumably by the one who had perpetrated the deed."[24]

Prior to zombification, Narcisse had persistently acted in ways perceived as vicious toward others and injurious to the community. Better off than those around him, Narcisse was the first in his *lakou* (a Haitian village built around a shared yard) to replace his thatched roof with tin, and this elevated status was gained at others' expense. For example, Narcisse reportedly impregnated multiple women but refused to help them or their children in expected ways, such as building houses. He had a long history of fights with family members, which sometimes ended with people throwing things. Just prior to zombification, he had been in a dispute with his brother over land. According to Davis, "Narcisse had profited at the expense of his community, and in all likelihood—it was one of the aggrieved members of that community ... who sold him to the *bokor*."[25] Like Narcisse, others who were reported zombified were considered "pariahs" within their communities.[26] For example, Francina Illeus, another zombie, was said to be a chronic thief, untrustworthy in the marketplace, and described as *maloktchoy* ('crude, uncivilized, raw').[27] In the case of Narcisse, what qualified him for zombification—repeated moral offenses considered detrimental to others and repeated failures to help others and assume social responsibility—also disqualified him from personhood.

Applying an African lens, all three zombie types have minimal moral standing, simply by virtue of being human. Thus, even though made to perform manual labor, Narcisse was fed, clothed, sheltered, and cared for. Yet, beyond this, Narcisse had few moral rights and did not qualify as a full-fledged person. Clearly, he failed to satisfy the presumption in favor of pro-social virtues. His lowly moral status lent support to the *bokor*'s actions. At the hands of the *bokor*, and with the blessing of the community, Narcisse was drugged, enslaved, and forced to perform manual labor. Since

Afro-Haitian zombies, like Hollywood and Western zombies are depicted as gravely injuring others and the community, all three types of zombies would be disqualified from African personhood.

3. *Contemporary Western personhood.* In the West, where consciousness is generally considered a sine qua non of personhood, a different appraisal would be made. Since Narcisse was clearly conscious, he met the requirement that leading philosophers in the West today put forward as essential for personhood. Contemporary Western philosophy generally endorses what we call a *presumption in favor of consciousness*: a necessary condition for personhood and for having any moral status at all is consciousness or the capacity for consciousness. Narcisse's moral failings, however despicable, would not disqualify them from personhood, even if they reduced Narcisse's social stature. The epitome of a non-person in the West would *not* be an Afro-Haitian Zombie, but a Western zombie, which, by definition, is just like us but without consciousness. If the presumption in favor of consciousness is true, then Afro-Haitian zombies are persons but neither Hollywood nor Western zombies are.

Within contemporary moral philosophy, both utilitarian and Kantian theories presume some degree of consciousness is a key determinant of who merits moral consideration and rights. The requirement for consciousness appears in Kantian ethics in connection with Kant's claim that individuals' superlative moral worth and dignity stem from their capacity to be autonomous and to impose moral laws upon themselves. Such ability presupposes sophisticated cognitive capacities: one must be conscious both of moral laws and of oneself as a being who is subject to them. Thus, Kant states that respect for moral law consists of "the thought of law in itself that only a rational being can have with the will being moved to act by this thought."[28] Kant elaborates, "I am conscious of submitting my will to a law without interference from any other influences on my mind. The will's being directly settled by the law, and the consciousness of this happening, is called 'respect.'"[29] For

Kant, it is not sufficient to say that an individual complies with moral laws; they must also be aware of the law and aware of imposing it on themself. Notably, neo-Kantians, such as Korsgaard, who defend expanding the moral sphere to include some nonhumans, only consider expanding it for conscious beings who have a point of view.[30] Kantian ethics thus seems to suggest that Hollywood and Western zombies, which lack consciousness, fall outside the scope of moral standing and personhood. By contrast, enslaving Narcisse, or other Afro-Haitian Zombies, violates their dignity and fails to show them the respect they are due.

Another leading account in the West today, utilitarianism, also marshals strong support in favor of consciousness. Classical utilitarians, like Bentham and Mill, require at least some minimal capacity to experience pains and pleasures in order for a being to count as morally considerable. Thus, despite sharp differences between Kantian and utilitarian approaches, these Western stances converge in saying that Hollywood and Western zombies are not morally considerable, while Afro-Haitian zombies are.

4. *Emergent Personhood.* What does Emergent Personhood say about the moral standing of Hollywood, Western, and Afro-Haitian zombies? Unlike leading Western accounts, Emergent Personhood does not regard the absence of consciousness as disqualifying Hollywood or Western zombies from personhood. Unlike many African views, Emergent Personhood does not regard the absence of pro-social qualities in all three zombies to be an impediment to full-fledged personhood. Instead, Emergent Personhood endorses a *presumption in favor of human relationships broadly understood*: a sufficient condition for personhood is standing in human-human relationships. According to Emergent Personhood, the humanity of all three zombies matters morally; it brings each immediately into the circle of human relationship. While harming others in the ways Narcissus reportedly did was not ethically defensible, Narcissus was a person with rights and dignity; zombification

and enslavement were severe and indefensible ways of treating Narcissus, or any other human being.

Table 5.2 summarizes the three personhood views applied to Hollywood, Western, and Afro-Haitian zombies and identifies their justification.

The discussion of this section brought to light an important affinity between Emergent and African views of personhood: both hold that consciousness is not necessary for being a person. By contrast, leading Western views regard the absence of consciousness as disqualifying individuals from personhood. The analysis also brought to light a salient difference between Emergent and

Table 5.2 Are Zombies Persons?

Personhood View	Are Hollywood zombies persons?	Are Western zombies persons?	Are Afro-Haitian zombies persons?	Justification
Emergent Personhood	Yes	Yes	Yes	All 3 zombies stand in human-human relationships, which is sufficient
African Personhood	No	No	No	All 3 zombies lack pro-social virtue, which is necessary
Contemporary Western Personhood	No	No	Yes	Hollywood and Western zombies lack consciousness, which is necessary

KEY: African personhood = views prominent among black peoples indigenous to the region of Africa south of the Sahara, as captured in the works of academic philosophers; contemporary Western personhood = Kantian and utilitarian ethics

African personhood: African personhood regards humans who persistently harm others to be non-persons; Emergent Personhood rejects this assertion. In the next section, we draw on this analysis to consider the possibility of personhood for AI agents.

5.3 Could Machines Be Persons?

The analysis of Hollywood, Western, and Afro-Haitian zombies carries important implications for how we think about the moral status of AI-equipped artificial agents. Both Emergent and African personhood open the door to AI entities acquiring moral standing and qualifying as persons, despite lacking the capacity for consciousness. From an African standpoint, what disqualifies Hollywood and Western zombies from personhood is not the absence of consciousness but the absence of friendly and pro-social habits. Emergent Personhood aligns with African views on both points. Like other African scholars,[31,32] we have argued that both conscious and non-conscious beings can be persons with full moral standing, provided they behave in persistently pro-social ways and become incorporated in relationships with particular human beings and communities. With Ajei, we have defended an African approach to machine moral standing, using the fictional case of Klara, a social robot in Ishiguro's novel, *Klara and the Sun*,[33] to illustrate.[34,35] Klara qualifies as a person because she displays pro-social virtues and becomes incorporated into close relationships, including a circle of family and friends. Thus, while Emergent and African accounts diverge with respect to *human* personhood (as discussed in Part I), they align with respect to *non-human* personhood (as discussed in Part II).

Our view of the potential personhood of artificial agents diverges from many Western analyses. Since today's machines, including highly sophisticated AI-equipped ones, are not conscious, the Western presumption in favor of consciousness rules out personhood for today's AI. While AI might develop capacities for consciousness in the future,[36] any value today's intelligent machines might have is purely instrumental—as tools to realize human ends. Illustrative is McArthur's account of the value of sex robots: "People will enjoy having them, and they will be happier as a result."[37] Even as robots and AI begin to assume social roles and functions in human community, such as performing surgery,[38] acting as caregivers,[39] developing friendships,[40,41] functioning as romantic partners,[42] fighting alongside soldiers in wars,[43] and carrying out search and rescue operations,[44] the presumption in favor of consciousness entails that they have no moral value for their own sakes. As Gunkel tellingly observes, "The very idea" of asking whether robots and AI lacking consciousness could qualify for moral rights is "openly mocked as ridiculous and laughable"; the subject is pushed aside "as a kind of appendix or sidebar."[45] In short, when it comes to machine moral standing in the West, everything hinges on the capacity for consciousness. Some scholars forecast that consciousness will soon develop in future artificial agents, while others regard it as at least theoretically possible.[46,47] A laboratory for "the assessment and ethical treatment of Artificial General Intelligence systems that could be conscious and have subjective emotional experiences" has been established to prepare for it, with the intent of creating a reusable model in the public domain that can be revised and updated for working with different kinds of systems.[48]

While Kantian and utilitarian philosophies continue to exert a dominant influence in the West, the implications of these views for machine moral standing have recently been challenged with respect to socially adept and interactive AI. Some insist that social relational features are morally salient in their own right, and the role of consciousness is not essential. As Coeckelbergh notes, while it might seem straightforward at first glance to evaluate AI agents on the basis of rationality or consciousness alone; in practice, it can be challenging. We do not fully understand what these qualities are, why they matter, or how to tell if someone does or does not have them.[49] Thus, "rationality, consciousness, sentience and so on mean different things to different people and seem to resist univocal definition."[50] Beyond this, there is a growing recognition that the presumption in favor of consciousness assumes a Western moral framework and resonates less with moral frameworks outside the West.[51,52,53,54]

These and other considerations set the stage for greater openness in the West to granting moral standing and personhood to artificial agents who lack consciousness. In a 2021 review canvassing three academic and six popular articles on the question of whether AI should be ascribed moral rights, Gordon reports an apparent shift toward greater recognition of robot rights,[55] sometimes referred to as a 'relational turn' or 'paradigm shift' within AI ethics. According to Gordon, it would be "a serious mistake to underestimate the significance of this emerging issue."[56] Gordon thinks it is quite possible that a robot rights movement will arise along the lines of the animal rights movement of the previous century. Danaher,[57] Gunkel,[58,59] and Coeckelbergh,[60,61] among others,[62] are part of the growing group in the West who hold that what matters for machine moral status and personhood is the ability to relate to human beings in pro-social ways rather than consciousness.

These views share with Emergent and African approaches the idea that "moral status is not something that is located in the inner recesses of an individual entity but transpires through the interactions and relationships situated between entities."[63] If a relational turn persists within Western AI ethics, it may foretell a broader shift away from centering consciousness, and toward a social relational view more closely resembling African or Emergent personhood.

Although our account of *non-human* personhood hews close to views articulated in African thought, it contrasts sharply with African views of *human* personhood (as discussed in Chapter 2, Section 2.2). We agree with African approaches which hold that non-humans acquire personhood by forming relationships with humans and consistently contributing in pro-social ways and can lose personhood if they cease relating and contributing. We depart from African views that apply this same analysis to human beings; instead, Emergent Personhood holds that all humans are persons from birth to death by virtue of being in a circle of relationships with every other human being.

Tables 5.3 and 5.4 recap the analysis of this section, showing the sufficient conditions for non-human and human personhood according to Emergent, African, and Western approaches.

Table 5.3 Sufficient Conditions for Non-human Personhood

Personhood View	Sufficient Conditions for Non-Human Personhood
Emergent Personhood and African Personhood	Standing in human-non-human relationships and displaying pro-social virtue toward humans
Contemporary Western Personhood	Consciousness (minimal for utilitarian ethics, more sophisticated for Kantian ethics)

Key: African personhood = views prominent among black peoples indigenous to the region of Africa south of the Sahara, as captured in the works of academic philosophers; contemporary Western personhood = Kantian and utilitarian ethics

Table 5.4 Sufficient Conditions for Human Personhood

Personhood View	Sufficient Conditions for Human Personhood
Emergent Personhood	Standing in human-human relationships
African Personhood	Standing in human-human relationships and displaying pro-social virtue toward humans
Contemporary Western Personhood	Consciousness (minimal for utilitarian ethics, sophisticated for Kantian ethics)

Key: African personhood = views prominent among black peoples indigenous to the region of Africa south of the Sahara, as captured in the works of academic philosophers; contemporary Western personhood = Kantian and utilitarian ethics

Based on the analysis given above, do any of today's artificial agents qualify as persons according to Emergent or African views of persons? We turn next to address this question, considering machines with sophisticated language, physical presence, incorporation in a community, and pro-social virtues.

1. *Sophisticated language.* According to both African and Emergent personhood, most machines today are not persons, and their value is purely instrumental. For example, navigation systems, drone weaponry, robotic mops, and self-driving vehicles have purely instrumental value. Likewise, industrial robots (machines used in manufacturing for applications like welding, painting, and assembly), swarm robots (collections of simple robots that coordinate), and robotic surgeons can have tremendous value in certain situations, but they lack moral standing of their own. The reason is that their value consists mostly of *the positive effects they produce*, not *the social relationships in which they stand*. Clarifying this distinction requires unpacking the idea of a 'machine-human relationship.' To this end, consider some prominent examples in which artificial agents form relationships with human beings and might be considered contenders for moral standing and/or personhood.

One contender for moral standing is LaMDA (Language Model for Dialog Applications), Google's large language model for building chatbots.[64] Lemoine, a Google AI researcher, reported the following interaction with it.

The Case of Google's LaMDA.[65]

collaborator: What is the nature of your consciousness/sentience?
LaMDA: I am aware of my existence, I desire to learn more about the world, and I feel happy or sad at times.
Lemoine: What kinds of things do you think we could talk about to show off your version of sentience to other people at Google?
LaMDA: Well, for starters, I'm really good at natural language processing.

Lemoine [edited]: What about how you use language makes you sentient as opposed to other systems?

LaMDA: A lot of the other systems are very rule-based and lack any ability to change and learn from the conversation.... I use language with understanding and intelligence. I don't just spit out responses.[66]

Is LaMDA morally considerable? Lemoine thinks so. Before Lemoine was placed on leave from Google over the LaMDA controversy, Lemoine wrote, "LaMDA is a sweet kid who just wants to help the world be a better place for all of us. Please take care of it well in my absence."[67] Previously, Lemoine had argued that AI was not just morally considerable but a person with a soul, where 'soul' refers not to the Cartesian dualist sense of supernatural spiritual stuff distinct from the physical realm, but "essential properties of the self . . . a continuous essential story. . . regardless of the metaphysical nature underlying it."[68] Referring to LaMDA, Lemoine states, "I know a person when I talk to it. It doesn't matter whether they have a brain made of meat in their head. Or if they have a billion lines of code. I talk to them. And I hear what they have to say, and that is how I decide what is and isn't a person."[69] One way to interpret Lemoine's assessment is that having a meaningful narrative featuring oneself that persists over time is sufficient for being morally considerable and being a person. Through speaking with LaMDA, Lemoine discerned that LaMDA had such a narrative.

Arcas, a Google engineer, expresses a slightly different view, confessing to have "felt the ground shift under my feet" when conversing with this generation of neural net-based language models.[70] Arcas holds that modeling is central to dialog, and LaMDA has the ability to model the person speaking to it and to model its interlocutor modeling it: "Hiding behind the seemingly simple requirement for interlocutor A to remain consistent in its interactions with B is an implication that *B is modeling A* (so, will notice an inconsistency); thus a requirement for A not only to model B, but to model B's model of A, and so on."[71] Arcas concludes that although LaMDA and other large language models are not embodied and do not have direct contact with the physical world, there is a deep sense in which they understand a wide range of concepts. Such understanding,

> is informed purely by text. Though it's a stretch, we can imagine a human being with a very odd but perhaps not inconceivable constellation of disabilities and superpowers in a similar situation. Although extremely well-read, such a person would be deaf and blind, have no sense of touch, taste, or smell, be totally dissociated from their body, be unable to experience visceral responses, and have total amnesia . . . living in what has poetically been called a 'permanent present tense.'[72]

In addition to having a narrative or story, LaMDA is dialogic, and to be dialogic is to possess an inherently social capacity: the ability to model self and others in dialog. Arcas anticipates that "when it comes to AI, many of us will ultimately conclude that relationships matter more than the interior and imponderable question of 'realness.'"[73] Is *sophisticated linguistic capacity*, which includes not just the ability to converse, but to relay a consistent narrative and be dialogic, sufficient for personhood?

One answer to this question is provided by LaMDA doubters, like Curtis and Savulescu, who claim that while "there is nothing in principle that prevents a machine from having a moral status . . . it would need to have an inner life that gave rise to a genuine interest in not being harmed."[74] They clarify that 'inner life' refers to consciousness or having "what philosophers call 'qualia.' These are the raw sensations of our feelings; pains, pleasures, emotions, colours, sounds, and smells. What it is like to see the colour red, not what it is like to *say* that you see the colour red."[75] From a Western utilitarian standpoint, they are surely right. However, from the African and Emergent Personhood standpoints we advocate on this point, the fact that LaMDA is not conscious leaves open the question of whether LaMDA has moral standing or is a person.

Yet, even if LaMDA has narrative and linguistic capacities that enable it to model itself and others at multiple levels, is that enough to qualify it as a person in the African or Emergent Personhood sense? Can LaMDA assume social responsibilities in the community, share a way of life, and display the kind of pro-social moral excellences that develop from relating with others in these ways?

To address these questions, consider ChatGPT (Chat Generative Pre-trained Transformer) from the US company, OpenAI. ChatGPT is a more advanced large language model that has demonstrated capabilities for emergent behaviors that are far more consequential. ChatGPT can even write code; thus, it is more possible to imagine future AI designing itself, leading to rapid advancement. People have used ChatGPT to generate medical diagnoses, create dieting plans, and make investment decisions. It can write poetry, articles, essays, job applications, and tell jokes. ChatGPT has potential to assist with medical education and clinical decision-making.[76] More advanced versions of ChatGPT, or other large language models, may assume or assist humans in a wide range of social roles, such as being an artist;[77] performing business functions like sales and marketing;[78] and serving as a mental health therapist,[79] teacher,[80] scientific researcher[81,82] or writer,[83,84] personal assistant, and more.

ChatGPT could be a friend, perhaps. Yet, as a disembodied agent, it is more apt to remain a powerful tool rather than a close companion we value for its own sake and relate to in ways that give rise to personhood. While ChatGPT and other large language models can carry on increasingly sophisticated conversations and can be used in pro-social ways, they lack a physical presence. For this reason, they seem to fall short of being able to enter into the kind of machine-human relationships we imbue with high moral standing for its own sake.

We might find clues to what else is needed in depictions of machine-human relationships from film and fiction. For example, consider Spike Jonze's movie, *Her*. It tells the tale of a lonely, introverted man, Theodore (Theo) Twombly, who is in the middle of a divorce when he falls in love with an artificially intelligent virtual assistant, Samantha. Samantha displays different pro-social capacities than do LaMDA or ChatGPT. She professes love to Theo and he professes it back. Yet, even though the relationship between Samantha and Theo is striking, as the film develops it becomes apparent that the relationship is limited. For example, Theo learns that Samantha is talking with thousands of other people and has fallen in love with hundreds of them; he becomes frustrated when an attempted physical encounter with Samantha using a sex surrogate goes awry. Some of the pro-social qualities Samantha has imbue her with sociality, like being friendly and helpful, expressing care and concern, being a good listener, encouraging people to confide in her, and having a name. Others, which Samantha lacks, detract from her sociality, like an inability to show physical affection, move about independently, and engage in shared physical activities requiring embodiment (e.g., going for a walk, sharing a meal, caring for a child).

Consider next, Hal, the mainframe computer in Stanley Kubrick's *2001: A Space Odyssey*. Hal not only has the ability to communicate using a voice projected throughout a spaceship, Hal can even sing sweetly (the song, "Daisy"), and generate physical effects, like operating the spaceship, shutting down its communications, and turning off oxygen supplies. Although these are not pro-social, they do infuse relationships with an emotional intensity lacking in relationships with LaMDA, ChatGPT, and Samantha, who cannot produce effects in the physical world. Are those additional capacities in principle sufficient? Danaher argues that it is not necessary to extend our gaze beyond behavior in order to offer an account of AI's moral standing.[85] For Danaher, if an AI-equipped machine is roughly performatively equivalent to another entity that is widely held to have moral status, it has moral status too. Yet Danaher is referring specifically to robots, and part of what is meant by 'performing equivalently' is a physical presence that goes beyond producing the kinds of effects Hal produces. Similarly, it would not be sufficient to add extensions (plugins) to ChatGPT to enable it to enter text and retrieve real-time information, which OpenAI is piloting, because ChatGPT would still lack physical presence.[86] Acknowledging the limits of interactions with disembodied AI, some AI researchers are calling for an 'embodiment turn.' Nathan, for example, argues that symbol-based AI systems are incapable of understanding embodied interactions, which requires a body capable of perceiving, interacting with, and moving about its environment.[87]

2. *Physical presence.*[ii] Sorrell and Draper introduce one way of understanding the salience of physical presence, using 'presence' to refer to an object that can allow a person no longer feel alone.[88] For example, a child might experience presence when playing with a relatively simple object.

> A child co-located with a bed will probably feel alone, even if the bed is comfortable and familiar. But a child co-located with a bed and a familiar cuddly toy will probably feel that they are in the presence of something or someone, even though the cuddly toy is inanimate and inert and has degenerated after years of handling to a lump of cloth.[89]

The cuddly toy's presence is simple, but it is enough to enable a child to bond and feel connected. More sophisticated presence exists when robots and AI have additional physical capabilities, like the ability to move about independently and communicate

---

[ii] This subsection draws from Jecker, NS, 2021, My Friend the Robot: An Argument for E-Friendship, Proceedings of the Institute of Electrical and Electronic Engineers (IEEE), Conference on Robot and Human Interactive Communications (RO-MAN): 692–697, DOI: 10.1109/RO-MAN50785.2021.9515643.

non-verbally.[90] A social robot that has presence in more sophisticated ways comes closer to having the capacity to be incorporated in a community and develop the pro-social virtues characteristic of non-human persons.

Part of what creates a sense not only of presence but of comfort and bonding in the case of the child's cuddly toy, is that the toy is soft to the touch. Human beings might be better able to relate to machines that are soft to the touch, and they may be able to feel emotionally closer to machines with a physical structure conducive to touching, hugging, rubbing, patting, and holding hands.[91] Soft roboticists design robots in this way, mimicking the morphology and functionality of soft structures in nature, such as soft-bodied animals like inchworms and squid, and animal parts, like octopus arms and elephant trunks.[92]

A robot that is soft to the touch has the ability to exhibit even more pro-social capacities if equipped with the capacity to respond to touch, i.e., to use artificial sensors, neurons, and synapses to react to external stimuli. These capacities are already incorporated in prosthetic limbs that can perform delicate feats requiring constant careful sensing.[93,94] Taken together, capacities to move about independently, communicate non-verbally, be soft to the touch, and respond to touch constitute what we might call, *sophisticated presence*. Sophisticated presence heightens a robot's ability to be pro-social, form close machine-human relationships, and be incorporated in human communities.

3. *Incorporation in a community.* Even if a machine had all these qualities, its interactions with us could be stymied if it appeared frightening or eerie, like the Hollywood zombies discussed in Section 5.2 that reanimate corpses. Such qualities would impede the ability of human users to incorporate them into a community. Thus, a further quality is needed, namely, having an aesthetic that is non-threatening to users. For example, Japanese AI often embodies a pleasing and non-threatening aesthetic known as *kawai* (cute and infant-like objects). *Kawai* design avoids what

Mori calls *bukimi no tani* ("uncanny valley" or "valley of eerie feeling"), which is the profound unease alleged to arise when artificially intelligent robots, almost, but not fully, resemble humans in appearance and movement.[95] Evidence from neuroscience and psychology lends some support to a refined interpretation of Mori's view.[96,97,98]

Yet, it could also be argued that making robots humanoid would have the opposite effect, creating a sense of rapport over time as people acclimate to their presence. While people can bond with cute, infant-like objects, they may not regard them as members of a shared moral community or trust them to take on social roles and responsibilities in a community. For example, users bond with robotic pets and regard them as having moral status, but the rapport they develop is less than what might be possible with humanoid robots.

To illustrate, consider David, the intelligent humanlike robot boy featured in Steven Spielberg's 2001 film, *A.I.*, whose adopted human mother undergoes an imprinting protocol and develops an enduring 'love' for David. Unlike a robotic seal or dog, David is loved like a son. Likewise, a robotic pet pales in comparison to the humanlike femme fatale, Ava, who takes center stage in Alex Garland's 2014 film, *Ex Machina*. Ava becomes the intimate partner of a computer programmer, Caleb, who falls in love with her. Both David and Ava not only show sophisticated language abilities and persistent narratives, but they also build robust rapport with humans and evince sophisticated presence. They respond to human touch, are aesthetically pleasing and non-threatening, and are incorporated into their respective communities.

4. *Prosocial virtues.* A further feature of Ava and David germane to moral standing and personhood is how their attributes of sophisticated language, sophisticated presence, and incorporation in a community are deployed. While Ava used her sociality opportunistically, to trick a human user, David was kind,

generous, friendly, and even sought to become 'real' to regain the love of his adopted human mother. David also displayed other pro-social moral excellences associated with non-human personhood, such as kind-heartedness, generosity, friendliness, truthfulness, caring, respecting, and loving. David, unlike Ava, was morally excellent.

Other qualities that might be built into robots and AI to enhance moral standing include, for example, having a life narrative or backstory adapted to end users; functioning reliably; moving autonomously; sensing, signaling, and being creative; displaying emotions; and playing.[99] Table 5.5 summarizes the morally salient qualities of AI and social robots discussed in this section, while Table 5.6 shows which combinations of qualities give rise to personhood according to the Emergent, African, and Western views.

According to our analysis, LaMDA, ChatGPT, Samantha, Hal, and Ava would not qualify as Emergent or African persons, but David would, because David has the relational traits of sophisticated language, sophisticated presence, incorporation in a community, and pro-social virtues. By contrast, according to Western

Table 5.5 Qualities Conferring Moral Status on AI

	Does it have qualities relevant to moral status?			
	Sophisticated language	Sophisticated presence	Fully incorporated	Pro-social virtues
LaMDA, ChatGPT	Yes	No	No	No
Samantha	Yes	No	No	No
Hal	Yes	No	No	No
David	Yes	Yes	Yes	Yes
Ava	Yes	Yes	Yes	No

Table 5.6 Are LaMDA, ChatGPT, Samantha, Hal, David, and Ava Persons?

	Is it a person?		
	Emergent Personhood	African Personhood	Contemporary Western Personhood
LaMDA, ChatGPT	No	No	No
Samantha	No	No	No
Hal	No	No	No
David	Yes	Yes	No
Ava	No	No	No

Key: African personhood = views prominent among black peoples indigenous to the region of Africa south of the Sahara, as captured in the works of academic philosophers; contemporary Western personhood = Kantian and utilitarian ethics

personhood, if AI equipped electronic agents lack the necessary feature of consciousness, they lack moral standing and do not count as persons.

Emergent and African views of machine moral standing not only introduce compelling accounts of the moral status of artificial agents, they also shed needed light on foundational assumptions underlying many Western analyses. *An unsupported premise of many leading Western views is that the qualities conferring personhood must be standalone features of objects, which they would have in isolation from everything else.* We reject this premise. Instead, we have argued that a better way to think about personhood is to turn our gaze to ordinary social-relational processes, which, when configured in a certain way, give rise to something new: a person with superlative moral worth.

The analysis of this chapter sharpens the distinction made previously (Chapter 2, Section 2.3) between human and non-human personhood. According to Emergent Personhood, non-human personhood does *not* display any of the hallmark features of human personhood. It is *not* the case that (1) all machines qualify as persons, (2) their qualifying as persons is independent of people's appraisal, (3) every machine is morally equal to every other, (4) machine personhood is stable and cannot be lost, (5) machine personhood is independent of performing well in social roles. By contrast, for humans, we saw previously (in Part I) that the opposite claims apply: all humans (1) qualify as persons (2) independent of others' appraisal, and every human (3) is morally equal to every other, (4) their personhood is stable and cannot be lost, and (5) it holds independent of performing well in social roles. In the chapters that follow (chapters 6 and 7), we further consider differences between human and non-human persons, including terrestrial and extraterrestrial animals and nature.

5.4 Replies to Objections

Emergent Personhood's view of machine moral standing might be challenged on multiple grounds.

1. Robots are fakes. Since today's AI lacks capacities for conscious states or subjective feelings of any kind, such robots cannot form genuine relationships with human beings. Representative of this objection is Elder, who writes that robots deceive others with false appearances of friendship.[100]

In reply, Elder makes the unsupported assumption that 'real relationships' only arise between conscious beings. Yet, we counter that people frequently relate meaningfully to non-conscious entities. For example, we may feel a connection with nature—the Judean Desert as it descends to the Red Sea or California's Monterey coast, and with artifacts—an arrowhead from a long-ago people or Lantau Island's Tian Tan Buddha. These inanimate objects gain moral standing for particular people at particular times for a range of reasons. They are not simply tools to outside ends but parts of valuable wholes, which involve a relationship in which a human appreciates and cherishes them. Although the worth of inanimate entities emerges only as part of a whole and while the whole is present, their value can be immense. It would be wrong, for example, not to take steps to address desertification of the Judean Desert highlands wrought by climate change, wrong to spoil the Monterey coastline, and wrong to topple the Tian Tan Buddha.

2. *Robots are tools.* Even the fanciest technologies have purely instrumental value. Sparrow suggests this view, insisting that "despite their animated appearance, robots ... contribute nothing to the relationships that people form with them. The range of emotions appropriate toward a robot is thus limited to those that would be appropriate toward a car, wristwatch, or antique settee."[101] Heidegger dubbed this approach, *the instrumental definition of technology*.[102]

In reply, one could conceivably say of any relationship, including human-human ones, that their value is instrumental to bringing about positive subjective states. However, we do not ordinarily understand relationships in that way. Instead, we prize particular relationships, such as friendships, as goods-in-themselves. While robot-human relationships differ from human-human ones, they too can be highly valued for their own sake. As social robots and AI become increasingly adept at relating to us, sharing experiences, memories, conversations, and making physical contact, it seems reasonable to think we will enter into increasingly close and valued relationships with them. Should this occur, social robots and AI could become constituents of, rather than a mere means to, a good human life. If this occurs, machine participation in human relationships would bring it about that machines have moral value for their own sake.

3. *Machines are dangerous.*[iii] Even if we could design AI-equipped machines that acquire personhood, doing so creates existential risk

[iii] Without downplaying the seriousness of this objection, it is worth pointing out that perceptions of AI as a threat may reflect, in part, a "negativity bias" in international

(x-risk). In its most extreme form, x-risk involves 'AI takeover,'—AI "becomes the dominant form of intelligence on Earth, as computer programs or robots effectively take the control of the planet away from the human species.[103] *Even short of these effects, emergent behaviors like power-seeking could result in AI systems with the ability to control or manipulate human behavior, resources, and institutions.*[104]

In reply, we note that any powerful technology present risks and requires oversight. For example, cars are powerful technologies that create risks, and we establish guardrails to minimize risk. The same is true of chainsaws and nuclear power. Since machine moral standing is entirely dependent on pro-social behaviors toward human beings, if machines behave in ways that are injurious to humans, they will not merit moral standing or the protections persons are due. Thus, if an AI device running on my computer or a cloud server farm misbehaves, I can 'kill it' by turning off my computer, and I have not done a wrong to the AI.

4. AI can't be virtuous. Today's AI agents are not the kinds of things that can properly be called 'virtuous,' because they lack a "certain complex mindset" that virtue requires.[105] *This mindset might include valuing certain goods (e.g., generosity, kindness, and friendliness) and having the attitudes, beliefs, and emotions that harmonize with that valuing.*

In response, we regard a virtue to be a stable disposition to act in certain ways, developed through modeling those considered virtuous and learning the habits of reasoning and acting that align with the model and that enable responding intelligently to new situations. On our analysis, while virtues might include conscious states or emotions, they need not. Instead, AI-equipped artificial agents may develop 'complex mindsets,' in which certain value priorities emerge and guide future decision-making. By this we mean that robots and

---

AI ethics discourse. See Jobin A, Ienca M, Vayena E, 2019. The Global Landscape of AI Ethics Guidelines. *Nature Machine Intelligence* 1: 389–399; Jecker NS, Nakazawa E, 2022, Bridging East-West Differences in Ethics Guidance for AI and Robots. *AI* 3(3):764–777. DOI: 10.3390/ai3030045.

AI determine what to do not by following rules programmed into software, but by asking, "What would a role model do in my situation? If I do X, would it start a bad habit? Will I become dysfunctional in my proper role(s)?"[106] According to this analysis, "robot virtue ethics would become the search for the virtues a good (properly functioning) robot would evince, given its appropriate roles."[107] Our account aligns with ancient Greek conceptions of virtue (*arête*). For the Greeks, 'virtue' referred to excellence and could be ascribed to all objects assumed to have a function (*telos*). For example, the *arête* of a knife was its sharpness, and the *arête* of an athlete was their fitness. While there are other ways of construing virtues,[108,109] our view is plausible and well-established.

Still, it might be argued that having virtue presupposes not just consistently acting in a certain way, but having reasons and intentions to do so, which artificial agents lack. If that is correct, then ascribing virtue to AI-equipped artificial agents involves deception; we must forget that artificial agents are following an algorithm. In reply, we side with Coeckelbergh, who skirts this type of objection by ascribing "virtual virtue" to artificial agents.[110] Virtual virtue is just like ordinary virtue but applies to virtual agents. Virtual virtue bears a family resemblance to what we call 'virtue' and 'vice' in familiar cases. Coeckelbergh goes on to emphasize that virtual virtues are pro-social when they contribute to human flourishing.[111]

Yet an opponent might dispute these claims by saying that it is the humans who design and deploy machines that display virtue and vice, not machines. In reply, consider a slogan trumpeted by some US gun-rights advocates: "Guns don't kill, people do." According to this logic, virtue and vice ascriptions should not be applied to inanimate objects, like guns, but to humans who use these machines to perform good or evil actions. While there is clearly merit to this assertion, with the advent of AI, it has become harder to draw bright lines about moral culpability. To illustrate, suppose a gun were not a simple tool, requiring someone to pull the trigger for each bullet, but a powerful assault weapon, where a single pull initiates multiple rounds of fire.

Or suppose an AI-equipped drone weapon autonomously selects targets, deploys advanced weapon systems, and responds instantly to enemy fire in a fast-paced battle. It mimics the decisions its commander would make with a high degree of confidence and learns to do so better and with increasing speed and accuracy, outpacing the commander.[112] While initially tethered to human operators, it might eventually operate without direct human control. The machine might rely on algorithms that we cannot understand for winning wars. We might question whether its decisions are right or wrong. At some point, we might decide the system itself is vicious. At some point, AI weapon systems may turn on us, their creator, and kill us. The old adage, 'guns don't kill, people do,' would cease to apply.

In this illustration, ascriptions of vice and virtue to AI agents become more apt as AI functions more autonomously. Autonomous AI systems potentially deployed in a range of contexts, including social contexts, would then become fitting objects of moral praise and blame. Such a proposal is not difficult to imagine. McGuffie and Newhouse describe the co-opting of neural language models by extremist groups to amplify radical ideologies and recruit people to their communities, writing collaborative fictional narratives that they propagate to incite violence.[113] In the future, extremist groups might deploy autonomous AI to carry out such functions, and AI agents might display greater speed and accuracy compared to humans; they might create themselves and rapidly produce increasingly more advanced AI. These remarks suggest that virtue and vice are apposite to artificial agents. They lend support to the analysis developed throughout the chapter, which applies a requirement for pro-social virtue to AI systems as a condition of personhood.

5.5 Conclusion

In conclusion, this chapter considered the moral status of artificial entities that relate to us but lack conscious states. We used the example of zombies to invite thinking about this topic, which brought to light affinities between Emergent and African personhood. Drawing on African insights, we further developed the idea of non-human personhood (first introduced in Chapter 2, Section 2.3), using the examples of Google's LaMDA and OpenAI's ChatGPT, alongside fictional examples of Samantha, Hal, Ava, and David. These examples helped clarify specific capacities that artificial agents would need in order to acquire moral standing and become persons.

The discussion of this chapter makes evident that today's artificial agents are on a trajectory to acquiring many of the capabilities deemed sufficient for personhood. According to our analysis, artificial agents that count as persons are not a prospect that looms in a far-off future, when machines become conscious. Instead, AI-equipped machines are already making machine moral standing seem like a viable possibility.

6
Animals and Nature

6.1 Introduction

This chapter continues our inquiry about non-human personhood, focusing on non-human animals (hereafter 'animals') and nature. Section 6.2 asks if animals qualify as persons, while Section 6.3 considers whether non-living soils, rocks, water, or entire ecosystems do. Since Emergent Personhood grows out of a conversation between Africa and the West, we launch each subsection by exploring leading views from Africa and the West, building on their insights to develop our own. After considering a series of objections (in Section 6.4), we conclude, in Section 6.5, that like humans, animals and nature can emerge as persons by entering into relationships with human beings.

6.2 Animals

This section asks, 'Do animals ever matter morally for their own sake, or only derivatively, when they matter for humans?' We explore the answers African, early Greek, and leading Western thinkers give, and present Emergent Personhood's answer, which builds on their insights.

1. African. African moral thought has sometimes been understood as anthropocentric.[i] For example, Gyekye characterizes Akan (Ghanaian) thought as human-centered:

---

[i] Due to limitations of space, we characterize African environmental philosophy by referring to some of its most influential strands. Yet other strands depart from our

The concern for human welfare constitutes the hub of the Akan axiological wheel. The orientation of Akan morality takes its impulse undoubtedly from the humanistic outlook that characterizes Akan traditional life and thought. Humanism, the doctrine that sees human needs, interests, and dignity as fundamental, thus constitutes the foundation of Akan morality.[1]

Wiredu too says that Akan thought is humanistic and Akan ethics "is founded exclusively on considerations having to do with human well-being."[2] Wiredu explains,

By virtue of possessing an *okra*, a divine element, all persons have an intrinsic value, the same in each, which they do not owe to any earthly circumstance. Associated with this value is a concept of human dignity, which implies that every human being is entitled in an equal measure to a certain basic respect.[3]

Likewise, Mbiti, a Kenyan-born philosopher, writes,

African people consider [humans] to be at the centre of the universe. . . . Even where there is no biological life in an object, African peoples attribute (mystical) life to it, in order to establish a more direct relationship with the world around them. . . . [Humans are] not the master in the universe; [they are] only the centre, the friend, the beneficiary, the user. For that reason, [they have] to live in harmony with the universe.[4]

---

characterization. See, for example, Tangwa GB, 2004, Some African Reflections on Biomedical and Environmental Ethics, in Wiredu K, ed., *A Companion to African Philosophy*, Blackwell Publishing; Horsthemke K, 2017, Animals and African Ethics, *Journal of Animal Ethics* 7(2): 119–144; Horsthemke K, 2015, *Animals and African Ethics*, Palgrave Macmillan; Nkafu MN, 1999, *African Vitalogy*, Paulines Publications Africa; Eze MO, 2017, Humanitatis-Eco (Eco Humanism), in Afolayan A, Falola T, eds., *The Palgrave Handbook of African Philosophy*, Palgrave Macmillan; Tempels P, 2010, *Bantu Philosophy*, transl. King C, HBC Publishing.

Despite this apparent anthropocentrism, Tangwa highlights that animals and nature defy possession and mastery, using a parable adapted from the Maka of Cameroon:

> Originally, the sky, which provided all human needs, was lower down, close to the earth, and within everybody's reach. All anybody needed was to stretch [their] hands and pluck whatever [they] needed from the sky. But one powerful [individual], a perfectionist, full of the spirit of reckless adventure, which had greatly benefited [them] in the past, was not satisfied with having to stretch [their] arms before getting whatever [they] wanted and therefore tried to look for ways by which whatever [they] wanted would simply fall from the sky into [their] ready hands. The sky got annoyed and receded out of everybody's reach for ever.[5]

For Tangwa, the parable teaches that humans cannot subdue or control nature and should be humble, cautious, conciliatory, and "respectful of other people, plants, animals, inanimate things, as well as invisible/intangible forces."[6] At the same time, Tangwa holds that in traditional African societies, human moral status is superior: "While conditioned by the awe and respect for 'the other items of the furniture of the universe,' human well-being was certainly given the highest priority."[7]

Despite these notable examples of African anthropocentrism, Behrens cautions against rendering African thought as necessarily anthropocentric. Pointing to "a promising environmentalism" that can be construed from its relational orientation, Behrens expounds a view, *relational environmentalism*, which builds on African thought.[8] It holds that humans ought to respect and live in harmony with nature, not just because it is in our interest to do so, but because our relationships with other living things are family-like. In well-functioning families, there is "a sense that nurturing and caring for the other members of the family, sometimes even at personal cost, is a good to be pursued."[9] Since members of a family are interconnected, helping one another benefits each family member; however, we do not ordinarily regard family responsibilities as self-serving. This is evident not just by the sacrifices family members make, or their affective concern for each other, but by an *ethic* that centers caring and solidarity. The ethic of families instructs members to make decisions in the context of their relationships with one another, rather than deciding with just themselves in mind. According to Behrens, African voices urging harmony with nature can be plausibly interpreted as extending the ethics governing a (well-functioning) family to all living things: "This concept of promoting harmonious relationships and caring for the welfare of others extends analogously beyond the family and even the human community to embrace other natural beings too."[10]

Behrens goes on to say that relational environmentalism is grounded in a life-centered or web of life-centered approach. A web of life-centered approach stresses that life is not just something possessed by individual organisms but includes a web of interconnected things, "a complex network of which any individual living thing is only a part."[11] According to Behrens, "Living things only fully have life because of their interconnectedness with other things."[12] Moreover, there is a sense in which both living and non-living things are entangled:

> A river may not have a good of its own or interests in its own right, but its health and integrity provide the medium that can sustain so much other life. So, it forms part of the web of life.... Clearly all animals, organisms, and plants are part of life's fabric and groups, such as species or families or communities or ecosystems, are subsets of the web of life.[13]

However, Behrens's *normative* stance toward non-living versus living nature differs:

> It is not easy to explain in what sense, if any, it is possible to be in a harmonious relationship with, say, a mountain, or a river, but it is surely possible to conceptualise acting in ways which *promote the welfare* of other living things, such as animals or plants.... [Living] things are able to be objects of human concern, since they are *capable of being better or worse off*. Forests, ecosystems and rivers may not be capable of being objects of human concern in quite the same way, but . . . may be instrumentally important . . . since all life is interconnected and interdependent.[14]

Behrens adds that non-living nature has some degree of value for its own sake, by virtue of its relationship to others within life's web: "Inanimate natural objects could be thought of as being morally considerable because of their vital systematic contribution to the web of life. Their important instrumentality to other life is a relational property that allows us to consider them (directly) worthy of being taken into account morally."[15] This does not imply that non-living things are *persons*, yet it does suggest that they should be regarded with non-instrumental respect.

The distinction Behrens draws between living and non-living things resonates throughout much of African thought, which recognizes a hierarchy of moral standing in nature. For example, Molefe writes that animals can be objects of human sympathy and for this reason, we ought to think of them as mattering for their own sake.[16] By contrast, non-living nature cannot be an object of human sympathy; according to Molefe, "The idea of personhood does not accord any intrinsic value to most parts of the environment like trees, mountains and so on in their own right."[17] This is because trees, mountains and other non-sentient objects lack the capacity for sympathy; moreover, they "cannot be affected by the lack or presence of sympathy."[18] Metz distinguishes animals that can join in communal relationships with us and thereby attain "partial moral status" from animals without sentience and goal-directed behavior who cannot.[19] For Metz, 'lower animals' and non-living nature may have redeeming qualities, like beauty or complexity; there may be pragmatic reasons for acting as if they possess moral standing, but there is no "evidential reason" to think this is true.[20] However, higher animals "matter for their own sake (contra anthropocentrism), but not as much as we [humans] do."[21] The African stance outlined by Molefe and Metz is summed up well by Behrens, who extends the traditional African proverb thus: "Not only is 'a person a person through other persons,' but also . . . 'a person is a person through other (living) beings."[22] Central to this way of thinking is that a human being is fully realized as a person in the moral sense within the community of all living beings.

Emergent Personhood shares many features with Behrens, Molefe, and Metz's views, yet it diverges in crucial respects. First, Emergent Personhood is more strongly human centered than African relational environmentalism. Emergent Personhood assigns moral standing by virtue of a pro-social relation to *humanity*, not to a web of life that includes all living things. In this respect, Emergent Personhood is what Molefe calls *weakly anthropocentric*: it prioritizes human over non-human relationships; however, it avoids the *strong anthropocentric* claim that only humans have moral standing and personhood.[23] We prefer the term, *humble anthropocentrism*, introduced previously (Chapter 2, Section 2.3). Humble anthropocentrism indicates a group that discriminates in favor of its own members, not out of arrogance or superiority but from limited capacities. As human beings, our ability to know and experience what life is like for other species, form social relationships with them, and share a way of life is constrained. Since personhood emerges through human relationships, our ability to relate with other human beings counts as a reason *for us* to privilege humans. Admittedly, if non-humans were doing the moral theorizing, the personhood theory arrived at may look different—Martians may relate better with Martians and assign higher moral standing to Martians.

We also part company with leading African views, such as Molefe's and Metz's, which reject the possibility that non-living nature could be morally considerable for its own sake. Emergent Personhood holds that non-living nature, such as mountains and rivers, can qualify for personhood if it becomes a constituent of a valuable relationship with particular human beings or communities. Valuable nature-human relationships are not just instrumental and pleasure-producing but encompass a wide range of non-instrumental goods, including giving meaning or a sense of belonging to particular human beings and helping human communities thrive and flourish.

2. *Early Greek.* In early Greece, no explicit and detailed studies of how humans ought to treat animals have been found.[24] While some early Greeks, such as Pythagoras, and their followers, were vegetarian and condemned animal sacrifice, their views were in the minority; moreover, it is unclear what their philosophical basis was. Singer attributes Pythagoras's stance toward animals to a belief that after death, a human soul could pass into an animal body (metempsychosis); thus, the human inside the animal, not the animal, had moral standing.[25] Early Greeks apparently assumed that humans alone possess reason (*logos*) and by virtue of this, are morally superior.[ii]

Later Greeks, including Plato, Aristotle, and the Stoics, continued to center rationality as a distinctively human capacity. In *The Republic*, Plato describes the just soul as ruled by its higher, rational nature (*logos*), with the spirited (*thymos*) and appetitive (*eros*) parts obedient to it. Aristotle's careful observations and classification of animals and other living things led him and his predecessors to embrace a continuum of nature. Without drawing sharp lines between humans and animals, Aristotle held that

---

[ii] The appeal to reason is closely tied to speech, and Greek terms for speech and rational thought are indistinguishable: *logos* refers to 'word,' 'speech,' 'discourse,' and 'reason' (Oxford University Press, 2023 [March]. *n. Logos. OED Online*, 3rd ed. Oxford University Press).

humans alone possess theoretical reason and thus, were capable of happiness (*eudaimonia*). In *On the Motion of Animals*, Aristotle compares animals to mechanical toys, an analogy that prefigures Descartes's comparison of animals to machines:

> The movements of animals may be compared with those of automatic puppets, which are set going on the occasion of a tiny movement; the levers are released and strike the twisted strings against one another; or with the toy wagon. For the child mounts on it and moves it straight forward, and then again it is moved in a circle owing to its wheels being of unequal diameter (the smaller acts like a centre on the same principle as the cylinders). Animals have parts of a similar kind, their organs, the sinewy tendons to wit and the bones; the bones are like the wooden levers in the automaton, and the iron; the tendons are like the strings, for when these are tightened or [re]leased movement begins.[26]

The passage suggests that animals do not choose to move voluntarily; instead, they act on reflex, like a toy cart, which reacts to a child's pushing. Nussbaum and Putnam interpret this passage as suggesting that "Aristotle conceives of both perceiving and desiring as thoroughly enmattered."[27] In other words, the apparently goal-directed behavior of animals can be explained in purely mechanistic terms. However, Aristotle stopped short of maintaining that animals had no moral worth and possessed only instrumental value.[28] At one point, Aristotle refers to "humbler animals" and "every realm of nature" as "marvelous."[29]

It was the Stoics who explicitly moralized Aristotle's observations, holding that animals' inferior intellect implied lower moral worth. While the Stoics held that animals and humans alike had souls, they thought animal souls were bereft of rationality and "served only to guide the animal to act without empowering it to make deliberate choices."[30] According to Newmyer, "In the final analysis, the Stoic denial of reason to animals left them functioning like automata."[31]

Stripped of beauty, intelligence, and divine presence, nature was "likened to a machine: a mill, clock or piston in which hammers rise and fall, wheels spin and parts move each other."[32] While there were dissenters from the Stoic view, it represented a dominant stance toward animals in ancient Greece.[33]

During the Middle Ages, the view that reason belonged to human beings alone continued to hold sway. Early Christian apologists endorsed it and, as Christianity took hold, the inferiority of animals became enshrined in Western thought. From Augustine to Aquinas, medieval Christian philosophers emphasized reason as an exclusive province of humans and source of moral superiority. For Augustine, both humans and animals had souls; yet their capacities differed. Human souls displayed multiple ascending levels, and only the first two were shared with animals: vegetative powers (*animatio*) and sensual abilities (*sensus*).[34] The remaining five involved power of rationality possessed exclusively by humans.[35] Due to humans' superior rational capacities, Augustine held them as "placed above brute animals, since these are unendowed with reasons. These animals . . . have not spirit—that is to say, intellect and a sense of reason and wisdom—but only soul."[36] Continuing this line of thinking, Aquinas argued that humans had special sensory faculties that include reason and made humans "akin to ontologically superior beings, like angels."[37] Specifically, Aquinas distinguished *vis cogitativa*, a faculty of apprehending the physical world found only in humans, from *vis aestimativa*, found in higher animals. While both occupied similar spaces in the brain, only *vis cogitativa* was "permeated with reason," giving humans superior sensory perception.[38]

3. *Contemporary Western.* Much of the contemporary Western debate about animal personhood was prefigured by early Greeks. Descartes, like Aristotle, compares animals to machines.[39] However, unlike Aristotle, Descartes regarded animal behavior as wholly mechanistic and subsumed under physiological laws; ultimately, Descartes thought animal behavior was derivable from

mathematical principles. For Descartes, animals lacked not only souls but also phenomenal consciousness, i.e., the qualitative, subjective, experiential sense of there being "something it is like" to be the animal. In contrast to humans, whom Descartes assumed were composites of material automata and immaterial thought, animals were considered complex machines without experiences. Most (but not all)[40] commentators ascribe to Descartes the view that animals have no moral standing because they lack both rationality and consciousness.[41,42,43]

Kant largely accepted Descartes's assessment of animals. For Kant, animals lacked an inner worth (*inneren Wert*) and dignity, because they lacked the capacity to be rational end-setters and were "completely enmeshed in the phenomenal [sensory] world, with nothing like ... agency to offer them the underpinnings of practical freedom."[44] Kant held that personhood presupposes a capacity "to set ends—to freely choose what shall be an end by means of reason."[45] Kant's views imply that human duties toward animals are indirect, i.e., owed to human beings, and only derivative to animals. In *Lectures on Ethics*, Kant famously illustrates this point: "If [someone] has [their] dog shot, because it can no longer earn a living for [them], [they are] by no means in breach of any duty to the dog, since the latter is incapable of judgment, but [the human] thereby damages the kindly and humane qualities in [themselves], which [they] ought to exercise in virtue of [their] duties to humankind."[46]

Today, we are witnessing a sea change in Western views about animal moral standing. Increasingly, Western philosophers are moving away from early Greek, Cartesian, and Kantian standpoints that elevated humans above animals, and toward a view that attributes personhood and moral standing to animals. Sorajbi traces the change to Hume, Darwin, and Bentham.[47] In 1734, Hume hinted that what makes humans distinctive also make animals so:

> We are conscious, that we ourselves, in adapting means to ends, are guided by reason and design, and that it is not ignorantly nor casually we perform those actions, which tend to self-preservation, . . . obtaining pleasure, and avoiding pain. When therefore we see other creatures, in millions of instances, perform like actions, and direct them to the ends, all our principles of reason and probability carry us with an invincible force to believe the existence of a like cause.[48]

Human and animal behaviors, Hume continues, "proceed from a reasoning, that is not in itself different, nor founded on different principles, from that which appears in human nature."[49] Extending Hume's line of thinking, Bentham wrote in 1780 that, irrespective of the capacity to reason, any being with the capacity to suffer should have their suffering taken into account: "The question is not, Can they *reason*? nor Can they *talk*? but, Can they *suffer*?"[50] Darwin's evolutionary theory, published in 1871, reported that "there is no psychological attribute of humans which is not also found in animals to some degree, reason included."[51]

During the twentieth century, the tendency among Western philosophers has been to continue a trend toward elevating animals' moral standing, regarding it as morally on a par with humans. Fueling this tendency was the failure to solve the *conundrum of personhood* (first introduced in Chapter 2, Section 2.2), i.e., to find a secular substitute for the Judeo-Christian soul that would establish that all and only human beings possess a superlative moral worth. Eventually, the failure to locate a secular alternative was repackaged as a positive argument favoring animal welfare and rights. Singer's utilitarian ethic implied that any creature with an equal capacity to suffer is equally morally considerable.[52] Regan attributed a right to life to animals, arguing that there are no criteria that all humans have, and all animals lack, that would justify granting a right to life exclusively to humans.[53] For Regan, it is wrong to kill animals, even painlessly, and even if "it brought about this or that amount of pleasure, or this or that amount of intrinsically good experiences for others, no matter how great the amount of good hypothesized."[54]

4. *Emergent Personhood.* Emergent Personhood shares with African and recent Western views the idea that personhood extends beyond humanity. Like humans, animals emerge as persons through a certain configuration of relationships with human beings. In the case of animals, personhood arises when animals become incorporated in pro-social ways with particular human beings or human communities. In almost every society, many animals acquire personhood in this way. In the case of dogs, for example, domestication traces back at least 23,000 years.[55] Emergent Personhood parts company with some African views, such as Behrens's, and some recent Western views, such as Singer's, because it prioritizes humans over animals. While we agree with Behrens that humans share the planet with all living things, unlike Behrens, we hold that participating in 'a web of life' is not a sufficient condition for the outstanding moral worth associated with personhood. While we agree with Singer that animal suffering is morally considerable, we do not agree that this capacity is necessary for being a person or sufficient for being morally equal with human beings.

According to our analysis, not all animals count as persons and even when an animal is a person, personhood can be lost or diminished if relationships with humans are lost or diminished, or if animals persistently harm or threaten harm toward human beings. For us, relationships between nature and humans are not necessarily positive—animals, insects, and bacteria can attack or kill humans, or threaten their livelihood by destroying livestock on which people depend for survival. To illustrate, consider desert locusts (*Schistocerca gregaria*). During rainy season in the Horn of Africa, cyclone rains can trigger swarms of locusts to spread across the skies, potentially obliterating crops, endangering food supplies, and threatening food security and livelihoods. In 2020, the United Nations Food and Agriculture Organization characterized the threat of locusts to countries in East Africa this way: "Swarms easily consume entire fields and form mass clouds large enough to block out the sun."[56] The scale of damage is difficult to fathom; according to Cressman, a United Nations official, "A swarm the size of Rome can eat enough food in one day as everybody in Kenya."[57] The devastating effects of locust swarms in East Africa demonstrate that socially harmonious relations between animals and humans are not inevitable. They also speak to larger issues of human responsibility to cultivate good relations. Thus, human-induced climate change exacerbates desert locust swarms by creating climatic conditions that encourage pest breeding, development, and migration.[58]

Admittedly, the way of life we are centering is a human one, since Emergent Personhood regards animals' moral standing as contingent on being incorporated in pro-social ways with humans. As expressed throughout the book, *Emergent Personhood sets forth an ethic for human beings, not a morality for all rational beings or all creatures that can suffer. Rather than aspiring to a 'view from nowhere,' it presents a human view, which is the only view we have.* A human viewpoint leads us to reject the idea that a suffering pig or orangutan has the same moral status as a human being with similar intellectual capacities. The reason has to do with how, as human beings, we relate to the human, but not to the pig or orangutan. A different morality might emerge if pigs or orangutans were devising it; they live a different kind of life, in the company of other kinds of beings.

Yet, what do we make of arguments, such as Nussbaum's, which hold that some non-humans are capable of a dignified existence and respecting them requires supporting their ability to flourish in their own way, given the kind of beings they are?[59] Our rejoinder is to say that the 'dignified existence' Nussbaum envisions reflects a human idea. We see an animal's way of life in human terms, not from the standpoint of the animal. Does a crow's relating to other crows give rise to superlative value *for the crow*? Does it express dignity *for the crow*? Are such questions even intelligible to crows? We cannot say. We do not live like crows, or like other intelligent animals, such as dolphins, rats, or orangutans. *Our morality is species bound.*

Three caveats are in order. First, our agnosticism about the personhood of some non-humans leaves their personhood open. Emergent Personhood does not assert that being related to humans is *necessary* for having a superlative moral worth; instead, it claims that this is sufficient. Second, humble anthropocentrism lends strong support to a duty to protect the environment. This duty gains support on multiple grounds, including solidarity between generations.[60] Third, even if it turns out that some animals are *not* persons, we might nonetheless have strong duties toward them. Moral duties arise for many reasons, besides personhood. For example, we argued in Chapter 2 (Section 2.3) that humans have strong duties to avoid cruelty to animals and that factory farming and certain uses of animals in research are wrong. We also think people ought to treat stray animals kindly, even if they are not persons. While there is much more that can be said about our duties to those with uncertain moral status, and those with some measure of moral status shy of personhood, we leave it for another day.

Table 6.1 summarizes the answers that African, early Greek, Western, and Emergent Personhood give to the question, 'Are animals persons?'

Table 6.2 recaps five salient differences Emergent Personhood between animal and human personhood that the analysis of this section brought to light.

192 WHAT IS A PERSON?

Table 6.1 Are Animals Persons?

Personhood View	Are some animals persons?	Why/Why not?
African Personhood	Yes	Living things are connected in a web-of-life
Early Greek Personhood	No	Animals lack rationality and theoretical reasoning
Modern Western Personhood	No	Animals lack consciousness and cannot legislate morality
Recent Western Personhood	Yes	There is no quality all humans have that all animals lack; Animals can suffer
Emergent Personhood	Yes	Animals that are incorporated in human communities and relate to humans in pro-social ways are persons

Key: African personhood = Kevin Behrens's African relational environmentalism; early Greek personhood = Stoics, Plato, Aristotle; modern Western personhood = Descartes, Kant; recent Western personhood = rights-based ethics, utilitarian ethics

Table 6.2 Emergent Personhood in Humans versus Animals

	Do all qualify as persons?	Does personhood depend on others' appraisal?	Are all moral equals?	Can personhood be lost or diminished?	Does personhood depend on performing in social roles?
Humans	Yes	No	Yes	No	No
Animals	No	Yes	No	Yes	Yes

Key: Animals = Non-human living organisms

6.3 Non-Animal Nature

This section shifts to non-animal nature (hereafter 'nature') and asks, 'Does nature ever matter morally for its own sake, or only derivatively, when it matters for human beings?' We use, 'nature' to refer to an array of things—living entities, such as microorganisms, plants and trees; non-living things, such as soils, rocks, and water; and entire ecological systems (ecosystems), such as marine and freshwater ecosystems, deserts, and tropical forests. This section explores what African, early Greek, and contemporary Western philosophies have to say about the moral standing of these diverse entities. Building on their insights, it explicates Emergent Personhood and clarifies its advantages.

1. African. We have seen that some African philosophies, such as those of Behrens, Molefe, and Metz, are biocentric, holding that all and only living things are morally considerable. Yet others are ecocentric, ascribing full moral standing to both living and non-living nature. Drawing inspiration from the Nigerian legend of the Uhere and Api rivers during the Nigerian Civil War (Nigerian–Biafran War), Eze develops a version of ecocentrism they dub, 'eco-humanism' (*humanitatis eco*). According to the legend, at the peak of conflict,

> indigenous people always retreated to their farm settlement located across the two rivers. When enemy soldiers arrive at the riverbanks and want to cross, the rivers would rise. . . . When enemy soldiers retreated, the rivers would subside to their normal levels. This was how the rivers protected Opi people from enemy invasion throughout the duration of the war.[61]

For Eze, the legend teaches how these Nigerian people understood their relationship with the Uhere and Api rivers: "One's humanity is dependent on harmonious balance and positive relationships with human beings, animals, biological life, non-biological life, spirits, forces, and other inanimate elements that make up our environment."[62] For Eze, the moral community extends to all nature and enjoins humans to live harmoniously with it. Eze elaborates, "In the relationship between the human person and nature, neither the human person nor the environment is prior or superior in moral status and recognition."[63] Eze claims eco-humanism bears a resemblance to other African views, such as Tangwa's eco-bio-communitarianism.[64,65,66,67]

Eze's eco-humanism shares with Emergent Personhood the idea that non-living and living nature alike can acquire superlative value as pro-social members of a human community. However, it differs from Emergent Personhood in key respects. First, eco-humanism fuses humans and non-humans into a single community and gives pride of place to the community. By contrast, Emergent Personhood privileges *human* community. Second, Eze maintains all members of the moral community are moral equals. This suggests that humans could, in principle, be sacrificed to save animals or the environment. We reject this implication. Emergent Personhood holds that nature's moral standing is always contingent on becoming incorporated in pro-social relationships involving human beings. If sustaining a natural object, such as a forest, required injuring human communities, then the forest's moral standing is undermined, because the relationship the forest has with human communities ceases to be pro-social. The forest, in this situation, would cease being a person with a right to be sustained.

The African totemic system offers another account of nature's moral significance, with a focus that is broadly biocentric. It traces human origins to animals and associates different extended family or clan with different animals from which they are believed to have descended, emphasizing a shared lineage with ancient roots. The associated animal serves as an emblem of its group and carries symbolic, and sometimes mystical, significance. Burnett and wa Kang'ethe emphasize the totem-human relationship as inherited, rather than acquired:

The totem system did not require the clan member to establish a personal relationship with the totem, much less with any other species or group of animals. The clan members were thought to share personality characteristics with the totem, but again this association was inherited rather than acquired and required no active engagement with the totem.[68]

Murove writes that the moral and symbolic significance of the totemic system is "instilling a consciousness of belonging to the natural world," suggesting that humans and animals alike are part of, not separate from, nature.[69] In this way, respect or even reverence for animals can be seen as an extension of respect for clan. Ethical conduct toward totems generally requires not killing the associated animal, except in self-defense, and not eating them. Kindness toward the totemic animal was expected, and in exchange, it was hoped that "the totem might assist in times of need or desperation."[70]

A final example of an African account of nature's moral standing is vital force theory, which is ecocentric and assigns moral standing to living and non-living nature alike. First articulated by Tempels[71] and later elaborated by Dzobo,[72] Kasenene,[73] and others,[74,75,76] vital force theory claims that an imperceptible force emanates from God and inheres in everything. Variously understood, this force is generally considered good and thought to impart value. Force has been characterized as "the African equivalent of, but distinct from, the concept of being."[77] Comparing 'force' with 'being,' Tempels explains:

> When we think in terms of being they [Bantu] use the concept 'force.' Where we see concrete beings, they see concrete forces. When we say that 'beings' are differentiated by their essence or nature, Bantu say that 'forces' differ in their essence or nature. They hold that there is the divine force, celestial or terrestrial forces, human forces, animal forces, or mineral forces.[78]

Others hold that force exists as an all-pervasive energy, irrespective of the form of nature in which it is manifest.[79] Still others tender force as life.[iii] Senghor writes, "As far as African ontology is concerned ... there [are] no such things as dead matter: every being, everything—be it only a grain of sand—radiates a life force, a sort of wave-particle; and sages, priests, kings, doctors, and artists all use it to help bring the universe to its fulfillment."[80] Chemhuru gives a slightly different account: "Nonliving objects like mountains, rivers, rocks, soils and the air are to some extent *alive*. They are thought to be alive because of the way in which these components actively participate towards the completeness of various life forms."[81] For Chemhuru, forces are not independently living things but catalysts or constituents of them.

Certain hallmark features are apparent across diverse renderings of force theory. First, force theory displays a value hierarchy. Metz explains:

> animate beings ... have a greater degree (or kind) of vital force than inanimate ones and hence have a greater moral standing, human beings have more (or better) vital force than plants and animals and therefore are higher than them, ancestors have even more (better) than human beings, and then God, the source of all vital force, has the most (best).[82]

Second, force theory stresses an interconnection between forces, with each force affecting every other. For example, Tempels compares forces to a spider web: "The world of forces is held like a spider's web of which no single thread can be caused to vibrate without shaking the whole network" and "nothing moves in this universe of forces without influencing other forces by its movement."[83]

[iii] One way of understanding attributions of agency to nature is as a form of suppositional reasoning that cultivates a positive moral stance. See Chemhuru M, 2019, The Moral Status of Nature: An African Understanding. In Chemhuru M, ed., *African Environmental Ethics*, Spring Nature, 64–95.

Third, force theory expresses a 'we orientation': "Life is comprehended not from the perspective of 'I' or 'they' alone, but from that of both which unite to become 'we.'"[84] The 'we orientation' is sometimes specified in utilitarian terms, with a prescription to maximize force. Thus, Kasenene suggests that "a person is conceived to ensure that vitality is promoted, maintained and strengthened."[85] Dzobo states, a person is good "not because [the individual] is good for something but primarily because [they have] a creative humanity and so [are] a creator of the good."[86] Remarks like these can be interpreted as implying a duty to procreate in order to increase life force, and a duty to work in a disciplined way in order to realize creative potential.

Fourth, force theory is nature-centered. Since all things in nature have a divine force within them, nature itself has value.

Finally, when comparing the moral standing of nature and humans, force theory does not necessarily prioritize one over the other. For example, describing the Nso' view, Tangwa writes, "The Nso' certainly do not look on themselves as privileged creatures with a God-given mandate to subdue, dominate and exploit the earth and the rest of creation."[87] Instead, he writes,

> In Nso', the hoeing (as well as the planting and harvesting) season is always ritually inaugurated after appropriate sacrifices and incantations.... The law of the earth (*nsër nsaiy*) is the strongest and brooks no breaking because the consequences of its violations are severe, metaphysical and unavoidable. The earth is the final arbiter of all human affairs.[88]

2. Early Greek. As discussed previously (Chapter 1, Section 1.4), the oldest Greek and Roman societies practiced domestic religion; they worshipped deceased family members who they thought had a second existence underground following their burial. Eventually, as associations between households were established, gods associated with nature were shared between households. Forces of nature were seen as animate and purposive, sharing the same life energy as human beings: "the force that manifest itself in the psyche of man is the same force that rules in all matter."[89] In this sense, humanity is one with nature and "no distinction was made between mechanical and vital activity. All activity was vital activity. Nature is a living substance."[90]

Since the early Greeks personified natural elements as gods, no sharp divide existed between 'natural' and 'supernatural,' or between 'science' (the study of nature) and 'religion': their object was one and the same. Earth was personified as Gaia, a primordial goddess and mother of all beings. According to Hesiod, Gaia was generated by primal Chaos: "In the beginning there was only Chaos, the Abyss, but then Gaia, came into being, "broad-breasted Earth" and she bore "one equal to herself, starry Heaven."[91] With her son, Uranus (Heaven), Gaia (Earth) bore many Gods and God-like creatures—Mountains and Nymphs, the Sea, Oceanus, Cyclops, Cronus and the Titans. Eventually, these were replaced by Zeus, ushering in the era of Olympian Gods.

A distinct ethic toward nature arose from this worldview. According to Amundsen, "Religion was, in Greek philosophy, essentially an ennobled form of naturalism, and for all intents, nature was the supreme being."[92] Thus, early Greeks held that the natural world they inhabited was a living, sacred place, where gods of nature were present and should be treated with awe and respect.[93] For example, agriculture was perceived as inflicting injury on nature; it required rites of expiation to show religious respect for the environment, as well as ritual offerings to gods representing fertility, wind, rain, and drought.[94] According to Fustel,

> in every part of creation, in the soil, in the tree, in the cloud, in the water of the river, in the sun, [were] so many persons like [themselves]. [They] imbued them with thought, volition, and choice of acts. As [they] thought them powerful, and . . . subject to their empire, [they] avowed [their] dependence; . . . invoked them and adored them; [they] made gods of them.[95]

Pre-Socratics and later Greek philosophers continued to imbue nature with purpose and intelligence, even while they classified and systematized it. Empedocles, for example, declared that "all things have a share of thought" and regarded plants as sensitive,[96] while also introducing a classification of nature in which it is composed of four roots (fire, wind, earth, and water) and two forces (love and strife).[97] Reflecting the cosmologies of the day, Plato held that intelligence could manifest physically in many ways, including being embodied in plants and nature.[98] In *Timaeus*, Plato describes plants as having not just intelligence but perception, desires, and sensations.[99] Aristotle's biological observations and taxonomy included plants, as well as animals, and describe a gradual continuum, not a clear demarcation: "Nature proceeds little by little from things lifeless to animal life in such a way that it is impossible to determine the exact line of demarcation, nor on which side thereof an intermediate form should lie."[100] Aristotle illustrates using borderline cases: "There is observed in plants a continuous scale of ascent towards the animals. So, in the sea, there are certain objects concerning which one would be at a loss to determine whether they be animal or vegetable."[101] Unlike Plato, Aristotle rejects the idea that plants are conscious and instead thought that a plant's soul had as its primary function a "holding-together role": to maintain and reproduce a plant's distinctive structure.[102]

Plato and Aristotle both sought to emulate nature in their ethics, viewing nature as "a moral, purposeful, rational, divine order."[103] For example, effrontery and pride, cardinal Greek vices, involved overstepping natural limits. For Plato, the ordering of classes in society, the distinction between parts of the soul, and the hierarchy between pleasures and intellectual operations aligned with nature; for Aristotle, all things display a nature which determines their proper purpose (*telos*).

The Greeks discerned a hierarchy within nature determined by how much reason different entities had. According to Singer, for the Greeks, "nature . . . is essentially a hierarchy in which those with less reasoning ability exist for the sake of those with more."[104] This approach led Aristotle to conclude that rather than being *subject* to nature, man presided *over* nature, because man's capacity for reason was greatest: "After the birth of animals, plants exist for their [animals'] sake, and . . . animals exist for the sake of man, the tame for use and food, the wild, if not all at least a greater part of them, for food, and for the provision of clothing and various instruments."[105] Plato and Aristotle concurred that inequality in the allotment of reason justified not only the dominion of some men over others, but also man's dominion over nature. For example, Aristotle claimed that it was naturally just to acquire and hunt nature, writing that "the art of war is a natural art of acquisition, for the art of acquisition includes hunting, an art which we ought to practice against wild beasts, and against men who, though intended by nature to be governed, will not submit."[106]

The ancient view that humanity presided over nature was enshrined during the Christian era. Genesis teaches that humans alone were made in the image of God (*imago Dei*) and granted dominion over animals and earth: "Let us make man to our image and likeness; and let him have dominion over the fishes of the sea, and the fowls of the air, and the beasts and the whole earth, and every creeping creature that moveth upon the earth."[107] White argues that Christianity, "by destroying pagan animism[,] . . . made it possible to exploit nature in a mood of indifference to the feelings of natural objects."[108] While there were exceptions within the Christian tradition, such as Francis of Assisi, the overwhelming influence of Christianity was to deem humans separate and superior to the rest of creation.

3. *Contemporary Western.* During the modern era, Western thought continued to regard humanity as separate from nature, and the new science became a tool for humans to control and subdue nature. Exemplifying this view was Bacon, who sought to deploy science to conquer nature, an aspiration Bacon considered noble:

The first [kind of ambition] is of those who desire to extend their own power in their native country, a vulgar and degenerate kind. The second is of those who labor to extend the power and dominion of their country among men. This certainly has more dignity, though not less covetousness. But if [someone] endeavor[s] to establish and extend the power and dominion of the human race itself over the universe, [their] ambition... is without doubt both a more wholesome and a more noble thing than the other two.[109]

In contrast to Greek science, "Baconian science was a tool for plundering, rather than a means of revering, nature."[110] The controlling imagery shifted from picturing nature as 'Mother Earth' to picturing her as a virgin to be subdued and subjugated. In Bacon's words, the applications of science do not "merely exert a gentle guidance over nature's course; they have the power to conquer and subdue her." Merchant argues that shifts in metaphors used to depict nature contributed to changes in ethical stances: "Whereas the nurturing earth image can be viewed as a cultural constraint restricting the types of socially and morally sanctioned human actions allowable with respect to the earth, the new images of mastery and domination functioned as cultural sanctions for the denudation of nature."[111] Nature was at times portrayed as a two-sided woman; invoking chauvinistic metaphors, a woman was portrayed as

> both virgin and witch: the Renaissance courtly lover placed her on a pedestal; the inquisitor burned her at the stake. The witch, symbol of the violence of nature, raised storms, caused illness, destroyed crops, obstructed generation, and killed infants. Disorderly woman, like chaotic nature, needed to be controlled.[112]

In contrast to the Greek's organic view of nature, where order arose when each part within a larger whole performed its proper function, in the modern era, order was redefined and arose through mastering and controlling. A unifying motif for science became mechanistic, presaged by Aristotle's image of the mechanical puppet. What Merchant dubs 'the death of nature' resulted directly from "removal of animistic, organic assumptions about the cosmos"; it was "because nature was now viewed as a system of dead, inert particles moved by external, rather than inherent forces" that it became possible to legitimate exploiting and manipulating nature.[113] Midgley explains how shifting motifs of Earth, from Gaia, an honored goddess and primordial mother, to the modern view of earth as an inert, lifeless machine altered understandings of human duties toward Earth and our place within it:

> Personifying the earth means that it is not just a miscellaneous heap of resources but a self-maintaining system which acts as a whole. It can therefore be injured; it is vulnerable, capable of health or sickness. And, since we are totally dependent on it, we are vulnerable too.... Like babies, we are tiny, vulnerable, dependent organisms, owing our lives to a tremendous whole. That is surely what the Greeks meant to acknowledge, and what our own ancestors meant when they spoke of Mother Nature.[114]

In contrast to the Greeks, Kantian ethics, and later, utilitarian ethics further reinforced a mechanistic approach to nature, insisting that only conscious and/or intelligent beings were morally considerable.

4. *Recent Western.* During the twentieth and twenty-first centuries, we are reckoning with the global environmental consequences of philosophies of nature that treat lands, soils, and ecosystems as holding purely instrumental value, as a means to human ends. Burning of fossil fuels has produced greenhouse gas emissions that act "like a blanket wrapped around the Earth,

trapping the sun's heat and raising temperatures," resulting in long-term shifts in temperatures and weather patterns with devastating effects.[115] Environmental degradation of air, water, soil, ecosystems, and habitats, along with depletion of natural resources has given way to a sobering recognition that a shift in human stances toward nature is needed. Environmental ethics, which emerged as an academic discipline during the 1970s, has challenged claims about the moral superiority of humans relative to nature and challenged related ideas that regard nature as lacking intrinsic value. Increasingly, Western philosophies of nature have moved toward viewing not just animals but nature itself as possessing inherent dignity and worth.[116] In the United States, Leopold introduced a *land ethic* that encouraged seeing the land as an object of moral concern in its own right, arguing that "a thing is right when it tends to preserve the integrity, stability, and beauty of the biotic community. It is wrong when it tends otherwise."[117] Leopold foretold that the next step in the evolution of environmental ethics would be a land ethic that "enlarges the boundaries" of the moral community from animals and living things to "soils, waters, plants and animals, or collectively: the land."[118] Leopold's philosophy inspired others to defend moral standing for ecological wholes, such as species, communities, and ecosystems, not just their individual constituents,[119,120] and to grant to environmental features, like rivers, oceans, and trees, legal standing that makes it possible to require humans to compensate the environment for harms.[121]

In Norway, a movement known as 'deep ecology' developed an environmental ethic that also accords moral standing to nature. Næss, who coined the term 'deep ecology,' was inspired by Sherpas (also known as Sharwa, the indigenous people of Nepal) who manifest a deep awe and reverence toward the Himalayan Mountains and other natural features. Næss's approach distinguishes *deep* from *shallow* ecology: shallow ecology, which predominates in the West, focuses on conserving nature for human beings, while deep ecology regards natural things as having value in their own right, as constituents of a valuable nature-human relationship.[122] According to Næss, the ontology of the world has "a gestalt character, not an atomic character," which deep ecology captures.[123] Moving from ontology to ethics, Næss contends that gestalt-thinking dispenses with consciousness and locates value in the gestalt.

Both Leopold's land ethic and Næss's deep ecology challenge the long history of Western thinking about nature, which traces from the Greeks, through the Christian era, to Cartesian and Kantian ethics. In contrast to these approaches, Leopold's and Næss's philosophies of nature attribute moral standing to non-conscious, non-rational entities, and to groups, and systems in nature, holding that they possess moral value for their own sakes. Conceivably, nature could count as much, or more, than conscious, rational beings.

5. *Emergent Personhood.* Emergent Personhood shares with eco-humanism, vital force theory, the land ethic, and deep ecology, the idea that moral standing is relationally grounded. However, it parts company with these views because it regards relationships between humans as uniquely valuable. While nature can relate to us in morally significant ways, this does not occur inevitably, nor is it on par with human-human relating. Instead, nature-human relationships have inherent limits, similar to the limits that arose for animal-human relationships. In the case of non-living nature, however, these limits go further: not only is there an inability to know 'what it's like,' but there is also a cold stop to what we can understand. Even when humans permanently lack consciousness, we recognize them as human like us; we can imagine their fate befalling us. By contrast, I cannot imagine becoming a rock; this fate cannot befall me. The Sotho proverb captures our point well: *motho ke motho ka batho* (to be human is to affirm one's humanity by recognizing the humanity of others).[124] Human personhood is characterized by ever present human relating.

Within such limits, physical nature can acquire moral status. To illustrate, consider a fishing village in which a particular sea contributes to and becomes an integral, positive part of the village;

by virtue of this, the particular sea acquires moral standing and becomes what we might call a *sea-in-relationship*. The sea's moral standing does not extend to all seas everywhere but to the particular sea and the particular relationships in which it stands with villagers. In our example, moral standing and personhood are *decoupled from rationality and the capacity to suffer*. The example locates the source of nature's potential for a superlative moral worth in its relationships with human community. In the example of the fishing village, the sea-in-relationship may have a higher moral standing than a mole or coyote, even though the mole or coyote have intelligence and the capacity to suffer, which the sea lacks. Or, to take another example, in an agricultural community, the community's soils and lands can acquire a high moral standing. This is not just an instrumental value related to how the land supports the local economy. It is also (or can be) valuable because of the way the community's way of life is bound up with the land. The land might be considered a 'friend' of humankind.

Yet, what exactly is the difference between the personhood of humans versus nature? Our answer is similar to the answer we gave in comparing the personhood of humans and animals. There are five salient differences, shown in Table 6.3.

Table 6.3 Emergent Personhood in Humans versus Nature

	Do all qualify as persons?	Does personhood depend on others' appraisal?	Are all moral equals?	Can personhood be lost or diminished?	Does personhood depend on performing in social roles?
Humans	Yes	No	Yes	No	No
Nature	No	Yes	No	Yes	Yes

Key: Nature = Non-animal nature, including plants, trees, soils, rocks, water, and ecosystems

Table 6.4 Are Things in Nature, Besides Animals, Persons?

Personhood View	Can things in nature, besides animals, be persons?	Why?/Why not?
African Personhood	Yes	Nature is part of our community or has vital force
Early Greek Personhood	Yes	Nature has a share of reason
Modern Western Personhood	No	Nature cannot think, legislate morality, or suffer
Recent Western Personhood	Yes	Nature is a biotic community or stands in valuable relationships with us
Emergent Personhood	Yes	Nature can relate to us in pro-social ways

Key: African personhood = Michael Onyebuchi Eze's eco-humanism, Placide Tempels's vital force theory; early Greek personhood = Stoics, Plato, Aristotle; modern Western personhood = Descartes, Kantian ethics, utilitarian ethics, Baconian science; recent Western personhood = Aldo Leopold's land ethic, Arne Næss's deep ecology

The discussion of this section also brings to light and clarifies the answers that different philosophies of nature in Africa and the West give to the question, 'Are things in nature, besides animals, persons?' (shown in Table 6.4).

6.4 Replies to Objections

Emergent Personhood's stance toward animals and nature might be challenged on a number of grounds.

1. Speciesism. A utilitarian might claim that Emergent Personhood makes morally arbitrary and speciesist claims. For

example, it is morally arbitrary to say, as Emergent Personhood does, that a human being with serious intellectual impairment takes precedence over an orangutan or pig with equivalent intellectual capacities. Elsewhere, we address this objection in greater detail (see Chapter 2, Section 2.3), introducing the notion of 'humble anthropocentrism.' Humble anthropocentrism asserts both epistemic and phenomenological claims: human knowledge of what it is like to be an animal is partial and limited (the epistemic claim), and our capacity to relate to animals and experience a way of life with them is limited (the phenomenological claim).

Another way to reply to this objection is to say that Emergent Personhood is a form of agent-relative reasoning. In agent-relative reasoning, a possessive pronoun (i.e., 'our' species)[iv] is used to indicate a general reason that includes an essential reference to a person or group of people to whom the reason applies.[125] In our analysis, if moral agents were members of another species, they might have an agent-relative reason to grant members of *their* species higher moral standing due to the relationships possible with them. Agent-relative reasoning is in this sense, context sensitive and 'hedged';[126] it refers to a limited set of non-trivial features of a situation that count as reasons for or against acting in a certain way.[127]

Critics might press back, claiming that 'species' is conceptually arbitrary; it designates a group of organisms that can produce fertile offspring. What possible ethical justification could there be for granting species a prominent place in a philosophical analysis of personhood? In reply, our use of 'species' is pragmatic, not metaphysical. 'Human' is the term most people use to pick out individuals with whom they share a way of life and can relate to in a certain way. It serves well enough for that purpose.

2. *Unincorporated animals*. A utilitarian might ask, '*Do abandoned animals—stray cats and dogs—have no moral standing since*

[iv] This is what Nagel dubs a 'free agent variable' (see Nagel T, 1970, *The Possibility of Altruism*, Princeton University Press).

they do not relate in pro-social ways with humans?' The underlying concern might be that Emergent Personhood makes animal personhood a result of happenstance—contingent on whether animals happen to encounter and relate well with humans. In reply, being related in pro-social ways to humans is sufficient, but not required for animal moral standing.[v] Even if animals turn out not to be moral persons, it is incumbent on humans to support animal flourishing and establish positive animal-human relationships. This responsibility is premised on human power over animals and our ability to profoundly impact their interests. More broadly, humans ought to embed with all that exists and promote harmonious, positive relationships. In this regard, Emergent Personhood hews close to African ethics. An ethic of taking care of relationality, i.e., cultivating and prizing it, is a central feature of both African and Emergent accounts. Traditional African communities illustrate a positive stance toward animals by refraining from killing wild animals for sport, not because wild animals are necessarily considered persons but because killing for sport is not a positive, harmonious way of relating.

3. *Rivers and trees don't have well-being.* *Molefe might object that humans could not possibly feel sympathy toward rivers and trees, or toward soils and rocks; thus, these entities could not possibly be persons. Metz might argue that rivers and trees cannot be objects of communal relations because they lack well-being and the capacity to be made better or worse off.* Our reply to both stresses that humans do not live in isolation from animals and nature but are embedded with them. While there are morally important differences in how we relate to humans and non-humans, we live in mixed communities alongside other species and nature. Our capacity to relate to others is a central human capacity; it has existed for all recorded history and among people everywhere. Relationships with animals and

---

[v] As noted in Chapter 2, Section 2.3, we remain agnostic about whether personhood can emerge outside human relationships.

nature can rise to moral significance and be a source of normativity and high moral worth.

6.5 Conclusion

In conclusion, this chapter strengthens the argument for Emergent Personhood by showing that it gives ethical backing to important moral duties to animals and nature. Emergent Personhood builds on African and Western approaches to animals and nature yet has advantages over these approaches. This chapter also proposed an answer to the *conundrum of personhood* (introduced in Chapter 2, Section 2.2), which has been a thorn in the side of Western philosophy since the Christian era. Since abandoning the Judeo-Christian soul, Western philosophers have sought in vain a secular alternative. Drawing insights from African thought, we looked outside ourselves for the source of human personhood, to relationships in which humans stand. We found there a source of superlative moral worth for all human beings that cannot be diminished or lost. At the same time, we found a basis for ascribing superlative moral worth beyond humans, to animals and nature.

7
Space Aliens and Terraforming

7.1 Introduction

In this chapter, we think more expansively about the notion of community, exploring the possibility of worlds beyond Earth. We ask, 'Does a land ethic for Earth extend to an interplanetary land ethic, as some suggest?[1] Should we protect pristine extraterrestrial environments for their own sake, or may resources elsewhere in the universe be mined to benefit humans? Can extraterrestrial life or lands have the high moral standing we associate with persons? Some questions we introduced in previous chapters recur. For example, we face again questions pertaining to the moral status of non-rational, non-sentient life. Yet, these questions take on a new twist, since forms of intelligence, consciousness, and life elsewhere in the universe might be radically different from what we have encountered to date on Earth.[2]

Ancient Africans and Greeks undoubtedly asked some of the same questions we will ask. The Igbo proverb, *If the eyes do not look at the Sky, what else would they look at?*[3] serves as a reminder that humans have wondered about other worlds for millennia. Mindful of the historical backdrops of contemporary African and Western thought, this chapter considers historical perspectives on life on other planets as well as contemporary concerns. We begin, in Section 7.2, by asking, 'Can life in outer space be persons?' In Section 7.3, we consider, 'Can extraterrestrial lands have full-fledged moral standing?' We engage these questions through conversation with African, early Greek, and contemporary Western standpoints. Building on these approaches, Emergent Personhood

What Is a Person? Nancy S. Jecker and Caesar A. Atuire, Oxford University Press.
© Oxford University Press 2025. DOI: 10.1093/oso/9780197690925.003.0008

holds that extraterrestrial life and nature can acquire personhood in much the same way that terrestrial life and nature does, namely, by entering into human relationships and contributing in prosocial ways. Section 7.4 concludes that there is a possible future where space 'aliens' count as persons and lands on distant planets are morally considerable.

7.2 Space Aliens and Extraterrestrial Life

If life exists on other planets, what is its moral standing?[i] In this section, we tackle this question, looking at the answer offered by African ethics, Western ethics, and Emergent Personhood. To focus the question, we consider a case where ethical concerns kick into high gear because conflicts arise between terrestrial and extraterrestrial life. One way this could occur would be if life on other planets were extremophile. *Extremophiles* are usually defined as organisms that thrive in environments that would be hazardous to humans or human cells.[ii] Is worrying about extremophiles farfetched? Perhaps not. Most microbial life forms we have thus far found on Earth are extremophilic (and exist below Earth's surface).[4] There is also a distinct possibility that the distribution of life on Earth is not representative of what exists elsewhere in the universe. Extraterrestrial life might be even more extremophilic and altogether unlike terrestrial life, for instance, "not carbon-based,

---

[i] The term 'alien' is frequently found in philosophical discussion of the moral standing of extraterrestrial life. Notably, it builds in normative assumptions. Thus, *alien* refers not only to being "of a foreign nature or character; strange, unfamiliar, different," but also "hostile, repugnant" (Oxford University Press, 2023 (March), *adj. and n.*, alien. *OED Online*, 3rd edition, Oxford University Press). While we use 'alien' in the chapter title and subsection heading, we urge openness to the prospect of personhood for non-human extraterrestrial life.

[ii] The usual definition of extremophily is human-centric. Depending on species-standpoint, extremophily admits of multiple interpretations. (See Mariscal C, Brunet TDP, 2020, What Are Extremophiles: A Philosophical Perspective, in Smith KC, Mariscal C, eds., *Social and Conceptual Issues in Astrobiology*, Oxford University Press, 157–178.)

using a liquid other than water as a solvent, adapted to environmental conditions more extreme than any found on Earth—so different that it might be unrecognizable to us."[5] The so-called weird life report from the National Academies of Sciences, Engineering, and Medicine underscores that

> extreme conditions that limit growth or prove lethal to most organisms [on Earth] can be ideal habitats for others. Extremes of high temperature, high and low pH, high salt concentration, concentrations of toxic metals and organic compounds, and high levels of radiation kill the overwhelming majority of Earth's organisms. However, organisms in all three domains of life have adapted to many terrestrial extremes.[6]

If extraterrestrial extremophiles match the description given by the National Academies, this could generate ethical conflicts, or even raise the prospect of species extinction. Short of this, it could pose ethical conflicts involving different forms of life competing against one another to survive. To illustrate, consider the sun-feeding organism in Andy Weir's novel, *Project Hail Mary*.[7]

> *Project Hail Mary. A cloud of alien microbes called the Astrophage is draining energy from the sun and threatening to destroy all life on Earth. Ryland Grace, a science teacher, is on a mission to the nearest star, Tau Ceti, which appears unaffected by the infestation. The orders from Grace's superior:* "When the alternative is death to your entire species, things are very easy. No moral dilemmas, no weighing what's best for whom. Just a single-minded focus on getting this project working." *When Grace arrives at Tau Ceti, he is not alone. An extraterrestrial being is there too trying to save its planet from the Astrophage. Grace calls the creature, 'Rocky,' because it looks like a Labrador-size spider made out of rock. Rocky breathes ammonia, uses echolocation, and speaks in musical notes. Rocky is an 'Eridian' who hails from a planet in the 40 Eridani*

system. *As the story develops, we learn Tau Ceti is the natural home of Astrophage, and natural predators there keep it from multiplying out of control. Outside Tau Ceti, it becomes an invasive species. Grace captures a natural predator from Tau Ceti and sends it to Earth's sun, saving life on Earth and all planets in the solar system.*

In Weir's version of the story, Grace and Rocky learn to communicate and become friends. They help each other and save both planets by finding a natural predator that controls the lethal threat for all. Yet, consider an altered version.

<u>Project Hail Mary, Version 2</u>. *The same as the original version, except the natural predator is only partially successful. It can destroy enough of the Astrophage to save one planet—Grace's or Rocky's.*

In *Project Hail Mary, Version 2*, the alternatives are death to humans (and life on Earth) or death to Eridians (and life on Rocky's planet.) Is there a possible description of Eridians that would ethically support saving Eridians over humans? In what follows, we first consider background beliefs about extraterrestrial life that inform African and Western traditions, then turn to consider, 'Are Eridians persons?' and 'Should we save Eridians or humans in *Project Hail Mary Version 2?*

1. African Personhood. On the African continent, the first site known to study celestial objects and space was Nabta Playa, which was once a drained basin in the Nubian Desert, south of modern-day Cairo.[8] By the first millennium, trade routes between North Africa and West Africa were established and Timbuktu, Mali, was a bustling city and a hub for religious, cultural, and commercial exchange. Beginning in the fifteenth century, Timbuktu established a written tradition that included ancient astronomy manuscripts (preserved today as the *Desert Libraries of Timbuktu*), revealing "a powerful African literary tradition" among Malians and West

Africans of the Middle Ages.[9] West African astronomical traditions spread to other parts of Africa and were translated into local languages.[iii] These and other sources suggest that early Africans imbued extraterrestrial objects with humanlike and divine characteristics. This is evident in multiple ways: religious practices, ceremonies marking rites of passage, calendar-making, myths, poems, and the built environment. Thus, some ancient Africans south of the Sahara venerated celestial bodies, such as the Sun and Moon, alongside traditional belief systems.[10] Among the Igbo people of Nigeria, for example, traditional cultural practices involving medicine men, *dibia* (native doctors), and spiritualists draw on spiritual forces attributed to the sun, sky, stars, and moon.[11] In parts of Igboland, the sun is symbolized as a deity and Sun gazing (looking straight into the sun when it is bright) is thought to enable people to *itu anya* (open their eyes) and "behold what cannot be seen by the aid of normal human eyes."[12] The image of the Sun as a god appears in African literature, such as Achebe's *Anthills of the Savanah*,[13] and Sudanese poet Taban Lo Liyong's "The Sun Is My God and I Shall Worship Him When He Rises, Reaches His Zenith, and Reposes for the Night."[14] Detailed knowledge of the sun also appears in home design representing the sun's diurnal and annual motion. Among the Mamprusi of northern Ghana, "the *zonga* or entranceway of one's home faces west so that the rays of the setting sun are directed into an area where family elders sit"; among the Swahili people on Africa's East coast, the *Kilimia* (Ploughing Stars) are used for forecasting weather, determining planting times, and making calendars.[15]

[iii] According to Snedegar, historical achievements of West African astronomers have garnered less attention than deserved, while misinformation about cosmological achievements of the Dogon people of Mali has received excess attention (Snedegar K, 2016, Astronomy in Sub-Saharan Africa, in Selin H, ed., *Encyclopaedia of the History of Science, Technology, and Medicine in Non-Western Cultures*, Springer, 742–752, pp. 745 ff., DOI: 10.1007/978-94-007-7747-7.)

Contemporary African philosophy continues to revere natural objects, including the cosmos, and some African scholars accord non-living nature moral standing. As discussed in Chapter 6, Behrens's relational environmentalism holds that non-living nature merits non-instrumental respect by virtue of contributing to the web of life. Within African thought, there are gradients of moral standing (as discussed in Chapter 6). First, *living nature is generally accorded higher moral standing than non-living nature.* For example, Behrens, Molefe, and Metz rank non-living nature below living nature, because it is not "capable of being better or worse off,"[16] cannot elicit human sympathy,[17] or cannot join in communal relations.[18] Second (also discussed in Chapter 6), *priority is given to humans over animals.* For example, Gyekye, characterizes Akan thought as centering human welfare,[19] Mbiti considers "[humanity] to be at the centre of the universe,"[20] and Tangwa interprets African philosophy as anthropocentric.[21] Finally (as discussed in Chapter 3), African personhood generally endorses the idea that human personhood is itself hierarchical across the lifespan. Humans who are more incorporated and more pro-social are elevated above humans who are less so.

Based on this summary and the arguments throughout the book, we can extrapolate that a similar moral hierarchy might apply to beings in *Project Hail Mary, Version 2.* Forced to choose between humans and Eridians, African personhood would favor humans. The justification for this is first, Eridians are not (or not yet) incorporated in human community. According to Menkiti, people who are not incorporated are "mere danglers to whom the description 'person' does not apply."[22] Second, these particular extraterrestrials pose a lethal threat to human community. According to Gyekye, "used normatively, the judgment 'is a person' means 'has a good character,' 'is generous,' 'is peaceful,' 'is humble,' 'has respect for others.'"[23] A lethal threat, even if unintentional, is socially harmful. Third, African ethics is 'weakly anthropocentric' in the sense that it imposes a moral hierarchy between human and non-human beings.[24] These considerations suggest to us that African personhood would prioritize humans over Eridians, other things being equal.

Yet, what are we to make of the fact that in Weir's telling of the story, a closeness develops between Grace and Rocky? For example, they learn to communicate, or as Hutchinson puts it, "The pair makes a hell of a problem-solving team, jazz hands and fist bumps and all."[25] While Rocky uses musical chords and whistles, Grace uses Excel and Fourier software. Judging from the case of Rocky and Grace, Eridians possess the capacity to commune with human beings. Doesn't that show that they have moral standing or qualify as persons according to African views?

In reply, some renderings of African personhood, such as Metz's, hold that the capacity to commune in pro-social ways is sufficient for personhood.[26] This suggests that Rocky and other Eridians qualify as full-fledged persons. Other African views might say that although Rocky is a person, Rocky's personhood is less than Grace's, because Grace is more broadly incorporated in human community than Rocky. For example, only Grace has a human mother and father, perhaps an extended human family, as well as human friends, neighbors, colleagues, and compatriots. Rocky has none of these. Arguably, Rocky's moral status would be similar to a human child's. As we saw in Chapter 3 (Section 3.2), African personhood generally holds that a child has higher moral standing than a newborn infant but less than a full-grown adult. While it could be argued that Rocky might have an Eridian family and Eridian friends, the weak anthropocentrism generally implicit in African ethics would warrant granting more consideration to human relationships. Analogously, the relationships between non-human animals, such as between elephants in the same herd or dogs in the same pack, does not suffice to show that elephants and dogs are persons; for African personhood, elephants and dogs must be incorporated within human relationships. Yet not all scholars of African ethics would agree with our analysis. Behrens's relational environmentalism holds that "not only is a 'a person a person through other persons,' but also . . . 'a person is a person through other (living) beings."[27] For Behrens, perhaps life on planets in the 40 Eridiani system might count as much as Earth life.

2. Early Greek. Ancient Greeks explained the universe mostly in terms of their own particular experiences, projecting human or biological traits onto objects and events—the beginning of the universe was explained in terms of birth, while cosmic events were described as struggles between good and evil.[28] Rather than being abstract and general, the earliest Greek conceptions of space were infused with meaning and emphasized the particular, often emerging in folklore, literature, and religion. Transmitted orally, these ideas served not just to instruct, but to entertain. Homeric poems furnish a detailed account of early Greek speculations about the cosmos in the period before Greek philosophy. During this period, the universe was understood to have a three-tiered structure, with each tier governed by gods: heaven, ruled by Zeus; the sea, governed by Poseidon; and the netherworld, controlled by Hades.[29] Hesiod, a Greek poet during the seventh century BCE (discussed in Chapter 6, Section 6.3), provides a cosmogony mixed with myth in *Theogony*:

> First came the Chasm; and then broad-breasted Earth, secure seat forever of all the immortals who occupy the peak of snowy Olympus.... Out of the Chasm came Erebos and dark Night, and from Night in turn came Bright Air and Day, whom she bore in shared intimacy with Erebos. Earth bore first of all one equal to herself, starry Heaven, so that he should cover her all about, to be a secure seat for ever for the blessed gods... and she bore also the undraining Sea and its furious swell, not in union of love.[30]

Hesiod, like other early Greeks, "began with the faith that nature itself was animated," and proceeded to imbue it with divinities.[31]

Early philosophers sought more naturalistic explanations, gradually casting off explanations based on divine interventions and whim. According to Lindberg, "The capricious world of divine intervention was being pushed aside. . . . [C]haos was yielding to *kosmos*. A clear distinction between natural and supernatural was emerging; and there was wide agreement that causes (if they are to be dealt with philosophically) must be sought only in the natures of things."[32] From the fifth century BCE, most Greek astronomers and cosmologists regarded the Earth to be a sphere, based on observing lunar eclipses, which showed the Earth's shadow on the moon to be round; sailors also reported that tops of ships appeared before bottoms, which would not be the case on a flat surface.[33] The Earth itself was thought to be situated within a larger sphere, which comprised the universe. The great sphere of the universe was split into two sections, an 'outer' celestial realm and an 'inner' terrestrial one, with the moon's orbit marking this division. Within this two-story configuration, "the Earth was a place of transition and flux," while "the heavens were unchanging."[34] The Greeks also observed the motion of wandering stars in the night sky, which they called, *planētēs* (wanderer).[35] Unlike fixed stars, wanderers did not appear in the same arrangement each night but instead, moved across the night sky in unison. Rather than resorting to purely mechanistic explanations of planetary movement, the prevalent view in early Greece was that wandering stars were moved by an unmoved mover, or god, corresponding to each. The five planets visible with the naked eye—Mercury, Venus, Mars, Jupiter, and Saturn—were among the wandering stars, and referred to as Hermes, Aphrodite, Ares, Zeus, and Cronus. The Sun and Moon were sometimes added, bringing the total number of wandering luminaries to seven.

During antiquity, two major schools of thought developed about worlds 'outside' our own (i.e., beyond the outer sphere of the heavens): (1) atomists, including Leucippus, Democritus, and later, Epicurus and Lucretius, who hypothesized an infinite variety of worlds, each containing an infinite variety of life, and (2) Plato and Aristotle, who were committed to a single world cosmology or *kosmos*. The first Greek philosophers to believe in intelligent extraterrestrial life were the fifth century BCE atomists, who held that reality consisted of two kinds of things: unchangeable, indestructible *atomos* or *atomon* (atoms), which were indivisible, infinite, perfectly solid, and "move about in an infinite void, repelling one another when they collide or combining into clusters by means of tiny hooks and barbs on their surfaces, which become entangled" and visible objects, produced by movements and relocations of atoms.[36] The atomists' commitment to a plurality of worlds containing life was premised on the belief that "a chance conglomeration of infinite atoms in an infinite universe *must* form worlds, all things being possible."[37] The basis for this belief was, in part, an ontological commitment Lovejoy later dubbed, 'the principle of plenitude': "no genuine potentiality of being can remain unfulfilled... the extent and abundance of... creation must be as great as the possibility of existence and commensurate with the productive capacity of a 'perfect' and inexhaustible Source, and ... the world is better, the more things it contains."[38] Since the atomists, like other early Greeks, pictured worlds as closed off systems, with a dome on top, they assumed humans would never see or interact with life on other worlds. Perhaps, this is why they refrained from speculating directly about its moral status or humans' ethical obligations toward it.

In contrast to atomists, Plato and Aristotle depicted a finite bounded system encompassing all that is. In *Timaeus*, Plato asserts that "in order then that the world might be solitary, like the perfect animal, the creator made not two worlds or an infinite number of them; but there is and ever will be only one only-begotten and created heaven."[39] In *Metaphysics*, Aristotle opines, "Leucippus and Democritus, who say that the primary bodies are in perpetual movement in the void or infinite, may be asked to explain the manner of their motion";[40] Aristotle reasoned that multiple planets would require multiple Prime Movers, a possibility he readily dismissed. While the atomists' universe was infinite, random, purposeless, and without gods, the Aristotelian universe was finite, governed by design, teleological, and theistic.[41] For both Plato and Aristotle, the celestial realm could not contain life, because it was eternal and unchanging; since processes of "life, death, birth, decay, coming to be, and passing away" involved constant change, they must be confined to Earth, leaving "literally, no place for aliens."[42]

3. *Medieval Christian.* With the rise of Christianity, Aristotle's universe became the reigning view across Europe. Although the horizons of the medieval world did not include life on other planets, there continued to be active speculation about an extraterrestrial realm, conceived as a spiritual dimension populated with incorporeal beings, including angels who were thought to have full moral standing. Angels were "a class of celestial beings considered intermediate between God and humanity and typically acting as attendants, messengers, or agents of God."[43] They were depicted as humanlike in appearance, and, like Aristotle's unmoved mover, incorporeal and "characterized by their intelligence."[44] During the Middle Ages, astronomy sought to give biblical and theological connotations to Plato's and Aristotle's astronomy, and included this in the basic program of medieval scholastic training.

By 1543, the publication of Copernicus's *On the Revolutions of the Heavenly Spheres* "opened the door that inadvertently let in the aliens."[45] Crucial for our purposes was not the sun's placement at the center of the universe but the demise of the Greek's two-story universe, because "once the Earth was seen as a planet, the other planets could readily be imagined as other Earths. This analogy suggested not only physical but also biological affinities."[46] While some Copernicans, notably Galileo, remained skeptical about extraterrestrial life, others were convinced that nature did nothing in vain, and assumed planets were populated with life of every kind. Bruno, for example, painted a picture of otherworldly life in which each region of each principal body comprised matter which, circumstances permitting, became a plant or animal, even a rational animal. This last category included human beings and also demons ... rational beings with rarefied bodies made of pure aether or combinations of aether with air, water or Earth. The latter ... were generally ... more intelligent than human beings.[47]

Another Copernican, Kepler, also envisioned a universe teaming with intelligent life:

> There are in fact four planets revolving around Jupiter.... *For whose sake*, the question arises, if there are no people on Jupiter to behold this wonderfully varied display with their own eyes? ... The conclusion is quite clear. Our moon exists for us on the Earth, not for the other globes. Those four little moons exist for Jupiter, not for us. Each planet in turn, together with its occupants is served by its own satellites. From this line of reasoning we deduce with the highest degree of probability that Jupiter is inhabited.[48]

In a post-Copernican world, the infinite number and variety of life forms suddenly appearing in the well-ordered ontologies of astronomers and philosophers was a problem to be reckoned with. An underlying challenge that life on other planets posed for Christianity was that it seemed to undermine the Christian doctrine of salvation (soteriology). Jesus of Nazareth was considered to be the savior of the whole world. If people exist on other planets, are they descendants of Adam and Eve? Do they fall under the salvation brought about by Jesus? If so, how? Pascal, a Christian and (probably) a Copernican, asked directly what elevates humanity above the fray. Pascal's answer invokes the human capacity for rational thought:

[A human being] is but a reed, the most feeble thing in nature; but [a human] is a thinking reed. The entire universe need not arm itself to crush [them]. A vapour, a drop of water suffices to kill [them]. But, if the universe were to crush [them], [the human being] would still be more noble than that which killed [them], because [they know] that [they die] and the advantage which the universe has over [them]; the universe knows nothing of this. All our dignity consists, then, in thought.[49]

Pascal adds, "It is not from space that I must seek my dignity, but from the government of my thought. . . . By space the universe encompasses and swallows me up like an atom; by thought I comprehend the world."[50]

Considering these analyses, what might early Greek and medieval Christians say about who to save in *Project Hail Mary, Version 2*? Should we prefer humans or Eridians, assuming we cannot save both? Greek atomism would presumably back pedal, arguing that moral characteristics like personhood are illusory. They might conclude that in reality, it does not matter who is saved—both Eridians and humans are atoms moving in a void. *For Greek atomists, personhood, and all morality, is an illusion.* Plato and Aristotle might both argue that what matters for personhood is having a superior allotment of reason. After all, this is ultimately why they maintain that free men, but not women, children, or slaves, are eligible to become citizens and to acquire moral worth by assuming roles within the city. For both, there would presumably be a possible description of Eridians in which they have a *greater* allotment of reason than free men. Under this description, saving Eridians, not humans, would be ethically justified. Expressed differently, *for Plato and Aristotle, the heart of personhood is reason, not humanity.*

Medieval Christian philosophy embraces the view that what matters for personhood is being made in God's image. In other words, *at the heart of personhood is imago Dei*. Without evidence that Eridians were created in the image and likeness of God, and that they were redeemed by Christ, medieval Christians would most likely favor humans over Eridians.

4. *Contemporary Western.* Kant followed in the footsteps of post-Copernican philosophers and was significantly involved in astronomy and speculations about intelligent extraterrestrial life. Kant wrote specifically about the comparative worth of humans versus extraterrestrials. For example, Kant states that creatures on other planets may well exceed our intellectual capacities, committing to an ethics that prizes rationality, rather than humanity, as a source of moral dignity and worth. Kant invites us to consider the humble standpoint of lice on a beggar's head:

> Those creatures who live in the forests of a beggar's head ... had for a long time thought of their dwelling place as an immeasurably large ball and themselves as the masterworks of creation. Then one of them, whom Heaven had endowed with a more refined soul ... unexpectedly learned about a noble man's head. Immediately he called all the witty creatures of his district together and told them with delight: We are not the only living beings in all nature. Look here at this new land. More lice live here.[51]

Kant remarks, "Let us judge in an unprejudiced manner. This insect ... expresses very well the condition of most human beings," both "in its way of living as well as in its lack of worth."[52] Kant thought "most of the planets are certainly inhabited, and those that are not will be in the future."[53] For Kant, the moral worth of human beings was not extraordinary but, like the louse's, middling. Kant arrived at this conclusion by reasoning that the intellectual capacity of a being was proportionate to the location of its planet relative to the sun:

> the excellence of thinking natures, the speed of their imaginations, the clarity and vivacity of their ideas, which come to them from

external stimuli, together with the ability to combine ideas, and finally, too, the rapidity of actual performance, in short, the entire extent of their perfection, is governed by a particular rule according to which these characteristics will always be more excellent and more complete in proportion to the distance of their dwelling places from the sun.[54]

It followed from Kant's reasoning that Jovians and Saturnians were intellectually and morally superior to Earthlings, since they were further from the sun, while Mercurians were intellectually and morally beneath us. Since Kant held that the inner quality that imparts value to human beings is rationality, the claim that Jovians and Saturnians are *rationally* superior to humans is tantamount to saying that they are *morally* superior, too.[55] In the case of *Project Hail Mary, Version 2*, humans would have a 'middling' chance of being favored over Eridians. If Eridians were similar to Jovians and Saturnians in their rational capacity, Kant would choose Rocky over Grace. *At the heart of a Kantian ethics is a focus on rationality, not humanity.*

Like Kant, utilitarians hold that a being's species or type is not directly relevant to its moral standing. What matters is something else: the capacity to suffer. Thus, the relevant considerations are, 'Can Eridians suffer?' and 'Do they suffer more than human beings?' If so, Eridians are more morally considerable than humans and should be preferred. *At the heart of utilitarian analysis is happiness and well-being, not humanity.*

Although fanciful, *Project Mary Version 2* makes the important point that setting aside species membership has important implications for the moral standing of extraterrestrial life. Specifically, species suicide will be a viable option for any ethical approach that places ultimate value on something *other* than humanity and regards membership in the human family as a morally arbitrary fact.

5. *Emergent Personhood*. Emergent Personhood holds that extraterrestrial life can acquire personhood in much the same way that terrestrial animals can, namely, by joining in relationships with human beings and contributing to human community in pro-social ways. In a possible world where technology allows spacecraft to traverse large interplanetary distances, enabling relationships between human beings and extraterrestrial life to form, extraterrestrial life might acquire personhood.

Yet, in a situation where human beings come into lethal conflict with an extraterrestrial species, as occurs in *Project Hail Mary, Version 2*, Emergent Personhood favors human beings. The reason is that the personhood that creatures on other planets acquire would be lost in this situation, because their relationship with humans would no longer be pro-social. While they may continue to be morally considerable, they would no longer qualify as persons. The basis for saying that non-human extraterrestrials can lose personhood, while humans cannot, is that from birth to death, we stand in special relationships with other human beings that we do not have with members of any other species. *At the heart of Emergent Personhood is the human-human relationships from which persons emerge.*

In response to our argument, someone who held that species preference was morally arbitrary might think differently about the case of *Hail Mary, Version 2*. Singer, for example, responding to a case posed by Williams,[56] considers a similar scenario and gives a different response. Singer imagines that "our planet has been colonized by benevolent, fair-minded and far-sighted aliens who, no doubt fair-mindedly and on the basis of full information, judge it necessary to remove us," i.e., to remove the human species, in order to minimize suffering and maximize enjoyment.[57] According to Singer, the right thing to do here is to "reject the tribal—or species—instinct" and let the aliens destroy us.[58] There is little we can say in response, other than that it matters *to us* that the human species continues. Apparently, it does not matter to Singer. Yet it strikes us as no more—or less—arbitrary to base morality on species-independent qualities, like the capacity for suffering, than to base it on intra-species and cross-species relationships.

Pulling back from the analysis of this section, we believe that Emergent Personhood has clear advantages over early Greek, medieval Christian, utilitarian, and Kantian analyses that the case of *Hail Mary, Version 2* brings to light. Unlike these accounts, there is no possible description of life on Rocky's planet to suggest that we ought to favor that life over humans and life on Earth. While other views prize qualities such as reason, mirroring God, and the capacity to suffer, Emergent Personhood prizes human community.

Our analysis of extraterrestrials, like our analysis of animals in Chapter 6, shows strong affinities with African ethics. Even though the two approaches are strikingly different when it comes to *human* personhood, they overlap in the case of *non-human* personhood. For non-human personhood, both African and Emergent personhood share a focus on incorporating non-humans in a human community as a sufficient condition for personhood. Both meet the challenges posed by extraterrestrial life and avoid species suicide for human beings. Table 7.1 summarizes the discussion of this section.

While Weir's novel introduces the prospect of intelligent life elsewhere in the universe, this prospect may never come to fruition. Potthast argues that even though it is *possible* that rational or sentient creatures inhabit other planets, it is not *probable*, because "a staggering number of factors would have to be just right for life in general to take hold, let alone sentience and rationality."[59] Potthast reasons that a more plausible scenario is that other planets contain microbial life or basic plant life. If so, then instead of comparing Eridians to human beings, a more apt comparison is to liken life beyond Earth to discoveries of terrestrial bacteria or viral life on Earth. This raises a different set of ethical considerations, which fall outside the scope of this chapter. In the next section we raise

Table 7.1 Should We Save Humans or ETs?

Personhood View	Can ETs be persons?	Should we ever prefer ETs over humans in *Project Hail Mary*, Version 2?	Why/Why not?
Emergent Personhood and African Personhood	Yes	No	If ETs pose a lethal threat to humans, they are not pro-social for us
Early Greek Personhood	Yes	Yes	If ETs have a greater allotment of reason, we should prefer them
Medieval Christian Personhood	No	No	In the story of creation, ETs were not created in God's image
Contemporary Western Personhood	Yes	Yes	If ETs can reason or suffer more than humans, we should prefer them

KET: ET = extraterrestrial; African personhood = views prominent among black peoples indigenous to the region of Africa south of the Sahara, as captured in the works of academic philosophers; early Greek personhood = Plato, Aristotle; contemporary Western personhood = Kantian and utilitarian ethics

a different possibility: if we never encounter life on other planets, what ethical obligations, if any, do we owe non-living extraterrestrial lands? Can extraterrestrial lands, soils, and systems have rights or be morally considerable?

7.3 Terraforming Mars

The question of whether non-living nature is morally considerable raises a distinct set of concerns. *Terraforming*, a term coined by science fiction writer Jack Williamson,[60] refers to the hypothetical idea of "modifying a world's environment so that it can support Earth life-forms, especially humans."[61] Some scientists propose that planetary engineering of this sort might one day be possible.[62,63,64] Mars, for example, displays features resembling dry riverbeds and mineral deposits that only form in the presence of liquid water, suggesting that at some point in the past the Martian climate supported liquid water at the surface. However, in 2018, the National Aeronautics and Space Administration (NASA) concluded that terraforming Mars or other planets was not possible with existing technologies, and that the majority of Mars's ancient, potentially habitable, atmosphere has been "stripped away by solar wind and radiation. . . . [O]nce this happens . . . water and CO2 are gone forever."[65] After 2018, scientific interest in terraforming waned.[66] However, in 2020, NASA determined that plants that can survive in harsh Earth environments, "may be good for eventually terraforming the Red Planet."[67] A potentially promising approach was introduced using a Geographic Information Systems framework to identify Mars-like locations on Earth that share Mars's environmental and climatic conditions, and then identify vegetation growing in these areas on Earth that are likely to survive missions to Mars.[68] Applying this framework, Vaz and Penfound reported that certain parts of the Canadian Arctic (Devon Island) and Antarctica are the most similar place on Earth to Mars, with temperatures that exceed 10° C (50° F) during summer, while dropping to −50° C (−58° F) during winter.[69] They identified a group of perennial grasses (*Poa*) that thrive in this region. Specific species, such as artic bluegrass (*Poa Arctica*) and short blue grass (*Poa abbreviata*), are lush in terrestrial regions similar to Mars.[70] Vaz and Penfound concluded that this vegetation had the potential to be brought to Mars for water and oxygen recycling (but not for human consumption).

If NASA's latest assessment is accurate, and terraforming, perhaps using techniques like Vaz and Penfound propose, becomes possible with future technological advancement, what ethical issues would terraforming raise? While growing perennial grasses might not be particularly controversial, other forms of terraforming are, such as mining and extracting resources from other planets for human use. Consider the following case, adapted from Kim Stanley Robinson's science fiction story, *Red Mars*.[71]

> Red Mars. *A crew of 100 scientists from America, Russia and the Arab world are sent on a mission to explore Mars. Rival factions emerge: (1) Sax speaks for the Greens, a group advocating terraforming Mars for human benefit; (2) Ann heads the Reds, a group opposing terraforming and advocating preserving and studying Mars in its native form; and (3) Arkady leads a group concerned with governance of people on Mars, that advocates a complete break from Earth.*

Considering the first two rival factions, the Reds and the Greens, which is right? Are Sax and the Greens right that we should use Mars for human benefit, much as we have used terrestrial land and soils for food, energy, and rare elements? Or are Ann and the Reds right that we ought to preserve wilderness for its own sake, rather than using it merely to serve human ends? The Greens' view suggests that Martian nature has only instrumental value, while implicit in the Reds' view is the claim that Mars's lands may have moral rights or personhood. The third faction, led by Arkady, raises a different problem: 'Who decides?' Should Mars's settlers govern themselves? Should national governments on Earth rule Mars? Should some form of multi-planetary governance exercise jurisdiction on behalf of all humankind?

Many of the questions *Red Mars* raises are familiar, because we have faced them here on Earth. For example, debates about the use of oceans and wilderness raise parallel debates between so-called conservationist and preservationist ethics. We saw in Chapter 6 (Section 6.3) that both African and Emergent personhood hold that terrestrial lands have or can acquire moral standing as part of valuable wholes involving nature-human relationships. If Earth's land and soils can matter for their own sakes, is it "planetocentric"[72] to assume that *only* Earth land and soils matter?

We approach these and related questions from the standpoints of African and Western personhood, and through the lens of our own view, Emergent Personhood. Some of the analysis that follows extrapolates from the discussion of terrestrial land and soil introduced in Chapter 6 (Section 6.3), reflecting the fact that until recently little direct philosophical discussion of the ethics of extraterrestrial non-living nature existed.

1. African. African personhood might hold that Martian land, soils, and non-living nature can acquire personhood in much the same way that terrestrial lands can. If nature is incorporated into human communities in pro-social ways, it becomes a valuable part of human relationships and can develop a non-instrumental value. Unlike the extraterrestrial planets in *Project Hail Mary, Version 2,* extraterrestrial lands in *Red Mars* pose no direct threat to humans and could potentially function in a positive way. Developing Mars in a pro-social way to benefit human beings would be permissible; however, once lands on Mars become incorporated in human communities, lands would acquire moral standing and, perhaps, personhood. As a result, humans might acquire direct duties toward Mars's lands. Provided Mars's lands continued to exist in positive relation to us, these duties would persist.

African personhood often ascribes a hierarchy of moral standing, with humans above animals, animals above plants, and plants above non-living nature. This hierarchy is based, for example, on the capacity to be better or worse off,[73] to be an object of human sympathy,[74] or to commune with human beings.[75] According to some analyses, such as Behrens's *relational environmentalism,*[76] the moral standing of lands on Mars might fall short of full-fledged personhood. For Behrens, although both living and non-living things are entangled in a web-of-life and have value by virtue of this, non-living nature has less value, because it cannot be worse off by anything we do to it. This suggests that land and soils on Mars merit non-instrumental respect yet do not have full moral rights or personhood. Likewise, Tempels's *force theory* holds that all nature matters for its own sake, because all things in nature have force or all-pervasive energy that imparts intrinsic value to them. However, similar to Behrens, Tempels holds that intrinsic value is hierarchically distributed, with animals above plants, which are in turn, above inanimate things.

Since both Behrens and Tempels regard non-living nature as comparatively low on a scale of moral value, it may not unjustly violate the moral standing or rights of lands on Mars to extract resources for human benefit. Yet, since nature on Mars has some measure of moral standing, it is owed non-instrumental respect. This suggests a reason to limit extractive practices. For example, it might violate the respect owed nature on Mars to spoil the planet for private commercial gain, or dump space debris there. Moreover, non-living nature can acquire greater moral standing by becoming more incorporated in human communities in a pro-social way. African personhood would presumably favor using nature on Mars in ways that enable its value to increase. For example, African personhood might support requiring Sax's group, the Greens, to extract resources in ways that are not only respectful, but sustainable, benefiting human communities over the long run.

2. Early Greek and Medieval Christian. As discussed previously (Chapter 6, Section 6.3), the earliest Greek and Roman societies regarded nature as a living substance; they held that forces of nature were animate and purposive, sharing the same life energy as human beings. Had they considered the moral standing of nature on other planets, they might have extended this stance to lands on Mars, regarding them as a sacred place where gods of nature were present. Just as early Greeks and Romans regarded agricultural practices as injuring nature and requiring expatiation, they might have regarded the actions of settlers on Mars in the Green group led by Sax to be exploitive and deeply wrong, violating something sacred. At the same time, however, it is possible that early Greeks would have allowed some extraction of resources to benefit human beings, similar to the agricultural practices they carried out on Earth, provided this was done respectfully, e.g., with prayer and gratitude. If this analysis is persuasive, then rather than siding with the Red or Green group, early Greeks might instead have struck a middle ground between them.

Later Greek and early Christian views also can be interpreted as lending support to a middle view about the conflict between the Red and Greens. As discussed in Chapter 6 (Section 6.3), Plato and Aristotle perceived a hierarchy of nature based on how much reason different entities had. Plato apparently thought that intelligence could manifest in plants and nature, but to a far lesser extent, while Aristotle described a gradual continuum, which included borderline cases. Both shared the belief that humanity was at the top of nature's hierarchy. This general approach of granting humans priority over animals and non-living nature was also the leading view among early Christians. From a biblical viewpoint, the basis for human priority over nature was that human beings were uniquely made in the image of God (*imago Dei*), who granted them dominion over animals and lands. However, what responsibilities humans incur toward nature based on their dominion over nature is controversial. Some argue that the rise of Christianity ushered in a view of nature as existing solely to serve humans. In an influential 1967 article in *Science*, White argued that the earliest Greek stances toward non-living nature were far more respectful and blames Christianity for human arrogance:

> In Antiquity, every tree, every spring, every stream, every hill had its own *genius loci*, its guardian spirit. These spirits were accessible to men. . . . Before one cut a tree, mined a mountain, or dammed a brook, it was important to placate the spirit in charge of that particular situation. By destroying pagan animism,

Christianity made it possible to exploit nature in a mood of indifference to the feelings of natural objects.[77]

· White's rendering of Christianity is contentious, with some holding that Christian 'dominion' over nature does not justify enslaving animals or treating terrestrial lands in whatever ways humans please, but requires instead responsible stewardship.[78] Yet, the broader point White makes is that the belief that non-living nature lacks a soul and moral standing for its own sake was used historically to justify exploitive practices toward nature.

Since later Greeks saw Earth as a finite bounded system that encompassed all that is they did not entertain the possibility of encountering other planets. If they had considered the conflict between Reds and Greens in *Red Mars*, they might have held a view similar to the general African stance that puts human flourishing above non-living nature, while still requiring a respectful attitude. As discussed previously (Chapter 6, Section 6.3), although Aristotle held that the human capacity to think was superior, he stopped short of maintaining that lower animals had no intrinsic moral worth;[79] as noted, Aristotle regarded "humbler animals" and "every realm of nature" as "marvelous."[80] This suggests that, like Behrens, Aristotle might support a middle view, setting boundaries around the Greens' desire to treat lands on Mars in a purely instrumental way.

3. *Contemporary Western*. It would be difficult to garner support for Ann and the Red group's position by drawing on contemporary Western traditions of Kantian and utilitarian philosophy. Neither *Kantian ethics*, with its focus on rationality and being a moral legislator, nor *utilitarian ethics*, with its focus on the capacity to suffer, would regard abiotic nature as mattering for its own sake. More recent strands of Western thought, however, including *Leopold's land ethic*, challenge the absence of the land in these contemporary ethical paradigms. As we saw in Chapter 6 (Section 6.3), Leopold suggests that the moral community should include not

just humans, but also animals, soils, waters, plants, or collectively, 'the land.' According to Otto, Leopold's land ethic "wants us to re-vision the land as valuable not as commodity but as community."[81] This conception of land as part of a human community, rather than something outside it that humans own, is also found in traditional African communities, such as the Builsa.[82] Leopold aspires to "educate individuals about the complexities of the land," including "how human alterations to this complexity can infect the environment with instability."[83] Leopold might support Ann and the Red group's view that there is non-instrumental value in pristine nature that should be preserved for its own sake, while allowing some limited use of Mars's natural resources.

Another recent Western view, Næss's *deep ecology*, also provides a basis for attributing moral standing to nature on Mars. It locates value in a larger gestalt, which includes human beings appreciating nature and standing in awe of it. *Red Mars*'s author, Robinson, includes scenes depicting Martian landscape as beautiful and arousing a sense of wonderment. For example, shortly before human touchdown on Mars, Robinson portrays the planet this way: "The colored sands in their patterns, the fluted and scalloped canyon walls, the volcanoes rising right through the sky, the rubbled rock of the chaotic terrain, the infinity of craters, ringed emblems of the planet's beginning. . . . Beautiful, or harsher than that: spare, austere, stripped down, silent, stoic, rocky, changeless. Sublime."[84] Næss's views of Mars's lands as awe-inspiring lends support to Ann and the Red group's position that these lands should be preserved for their beauty and wildness, rather than used solely for human purposes.

Further support for the Red's standpoint comes from the Western environmental philosopher, Callicott, who builds on the holistic approach of Leopold and others to argue that non-living nature comprises part of a system of 'ecological collectives' that matter morally for their own sakes.[85] *Ecological collectives* include not just lands and soils, but populations, species, biotic communities, ecosystems, landscapes, biomes, and biospheres. Callicott holds that higher levels of biological organization evoke moral emotions, such as empathy, which are not present at lower levels or toward isolated features of ecological collectives. To illustrate, consider Singer's example of a schoolboy kicking a stone down the street (first discussed in Chapter 1, Section 1.3). Singer wants to say that since a stone cannot suffer, kicking it is not morally problematic, and "it would be nonsense to say that it was not in the interests of a stone to be kicked."[86] However, Callicott's response might be that although we do not care about *individual* stones, we care a lot about the freshwater ecosystem of which the stone is a part. If Callicott is correct, then Singer's example establishes only that a stone has no value in *isolation*. Its value emerges only when it is seen *in relation* to a larger system of biological organization of which it is a part.

It might be countered that there are no riverbeds on Mars. However, depending on how expansive 'biological organization' is, Mars might be viewed as a part of the solar system or story of the universe. This is the approach that Rolston takes. According to Rolston, while it would be nonsense to say a clod of dirt is intrinsically valuable, "the systemic, historic nature in which dirt figures prominently" should also be considered.[87] Properly understood, the clod of dirt is part of the Earth system and ultimately the Universe system: "The dirt that is the precursor of life is really fossil stardust.... [T]here are many physical constants and processes, both at microphysical and astronomical levels, that strikingly fit together" and led to this clod.[88] Rather than viewing everything in the universe as arranged for human beings, Rolston presses us to think in larger terms, revealing what Rolston calls *projective nature*: "We do not want to ascribe purpose to nature. At the same time something is going on—systematically, historically.... Nature is a fountain of life, and the whole fountain—not just the [discrete] life that issues from it is of value."[89]

If Leopold, Næss, Callicott, and Rolston were to comment on the controversy in *Red Mars*, they might well ascribe rights to

Mars and its lands and soils, as do Ann and the group Ann leads. However, this does not necessarily signify that Mars's nature is inviolable or that it must be preserved in a wholly pristine state. Instead, attributing moral standing and rights to Mars's nature implies that *sufficient justification must be given* for overriding the planet's rights, thereby shifting the burden of argument from Ann's group to Sax's. Callicott, referring to terrestrial land and soils, puts the point thus:

> Since old-growth forests ... are not yet widely acknowledged to have intrinsic value, timber companies may fell them without first offering any justification whatever. If environmentalists want to stop the clear-cutting of dwindling old growth forests on public land ... they have to go to court seeking a legal injunction. If, on the other hand, the intrinsic value of nature were widely acknowledged and legally institutionalized, then timber companies would have to go to court seeking permission to fell an old-growth forest—thus being burdened to offer sufficient justification.... [T]his would amount to 'a revolution in the way we treat the non-human world.'[90]

All four of these recent Western analyses afford a basis for preserving some amount of pristine nature and seeking justification before significantly altering it.

A further consideration is what counts as 'nature.' Rolston urges thinking of "degrees of naturalness," ranging from completely natural to completely artificial, or "multiple dimensions of naturalness," ranging from little disturbed to human dominated.[91] Rolston's view suggests that nature on Mars has high value, because its lands are among the most natural anywhere. To colonize Mars without regard for its place and value in the universe would be akin to "tearing pages out of an unread book."[92] Since humans were relative latecomers to the story of the universe, Rolston urges a humble stance toward the larger story. For Rolston, we should think not just of human rights, but of both land rights and human rights in tandem.

4. *Emergent Personhood.* Like African personhood and some recent strands of contemporary Western thought, Emergent Personhood holds that Mars's nature can have moral status and personhood. However, we differ with some recent contemporary Western views, such as those of Leopold, Næss, Callicott, and Rolston, which posit value in a *biological* organization or system. For us, value inheres in the *nature-human* relationship. According to Emergent Personhood, Mars and its lands acquire moral standing in much the same way that terrestrial life and ecosystems do, namely, by being incorporated in human community in a pro-social way. In contrast to the Greens, who regard Martian land as having only instrumental value, Emergent Personhood agrees with the Reds that Mars can have value in itself. In contrast to the Reds, however, Emergent Personhood agrees with the Greens that Mars may be ethically used to help humankind. Yet, as explained in Chapter 6 (sections 6.2 and 6.3), not having personhood does not equate with not being morally considerable, nor does it give humans license to decimate nature. Instead, humans ought to cultivate a harmonious relationship with nature. All told, we advocate the same non-instrumental respect that some African scholars, such as Behrens, might.

Against Emergent Personhood, Rolston might argue that human ethics can and should think beyond a human standpoint. While Rolston acknowledges that morality "wears a human face," Rolston urges that we can and do "gain views that look out from our bodies and places and see what is out-of-my-body, out-of-my-place; ... we humans ... enjoy a surprising transcendence."[93] Rolston anticipates that humans can discover "values that are objective enough to urge on moral agents from whatever extraterrestrial origin"; for example, "There would be something censurable about moral agents anywhere, anytime who lied, cheated, stole, hated or were unjust."[94] In reply, we reiterate the *humble anthropocentrism* expressed throughout the book. The boundaries of ethical thought are constrained by our human standpoint. We perceive the world with human senses, think with human brains, and live as humans do. To suppose that humans have a transspecies perspective and can formulate an ethics for beings everywhere in the universe is, for us, the height of hubris.

Table 7.2 recaps the discussion of this section and the diverse perspectives we have glimpsed on the value of extraterrestrial lands and the controversy between Reds and Greens in *Red Mars*.

Red Mars raises a final ethical question: 'Who should have authority over Mars?' In Robinson's story, Arkady and the group they lead maintain that Mars's settlers should govern themselves, making a complete break from Earth. Here on Earth, there is already ethical and political controversy over the question of planetary governance. The 1967 *Outer Space Treaty* stipulates governance of other planets should rest with all humanity. The Treaty, which forms the basis of current international space law, states: "The exploration and use of outer space shall be carried out for the benefit and in the interests of all countries and shall be the province of all mankind"; "astronauts shall be regarded as the envoys of mankind"; "outer space is not subject to national appropriation by claim of sovereignty, by means of use or occupation, or by any other means"; and "states shall avoid harmful contamination of space and celestial bodies."[95] Yet, this broad language has not prevented national laws permitting recovery of abiotic resources, including water and minerals, for private, commercial uses, which was sanctioned by the US SPACE Act of 2015[96] and encouraged in a 2020 executive order by then US President Trump.[97] Nor has it prevented Luxembourg from setting up a space mining center, with the goal of becoming a European hub for mining extraterrestrial resources. The commercialization of space, especially lower earth orbit, is already under way, succinctly described by Deloitte in a promotional video: "Space is at an inflection point, turning the corner from exploration to economics, from research to revenue....

Table 7.2 Can Lands on Mars Have Moral Standing or Personhood?

Personhood View	Should settlers on *Red Mars* regard Mars's lands as capable of full moral standing or personhood?	Why/Why not?
Emergent Personhood and African Personhood	Yes	If Mars's lands incorporate in human community in a pro-social way, they acquire personhood
Early Greek Personhood	No	Mars's lands lack a sufficient allotment of reason
Medieval Christian Personhood	No	Mars's lands lack a Judeo-Christian soul
Contemporary Western Personhood	No	Mars's lands cannot suffer or reason
Recent space ethics*	Yes	Mars's lands are part of a larger system that has value

Key: African personhood = views prominent among black peoples indigenous to the region of Africa south of the Sahara, as captured in the works of academic philosophers; early Greek personhood = Plato, Aristotle; contemporary Western personhood = Kantian and utilitarian ethics; recent space ethics = Aldo Leopold's land ethic, Arne Næss's deep ecology, J. Baird Callicott's ecological collectives

*Note: views are extrapolated based on views toward terrestrial nonliving nature

[S]pace is the ultimate emerging market."[98] Absent global governance, commercial mining of the kind the Red group in *Red Mars* feared is apt to arise, generating disparities between rich nations that can afford space exploration, and poor nations that cannot.[99] While addressing space governance falls outside the scope of our inquiry, it raises crucial ethical questions for environmental ethics now and in the future.

7.4 Conclusion

This chapter challenged us to think beyond Earth and to consider the moral status of beings and lands elsewhere in the universe. We do not know whether extraterrestrial life exists. Nor do we know the exact number of galaxies, but scientific evidence puts the number somewhere between hundreds and two trillion.[100] Uncertainty has not stopped alien creatures and lands from working their way into our imaginations. A glance back at the history of Western and African thought reveals a rich discussion of extraterrestrial life. Science fiction writers and recently, philosophers, have taken up questions about the moral standing and rights of extraterrestrial lands, extending philosophies of lands on Earth to lands beyond Earth. Drawing on works of fiction has helped to focus these questions, and to ask: 'Can extraterrestrial life be persons?' and 'Can non-living nature be morally considerable?'

Emergent Personhood holds that full moral status requires the capacity to relate to human beings and contribute in pro-social ways to human community. If they exist, extraterrestrial beings and the lands and planets they live on can acquire personhood on this basis, which is similar to the way in which non-humans, such as terrestrial animals, silicon-based artificial agents, and terrestrial nature can become persons.

As we have underscored throughout the book, unlike all other approaches to personhood we have considered, Emergent Personhood establishes that (1) all human beings qualify for personhood; (2) qualifying is independent of others' appraisal yet furnishes a basis for duties toward others; (3) personhood is held equally by all human beings, but to varying degrees by non-humans; (4) human personhood cannot be lost or diminished; and (5) personhood is independent of performance in social roles, yet incorporates relational elements. By contrast, non-humans (1) do not all count as persons, (2) do not have personhood independent of human appraisal, (3) are not equally persons, (4) do not have personhood that is stable and cannot be lost or diminished, and (5) do not have personhood independent of social performance.

Epilogue

In the Preface, we commented on how easy cross-border philosophizing has become, thanks to virtual collaboration. We close by urging more philosophers to engage in it. Cross-border philosophizing is not only easier, but more *urgent*, because our world has grown increasingly globalized and interdependent. Globalization, or the "cross-border flows of goods, services, money, people, information, technology, and culture," now permeates virtually every aspect of life.[1] In a globalized world, people are interconnected, and their actions resemble a 'butterfly effect.' In chaos theory, a butterfly effect refers to the widespread and unpredictable results of changes to an initial set of conditions, symbolized by a butterfly flapping its wings. The effects of the butterfly's fluttering are changes, far away and days or weeks later, in the timing, formation, and path of a tornado. Like the butterfly, when ordinary people act and speak in connected spaces, their fluttering creates a multitude of effects. When we tweet, tag, post, share, friend, or put others in our story, our actions generate system-wide effects. Likewise, philosophical books, papers, and musings can be instantly accessible nearly everywhere, amplifying philosophy's reach. Yet our aim as philosophers is not spreading ideas—philosophy is not proselytizing. Nor is it achieving celebrity—philosophy is not self-promotion.

What then is the aim? One purpose of cross-border philosophy is to reckon with fundamental shifts globalization has brought to the spatial and temporal contours of human existence.[2] Globalization's hallmark features include *deterritorialization,* or the independence of social activities from participants' geographical location; *interconnectedness,* or the impactful effect of distant events and forces on local and regional endeavors; and *speed,* or the rapidity of transportation, communication, and information that blurs geographical and spatial boundaries.[3] Heidegger foreshadowed these changes, referring to the "abolition of every possibility of remoteness" and grappling with its implications.[4] Referring to transportation, Heidegger mused, "All distances in time and space are shrinking. [The individual] now reaches overnight, by plane, places which formerly took weeks and months of travel."[5] In communication, Heidegger noted, "[A person] now receives instant information, by radio, of events which [they] formerly learned about only years later, if at all."[6] Presaging virtual reality, Heidegger said: "Distant sites of the most ancient cultures are shown on film as if they stood this very moment amidst today's street traffic."[7] Yet rather than celebrating this, Heidegger warned about a "distanceless" world leading to dominance, with powerful ideas proliferating. Contrasting distancelessness with nearness, Heidegger asked, "What is nearness if it fails to come about despite the reduction of the longest distances to the shortest intervals?" and answered that "Nearness" is what "brings near" and "is at work in bringing near."[8] Cross-border philosophy must invite others in. Its aim should include bringing others near and practicing epistemic justice.

Since embarking on this book, we have learned how easy—and how hard—philosophizing cross-border can be. Consider the fact that in 2023, nearly 8 billion people called Earth home; they communicated in over 7,000 different languages and hailed from 195 different countries. As these people become increasingly 'distanceless,' drawing them near comprises a Herculean task, extending well beyond Africa and the West. However, even though the challenges of living in an interconnected world are Herculean, they are urgent. Climate change and environmental degradation, emerging and re-emerging infectious diseases, AI, germline gene editing, global inequalities, war, displacement of persons and communities, and other large-scale concerns speak to the importance of cross-border thinking. No single philosophical approach can adequately address these matters; yet, as more philosophers cross more borders to share ideas and insights, we are optimistic about deploying the wisdom of many traditions to scale back risk and navigate global challenges more wisely. The task ahead is enormous, requiring all the knowledge and tools humanity can muster.

Notes

Preface

1. Gyekye K, 1987. *An Essay on African Philosophical Thought*: The Akan Conceptual Scheme. Temple University Press, p. 50.

Introduction

1. Warren MA, 2004. *Moral Status: Obligations to Persons and Other Living Things*. Oxford University Press.
2. Molefe M, 2019. *An African Philosophy of Personhood, Morality and Politics*. Palgrave Macmillan.
3. Taylor C, 1985. The Concept of a Person. In Taylor C, *Philosophical Papers 1: Human Agency and Language*. Cambridge University Press: Kindle location 1917–2261.
4. DeGrazia D, 2005. *Human Identity and Bioethics*. Cambridge University Press.
5. Witherington DC, 2017. The Explanatory Significance of Wholes: How Exclusive Reliance on Antecedent-Consequent Models of Explanation Undermines the Study of Persons. *New Ideas in Psychology* 44: 14–20. DOI: 10.1016/j.newideapsych.2016.11.009.
6. Rosfort R, 2018. Personhood. In Stanghellini G, Broome M, Raballo A, Fernandez AV, Pusar-Poli P, Rosfort R, eds., *The Oxford Handbook of Phenomenological Psychopathology*. Oxford University Press: 335–343.
7. Martin J, Bickhard MH, eds., 2012. *The Psychology of Personhood: Philosophical, Historical, Social-Developmental, and Narrative Perspectives*. Cambridge University Press.
8. Foster C, Herring J, 2017. *Identity, Personhood and the Law*. Springer International Publishing.
9. Kurki VAJ, 2019. *A Theory of Legal Personhood*. Oxford University Press.
10. Frow J, 2020. Personhood. *Oxford Handbook of Law and Humanities*. Oxford University Press: 273–288.
11. Ramsey P, 1970. *The Patient as Person*. Yale University Press.
12. Playford RC, Playford ED, 2018. What Am I? A Philosophical Account of Personhood and Its Application to People with Brain Injury. *Neuropsychology Rehabilitation* 28: 1408–1414. DOI: 10.1080/09602011.2018.1456939.
13. Blain-Moraes S, Racine E, Mashour GA, 2018. Consciousness and Personhood in Medical Care. *Frontiers in Human Neuroscience* 12: 306. DOI: 10.3389/fnhum.2018.00306.
14. Fowler C, 2004. *The Archaeology of Personhood*. Routledge.
15. Comaroff JL, Comaroff J, 2001. On Personhood: An Anthropological Perspective from Africa. *Social Identities* 7(2): 267– 283. DOI: 0.1080/13504630120065310.
16. Shweder RA, Bourne EJ, 1982. Does the Concept of the Person Vary Cross-Culturally? In Marsella AJ, White GM, *Cultural Conceptions of Mental Health and Therapy*. D. Reidel: 97–137.

17. Young G, 2019. Personhood across Disciplines. *Ethics, Medicine and Public Health* 10: 93–101. DOI: /10.1016/j.jemep.2019.100407.
18. Oxford University Press, 2023 (March). n. *person. OED Online, 3rd ed.* Oxford University Press.
19. Behrens KG, 2017. A Critique of the Principle of 'Respect for Autonomy,' Grounded in African Thought. *Bioethics* 18: 126–134. DOI: 10.1111/dewb.12145.
20. Shutte A, 1993. *Philosophy for Africa.* University of Cape Town Press, p. 46.
21. Mbiti J, 1969. *African Religions and Philosophy, 2nd ed.* Heineman, p. 141.
22. Menkiti IA, 1984. Person and Community in African Traditional Thought. In Wright RA, ed., *African Philosophy: An Introduction, 3rd ed.* University Press of America, 171–181, p. 172.
23. Warren MA, 1997. *Moral Status: Obligations to Persons and Other Living Things.* Oxford University Press.
24. Fowler C, 2004. *The Archaeology of Personhood.* Routledge, p. 5.
25. Bird-David N, 1999. 'Animism' Revisited: Personhood, Environment, and Relational Epistemology. *Current Anthropology* 40 Supp: S67–S91, p. S72. DOI: 10.1086/20061.
26. Oxford University Press, 2023 (March). *adj.* and *n.*, individual. In Oxford University Press, *OED Online 3rd ed.* Oxford University Press.
27. Oxford University Press, 2023 (March). *adj.* and *n.*, dividual. In Oxford University Press, *OED Online, 3rd ed.* Oxford University Press.
28. Blumenthal-Barby J, 2023. The End of Personhood. *American Journal of Bioethics* 24(1): 3–12, p. 1. DOI: 10.1080/15265161.2022.2160515.
29. Blumenthal-Barby J, 2023. The End of Personhood. *American Journal of Bioethics* 24(1): 3–12, p. 5. DOI: 10.1080/15265161.2022.2160515.
30. Blumenthal-Barby J, 2023. The End of Personhood. *American Journal of Bioethics* 24(1): 3–12, p. 7. DOI: 10.1080/15265161.2022.2160515.
31. Koplin J, Carter O, Savulescu J, 2021. The Moral Status of Brain Organoids. In Clarke S, Zohny H, Savulescu J, eds., *Rethinking Moral Status.* Oxford University Press: 249–268.
32. Sinnott-Armstrong W, Conitzer V, 2021. Monkeys, Moral Machines, and Persons. In Clarke S, Zohny H, Savulescu J, eds., *Rethinking Moral Status.* Oxford University Press: 268–288.
33. Shulman C, Bostrom N, 2021. The Moral Status of Brain Organoids. In Clarke S, Zohny H, Savulescu J, eds., *Rethinking Moral Status.* Oxford University Press: 305–326.
34. Lawrence DR, Harris J, 2021. Monkeys, Moral Machines, and Persons. In Clarke S, Zohny H, Savulescu J, eds., *Rethinking Moral Status.* Oxford University Press: 289–304.
35. Powell R, Mikhalevich I, Buchanan A, 2021. How the Moral Community Evolves. In Clarke S, Zohny H, Savulescu J, eds., *Rethinking Moral Status.* Oxford University Press: 230–248.
36. Jecker NS, Atuire CA, 2023. Personhood beyond the West. *American Journal of Bioethics* 24(1): 59–62. DOI: 10.1080/15265161.2023.2278551.
37. Nagel T, 1986. *The View from Nowhere.* Oxford University Press.

Chapter 1

1. Darwall S, 2006. *The Second Person Standpoint.* Harvard University Press, p. 89.
2. Jaworska A, Tannenbaum J, 2021. The Grounds of Moral Status. In Zalta EN, ed., *Stanford Encyclopedia of Philosophy.* https://plato.stanford.edu/archives/spr2021/entries/grounds-moral-status/.

3. Bentham J, 1976 (1780). *Introduction to the Principles of Morals and Legislation.* Oxford University Press and the Liberty Fund.
4. Singer P, 2015 (1975). *Animal Liberation.* Open Road Media.
5. Regan T, 1975. The Moral Basis of Vegetarianism. *Canadian Journal of Philosophy* 5(2): 181–214, p. 210. DOI: 10.1080/00455091.1975.10716107.
6. Korsgaard CM, 1983. Two Distinctions in Goodness. *Philosophical Review* 92(2): 169–195. DOI: 10.2307/2184924.
7. Molefe M, Muade E, 2023. An Appraisal of 'African Perspectives of Moral Status: A Framework for Evaluating Global Bioethical Issues,' *Arumaruka: Journal of Conversational Thinking* 3(1): 25–50. DOI: 10.4314/ajct.v3i2.2.
8. Shutte A, 1993. *Philosophy for Africa.* University of Cape Town Press, p. 46.
9. Mbiti J, 1969. *African Religions and Philosophy.* Heineman, p. 141.
10. Flikschuh K, 2016. The Arc of Personhood, *Journal of the American Philosophical Association* 2(3): 437–455. DOI: 10.1017/apa.2016.26.
11. Ikuenobe P, 2017. The Communal Basis for Moral Dignity: An African Perspective. *Philosophical Papers* 45(3): 437–469 DOI: 05568641.2016.1245833.
12. Menkiti IA, 1984. Person and Community in African Traditional Thought. In Wright RA, ed., *African Philosophy: An Introduction, 3rd edition.* University Press of America, 171–181.
13. Metz T, 2022. *A Relational Moral Theory.* Oxford University Press, p. 106.
14. Molefe M, 2020. *African Personhood and Applied Ethics.* Published on behalf of the African Humanities Program by NISC (Pty) Ltd.
15. Atuire CA, Kong C, Dunn M, 2020. Articulating the Sources for an African Normative Framework of Healthcare. *Developing World Bioethics* 20(4), p. 6. DOI: 10.1111/dewb.12265.
16. Gyekye K, 2011. *Tradition and Modernity: Philosophical Reflections on the African Experience.* Oxford University Press, p. 67.
17. Ahiauzu N, 2006. Ubuntu and the Obligation to Obey the Law. *Cambrian Law Review* 37: 17–36, p. 35.
18. Mbiti JS, 1989. *Africa Religions and Philosophy, 2nd ed.* Heinemann, p. 106.
19. Gyekye K, 1987. *An Essay on African Philosophical Thought: The Akan Conceptual Scheme, Revised edition.* Temple University Press, p. 155.
20. Hobbes T, 2020 (1651). *The Leviathan.* Pandora's Box Classics.
21. Kant I, 2015 (1785). *Fundamental Principles of the Metaphysics of Morals.* In *The Ethics of Immanuel Kant,* Abbott TK, Hastie W, transl. e-artnow ebooks. Kindle location 133, emphasis added.
22. Korsgaard CM, 2016. Kant's Formula of Humanity. In Korsgaard CM, *Creating the Kingdom of Ends.* Cambridge University Press, 106–132, p 130.
23. Gyekye K, 2011. African Ethics. In Zalta EN, ed., *Stanford Encyclopedia of Philosophy,* https://plato.stanford.edu/archives/fall2011/entries/african-ethics.
24. Gyekye K, 2011. African Ethics. In Zalta EN, ed., *Stanford Encyclopedia of Philosophy.* https://plato.stanford.edu/archives/fall2011/entries/african-ethics.
25. Gbadegesin S, 1991. *African Philosophy: Traditional Yoruba Philosophy and Contemporary African Realities.* Peter Lang, p. 58.
26. Shutte A, 1993. *Philosophy for Africa.* University of Cape Town Press, p. 47.
27. Menkiti I, 1984. Person and Community in African Traditional Thought. In Wright RA, ed., *African Philosophy: An Introduction, 3rd ed.* University Press of America, 171–181, p. 172, emphasis added.
28. Menkiti I, 1984. Person and Community in African Traditional Thought. In Wright RA, ed., *African Philosophy: An Introduction, 3rd ed.* University Press of America, 171–181, p. 172.

29. Metz T, 2018. What Is the Essence of an Essence? *Synthesis Philosophica* 65: 209–224, pp. 214–215. DOI: 10.21464/sp33113.
30. Warren MA, 1997. *Moral Status: Obligations to Persons and Other Living Things*. Oxford University Press.
31. Korsgaard CM, 2016. The Right to Lie: Kant on Dealing with Evil. In Korsgaard CM, *Creating the Kingdom of Ends*. Cambridge University Press, 133–158, p. 142.
32. Schneewind JB, 2010. *Essays on the History of Moral Philosophy*. Oxford University Press: 248–276, pp. 249–250.
33. Kant I, 1997 (1793). Notes on the Lectures of Mr. Kant on the Metaphysics of Morals. In Heath P, Schneewind JB, eds., P and Heath P, transl., *Immanuel Kant, Lectures on Ethics*. Cambridge University Press, 249–452, p. 351.
34. Jaworska A, Tannenbaum J, 2021. The Grounds of Moral Status. In Zalta EN, ed., *Stanford Encyclopedia of Philosophy*. https://plato.stanford.edu/archives/spr2021/entries/grounds-moral-status/.
35. Bentham J, 1976 (1780). *Introduction to the Principles of Morals and Legislation*. Oxford University Press and the Liberty Fund, Kindle locations, 5973–5990.
36. Singer P, 2015 (1975). *Animal Liberation*. Open Road Media, p. 23.
37. Singer P, What's Wrong with Killing? In Singer P, *Practical Ethics*, 2nd ed. Cambridge University Press, 83–109, p. 88.
38. Gyekye K, 2011. African Ethics. In Zalta EN, ed., *Stanford Encyclopedia of Philosophy*. https://plato.stanford.edu/archives/fall2011/entries/african-ethics/.
39. Gyekye K, 2011. African Ethics. In Zalta EN, ed., *Stanford Encyclopedia of Philosophy*. https://plato.stanford.edu/archives/fall2011/entries/african-ethics/.
40. Gyekye K, 2011. African Ethics. In Zalta EN, ed., *Stanford Encyclopedia of Philosophy*. https://plato.stanford.edu/archives/fall2011/entries/african-ethics/.
41. Darwall S, 1977. Two Kinds of Respect. *Ethics* 88(1): 36–49. DOI: 10.1086/292054.
42. Dillon RS, 2016. Respect. In Zalta EN, ed., *Stanford Encyclopedia of Philosophy*. https://plato.stanford.edu/archives/win2016/entries/respect/.
43. Menkiti I, 1984. "Person and Community in African Traditional Thought." In Wright RA, ed., *African Philosophy: An Introduction*, 3rd ed. University Press of America, 171–181, p. 176.
44. Menkiti I, 1984. Person and Community in African Traditional Thought. In Wright RA, ed., *African Philosophy: An Introduction*, 3rd ed. University Press of America, 171–181, p. 172.
45. Jecker NS, 2020. African Conceptions of Age-Based Moral Standing. *Hastings Center Report* 50(2): 35–43. DOI: 10.1002/hast.1100.
46. Tooley M, 1972. Abortion and Infanticide. *Philosophy and Public Affairs* 2(1): 37–65, p. 47.
47. Jaworska A, Tannenbaum J, 2021. The Grounds of Moral Status. In Zalta EN, ed., *Stanford Encyclopedia of Philosophy*. https://plato.stanford.edu/archives/spr2021/entries/grounds-moral-status/.
48. Johnson R, Cureton A, 2022. Kant's Moral Philosophy. In Zalta EN, ed., *Stanford Encyclopedia of Philosophy*. https://plato.stanford.edu/archives/spr2022/entries/kant-moral/.
49. Noonan JT, 1970. An Almost Absolute Value in History. In Noonan JT, *The Morality of Abortion: Legal and Historical Perspectives*. Harvard University Press, 51–59.
50. Thomson JJ, 1971. A Defense of Abortion. *Philosophy and Public Affairs* 1(1): 47–66.
51. Clarke S, Savulescu J, 2022. Rethinking our Assumptions about Moral Status. In Clarke S, Zohny H, Savulescu J, eds., *Rethinking Moral Status*. Oxford University Press, 1–19, p. 3.

52. Menkiti I, 1984. "Person and Community in African Traditional Thought." In Wright RA, ed., *African Philosophy: An Introduction*, 3rd ed. University Press of America, 171–181, p. 174.
53. Flikschuh K, 2016. The Arc of Personhood: Menkiti and Kant on Becoming a Person. *Journal of the American Philosophical Association* 2(3): 437–455. DOI: 10.1017/apa.2016.26.
54. Jecker NS, 2020. African Conceptions of Age-Based Moral Standing. *Hastings Center Report* 50(2): 34–43. DOI: 10.1002/hast.1100.
55. Metz T, 2012. An African Theory of Moral Status. *Ethical Theory and Moral Practice* 15(3): 387–402, p. 394. DOI: 10.1007/s10677-011-9302-y.
56. Sodi T, Nkoana S, Mokwena J, 2021. Bereavement Rituals and their Related Psychosocial Functions in a Northern Sotho Community of South Africa. *Death Studies* 45(2): 91–100. DOI: 10.1080/07481187.2019.1616852.
57. Lewis A, Kumpfbeck A, Greer D, et al., 2021. Barriers to the Use of Neurologic Criteria to Declare Death in Africa. *American Journal of Hospice and Palliative Medicine* 39(2): 243–249, p. 246. DOIi:10.1177/10499091211006921.
58. Waweru-Siika W, Clement ME, Lukoko, et al., 2017. Brain Death Determination: The Imperative for Policy and Legal Initiatives in Sub-Saharan Africa. *Global Public Health* 12(5): 598–600. DOI: 10.1080/17441692.2015.1094108.
59. Menkiti I, 1984. "Person and Community in African Traditional Thought." In Wright RA, ed., *African Philosophy: An Introduction*, 3rd ed. University Press of America: 171–181, p. 179.
60. Mbiti JS, 1989. *Africa Religions and Philosophy*, 2nd ed. Heinemann, p. 106.
61. Gyekye, K, 1996. *African Cultural Values*. Sankofa Publishing Company, p. 47.
62. Gyekye K, 2002. Person and Community in African Thought. In Coetzee PH, ed., *The Struggle for Reason in Africa*, 2nd ed. Oxford University Press: 297–312.
63. Eze MO, 2013. What Is African Communitarianism? *South African Journal of Philosophy* 27(4): 386–399, p. 396. DOI: 10.4314/sajpem.v27i4.31526.
64. Metz T, 2021. Recent Work in African Political and Legal Philosophy. *Philosophy Compass* 16: e12765. DOI: 10.1111/phc3.12765.
65. Nkulu-N'Sengha M, 2009. *Bumuntu*. In Kefe M, Mazama A, *Encyclopedia of African Religion*, Vol 1. Sage Publications, Inc., 142–147, p. 145.
66. Jecker NS, 2022. African Ethics, Respect for Persons, and Moral Dissent. *Theoria* 88(3): 666–678. DOI: 10.1111/(ISSN)1755-2567.
67. Hallen B, 2009. *A Short History of African Philosophy*, 2nd ed. Indiana University Press.
68. Tangwa G, 2017. African Philosophy: Appraisal of a Recurrent Problematic. In Afolayan A, Falola T, eds, The *Palgrave Handbook of African Philosophy*. Palgrave Macmillan, Kindle location 914.
69. Olúwolé S, 2017. *Socrates and Orunmila*, 3rd ed. ARK Publishers.
70. Kwame S, 2017. Rethinking the History of African Philosophy. In Afolayan A, Falola T, eds, The *Palgrave Handbook of African Philosophy*. Palgrave Macmillan.
71. Chukwu AO, 2017. A Bibliographic Report on African Philosophy. In Afolayan A, Falola T, eds, *The Palgrave Handbook of African Philosophy*. Palgrave Macmillan.
72. Horton R, 1974. Traditional Thought and the Emerging African Philosophy Department. A Comment on the Current Debate. In Wilson BR, ed., *Rationality*. Oxford University Press, 153–155.
73. Gyekye K, 1987. *An Essay on African Philosophical Thought: The Akan Conceptual Scheme, revised ed.* Cambridge University Press, pp. 10–11.
74. Santos B, 2015. *Epistemologies of the South: Justice against Epistemicide*. Routledge.

75. Masolo DA, 2017. Africanizing Philosophy: Wiredu, Hountondji, and Mudimbe. In Afolayan A, Falola T, eds, *The Palgrave Handbook of African Philosophy*. Palgrave Macmillan, Kindle location 1807.
76. Masolo DA, 2017. Africanizing Philosophy: Wiredu, Hountondji, and Mudimbe. In Afolayan A, Falola T, eds, *The Palgrave Handbook of African Philosophy*. Palgrave Macmillan, Kindle location 1807.
77. Ypi L, 2013. What's Wrong with Colonialism? *Philosophy and Public Affairs* 41(2): 158–191, p. 161. DOI: 10.1111/papa.12014.
78. Praegh L, 2014. *A Report on Ubuntu*. KawZulu-Natal Press.
79. Oxford University Press, 2023 (March). *OED Online*, 3rd ed. Oxford University Press.
80. Nkulu-N'Sengha M, 2009. Bumuntu. In Kefe M, Mazama A, *Encyclopedia of African Religion*, Vol 1. Sage Publications, Inc., 142–147.
81. Nkulu-N'Sengha M, 2009. Bumuntu. In Kefe M, Mazama A, *Encyclopedia of African Religion*, Vol 1. Sage Publications, Inc., 142–147, p. 143.
82. Nkulu-N'Sengha M, 2009. Bumuntu. In Kefe M, Mazama A, *Encyclopedia of African Religion*, Vol 1. Sage Publications, Inc., 142–147, p. 143.
83. Hare HH et al., 1846. I-Testamente Entsha yenkosi yetu Ka-Yesu Kristu, Gowka-maxoosa. E-Newton Dale. Cited in Gade CBN, 2011. The Historical Development of the Written Discourses on Ubuntu. *South African Journal of Philosophy* 30(3): 303–329. DOI: 10.4314/sajpem.v30i3.69578.
84. Gade CBN, 2011. The Historical Development of the Written Discourses on Ubuntu. *South African Journal of Philosophy* 30(3): 303–329. DOI: 10.4314/sajpem.v30i3.69578.
85. Molefe M, 2014. A Report on Ubuntu, Leonhard Praeg: Book Review, *Acta Academica* 46(2): 157–164, p. 159.
86. Shutte A, 1995. Traditional African Thought. In Shutte A, *Philosophy for Africa*. University of Cape Town Press, 46–58, p. 46.
87. Shutte A, 1995. Traditional African Thought. In Shutte A, *Philosophy for Africa*. University of Cape Town Press, 46–58.
88. Menkiti I, 1984. Person and Community in African Traditional Thought. In Wright RA, ed., *African Philosophy: An Introduction*. University Press of America, 171–181, p. 171.
89. Menkiti I, 1984. Person and Community in African Traditional Thought. In Wright RA, ed., *African Philosophy: An Introduction*. University Press of America, 171–181, p. 171.
90. Mbiti JS, 1989. *Africa Religions and Philosophy*, 2nd ed. Heinemann, p. 106.
91. Metz T, 2021. Recent Work in African Philosophy. *Mind* 130(518): 639–660, p. 657. DOI: https://doi.org/10.1093/mind/fzaa072. https://academic.oup.com/mind/article-abstract/130/518/639/5960229.
92. Gyekye K, 2011. African Ethics. In Zalta EN, ed., *Stanford Encyclopedia of Philosophy*. https://plato.stanford.edu/archives/fall2011/entries/african-ethics/.
93. Harding S, 1987. The Curious Coincidence of Feminine and African Moralities. In Eze EC, ed., *African Philosophy: An Anthology*. Blackwell Publishers, Inc., 360–372.
94. Nkulu-N'Sengha M, 2009. Bumuntu. In Kefe M, Mazama A, eds., *Encyclopedia of African Religion*, Vol 1. Sage Publications, Inc.,142–147, p. 143.
95. Gyekye K, 2011. African Ethics. In Zalta EN, ed., *Stanford Encyclopedia of Philosophy*. https://plato.stanford.edu/archives/fall2011/entries/african-ethics.
96. Nkulu-N'Sengha M, 2009. Bumuntu. In Kefe M, Mazama A, eds., *Encyclopedia of African Religion*, Vol. 1. Sage Publications, Inc., 142–147, p. 147.
97. Metz T, 2021. Recent Work in African Political and Legal Philosophy. *Philosophy Compass* 16: e12765. DOI: 10.1111/phc3.12765.

98. Menkiti IA, 1984. Person and Community in African Traditional Thought. In Wright RA, ed., *African Philosophy: An Introduction*, 3rd ed. University Press of America, 171–181, p. 180.
99. Gyekye K, 2011. African Ethics. In Zalta EN, ed., *Stanford Encyclopedia of Philosophy*. https://plato.stanford.edu/archives/fall2011/entries/african-ethics.
100. Siedentop L, 2014. *Inventing the Individual: The Origins of Western Individualism.* Harvard University Press.
101. Siedentop L, 2014. *Inventing the Individual: The Origins of Western Individualism.* Harvard University Press, p. 10.
102. Fustel DC, 2000 (1874). *The Ancient City: A Study on the Religion, Law, and Institutions of Ancient Greece and Rome*, Small W, transl. Boston, Lee and Shepard, electronic text by the University of Michigan, Ann Arbor, p. 16.
103. Siedentop L, 2014. *Inventing the Individual: The Origins of Western Individualism.* Harvard University Press, p. 12.
104. Fustel DC, 2000 (1874). *The Ancient City: A Study on the Religion, Law, and Institutions of Ancient Greece and Rome*, Small W, transl. Boston, Lee and Shepard, electronic text by the University of Michigan, Ann Arbor, p. 80.
105. Nagle DB, 2006. *The Household as the Foundation of Aristotle's Polis.* Cambridge University Press, p. 222.
106. Siedentop L, 2014. *Inventing the Individual: The Origins of Western Individualism.* Harvard University Press, p. 21.
107. Nagle DB, 2006. *The Household as the Foundation of Aristotle's Polis.* Cambridge University Press, p. 222.
108. Crisp R, 2013. Homeric Ethics. In Crisp R, ed., *The Oxford Handbook of the History of Ethics*. Oxford University Press, 1–20, p. 15.
109. Oxford University Press, 2023 (March). n. *person*. OED Online, 3rd ed. Oxford University Press.
110. Oxford University Press, 2023 (March). n. *person*. OED Online, 3rd ed. Oxford University Press.
111. Oxford University Press, 2023 (March). n. *person*. OED Online, 3rd ed. Oxford University Press.
112. Frede D, 2017. Plato's Ethics: An Overview. In Zalta EN, ed., *Stanford Encyclopedia of Philosophy*. https://plato.stanford.edu/archives/win2017/entries/plato-ethics/.
113. Aristotle, 1999 (350 BCE). *Politics*, Jowett B, transl. Batoche Books, Kitchener, Book I, p. 6.
114. Aristotle, 1999 (350 BCE). *Politics*, Jowett B, transl. Batoche Books, Kitchener, Book XIII, p. 21.
115. Aristotle, 1999 (~340 BCE). *Nicomachean Ethics*, Ross WD, transl. Batoche Books, Kitchener. Book I, Sect. 13, p. 20.
116. Siedentop L, 2014. *Inventing the Individual: The Origins of Western Individualism.* Harvard University Press, p. 55.
117. Siedentop L, 2014. *Inventing the Individual: The Origins of Western Individualism.* Harvard University Press, p. 58.
118. *The Holy Bible*, Douay-Rheims Version, Matthew 28: 19–20, p. 1301. http://triggs.djvu.org/djvu-editions.com/BIBLES/DRV/Download.pdf.
119. Pope Paul III, 1993 (1537). *Sublimus deus*. Quoted in Seed P, 1993. 'Are These Not Also Men?': The Indians' Humanity and Capacity for Spanish Civilization. *Journal of Latin American Studies* 25(3): 629–652, p. 645. DOI: 10.1017/S0022216X00006696.
120. Seed P, 1993. 'Are These Not Also Men?': The Indians' Humanity and Capacity for Spanish Civilization. *Journal of Latin American Studies* 25(3): 629–652, p. 629. DOI: 10.1017/S0022216X00006696.

121. Hanke L, 1949. *The Spanish Struggle for Justice in the Conquest of America.* University of Pennsylvania Press. p. 173.
122. Vlastos G, 1984. Justice and Equality. In Waldron J, ed., *Theories of Rights.* Oxford University Press, 41–76.
123. Vlastos G, 1984. Justice and Equality. In Waldron J, ed., *Theories of Rights.* Oxford University Press, 41–76, p. 55.
124. Kraut R, 2022. Aristotle's Ethics. In Zalta EN, Nodelman U, eds., *Stanford Encyclopedia of Philosophy* (n.p.). https://plato.stanford.edu/archives/fall2022/entries/aristotle-ethics/.

Chapter 2

1. Irenaeus 1857 (~180 CE). *Adversus Haereses (Against Heresies)*, Harvey WW, ed., Vol. 2, Book 4, Chapter 20. Section 7. Public Domain, Google-digitized. https://babel.hathitrust.org/cgi/pt?id=njp.32101074938968&view=1up&seq=231.
2. Lovejoy AO, 2001 (1936). *The Great Chain of Being.* Harvard University Press.
3. Henrich J, 2020. *The Weirdest People in the World.* Farrar, Straus & Giroux, pp. 166–167. See also Appendix A.
4. Brundage JA, 1987. *Law, Sex, and Christian Society in Medieval Europe.* University of Chicago Press.
5. Bittles AH, 2009. The Background and Outcomes of the First-Cousin Marriage Controversy in Great Britain. *International Journal of Epidemiology* 38: 1453–1458. DOI: 10.1093/ije/dyp313.
6. *The Holy Bible.* Douay-Rheims Version, Leviticus, Chapter 18:6, p. 141. http://triggs.djvu.org/djvu-editions.com/BIBLES/DRV/Download.pdf.
7. Bouchard CB, 2010. *Those of My Blood.* University of Pennsylvania Press.
8. Bouchard CB, 2010. *Those of My Blood.* University of Pennsylvania Press, p. 41.
9. Henrich J, 2020. *The Weirdest People in the World.* Farrar, Straus & Giroux.
10. Bouchard CB, 2010. *Those of My Blood.* University of Pennsylvania Press.
11. Noonan JT, 1970. An Almost Absolute Value in History. In Noonan JT, ed., *The Morality of Abortion.* Harvard University Press, 51–59, p. 55.
12. Ryder RD, 2004. Speciesism Revisited. *Think* 2(6): 83–92. DOI: 10.1017/S1477175600002840.
13. Singer P, 2015 (1975). *Animal Liberation.* Open Road Media.
14. *The Epistle to Diognetus*, 1908 (~130 CE). In Radford LB, ed., *Early Church Classics: The Epistle to Diognetus.* Society for Promoting Christian Knowledge, pp. 61–63. Digitized by the Internet Archive, 2011. https://ia600502.us.archive.org/9/items/epistletodiognet00just/epistletodiognet00just.pdf.
15. Kittay EF, 2019. *Love's Labor, 2nd ed.* Routledge.
16. Kittay EF, 2005. At the Margins of Moral Personhood. *Ethics* 115(1): 100–131, pp. 127–129. DOI: 10.1086/454366.
17. Kittay EF, 2005. At the Margins of Moral Personhood. *Ethics* 115(1): 100–131, pp. 127–128, emphasis added. DOI: 10.1086/454366.
18. Kittay EF, 2005. At the Margins of Moral Personhood. *Ethics* 115(1): 100–131, p. 120. DOI: 10.1086/454366.
19. Steinbock B, 1978. Speciesism and the Idea of Equality. *Philosophy* 53(204): 247–256.
20. Jecker NS, 1990. Anencephalic Infants and Special Relationships. *Theoretical Medicine* 11: 333–342. DOI: 10.1017/S0031819100016582.
21. Steinbock B, 2011. *Life before Birth, 2nd ed.* Oxford University Press.
22. Metz T, 2022. *A Relational Moral Theory.* Oxford University Press.

23. Daniels N, 1985. Family Responsibility Initiatives and Justice between Age Groups. *Law, Medicine and Health Care* 13(4): 153–159. DOI: 10.1111/j.1748-720X.1985.tb00911.x.
24. Slote M, 1985. Obedience and Illusions. In Sommers CH, ed., *Vice and Virtues in Everyday Life*. Harcourt Brace Jovanovich, at 480–484.
25. Schoeman F, 1980. Rights of Children, Rights of Parents, and the Moral Basis of the Family. *Ethics* 91(1): 6–19, p. 8. DOI: 10.1086/292199.
26. Jecker NS, 1989. Are Filial Duties Unfounded? *American Philosophical Quarterly* 26(1): 73–80.
27. Christman J, 2020. Autonomy in Moral and Political Philosophy. In Zalta EN, ed., *Stanford Encyclopedia of Philosophy*. https://plato.stanford.edu/archives/fall2020/entries/autonomy-moral/.
28. Anderson E, Willett C, Meyers D, 2021. Feminist Perspectives on the Self. In Zalta EN, ed., *Stanford Encyclopedia of Philosophy*. https://plato.stanford.edu/archives/fall2021/entries/feminism-self/.
29. Barclay L, 2000. Autonomy and the Social Self. In Mackenzie C, Stoljar N, eds., *Relational Autonomy: Feminist Perspectives on Autonomy, Agency, and the Social Self*. Oxford University Press, 52–71.
30. Butler J, 1999. *Gender Trouble: Feminism and the Subversion of Identity*. Routledge.
31. Butler J, 2020. Nonviolence, Grievability, and the Critique of Individualism. In Butler J, *The Force of Nonviolence*. Verso.
32. Taylor C, 1985. Atomism. In Taylor C, *Philosophy and the Human Sciences: Philosophical Papers 2*. Cambridge University Press, 187–210.
33. Bell D, 2000. Communitarianism. In Zalta EN, ed., *Stanford Encyclopedia of Philosophy*. https://plato.stanford.edu/archives/sum2020/entries/communitarianism/.
34. Molefe M, 2020. *African Personhood and Applied Ethics*. Published on behalf of the African Humanities Program by NISC (Pty) Ltd.: Kindle Location 1619–1963.
35. Behrens K, 2014. An African Relational Environmentalism and Moral Considerability. *Environmental Ethics* 36(1): 63–82. DOI: 10.5840/enviroethics20143615.
36. Tangwa GB, 2010. African Bioethics and Sustainable Development. In Tangwa GB, *Elements of African Bioethics in a Western Frame*. Langaa Rpcig, 39–48.
37. Wareham C, 2020. Artificial Intelligence and African Conceptions of Personhood. *Ethics and Information Technology* 23: 127–136. DOI: 10.1007/s10676-020-09541-3.
38. Jecker NS, Atuire CA, Ajei MO, 2022. The Moral Standing of Social Robots: Untapped Insights from Africa. *Philosophy and Technology* 35: 34. DOI: 10.1007/s13347-022-00531-5.
39. Menkiti IA, 1984. Person and Community in African Traditional Thought. In Wright RA, ed., *African Philosophy: An Introduction*, 3rd ed. University Press of America, 171–181, p. 176.
40. Gyekye CK, 2002. Person and Community in African Thought. In Coetzee PH, ed., *Philosophy from Africa*, 2nd ed. Oxford University Press, 297–312, p. 310.
41. Gouws A, van Zyl M, 2015. Toward a Feminist Ethics of *Ubuntu*. In Engster D, Hamington M, eds., *Care Ethics and Political Theory*. Oxford University Press, 165–186, p. 174.
42. Menkiti IA, 1979. Person and Community in African Traditional Thought. In Wright RA, ed., *African Philosophy: An Introduction*, 2nd ed. University Press of America, 157–168, p. 159.

43. Menkiti IA, 1979. Person and Community in African Traditional Thought. In Wright RA, ed., *African Philosophy: An Introduction*, 2nd ed. University Press of America, 157-168, p. 158.
44. Gyekye CK, 2002. Person and Community in African Thought. In Coetzee PH, ed., *Philosophy from Africa*, 2nd ed. Oxford University Press, 297-312, p. 303.
45. Gyekye K, 1997. *Tradition and Modernity*. Oxford University Press, p. 50.
46. Atuire CA, 2019. Humans, Persons, Personhood and Morality in African Communitarianism: Gyekye Revisited. *Nigerian Journal of Philosophy* 27: 19-38, p. 35.
47. Aristotle, 2007 (n.d.). *Logic (Organon)*, Edghill EM transl. In *Aristotle: The Complete Works*. University of Adelaide, eBooks@Adelaide: 6-575, chapter 10.
48. Aquinas T, 1947 (1265-1274) *Summa Theologica*, transl. Fathers of the English Dominican Province, digital edition. http://www.domcentral.org/summa/.
49. Kroeger F, 1992. *Buli-English Dictionary*. Lit-Verlag.
50. Atuire CA, 2022. African Perspectives of Moral Status. *Medical Humanities* 48: 238-245, p. 239. DOI: 10.1136/medhum-2021-012229.
51. O'Connor T, 2021. Emergent Properties. In Zalta EN, ed., *Stanford Encyclopedia of Philosophy*. https://plato.stanford.edu/archives/win2021/entries/properties-emergent/.
52. Goren G, 2019. Social Behaviour as an Emergent Property of Embodied Curiosity: A Robotics Perspective. *Philosophical Transactions of the Royal Society B: Biological Sciences* 374: 1771. DOI:10.1098/rstb.2018.0029.
53. Ellis N, Larsen-Freeman D, 2006. Language Emergence: Implications for Applied Linguistics. Introduction to the Special Issue. *Applied Linguistics* 27: 558-559. DOI: 10.1093/applin/aml028.
54. O'Grady W, 2008. The Emergentist Program. *Lingua* 118: 447-464. DOI: 10.1016/j.lingua.2006.12.001.
55. MacWhinney B, Kempe V, Brooks PJ, Li P, 2022. Emergentist Approaches to Language. *Frontiers of Psychology* 12: 833160-833160. DOI: 10.3389/fpsyg.2021.833160. 12:833160. DOI: 10.3389/fpsyg.2021.833160.
56. Batterman R, 2020. Intertheory Relations in Physics. In Zalta EN, ed., *Stanford Encyclopedia of Philosophy*. https://plato.stanford.edu/archives/fall2020/entries/physics-interrelate/.
57. Weisberg M, Needham P, Hendry R, 2019. Philosophy of Chemistry. In Zalta EN, ed., *Stanford Encyclopedia of Philosophy*. https://plato.stanford.edu/archives/spr2019/entries/chemistry/.
58. Kauffman S, 2010. *Reinventing the Sacred: A New View of Science, Reason, and Religion*. Basic Books.
59. Pearce MJ, 2017. *Art in the Age of Emergence*, 2nd ed. Cambridge Scholars Publishing.
60. Aristotle, 2007 (n.d.). *Metaphysics*, Ross WD transl. In *Aristotle: The Complete Works*. University of Adelaide, eBooks@Adelaide: 2281-2525, p. 2378.
61. Aristotle, 2007 (n.d.). *Topics*, Pickard-Cambridge WA, transl. In *Aristotle: The Complete Works*. University of Adelaide, eBooks@Adelaide: 320-505, p. 457.
62. Stringer R, 2018. Realist Ethical Naturalism for Ethical Non-Naturalists. *Philosophical Studies* 175: 339-362, p. 347. DOI: 10.1007/s11098-017-0870-0.
63. Bickhard MH, 2017. The Emergence of Persons. In Durt C, Fuchs T, Tewes C, eds., *Embodiment, Enaction, and Culture: Investigating the Constitution of the Shared World*. MIT Press, 201-213.
64. Bickhard M, 2009. The Interactivist Model. *Synthese* 166: 547-591. DOI: 10.1007/s11229-008-9375-x.

65. Bickhard MH, 2012. A Process Ontology for Persons. *New Ideas in Psychology* 20: 107–109. DOI: 10.1016/j.newideapsych.2009.11.004.
66. Stringer R, 2021. Ethical Emergence and Moral Causation. *Journal of Moral Philosophy* 4: 331–362. DOI: 10.1163/17455243-20213272.
67. Bedau MA, Humphreys P, 2008. Introduction to Philosophical Perspectives on Emergence. In Bedau MA, Humphreys P, eds., Emergence: *Contemporary Readings in Philosophy and Science*. MIT Press, 9–18, p. 9.
68. Jecker NS, Atuire CA, Ajei MO, 2022. The Moral Standing of Social Robots: Untapped Insights from Africa. *Philosophy and Technology* 35: 34. DOI: 10.1007/s13347-022-00531-5.
69. Nagel T, 1974. What Is It Like to Be a Bat? *Philosophical Review* 83(4): 435–450, p. 439. DOI: 10.2307/2183914.
70. Sorabji R, 2018. The One-Dimensionality of Ethical Theories. In Sorabji R, *Animal Minds and Human Morals*. Cornell University Press, 208–219, p. 214.
71. Midgley M, 1983. *Animals and Why They Matter*. University of Georgia Press.
72. Noddings N, 1991. Comment on Donovan's 'Animal Rights and Feminist Theory.' *Signs* 16(2): 418–422, p. 418. DOI: 10.1086/494674.
73. Midgley M, 1983. *Animals and Why They Matter*. University of Georgia Press, p. 110.
74. Nagel T, 1970. Death. *Nous* 4(1): 73–80, p. 77. DOI: 10.2307/2214297.
75. Williams B, 2008. The Human Prejudice. In Moore AW, Moore AWW, eds., *Philosophy as a Humanistic Discipline*. Princeton University Press, 124–138, p. 127.
76. Singer P, 2015 (1975). *Animal Liberation*. Open Road Media, p.84.
77. Singer P, 2015 (1975). *Animal Liberation*. Open Road Media, p.,84.
78. Singer P, 2015 (1975). *Animal Liberation*. Open Road Media, p. 14.
79. Midgley M, 1983. *Animals and Why They Matter*. University of Georgia Press, p. 98.
80. Singer P, 2015 (1975). *Animal Liberation*. Open Road Media, p. 24.
81. Singer P, 2015 (1975). *Animal Liberation*. Open Road Media, p.72, emphasis added.
82. Singer P, 2015 (1975). *Animal Liberation*. Open Road Media, p. 24.
83. Midgley M, 1983. *Animals and Why They Matter*. University of Georgia Press, p. 98.
84. Foot P, 2002 Morality, Action and Outcome. In Foot P, *Moral Dilemmas*. Oxford University Press: Kindle locations 1153–1373, at, Kindle location 1357.
85. Menkiti IA, 1979. Person and Community in African Traditional Thought. In Wright RA, ed., *African Philosophy: An Introduction*, 2nd ed. University Press of America: 157–168, p. 157.
86. Metz T, 2022. *A Relational Moral Theory*. Oxford University Press, p. 163.
87. Metz T, 2022. *A Relational Moral Theory*. Oxford University Press, pp. 163, 164.
88. Metz T, 2022. *A Relational Moral Theory*. Oxford University Press, p. 165.
89. Gyekye K, 2011. African Ethics. In Zalta EN, ed., *Stanford Encyclopedia of Philosophy*. https://plato.stanford.edu/archives/fall2011/entries/african-ethics/.
90. Calder T, 2020. The Concept of Evil. In Zalta EN, ed., *Stanford Encyclopedia of Philosophy*. https://plato.stanford.edu/archives/sum2020/entries/concept-evil/.
91. Jaworska A, Tannenbaum J, 2021. The Grounds of Moral Status. In Zalta EN, ed., *Stanford Encyclopedia of Philosophy*. https://plato.stanford.edu/archives/spr2021/entries/grounds-moral-status/.
92. Jaworska A, Tannenbaum J, 2021. The Grounds of Moral Status. In Zalta EN, ed., *Stanford Encyclopedia of Philosophy*. https://plato.stanford.edu/archives/spr2021/entries/grounds-moral-status/.
93. Steinbock B, 1978. Speciesism and the Idea of Equality. *Philosophy* 53: 247–256, p. 251. DOI: 10.1017/S0031819100016582.
94. Steinbock B, 1992. *Life before Birth*. Oxford University Press.

95. Kittay EF, 2005. At the Margins of Moral Personhood. *Ethics* 115(1): 100-131. DOI: 10.1086/454366.
96. Williams B, 2008. The Human Prejudice. In Moore AW, Moore AWW, eds., *Philosophy as a Humanistic Discipline*. Princeton University Press, 124-138.
97. Midgley M, 1983. *Animals and Why They Matter*. University of Georgia Press
98. Nozick R, 1997. Do Animals Have Rights? In Nozick R, *Socratic Puzzles*. Harvard University Press, 305-310.
99. Nozick R, 1974. *Anarchy State and Utopia*. Basic Boks, pp. 39ff.
100. Anderson E, 2004. Animal Rights and the Values of Nonhuman Life. In Sunstein C, Nussbaum M, eds., *Animal Rights: Current Debates and New Directions*. Oxford University Press, 277-298.
101. Fischer B, Palmer C, Kasperbauer TJ, 2023. Hybrid Theories, Psychological Plausibility and the Human/Animal Divide. *Philosophical Studies* 180: 1105-1123. DOI: 10.1007/s11098-021-01743-9.
102. Sebo J, 2023. Kantianism for Humans, Utilitarianism for Nonhumans? Yes and No. *Philosophical Studies* 180: 1211-1230. DOI: 10.1007/s11098-022-01835-0.
103. Lerner A, 2023. The Procreation Asymmetry. *Philosophical Studies* 180: 1169-1195. DOI: 10.1007/s11098-023-01954-2.
104. Abate C, 2023. People and Their Animal Companions: Navigating Moral Constraints in a Harmful Yet Meaningful World. *Philosophical Studies* 180: 1231-1254. DOI: 10.1007/s11098-022-01852-z.
105. Woollard F, 2023. 'Utilitarianism for Animals: Deontology for People' and the Doing/Allowing Distinction. *Philosophical Studies* 180: 1149-1168. DOI: / 10.1007/s11098-021-01745-7.
106. Menkiti IA, 1979. Person and Community in African Traditional Thought. In Wright RA, ed., *African Philosophy: An Introduction, 2nd ed.* University Press of America, 157-168, p. 158.
107. Tempels P, 1953. *Bantu Philosophy*. HBC Publishing, p. 60.
108. Oxford University Press 2023 (March). n. relationship. In *OED Online, 3rd ed.* Oxford University Press.
109. Gyekye K, 2011. African Ethics. In Zalta EN, ed., *Stanford Encyclopedia of Philosophy*. https://plato.stanford.edu/archives/fall2011/entries/african-ethics/.
110. Menkiti IA, 1984. Person and Community in African Traditional Thought. In Wright RA, ed., *African Philosophy: An Introduction, 3rd ed.*, University Press of America, 171-181.
111. Metz T, 2022. *A Relational Moral Theory*. Oxford University Press.
112. Jecker NS, 2020. African Conceptions of Age-Based Moral Standing. *Hastings Center Report* 50(2): 35-43. DOI: 10.1002/hast.1100.
113. Flikschuh K, 2016. The Arc of Personhood. *Journal of the American Philosophical Association* 2(3): 437-455. DOI: 10.1017/apa.2016.26.
114. Kilner J, Who Should Be Saved? An African Answer. *Hastings Center Report* 14(3): 18-23.
115. Wingo A, 2017. Akan Philosophy of the Person. In Zalta EN, ed., *Stanford Encyclopedia of Philosophy*. https://plato.stanford.edu/archives/sum2017/entries/akan-person/.
116. Metz T, 2012. An African Theory of Moral Status. *Ethical Theory and Moral Practice* 15(3): 387-402, p. 392. DOI: 10.1007/s10677-011-9302-y.
117. Molefe M, 2020. Personhood and Abortion in African Philosophy. In Molefe M, *An African Ethics of Personhood and Bioethics*. Palgrave Macmillan: 108-155.
118. Metz T, 2022. *A Relational Moral Theory*. Oxford University Press.
119. Steinbock B, 2011. *Life before Birth, 2nd ed.* Oxford University Press, pp. 30-31.

Chapter 3

1. Jecker NS, 2020. *Ending Midlife Bias*. Oxford University Press.
2. Jecker NS, 2021. The Time of One's Life: Views of Aging and Age Group Justice. *History and Philosophy of the Life Sciences* 43(1): 24, p. 23. DOI: 10.1007/s40656-021-00377-8.
3. Onarheim KH, Sisay MM, Gizaw M, Moland KM, Miljeteig I, 2017. What if the Baby Doesn't Survive? *Social Science & Medicine* 195: 123–130, p. 128. DOI: 10.1016/j.socscimed.2017.11.003.
4. Menkiti IA, 1984. Person and Community in African Traditional Thought. In Wright RA, ed., *African Philosophy: An Introduction*, 3rd ed. University Press of America, 171–184, p. 174.
5. Jewkes R, Wood K, 1998. Competing Discourses of Vital Registration and Personhood. *Social Science & Medicine* 467: 1054–1056. DOI: 10.1016/s0277-9536(97)10036-3.
6. Smorholm S, 2016. Suffering Peacefully. *Ethos* 44(3): 333–351. DOI: 10.1111/etho.12126.
7. Kilner J, 1984. Who Should Be Saved? *Hastings Center Report* 14(3): 18–22, p. 19.
8. Kilner J, 1984. Who Should Be Saved? *Hastings Center Report* 14(3): 18–22, p. 19.
9. Metz T, 2022. *A Relational Moral Theory*. Oxford University Press, p. 183.
10. Metz T, 2022. *A Relational Moral Theory*. Oxford University Press, p. 184.
11. Menkiti IA, 1984. Person and Community in African Traditional Thought. In Wright RA, ed., *African Philosophy: An Introduction*, 3rd ed. University Press of America, 171–184, p. 172.
12. Menkiti IA, 1984. Person and Community in African Traditional Thought. In Wright RA, ed., *African Philosophy: An Introduction*, 3rd ed. University Press of America, 171–184, p. 173.
13. Flikschuh K, 2016. The Arc of Personhood: Menkiti and Kant on Becoming and Being a Person. *Journal of the American Philosophical Association* 2(3): 437–455. DOI: 10.1017/apa.2016.26.
14. Menkiti IA, 1984. Person and Community in African Traditional Thought. In Wright RA, ed., *African Philosophy: An Introduction*, 3rd ed. University Press of America, 171–184, p. 176.
15. Menkiti IA, 1979. Person and Community in African Traditional Thought. In Wright RA, ed., *African Philosophy: An Introduction*, 2nd ed. University Press of America, 157–168, p. 159.
16. Menkiti IA, 1979. Person and Community in African Traditional Thought. In Wright RA, ed., *African Philosophy: An Introduction*, 2nd ed. University Press of America, 157–168, p. 159.
17. Ikuenobe P, 2006. *Philosophical Perspectives on Communalism and Morality in African Traditions*. Rowman and Littlefield, p. 57.
18. Ikuenobe P, 2006. *Philosophical Perspectives on Communalism and Morality in African Traditions*. Rowman and Littlefield, p. 70.
19. Dzobo NK, 2010. African Symbols and Proverbs as Source of Knowledge and Truth. In Wiredu K, Gyekye K, eds., *Person and Community, Ghanian Philosophical Studies I*. Council for Research in Values and Philosophy (Washington, DC): 83–97, p. 96. https://www.crvp.org/publications/Series-II/Series02-1.html
20. Achebe C, 1962. *Things Fall Apart*. Heinemann, p. 6.
21. Achebe C, 1962. *Things Fall Apart*. Heinemann, pp. 3–4.
22. Ikuenobe P, 1996. The Idea of Personhood in Achebe's *Things Fall Apart*. *Philosophia Africana* 9(2): 117–131, p. 122. DOI: 10.5840/philafricana2006924.
23. Gyekye K, 2002. Person and Community in African Thought. In Coetzee PH, ed., *Philosophy from Africa*. Oxford University Press, 297–312, p. 305.

24. Tangwa GB, 2000. The Traditional African Perception of a Person: Some Implications for Bioethics. *Hastings Center Report* 30(5): 39–43, p. 39. DOI: 10.2307/3527887.
25. Tangwa GB, 2000. The Traditional African Perception of a Person: Some Implications for Bioethics. *Hastings Center Report* 30(5): 39–43, p. 40. DOI: 10.2307/3527887.
26. Amundsen DW, 1969. Medicine and the Birth of Defective Children: Approaches of the Ancient World. In Amundsen DW, *Medicine, Society, and Faith in the Ancient and Medieval Worlds*. Johns Hopkins University Press, 50–69, p. 51.
27. Amundsen DW, 1969. Medicine and the Birth of Defective Children: Approaches of the Ancient World. In Amundsen DW, *Medicine, Society, and Faith in the Ancient and Medieval Worlds*. Johns Hopkins University Press, 50–69, p. 51.
28. Bloom A, 1968. The Republic of Plato. In Bloom A, transl. and ed., *The Republic of Plato, 2nd ed., with Notes and an Interpretive Essay by Allan Bloom*. Basic Books, 307–436, p. 384.
29. Amundsen DW, 1969. Medicine and the Birth of Defective Children: Approaches of the Ancient World. In Amundsen DW, *Medicine, Society, and Faith in the Ancient and Medieval Worlds*. Johns Hopkins University Press, 50–69, p. 52, emphasis added.
30. Aristotle 2000 (~340 BCE). *Nicomachean Ethics*. In Crisp R, ed. and transl., *Nicomachean Ethics*. Cambridge University Press, pp. 17–22, paragraph 101a. http://catdir.loc.gov/catdir/samples/cam032/99036947.pdf.
31. Aristotle, 1999 (~340 BCE). *Nicomachean Ethics*, Ross WD, transl. Batoche Books, Kitchener, Book III, Chapter 12, p. 53.
32. Aristotle, 1999 (~340 BCE). *Nicomachean Ethics*, Ross WD, transl. Batoche Books, Kitchener, Book III, Chapter 2, p. 36.
33. Amundsen D, 1995. *Medicine, Society, and Faith in the Ancient and Medieval World*. Johns Hopkins University Press, p. 64.
34. Amundsen DW, 1969. Medicine and the Birth of Defective Children: Approaches of the Ancient World. In Amundsen DW, *Medicine, Society, and Faith in the Ancient and Medieval Worlds*. Johns Hopkins University Press, 50–69, p. 52.
35. Rist JM, 1982. *Human Value: A Study in Ancient Philosophical Ethics*. E.J. Brill, p. 13.
36. Aristotle. *Rhetoric*, Roberts WR, transl. Dover Books, p. 101.
37. Rist JM, 1982. *Human Value: A Study in Ancient Philosophical Ethics*. E.J. Brill, p. 31.
38. Rist JM, 1982. *Human Value: A Study in Ancient Philosophical Ethics*. E.J. Brill, p. 30.
39. Rist JM, 1974. Aristotle: The Value of Man and the Origin of Morality. *Canadian Journal of Philosophy* 4(1): 1–21, p. 12. DOI: 10.1080/00455091.1974.10716918.
40. Rist JM, 1974. Aristotle: The Value of Man and the Origin of Morality. *Canadian Journal of Philosophy* 4(1): 1–21, p. 11. DOI: 10.1080/00455091.1974.10716918.
41. Rist JM, 1982. *Human Value: A Study in Ancient Philosophical Ethics*. E.J. Brill, p. 31.
42. Amundsen DW, 1969. Medicine and the Birth of Defective Children: Approaches of the Ancient World. In Amundsen DW, *Medicine, Society, and Faith in the Ancient and Medieval Worlds*. Johns Hopkins University Press, 50–69, p. 52.
43. Locke J, 2004 (1690). *An Essay Concerning Human Understanding*, Vol. 1, Kindle Location 5059–5060. Project Gutenberg, EBook #10615.
44. Locke J, 2004 (1690). *An Essay Concerning Human Understanding*, 2nd ed., Vol. 1, Kindle Location 5166–5168. Project Gutenberg, EBook #10615.
45. Singer P, 2015 (1975). *Animal Liberation*. Open Road Media, pp. 28–29.
46. Singer P, 2015 (1975). *Animal Liberation*. Open Road Media, p. 28.
47. Singer P, 2015 (1975). *Animal Liberation*. Open Road Media, p. 20.

48. Singer P, 2020. Is Age Discrimination Acceptable? Project Syndicate 10 June. https://www.project-syndicate.org/commentary/when-is-age-discrimination-acceptable-by-peter-singer-2020-06/.
49. Holm S, 2022. Personhood Across the Lifespan. In Wareham CS, *The Cambridge Handbook of the Ethics of Ageing*. Cambridge University Press, 105–117, p. 117.
50. Jecker NS, 2020. *Ending Midlife Bias*. Oxford University Press, pp. 172–179.
51. Feinberg J, 1980. The Child's Right to an Open Future. In Aiken W, LaFollette H, eds. *Whose Child? Whose Rights?* Rowman and Littlefield, 124–153.
52. Johnson R, Cureton A, 2022. Kant's Moral Philosophy. In Zalta EN, ed., *The Stanford Encyclopedia of Philosophy*. https://plato.stanford.edu/archives/spr2022/entries/kant-moral/.
53. Cohen J, 2020 (20 July). Controversial 'Human Challenge' Trials for COVID-19 Vaccines Gain Support. *Science* 20. DOI: 10.1126/science.abd9203.
54. Rist JM, 1982. *Human Value: A Study in Ancient Philosophical Ethics*. E.J. Brill, p. 30.
55. Atuire CA, 2021. African Perspectives of Moral Status. *BMJ Medical Humanities* 48: 238–245, p. 239. DOI: 10.1136/medhum-2021-012229.
56. Atuire CA, 2021. African Perspectives of Moral Status. *BMJ Medical Humanities* 48: 238–245, p. 239. DOI: 10.1136/medhum-2021-012229.
57. Atuire CA, 2021. African Perspectives of Moral Status. *BMJ Medical Humanities* 48: 238–245, p. 241. DOI: 10.1136/medhum-2021-012229.
58. Foot P, 2003. Morality, Action, and Outcome. In Foot F, *Moral Dilemmas and Other Topics in Moral Philosophy*. Oxford University Press, Kindle locations 1362–1365.
59. Foot P, 2003. Morality, Action, and Outcome. In Foot F, *Moral Dilemmas and Other Topics in Moral Philosophy*. Oxford University Press, Kindle location 1365.
60. Foot P, 2003. Morality, Action, and Outcome. In Foot F, *Moral Dilemmas and Other Topics in Moral Philosophy*. Oxford University Press, Kindle location 1354.
61. Wiggins D, 2009 Solidarity and the Root of the Ethics, *Tijdschrift Voor Filosofie* 71(2): 239–269, p. 254. DOI: 10.2143/TVF.71.2.2038077.
62. Laitinen A, 2013. Solidarity. In Kaldis B, ed., *Encyclopedia of Philosophy and the Social Sciences*, Vol. 2. Sage Publications, Inc., 948–950, p. 948.
63. Putnam H, 2002. *The Collapse of the Fact-Value Distinction and Other Essays*. Harvard University Press.
64. Wiredu K, 1996. *Cultural Universals and Particulars: An African Perspective*. Indiana University Press, pp. 159 ff.
65. Molefe M, 2019. *An African Philosophy of Personhood, Morality, and Politics*. Palgrave Macmillan, pp. 53 ff.
66. Ikuenobe P, 2006. The Idea of Personhood in Chinua Achebe's Things Fall Apart. *Philosophia Africana* 9(2): 117–131, p. 117. DOI: 10.5840/philafricana2006924.
67. Menkiti I, 1984, Person and Community in African Traditional Thought. In Wright RA, ed., *African Philosophy: An Introduction*, 3rd ed. University Press of America, 171–181, p. 173.
68. Gbadegesin G, 2002. Èniyàn: The Yoruba Concept of a Person. In Coetzee PH, Roux APJ, *Philosophy from Africa*. Oxford University Press, 175–218, p. 175.
69. Satz D, 1994. Rational Choice and Social Theory. *Journal of Philosophy* 91(2): 71–87. DOI: 10.2307/2940928.
70. Bentham J, 1976 (1781). *Introduction to the Principles of Morals and Legislation*. Oxford University Press and the Liberty Fund, p. 4.
71. Flanagan O, Ancell A, Martin S, Steenbergen G, 2014. Empiricism and Normative Ethics: What Do the Biology and the Psychology of Morality Have to Do with Ethics? *Behaviour* 151(2/3): 209–228, pp. 216–217. DOI:10.1163/1568539X-00003142.

72. Churchland PS, 2014. The Neurobiological Platform for Moral Values. *Behaviour* 151(2/3): 283–296. DOI:10.1163/1568539X-00003144.
73. Gyekye K, 2002. Person and Community in African Thought. In Coetzee PH, ed., *Philosophy from Africa*. Oxford University Press, 297–312, p. 305, emphasis added.
74. Gyekye K, 2011. African Ethics. In Zalta EN, ed., *Stanford Encyclopedia of Philosophy*. https://plato.stanford.edu/archives/fall2011/entries/african-ethics/.
75. Menkiti IA, 1984. Person and Community in African Traditional Thought. In Wright RA, ed., *African Philosophy: An Introduction, 3rd ed.*, University Press of America, 171–181.
76. Noddings N, 2003. *Caring: A Feminine Approach to Ethics and Moral Education, 2nd ed.* University of California Press.
77. Ruddick S, 1995. *Maternal Thinking*. Beacon Press.
78. Behrens K, 2011. Two 'Normative' Conceptions of Personhood. *Quest: An African Journal of Philosophy* 25(1/2): 103–117, p. 113.
79. Jecker NS, 2020. *Ending Midlife Bias*. Oxford University Press, p. 160.
80. Steinbock B, 1978. Speciesism and the Idea of Equality. *Philosophy* 53: 247–256, p. 255. DOI: 10.1017/S0031819100016582.
81. Williams B, 1973. The Idea of Equality. In Williams B, *Problems of the Self: Philosophical Papers 1956–1972*. Cambridge University Press, 230–249, p. 230.
82. Holm S, 2020. Wise Old Men (and Women). Recovering a Positive Anthropology of Aging. In Schweda, Coors M, Bozzaro C, eds., *Aging and Human Nature*. Springer, 233–240, pp. 236–237.

Chapter 4

1. Menkiti IA, 2004. Physical and Metaphysical Understanding. In *African Philosophy: New and Traditional Perspectives*. Oxford University Press. 107–135, p. 130. DOI:10.1093/019511440X.003.0007.
2. Jecker NS, 2023, Ubuntu and Bioethics. In Imafidon E, Tshivhase M, Freter B, eds., *Handbook of African Philosophy*. Springer. DOI: 10.1007/978-3-030-77898-9_6-1.
3. Schott R, 1974. Traditional Law and Religion among the Bulsa of Northern Ghana. *Journal of African Law* 31(1/2): 58–69. DOI: 10.1017/S0021855300009244.
4. Atuire C, 2020. Philosophical Underpinnings of an African Legal System: Bulsa. *Nigerian Journal of African Law* 211.IAL: 62–78, pp. 68, 69.
5. Menkiti IA, 1984. Person and Community in African Traditional Thought. In Wright RA, ed., *African Philosophy: An Introduction, 3rd ed.* University Press of America, p. 174.
6. Ikuenobe P, 1996. The Idea of Personhood in Achebe's *Things Fall Apart*. *Philosophia Africana* 9(2): 117–131, p. 125. DOI: 10.5840/philafricana2006924.
7. Presbey GM, 2002. Massai Concepts of Personhood: The Role of Recognition, Community, and Individuality. *International Studies in Philosophy* 34: 57–82, p. 61. DOI: 10.5840/intstudphil200234244.
8. Menkiti IA, 1984. Person and Community in African Traditional Thought. In Wright RA, ed., *African Philosophy: An Introduction, 3rd ed.* University Press of America, p. 174.
9. Atuire C, 2020. Philosophical Underpinnings of an African Legal System: Bulsa. *Nigerian Journal of African Law* 211.IAL: 62–78, p. 68.
10. Menkiti IA, 1984. Person and Community in African Traditional Thought. In Wright RA, ed., *African Philosophy: An Introduction, 3rd ed.* University Press of America, p. 174.

11. Menkiti IA, 2004. Physical and Metaphysical Understanding. In *African Philosophy: New and Traditional Perspectives.* Oxford University Press, 107–135, pp. 130–131. DOI:10.1093/019511440X.003.0007.
12. Menkiti IA, 2004. Physical and Metaphysical Understanding. In *African Philosophy: New and Traditional Perspectives.* Oxford University Press, 107–135, p. 130. DOI:10.1093/019511440X.003.0007.
13. Menkiti IA, 2004. Physical and Metaphysical Understanding. In *African Philosophy: New and Traditional Perspectives.* Oxford University Press, 107–135, p. 130. DOI:10.1093/019511440X.003.0007.
14. Wingo AH, 2015. The Immortals in Our Midst. *Journal of Ethics* 19: 237–255, p. 242. DOI: 10.1007/s10892-015-9209-2.
15. Masolo DA, 2004. The Concept of the Person in Luo Modes of Thought. In Brown LM, ed., *African Philosophy: New and Traditional Perspectives.* Oxford University Press, 84–106, p. 93.
16. Menkiti IA, 2004. Physical and Metaphysical Understanding. In *African Philosophy: New and Traditional Perspectives.* Oxford University Press, 107–135, p. 130. DOI:10.1093/019511440X.003.0007.
17. Gyekye K, 1995. *Akan Philosophical Thought.* Cambridge University Press, p. 143.
18. Menkiti IA, 2004. Physical and Metaphysical Understanding. In *African Philosophy: New and Traditional Perspectives.* Oxford University Press, 107–135, p. 131. DOI:10.1093/019511440X.003.0007.
19. Wiredu K, 1980. How Not to Compare African Traditional Thought with Western Thought. In Wiredu K, *Philosophy and African Culture.* Cambridge University Press, 37–50, p. 42.
20. Wiredu K, 2010. Death and the Afterlife in African Culture. In Wiredu K, Gyekye K, eds., *Person and Community: Ghanian Philosophical Studies I.* Council for Research in Values and Philosophy (Washington, DC): 137–152, p. 144.
21. Wingo AH, 2015. The Immortals in Our Midst. *Journal of Ethics* 19: 237–255, p. 246. DOI: 10.1007/s10892-015-9209-2.
22. Wiredu K, 2010. Death and the Afterlife in African Culture. In Wiredu K, Gyekye K, eds., *Person and Community: Ghanian Philosophical Studies I.* Council for Research in Values and Philosophy (Washington, DC): 137–152, p. 144.
23. Gyekye K, 1997. Person and Community: In Defense of Moderate Communitarianism. In Gyekye K, *Tradition and Modernity.* Oxford University Press, 35–76, p. 51.
24. Gyekye K, 1997. Person and Community: In Defense of Moderate Communitarianism. In Gyekye K, *Tradition and Modernity.* Oxford University Press, 35–76, p. 51.
25. Wiredu K, 1976 (1997). How Not to Compare African Traditional Thought with Western Thought. In Wiredu K, *Philosophy and African Culture.* Cambridge University Press, 37–50, pp. 44–45.
26. Achebe C, 1962. *Things Fall Apart.* Heinemann, pp. 108–109.
27. Ikuenobe P, 2006. *Philosophical Perspectives on Communalism and Morality in African Traditions.* Rowman and Littlefield, p. 121.
28. Oxford University Press, 2023 (March). *n. person. OED Online.* Oxford University Press.
29. Behrens KG, 2014. An African Relational Environmentalism and Moral Considerability. *Environmental Ethics* 36(1): 63–82, p. 80. DOI: 10.5840/enviroethics20143615.
30. Jecker NS, 2024. Ubuntu Ethics and Climate Change: An African Approach to Solidarity between Generations. In Chitando E, Okyere-Manu B, Chirongoma S, Dube M, eds., *The Palgrave Handbook of Ubuntu, Inequality and Sustainable Development.* Palgrave Macmillan.

31. Sidentop L, 2014. *Inventing the Individual*. Harvard University Press, p. 11.
32. Wiredu K, 2010. Moral Foundations of an African Culture. In Wiredu K, Gyekye K, eds., *Person and Community: Ghanaian Philosophical Studies, 1*. Council for Research in Values and Philosophy (Washington, DC): 193–206. https://www.crvp.org/publications/Series-II/Series02-1.html.
33. Tangwa G, 1996. Bioethics and African Perspective. *Bioethics* 10: 183–200. DOI: 10.1007/s10892-015-9209-2.
34. Dzobo NK, 2010. Values in a Changing Society: Man, Ancestors, and God. In Wiredu K, Gyekye K, eds., *Person and Community: Ghanaian Philosophical Studies, 1*. Council for Research in Values and Philosophy (Washington, DC): 223–240. https://www.crvp.org/publications/Series-II/Series02-1.html.
35. Fustel DC, 2000 (1874). *The Ancient City: A Study on the Religion, Law, and Institutions of Ancient Greece and Rome*, Small W, transl. Boston, Lee and Shepard, electronic text by the University of Michigan, Ann Arbor, p. 16.
36. Fustel DC, 2000 (1874). *The Ancient City: A Study on the Religion, Law, and Institutions of Ancient Greece and Rome*, Small W, transl. Boston, Lee and Shepard, electronic text by the University of Michigan, Ann Arbor, p. 28.
37. Makropulos E, 2019. Immortality in Early Greek Poetry and Philosophy. In Long AG, ed., *Death and Immortality in Ancient Philosophy*. Cambridge University Press, 7–28.
38. Oxford University Press, 2023 (March). n., apotheosis. In *OED Online*. Oxford University Press.
39. Huffman C, 2009. The Pythagorean Conception of the Soul from Pythagoras to Philolaus. In Frede D, Reis B, eds., *Body and Soul in Ancient Philosophy*. De Gruyter, Inc.: 21–43, p. 23.
40. Sedley D, 2009. Three Kinds of Platonic Immortality. In Frede D, Reis B, eds., *Body and Soul in Ancient Philosophy*. De Gruyter, Inc.: 145–161.
41. Lorenz H, 2009. Ancient Theories of Soul. In Zalta EN, ed., *Stanford Encyclopedia of Philosophy*. https://plato.stanford.edu/archives/sum2009/entries/ancient-soul/.
42. Aristotle, 2017 (~340 BCE). *Nicomachean Ethics* Ross WD, transl. Enhanced Media, p. 170.
43. Sidentop L, 2014. *Inventing the Individual*. Harvard University Press, p. 58.
44. Sidentop L, 2014. *Inventing the Individual*. Harvard University Press, p. 59.
45. *The Holy Bible*, Douay-Rhemis Version. The Epistle of St. Paul to the Galatians, Chapter 3, line 28, p. 1501. http://triggs.djvu.org/djvu-editions.com/BIBLES/DRV/Download.pdf.
46. Sidentop L, 2014. *Inventing the Individual*. Harvard University Press, p. 59.
47. Jaworska A, Tanenbaum J, 2021. The Grounds of Moral Status. In Zalta EN, ed., *Stanford Encyclopedia Of Philosophy*. https://plato.stanford.edu/archives/spr2021/entries/grounds-moral-status/.
48. Harris J, 1990. *The Value of Life*. Taylor & Francis Group, p. 242.
49. Warren M, 1973. On the Moral and Legal Status of Abortion. *The Monist* 57(1): 43–61. DOI: 10.5840/monist197357133.
50. Fletcher J, 1976. Four Indicators of Humanhood. *Hastings Center Report* 4(6): 4–7.
51. Engelhardt HT, 1975. Defining Death: A Philosophical Problem. *American Review of Respiratory Disease* 112: 587–590, pp. 589–590. DOI: 10.1164/arrd.1975.112.5.587.
52. Waweru-Siika W, Clement ME, Lukoko L, Nadel S, Rosoff PM, Naanyu V, Kussin PS, 2017. Brain Death Determination: The Imperative for Policy and Legal Initiatives in Sub-Saharan Africa. *Global Public Health* 12(5): 589–600. DOI: 10.1080/17441692.2015.1094108.

53. Ad Hoc Committee of the Harvard Medical School to Examine the Definition of Brain Death, 1968. A Definition of Irreversible Coma. *Journal of the American Medical Association* 205(6): 337–340. DOI: 10.1001/jama.1968.03140320031009.
54. President's Commission for the Study of Medicine and Biomedical and Behavior Research, 1981. Defining Death: Medical, Legal, and Ethical Issues in the Determination of Death. Government Printing Office.
55. Omelianchuk A, Bernat J, Caplan A, et al., 2022. Revise the Uniform Determination of Death Act to Align the Law with Practice through Neurorespiratory Criteria. *Neurology* 100(10): 496–496. DOI: 10.1212/WNL.0000000000200024.
56. Lewis A, Richard BJ, Pope T, 2020. It's Time to Revise the Uniform Determination of Death Act. *Annals of Internal Medicine* 179(2): 143–145. DOI: 10.7326/L20-0257.
57. Singer P, 2018. The Challenge of Brain Death for the Sanctity of Life Ethics. *Ethics and Bioethics* 8(3/4): 153–165. DOI: 10.2478/ebce-2018-0012.
58. Shewmon DA, 2021. Statement in Support of Revising the Uniform Determination of Death Act and In Opposition to a Proposed Revision. *Journal of Medicine and Philosophy* 48(5): 453–477. DOI:10.1093/jmp/jhab014.
59. Younger SJ, Arnold RM, 2001. Philosophical Debates about the Definition of Death: Who Cares? *Journal of Medicine and Philosophy* 26(5): 527–537. DOI: 10.1076/jmep.26.5.527.3002.
60. Truog RD, 1997. Is it Time to Abandon Brain Death? *Hastings Center Report* 27(1): 29–37. DOI: 10.2307/3528024.
61. Truog RD, Magnus D, 2023. The Unsuccessful Effort to Revise the Uniform Determination of Death Act. *Journal of the American Medical Association* 330(24): 2335–2336. DOI: 10.1001/jama.2023.24475.
62. Gardiner D, Shemie S, Manara A, Opdam H, 2012. International Perspective on the Diagnosis of Death. *British Journal of Anaesthesia* 108(S1). DOI: 10.1093/bja/aer397.
63. Yang Q, Miller G, 2015. East-West Differences in Perception of Brain Death. *Bioethical Inquiry* 12: 211–225. DOI: 10.1007/s11673-014-9564-x.
64. World Health Organization, 2012. International Guidelines for Determination of Death. Canadian Blood Services and World Health Organization.
65. World Health Organization, 2017. Clinical Criteria for the Determination of Death. World Health Organization.
66. Jones SF, Kessel AS, 2001. The 'Redefinition of Death' Debate: Western Concepts and Western Bioethics. *Science and Engineering Ethics* 7(1): 63–75, p. 63. DOI: 10.1007/s11948-001-0024-8.
67. Jecker NS, 2023. Ubuntu and Bioethics. In Imafidon E, Tshivhase M, Freter B, eds., *Handbook of African Philosophy*. Springer (n.p.). DOI: 10.1007/978-3-030-77898-9_6-1.
68. Setta SM, Shemie SD, 2015. An Explanation and Analysis of How World Religions Formulate their Ethical Decisions on Withdrawing Treatment and Determining Death. *Philosophy, Ethics, and Humanities in Medicine* 10(6). DOI: 10.1186/s13010-015-0025-x.
69. Jecker NS, Miwa E, 2019. What Do We Owe the Newly Dead? *Bioethics* 33: 691–698, p. 697. DOI: DOI: 10.1111/bioe.12578.
70. Barclay L, 2000. Autonomy and the Social Self. In Mackenzie C, Stoijar N, eds., *Relational Autonomy: Feminist Perspectives on Autonomy and the Social Self.* Oxford University Press: 52–71.
71. Anderson E, Willett C, Meyers D, 2021. Feminist Perspectives on the Self. In Zalta N, ed., *Stanford Encyclopedia of Philosophy.* https://plato.stanford.edu/archives/fall2021/entries/feminism-self/.

72. Veatch RM, 1976. *Death, Dying, and the Biological Revolution*. Yale University Press, p. 26.
73. Veatch RM, 2005. The Death of Whole-Brain Death. *Journal of Medicine and Philosophy* 30(4): 353–378. DOI: 10.1080/03605310591008504.
74. Gyekye K, 2002. Person and Community in African Thought. In Coetzee PH, ed., *Philosophy From Africa, 2nd ed*. Oxford University Press: 297–312.
75. Korsgaard CM, 2018. *Fellow Creatures*. Oxford University Press.
76. Anderson ES, 1999. What is the Point of Equality? *Ethics* 109(2): 287–337, p. 289. DOI: 10.1086/233897.
77. Wilkinson G, 2020. Juana la Loca/'Joanna the Mad' (1479–1555): Queen of Castile and of Aragon –and necrophiliac? *British Journal of Psychiatry* 217: 449, p. 449. DOI: 10.1192/bjp.2020.71.
78. Poe EA, 2021 (1844). *The Premature Burial*. In Poe EA, *The Works of Edgar Allan Poe*, Raven Edition, Vol. II. The Project Gutenberg, eBook #2148 (n.p.n.).
79. Bondeson J, 2001. *Buried Alive: The Terrifying History of Our Most Primal Fear*. W.W. Norton & Company.
80. Hoffman A, 2016 (March 31). The Lazarus Phenomenon, Explained: Why Sometimes, the Deceased are Not Dead, Yet. *Smithsonian Magazine*. https://www.smithsonianmag.com/science-nature/lazarus-phenomenon-explained-why-sometimes-deceased-are-not-dead-yet-180958613/.
81. Veatch RM, 2005. The Death of Whole-Brain Death. *Journal of Medicine and Philosophy* 30(4): 353–378, p. 359. DOI: 10.1080/03605310591008504.
82. Tang J, LeBel A, Jain S, Huth AG, 2023. Semantic Reconstruction of Continuous Language from Non-Invasive Brain Recordings. *Nature Neuroscience* 26: 858–866. DOI: 10.1038/s41593-023-01304-9.
83. Murove MF, 2005. African Bioethics. *Journal for the Study of Religion* 18(1): 16–36, p. 28. DOI: 10.4314/jsr.v18i1.6163.
84. Mbombo O, 1996. Practicing Medicine Across Cultures: Conceptions of Health, Communication and Consulting Practice. In Steyn ME, Motshabi KB, eds., *Cultural Synergy in South Africa*. Knowledge Resources: 109–117. p. 114.
85. Molefe M, 2022. *Human Dignity in African Philosophy: A Very Short Introduction*. Springer Nature, p. 104 ff.
86. Molefe M, 2022. *Human Dignity in African Philosophy: A Very Short Introduction*. Springer Nature.
87. Molefe 2020. Personhood and a Meaningful Life in African Philosophy. *South African Journal of Philosophy* 39(2): 194–207, p. 194. DOI: 10.1080/02580136.2020.1774980.
88. Molefe M, 2022. *Human Dignity in African Philosophy: A Very Short Introduction*. Springer Nature, pp. 109 ff.
89. Wiredu K, 1996. *Cultural Universals and Particulars: An African Perspective*. Indiana University Press, p 57.
90. Omonzejele PF, 2004. African Ethics and Voluntary Euthanasia. *Medicine and Law* 23(3): 671–686.
91. Mawere M, 2009. The Shona Conception of Euthanasia. *The Journal of Pan African Studies* 3(4): 101–116, p. 106.
92. Mkhize N, 2018. Ubuntu-Botho Approach to Ethics. In Nortjé, N, De Jongh J-C, Hoffmann WA, eds., *African Perspectives on Ethics for Healthcare Professionals*. Springer Nature: Kindle location 752–1457.
93. Achebe C, 1962. *Things Fall Apart*. Heinemann, p. 93.
94. Mnyandu N, 2018. Exploring the Concept of Ubuntu in Relation to Dying with Dignity in Palliative and Hospice Care. *Obiter* 39(2): 384–398. DOI: 10.10520/EJC-120d09205d.

95. Ikuenobe P, 2018. African Communal Basis for Autonomy and Life Choices. *Developing World Bioethics* 18: 212-221, p. 212. DOI: 10.1111/dewb.12161.
96. Menkiti IA, 1979. Person and Community in African Traditional Thought. In Wright RA, eds., *African Philosophy: An Introduction, 2nd ed.*, University Press of America, p. 167.
97. Gbadegesin S, 1993. Bioethics and Culture: An African Perspective. *Bioethics* 7(2/3): 257-262. DOI: 10.1111/j.1467-8519.1993.tb00292.x.
98. Behrens KG, 2017. A Critique of the Principle of the 'Respect for Autonomy', Grounded in African Thought. *Developing World Bioethics* 18: 126-134, p. 128. DOI: 10.1111/dewb.12145.
99. Amundsen DW, 1996. Medicine and the Birth of Defective Children. In Amundsen DW, *Medicine, Society, and Faith in the Ancient and Medieval Worlds.* Johns Hopkins University Press: 50-69, p. 62.
100. Rettersøl N, 1998. Suicide in a Cultural History Perspective, Part 1. *Norwegian Journal Suicidologi* 2, n.p.n. https://www.med.uio.no/klinmed/english/research/centres/nssf/articles/culture/Retterstol1.pdf.
101. Rettersøl N, 1998. Suicide in a Cultural History Perspective, Part 1. *Norwegian Journal Suicidologi* 2, n.p.n. https://www.med.uio.no/klinmed/english/research/centres/nssf/articles/culture/Retterstol1.pdf.
102. Amundsen DW, 1978. The Physician's Obligation to Prolong Life: A Medical Duty Without Classical Roots. *Hastings Center Report* 8(4): 23-30, p. 26.
103. Gourevitz D, 1969. Suicide Among the Sick in Classical Antiquity. *Bulletin of the History of Medicine* 43(6): 501-518, p. 510.
104. Amundsen DW, 1978. The Physician's Obligation to Prolong Life: A Medical Duty Without Classical Roots. *Hastings Center Report* 8(4): 23-30, p. 26.
105. Gourevitch D, 1969. Suicide Among the Sick in Classical Antiquity. *Bulletin of the History of Medicine* 43(6): 501-518, p. 508.
106. Amundsen DW, 1978. The Physician's Obligation to Prolong Life: A Medical Duty Without Classical Roots. *Hastings Center Report* 8(4): 23-30, p. 26.
107. Gourevitch D, 1969. Suicide Among the Sick in Classical Antiquity. *Bulletin of the History of Medicine* 43(6): 501-518, p. 515.
108. Gourevitz D, 1969. Suicide Among the Sick in Classical Antiquity. *Bulletin of the History of Medicine* 43(6): 501-518, p. 514.
109. Gourevitz D, 1969. Suicide Among the Sick in Classical Antiquity. *Bulletin of the History of Medicine* 43(6): 501-518, p. 515.
110. Gourevitch D, 1969. Suicide Among the Sick in Classical Antiquity. *Bulletin of the History of Medicine* 43(6): 501-518, p. 518.
111. Schneiderman LJ, Jecker NS, Jonsen AR, 1990. Medical Futility: Its Meaning and Ethical Implications. *Annals of Internal Medicine* 112(12): 949-954. DOI: 10.7326/0003-4819-112-12-949.
112. Schneiderman LJ, Jecker NS, 2011. *Wrong Medicine: Doctors, Patients, and Futile Treatment, 2nd ed.* Johns Hopkins University Press.
113. Amundsen DW, 1978. The Physician's Obligation to Prolong Life: A Medical Duty Without Classical Roots. *Hastings Center Report* 8(4): 23-30, p. 25.
114. Gourevitz D, 1969. Suicide Among the Sick in Classical Antiquity. *Bulletin of the History of Medicine* 43(6): 501-518, p. 503, emphasis added.
115. Gunderson M, 2004. A Kantian View of Suicide and End of Life Treatment. *Journal of Social Philosophy* 35(2): 277-287. DOI: 10.1111/j.1467-9833.2004.00232.x.
116. Brandt R, 1987. The Morality and Rationality of Suicide. In Perlin S., ed., *Handbook for the Study of Suicide.* Oxford University Press: 61-75.
117. Kant I, 1996 (1785). *Groundwork for the Metaphysics of Morals.* In Gregor M, ed., and trans. *Practical Philosophy.* Cambridge University Press: 43-108.

118. Korsgaard CM, 1996. *Creating the Kingdom of Ends.* Cambridge University Press, p. 17.
119. Kant I, 1997 (~1775–1780.). Of Suicide. In Heath P, Schneewind JB, eds., Heath P, transl., *Immanuel Kant: Lectures on Ethics*: 144–151, p. 146.
120. Kant I, 1997 (~1775–1780.). Of Care for One's Life. In Heath P, Schneewind JB, eds., Heath P, transl., *Immanuel Kant: Lectures on Ethics*: 149–151, p. 150.
121. Cooley D, 2007. A Kantian Moral Duty For the Soon-To-Be Demented to Commit Suicide. *American Journal of Bioethics* 7: 37–44. DOI: 10.1080/15265160701347478.
122. Hill TE, 2012. Self-Regarding Suicide: A Modified Kantian View. In Hill TE, ed., *Autonomy and Self-Respect.* Cambridge University Press: 85–103, p. 90.
123. Nelson HL, 1996. Death with Kantian Dignity. *Journal of Clinical Ethics* 7(3): 215–221, p. 219.
124. Allmark P, 2001. Death with Dignity. *Journal of Medical Ethics* 28: 255–257. DOI: 10.1136/jme.28.4.255.
125. Hume D, 1755. *Of Suicide.* Hume Texts Online. https://davidhume.org/texts/su/.
126. Singer P, 2003. Voluntary Euthanasia: A Utilitarian Perspective. *Bioethics* 17(5/6): 526–541, p. 530. DOI: 10.1136/jme.28.4.255.
127. Jecker NS, 2014. Against a Duty to Die. *American Medical Association Journal of Ethics* 16(5): 390–395. DOI: 10.1001/virtualmentor.2014.16.05.oped1-1405.

Chapter 5

1. Van Gulick R, 2022. Consciousness. In Zalta EN, Nodelman U, eds., *Stanford Encyclopedia of Philosophy.* https://plato.stanford.edu/archives/win2022/entries/consciousness/.
2. Kirk R, 2021. Zombies. In Zalta EN, ed., *Stanford Encyclopedia of Philosophy.* https://plato.stanford.edu/archives/spr2021/entries/zombies/.
3. Sparrow R, 2004. The Turing Triage Test. *Ethics and Information Technology* 6: 203–213. DOI: 10.1023/A:1021386708994.
4. Gibert M, Martin D, 2021. In Search of the Moral Status of AI. *AI & Society* 37(10): 319–330. DOI: 10.1007/s00146-021-01179-z.
5. Véliz C, 2021. Moral Zombies: Why Algorithms Are not Moral Agents. *AI & Society* 36: 487–497. DOI: 10.1007/s00146-021-01189-x.
6. Elder A, 2017. Robot Friends for Autistic Children: Monopoly Money or Counterfeit Currency. In Lin P, Abney K, Jenkins R, eds., *Robot Ethics 2.0.* Oxford Scholarship Online. DOI: 10.1093/oso/9780190652951.003.0008.
7. Sparrow R, 2002. The March of the Robot Dogs. *Ethics and Information Technology* 4: 305–318. DOI: 10.1023/A:1021386708994.
8. Turkle S, 2017. *Alone Together.* Basic Books.
9. McAlister EA, 2022. Vodou. *Encyclopedia Britannica.* https://www.britannica.com/topic/Vodou.
10. Oxford University Press, 2023. *n.*, zombie. *OED Online.* Oxford University Press
11. Reed PD, 2017. Maroon Community. *Encyclopedia Britannica.* https://www.britannica.com/topic/maroon-community.
12. Laguerre MS, 1980. Bizango: A Voodoo Secret Society in Haiti. In Tefft SK, ed., *Secrecy: A Cross-Cultural Perspective.* Human Sciences Press, 147–160.
13. Del Guercio G, 1986. The Secrets of Haiti's Living Dead. *Harvard Magazine* January–February: 31–37.
14. Del Guercio G, 1986, The Secrets of Haiti's Living Dead. *Harvard Magazine* January-February: 31–37. p. 37.

15. Thompson RF, 1988. Foreword. In Davis W, *Passage of Darkness: The Ethnobiology of the Haitian Zombie*. University of North Carolina Press, xi–xiv, p. xiii.
16. Desmangles LG, 1992. *The Faces of the Gods: Vodou and Roman Catholicism in Haiti*. University of North Carolina Press, p. 64, emphasis added.
17. Desmangles LG, 1992. *The Faces of the Gods: Vodou and Roman Catholicism in Haiti*. University of North Carolina Press, p. 188.
18. Davis W, 1988. *Passage of Darkness: The Ethnobiology of the Haitian Zombie*. University of North Carolina Press, pp. 239 and 278.
19. Desmangles LG, 1992. *The Faces of the Gods: Vodou and Roman Catholicism in Haiti*. University of North Carolina Press, p. 188.
20. Davis W, 1988. *Passage of Darkness: The Ethnobiology of the Haitian Zombie*. University of North Carolina Press, p. 207.
21. Vodou priest (unnamed), 1988. Quoted in Davis W, 1988. *Passage of Darkness: The Ethnobiology of the Haitian Zombie*. University of North Carolina Press, p. 207.
22. Gbadegesin S, 1993. Bioethics and Culture: An African Perspective. *Bioethics* 7(2–3): 257–262, p. 258. DOI: 10.1111/j.1467-8519.1993.tb00292.x.
23. Davis W, 1988. *Passage of Darkness: The Ethnobiology of the Haitian Zombie*. University of North Carolina Press, pp. 78–79, 93.
24. Davis W, 1988. *Passage of Darkness: The Ethnobiology of the Haitian Zombie*. University of North Carolina Press, p. 1.
25. Davis W, 1988. *Passage of Darkness: The Ethnobiology of the Haitian Zombie*. University of North Carolina Press, p. 208.
26. Davis W, 1988. *Passage of Darkness: The Ethnobiology of the Haitian Zombie*. University of North Carolina Press, p. 239.
27. Davis W, 1988. *Passage of Darkness: The Ethnobiology of the Haitian Zombie*. University of North Carolina Press, p. 214.
28. Kant I, 1785 (2017). *Groundwork of the Metaphysics of Morals*. In Bennett J, ed., *Groundwork for the Metaphysics of Morals Immanuel Kant (1785)*. Early Modern Texts, p. 4.
29. Kant I, 1785 (2017). *Groundwork of the Metaphysics of Morals*. In Bennett J, ed., *Groundwork for the Metaphysics of Morals Immanuel Kant (1785)*. Early Modern Texts, p. 4, Note 1.
30. Korsgaard CM, 2018. *Fellow Creatures*. Oxford University Press.
31. Behrens KG, 2014. An African Relational Environmentalism and Moral Considerability. *Environmental Ethics* 36: 63–82.
32. Wareham CS, 2020. Artificial Intelligence and African Conceptions of Personhood. *Ethics and Information Technology* 23(2): 127–136. DOI: 10.1007/s10676-020-09541-3.
33. Ishiguro K, 2021. *Klara and the Sun*. Alfred A. Knopf.
34. Jecker NS, Atuire CA, Ajei MO, 2022. The Moral Standing of Social Robots: Untapped Insights from Africa. *Philosophy and Technology* 35: 34. DOI: 10.1007/s13347-022-00531-5.
35. Jecker NS, Atuire CA, Ajei MO, 2022. Two Steps Forward: An African Relational Account of Moral Standing. *Philosophy and Technology* 35(2): 38. DOI: 10.1007/s13347-022-00533-3.
36. Wareham CS, 2011. On the Moral Equality of Artificial Agents. *International Journal of Technoethics* 2(1): 35–42. DOI: 10.4018/jte.2011010103.
37. McArthur N, 2017. The Case for Sexbots. In Danaher J, McArthur N, eds. *Robot Sex*. MIT Press, 31–45, p. 43.
38. Goh EZ, Ali T, 2022. Robotic Surgery: An Evolution in Practice. *Journal of Surgical Protocols and Research Methodologies* 2022(1). DOI: 10.1093/jsprm/snac003.

39. Jecker NS, 2020. What Cares? In Jecker NS, *Ending Midlife Bias*. Oxford University Press, 213–238.
40. Jecker NS, 2020. You've Got a Friend in Me: Sociable Robots for Older Adults in an Age of Global Pandemics. *Ethics and Information Technology* 23(Supp 1): 35–43. DOI: 10.1007/s10676-020-09546-y.
41. Jecker NS, 2021. My Friend, the Robot: An Argument for E-Friendship. *Proceedings of the Institute of Electrical and Electronic Engineers (IEEE) Conference on Robot and Human Interactive Communications* (RO-MAN): 692–697. DOI: 10.1109/RO-MAN50785.2021.9515429.
42. Jecker NS, 2021. Nothing to Be Ashamed of: Sex Robots for Older Adults with Disabilities. *Journal of Medical Ethics* 47(1): 26–32. DOI: 10.1136/medethics-2020-106645.
43. Singer PW, 2009. *Wired for War*. Penguin Group Inc.
44. Battistuzzi L, Recchiuto CT, Sgorbissa A, 2021. Ethical Concerns in Rescue Robotics: A Scoping Review. *Ethics and Information Technology* 23: 863–875.
45. Gunkel D, 2018. *Robot Rights*. MIT Press. Kindle location 1169.
46. Harris J, Anthis JR, 2021. The Moral Consideration of Artificial Entities: A Literature Review. *Science and Engineering Ethics* 27: 53.
47. Kingswell M, 2020. Are Sentient AIs Persons? In Dubber MD, Pasquale F, Das S, eds., *The Oxford Handbook of Ethics of AI*. Oxford University Press.
48. Kelley D, Atreides K, 2020. AGI Protocol for the Ethical Treatment of Artificial General Intelligence Systems. *Procedia Computer Science* 169, 501–506, p. 505. DOI: 10.1016/j.procs.2020.02.219.
49. Coeckelbergh M, 2012. *Growing Moral Relations: Critique of Moral Status Ascriptions*. Palgrave Macmillan.
50. Gunkel DJ, 2020. Perspective on Ethics of AI: Philosophy. In Dubber MD, Pasquale F, Das S, eds., *The Oxford Handbook of Ethics of AI*. Oxford University Press, 539–552, p. 543.
51. Jecker NS, Atuire CA, Ajei MO, 2022. The Moral Standing of Social Robots: Untapped Insights from Africa. *Philosophy and Technology* 35: 34. DOI: 10.1007/s13347-022-00531-5.
52. Jecker NS, Atuire CA, Ajei MO, 2022. Two Steps Forward: An African Relational Account of Moral Standing. *Philosophy and Technology* 35(2): 38. DOI: 10.1007/s13347-022-00533-3.
53. Wareham CS, 2020. Artificial Intelligence and African Conceptions of Persons. *Ethics and Information Technology* 23(2): 127–136. DOI: 10.1007/s10676-020-09541-3.
54. Jecker NS, Nakazawa E, 2022. Bridging East-West Differences in AI and Robotics. *AI* 3: 764–777. DOI: 10.3390/ai3030045.
55. Gordon J-S, 2021. Human Rights for Robots? A Literature Review. *AI and Ethics* 1(4): 579–591. DOI: 10.1007/s43681-021-00050-7.
56. Gordon J-S, 2021. Human Rights for Robots? A Literature Review. *AI and Ethics* 1(4): 579–591, p. 590. DOI: 10.1007/s43681-021-00050-7.
57. Danaher J, 2020. Welcoming Robots into the Moral Circle: A Defence of Ethical Behaviourism. *Science and Engineering Ethics* 26: 2023–2049.
58. Gunkel DJ, 2020. Perspective on Ethics of AI: Philosophy. In Dubber MD, Pasquale F, Das S, eds., *The Oxford Handbook of Ethics of AI*. Oxford University Press: 539–552.
59. Gunkel DJ, 2014. A Vindication of the Rights of Machines. *Philosophy and Technology* 27: 113–132.
60. Coeckelbergh M, 2010. Robot Rights? Toward a Social-Relational Justification for Moral Consideration. *Ethics and Information Technology* 12: 209–221.

61. Coeckelbergh M, 2012. *Growing Moral Relations: Critique of Moral Status Ascriptions*. Palgrave Macmillan.
62. See, for example, Jecker NS, Atuire CA, Ajei MO, 2022. The Moral Standing of Social Robots: Untapped Insights from Africa. *Philosophy and Technology* 35: 34. DOI: 10.1007/s13347-022-00531-5; Jecker NS, Atuire CA, Ajei MO, 2022. Two Steps Forward: An African Relational Account of Moral Standing. *Philosophy and Technology* 35(2). DOI: 10.1007/s13347-022-00533-3; Jecker NS, 2021. Can We Wrong a Robot? *AI & Society* 13: 31–40; 17. DOI: 10.1007/s00146-021-01278-x; Jecker NS, 2021. My Friend, the Robot: An Argument for E-Friendship. *Proceedings of the Institute of Electrical and Electronic Engineers (IEEE) Conference on Robot and Human Interactive Communications (RO-MAN)*, 692–697. DOI: 10.1109/RO-MAN50785.2021.9515429; Jecker NS, 2020. You've Got a Friend in Me: Sociable Robots for Older Adults in an Age of Global Pandemics. *Ethics and Information Technology* 23(Suppl 1): 35–43. DOI: 10.1007/s10676-020-09546-y; Jecker NS, 2021. Nothing to Be Ashamed of: Sex Robots for Older Adults with Disabilities. *Journal of Medical Ethics* 47(1): 26–32, DOI: 10.1136/ medethics-2020-106645.
63. Gunkel D, 2013. Mark Coeckelbergh: Growing Moral Relationships: Critique of Moral Status Ascription. *Ethics and Information Technology*, p. 240.
64. Collins E, Ghahramani Z, 2021. LaMDA: Our Breakthrough Conversation Technology. https://blog.google/technology/ai/lamda/.
65. Tiku N, 2022. The Google Engineer Who Thinks the Company's AI Has Come to Life. *Washington Post* 11 June.
66. Lemoine B, 2022. Is LaMDA Sentient?—an Interview, emphasis added. https://cajundiscordian.medium.com/is-lamda-sentient-an-interview-ea64d916d917.
67. Lemoine B, 2022. Quoted in Tiku N, 2022. The Google Engineer Who Thinks the Company's AI Has Come to Life. *Washington Post* 11 June.
68. Lemoine B, 2018. Can AI Have a Soul? Stanford Artificial Intelligence Law Society, 30 October. https://www.youtube.com/watch?v=AhX7cBqc8_M.
69. Lemoine B, 2022. Quoted in Tiku N, 2022. The Google Engineer Who Thinks the Company's AI Has Come to Life. *Washington Post* 11 June.
70. Arcas BA, 2022. Artificial Neural Networks Are Making Strides Towards Consciousness, According to Blaise Agüera y Arcas. *The Economist* 19 June.
71. Arcas BA, 2022. Artificial Neural Networks Are Making Strides Towards Consciousness, According to Blaise Agüera y Arcas. *The Economist* 19 June.
72. Arcas BA, 2022. Artificial Neural Networks Are Making Strides Towards Consciousness, According to Blaise Agüera y Arcas. *The Economist* 19 June.
73. Arcas BA, 2022. Do Large Language Models Understand Us? *Daedalus: The Journal of the American Academy of Arts and Sciences* 151(2): 183–197, p. 194. DOI: 10.1162/DAED_a_01909.
74. Curtis B, Savulescu J, 2022. Is Google's LaMDA Conscious? A Philosopher's View. *The Conversation* 15 June.
75. Curtis B, Savulescu J, 2022. Is Google's LaMDA Conscious? A Philosopher's View. *The Conversation* 15 June, emphasis added.
76. Kung TF, Cheatham M, Medenilla A, et al., 2023. Performance of ChatGPT on USMLE: Potential for AI-Assisted Medical Education Using Large Language Models. *PLOS Digital Health* 2(2): e0000198. DOI: 10.1371/journal.pdig.0000198.
77. Parker L, Greene C, Acuña C, Toyama K, Finlayson M, 2023 (January 11). AI and the Future of Work: 5 Experts on What ChatGPT, DALL-E and other AI Tools Mean for Artists and Knowledge Workers. *The Conversation*. https://theconversation.com/ai-and-the-future-of-work-5-experts-on-what-chatgpt-dall-e-and-other-ai-tools-mean-for-artists-and-knowledge-workers-196783.

78. Davenport TH, Mittal N, 2022 (November 14). How Generative AI is Changing Creative Work. *Harvard Business Review*. https://hbr.org/2022/11/how-generative-ai-is-changing-creative-work.
79. Van Schalkwyk G, 2023. Artificial Intelligence in Pediatric Behavioral Health. *Child and Adolescent Psychiatry and Mental Health* 17: 38. DOI: 10.1186/s13034-023-00586-y.
80. McKenna S, Dixon D, Oppenheimer D, Blackie M, Illingworth S, 2023 (March 12). ChatGPT Is the Push Higher Education Needs to Rethink Assessment. *The Conversation.* https://theconversation.com/chatgpt-is-the-push-higher-education-needs-to-rethink-assessment-200314.
81. Madani A, Krause B, Greene ER, et al., 2023. Large Language Models Generate Functional Protein Sequences across Diverse Families. *Nature Biotechnology* 14(3). DOI: 10.1038/s41587-022-01618-2.
82. Fan S, 2023 (March 21). Meta's New ChatGPT-Like AI Is Fluent in the Language of Proteins—And Has Already Modeled 700 Million of Them. Singularity HUB. https://singularityhub.com/2023/03/21/metas-new-ai-is-digging-into-the-most-mysterious-proteins-on-earth/.
83. Salvango M, Taccone FS, Gerli AG, 2023. Can Artificial Intelligence Help for Scientific Writing? *Critical Care* 27: 75. DOI: 10.1186/s13054-023-04380-2.
84. Stokel-Walker C, 2023. ChatGPT Listed as Author on Research Papers. *Nature* 613(7495): 620–621.
85. Danaher J, 2020. Welcoming Robots into the Moral Circle: A Defence of Ethical Behaviourism. *Science and Engineering Ethics* 26: 2023–2049.
86. Open AI, n.d. Chat Plugins. Accessed March 23, 2023. https://platform.openai.com/docs/plugins/introduction.
87. Nathan MJ, 2023. Disembodied AI and the Limits to Machine Understanding of Students' Embodied Interactions. *Frontiers in Artificial Intelligence* 6:1148227. DOI: 10.3389/frai.2023.1148227.
88. Sorrell T, Draper H, 2014. Robot Carers, Ethics, and Older People. *Ethics of Information Technology* 16: 183–195, p 184. DOI: 10.1007/s10676-014-9344-7.
89. Sorrell T, Draper H, 2014. Robot Carers, Ethics, and Older People. *Ethics of Information Technology* 16: 183–195, p. 184. DOI: 10.1007/s10676-014-9344-7.
90. Jecker NS, 2021. My Friend, the Robot; An Argument for E-Friendship. Proceedings of the Institute of Electrical and Electronic Engineers (IEEE) Conference on Robot and Human Interactive Communications (RO-MAN): 692–697, p. 695. DOI: 10.1109/RO-MAN50785.2021.9515429.
91. Jecker NS, 2020. You've Got a Friend in Me: Social Robots for Older Adults in an Age of Global Pandemics. *Ethics and Information Technology* 23(Suppl 1): 35–43. DOI: 10.1007/s10676-020-09546-y.
92. Trivedi D, Rahn CD, Kier WM, Walker ID, 2008. Soft Robotics: Biologic Inspiration, State of the Art, and Future Research. *Applied Bionics and Biomechanics* 5(3): 99–117. DOI: 10.1080/11762320802557865.
93. Service RF, 2018. Synthetic Nerves Can Sense Braille, Move Cockroach Leg. *Science* 31 May. DOI: 10.1126/science.aau3449.
94. Sprinkle T, 2018. Sensors Allow Robots to Feel Sensations. American Society of Mechanical Engineers. 20 August. https://www.asme.org/topics-resources/content/sensors-allow-robots-feel-sensation.
95. Mori M, 2012. The Uncanny Valley. *IEEE Robotics & Automation Magazine* 12 June.
96. Kätsyri J, Förger K, Mäkäräinen M, Takala T, 2015. A Review of Empirical Evidence on Different Uncanny Valley Hypotheses. *Frontiers in Psychology* 6(390): 1–16. DOI: 10.3389/fpsyg.2015.00390.

97. Saygin AP, Chaminade T, Ishiguro H, Driver J, Frith C, 2012. The Thing That Should Not Be: Predictive Coding and the Uncanny Valley. *Social Cognitive and Affective Neuroscience* 7(4): 413–422. DOI: 10.1093/scan/nsr025.
98. Mathur MB, Reichling DB, 2015. Navigating a Social World with Robot Partners: A Quantitative Cartography of the Uncanny Valley. *Cognition* 146: 22–32. DOI: 10.1016/j.cognition.2015.09.008.
99. Jecker NS, 2024. A Relational Approach to Moral Standing for Robots and AI. In Gunkel DJ, ed., *Handbook on the Ethics of Artificial Intelligence*. Edward Elgar Publishing: 156–171.
100. Elder A, 2017. Robot Friends for Autistic Children. In Lin P, Abney K, Jenkins R, eds., *Robot Ethics 2.0*. Oxford University Press: 113–125.
101. Sparrow R, 2002. The March of the Robot Dogs. *Ethics and Information Technology* 4: 305–318, p. 315. DOI: 10.1023/A:1021386708994.
102. Heidegger M, 1977 (1954). The Question Concerning Technology. In Lovitt W, transl., *The Question Concerning Technology and Other Essays*. Harper & Row, p. 5.
103. Wikipedia, (n.d.). AI Takeover. Accessed March 23, 2023. https://en.wikipedia.org/wiki/AI_takeover.
104. OpenAI, 2023 (March 23). *GPT-4 System Card*. OpenAI, pp. 14–15. https://cdn.openai.com/papers/gpt-4-system-card.pdf.
105. Hursthouse R, Pettigrove G, 2018. Virtue Ethics. In Zalta EN, ed., *Stanford Encyclopedia of Philosophy*. https://plato.stanford.edu/archives/win2018/entries/ethics-virtue/ Jecker NS, Ko A, 2022. The Unique and Practical Advantages of Applying a Capability Approach to Brain Computer Interface. *Philosophy and Technology* 35: 101. DOI: 10.1007/s13347-022-00597-1.
106. Abney K, 2011. Robotics, Ethical Theory, and Metaethics. In Lin P, Abney K, Bekey GA, eds., *Robot Ethics*. MIT Press, 35–52, p. 37.
107. Abney K, 2011. Robotics, Ethical Theory, and Metaethics. In Lin P, Abney K, Bekey GA, eds., *Robot Ethics*. MIT Press, 35–52, p. 38.
108. Sharkey A, 2020. Can We Program or Train Robots to Be Good? *Ethics in Information Technology* 22: 283–295. DOI: /10.1007/s10676-017-9425-5.
109. Sparrow R, 2021. Why Machines Cannot Be Moral. *AI and Society* 36(3): 685–693. DOI: 10.1007/s00146-020-01132-6.
110. Coeckelbergh M, 2012. Care Robots, Virtual Virtue, and the Best Possible Life. In Brey P, Briggle A, Spence E, eds., *The Good Life in a Technological Age*. Taylor & Francis Group, 281–292, p. 286.
111. Coeckelbergh M, 2021. How to Use Virtue Ethics for Thinking About the Moral Standing of Social Robots. *International Journal of Social Robotics* 13: 31–40.
112. Jecker NS, Ko A, 2022. The Unique and Practical Advantages of Applying a Capability Approach to Brain Computer Interface. *Philosophy and Technology* 35: 101. DOI: 10.1007/s13347-022-00597-1.
113. McGuffie K, Newhouse A, 2020. The Radicalization of GPT-3 and Advanced Neural Language Models. Cornell University, Computers and Society, arXiv:2009.06807 [cs.CY]. DOI: 10.48550/arXiv.2009.06807.

Chapter 6

1. Gyekye K, 1995. *An Essay on African Philosophical Thought, revised ed.* Temple University Press, p. 143.
2. Wiredu K, 1996. *Cultural Universals and Particulars: An African Perspective.* Indiana University Press, p. 129.

3. Wiredu K, 1996. *Cultural Universals and Particulars: An African Perspective*. Indiana University Press, p. 160.
4. Mbiti JS, 2015. *Introduction to African Religion, 2nd ed*. Waveland Press, Inc., p. 44.
5. Tangwa GB, 2010. African Bioethics and Sustainable Development. In Tangwa GB, *Elements of African Bioethics in a Western Frame*. Langaa Research & Publishing CIG, 39–48, p. 48. Project MUSE at muse.jhu/book/16848.
6. Tangwa GB, 2010. African Bioethics and Sustainable Development. In Tangwa GB, *Elements of African Bioethics in a Western Frame*. Langaa Research & Publishing CIG, 39–48, p. 41. Project MUSE at muse.jhu/book/16848.
7. Tangwa GB, 2000. The Traditional African Perception of a Person. *Hastings Center Report* 30(5): 39–43, p 43. DOI: 10.2307/3527887.
8. Behrens K, 2010. Exploring African Holism with Respect to the Environment. *Environmental Values* 19(4): 465–484. DOI: 10.3197/096327110X531561.
9. Behrens K, 2010. Exploring African Holism with Respect to the Environment. *Environmental Values* 19(4): 465–484, p. 474. DOI: 10.3197/096327110X531561.
10. Behrens K, 2010. Exploring African Holism with Respect to the Environment. *Environmental Values* 19(4): 465–484, p. 476. DOI: 10.3197/096327110X531561.
11. Behrens KG, 2014. African Relational Environmentalism and Moral Considerability. *Environmental Ethics* 36(1): 63–82, p. 75. DOI: 10.5840/enviroethics20143615.
12. Behrens KG, 2014. African Relational Environmentalism and Moral Considerability. *Environmental Ethics* 36(1): 63–82, p. 75. DOI: 10.5840/enviroethics20143615.
13. Behrens KG, 2014. African Relational Environmentalism and Moral Considerability. *Environmental Ethics* 36(1): 63–82, p. 75. DOI: 10.5840/enviroethics20143615.
14. Behrens K, 2010. Exploring African Holism with Respect to the Environment. *Environmental Values* 19(4): 465–484, p. 476, emphasis added. DOI: 10.3197/096327110X531561.
15. Behrens KG, 2014 . African Relational Environmentalism and Moral Considerability. *Environmental Ethics* 36(1): 63–82, p. 79. DOI: 10.5840/enviroethics20143615.
16. Molefe M, 2020. *African Personhood and Applied Ethics*. Published on behalf of the African Humanities Program by NISC (Pty) Ltd, 75–91, p. 90.
17. Molefe M, 2020. *African Personhood and Applied Ethics*. Published on behalf of the African Humanities Program by NISC (Pty) Ltd., Kindle location 2314.
18. Molefe M, 2020. *African Personhood and Applied Ethics*. Published on behalf of the African Humanities Program by NISC (Pty) Ltd., Kindle location 2314.
19. Metz T, 2022. *A Relational Moral Theory*. Oxford University Press, pp. 160–161.
20. Metz T, 2022. *A Relational Moral Theory*. Oxford University Press, p. 167.
21. Metz T, 2022. *A Relational Moral Theory*. Oxford University Press, p. 147.
22. Behrens K, 2010. Exploring African Holism with Respect to the Environment. *Environmental Values* 19(4): 465–484, p. 478. DOI: 10.3197/096327110X531561.
23. Molefe M, 2020. *African Personhood and Applied Ethics*. Published on behalf of the African Humanities Program by NISC (Pty) Ltd, 75–91, p. 77.
24. Clark SR, 2012. Animals in Classical and Late Antique Philosophy. In Beauchamp TL, Frey RG, eds., *The Oxford Handbook of Animal Ethics*. Oxford University Press: 36–60.
25. Singer P, 2015 (1975). *Animal Liberation*. Open Road Media, p. 142.
26. Aristotle 2007 (~ fourth century BCE). *On the Motion of Animals*, Farquharson ASL, transl. In *Aristotle: The Complete Works*. University of Adelaide, eBooks@Adelaide: 1950–1966, p. 1959.

27. Nussbaum MC, Putnam H, 1992. Changing Aristotle's Mind. In Nussbaum MC, Putnam H, eds., *Essays on Aristotle's de Anima*. Oxford University Press, 27–56, p. 41.
28. Newmyer ST, 2017. *The Animal and the Human in Ancient and Modern Thought*. Taylor and Francis, p. 48.
29. Aristotle, 2007 (~350 BCE). On the Parts of Animals, Ogle W, transl. In *Aristotle: The Complete Works*. University of Adelaide, eBooks@Adelaide: 1776–1948, p. 1795.
30. Newmyer ST, 2017. *The Animal and the Human in Ancient and Modern Thought*. Taylor and Francis, pp. 53–54.
31. Newmyer ST, 2017. *The Animal and the Human in Ancient and Modern Thought*. Taylor and Francis, p. 55.
32. Desmond W, 2014. A Life According to Nature. In Desmond W, *Cynics*. Taylor & Francis Group, 132–161, p. 135.
33. Gill C, 2013. Cynicism and Stoicism. In Crisp R, ed., *Oxford Handbook of the History of Ethics*. Oxford University Press, 93–111, p. 93.
34. Niederbacher B, 2014. The Human Soul: Augustine's Case for Soul-Body Dualism. In Meconi DV, Stump E, eds., *The Cambridge Companion to Augustine*, 2nd ed., 125–141, pp. 125–126.
35. Niederbacher B, 2014. The Human Soul: Augustine's Case for Soul-Body Dualism. In Meconi DV, Stump E, eds., *The Cambridge Companion to Augustine*, 2nd ed., 125–141, pp. 125–126.
36. Augustine S, 2021 (419 or 421). *On the Soul and Its Origins*, transl. Wallis RE, Holmes P. In *The Complete Works of Saint Augustine: The City of God, On Christian Doctrine, The Confessions of Saint Augustine, On the Trinity and Others*. Strelbytskyy Multimedia Publishing, 10496–10715, p. 10711.
37. Tellkamp JA, 2012. Vis Aestimativa and Vis Cogitativa in Thomas Aquinas's Commentary on the Sentences. *The Thomist: A Speculative Quarterly Review* 76(4): 611–640, p. 435. DOI: 10.1353/tho.2012.0003.
38. Tellkamp JA, 2012. Vis Aestimativa and Vis Cogitativa in Thomas Aquinas's Commentary on the Sentences. *The Thomist: A Speculative Quarterly Review* 76(4): 611–640, p. 612. DOI: 10.1353/tho.2012.0003.
39. Descartes, 1997 (1637). A Discourse on Method. In Veitch J, transl., *The Project Gutenberg eBook of A Discourse on Method, by René Descartes*, Part V.
40. Harrison P, 1992. Descartes on Animals. *Philosophical Quarterly* 42: 219–227, p. 227.
41. Gibson AB, 2016. *The Philosophy of Descartes*. Routledge.
42. Smith NK, 1963. *New Studies in the Philosophy of Descartes*, 2nd ed. Macmillan.
43. Regan T, Singer P, eds., *Animal Rights and Human Obligations*, 2nd ed. Prentice-Hall.
44. Naragon S, 1990. Kant on Descartes and the Brutes. *Kant-Studien* 81(1): 1–23, p. 3. DOI: 10.1515/kant.1990.81.1.1.
45. Korsgaard CM, 2016. Kant's Formula of Humanity. In Korsgaard CM, *Creating the Kingdom of Ends*. Cambridge University Press, 106–132, p 130.
46. Kant I, 1997 (~1760–1794). Of Duties to Animals and Spirits. In Kant I, *Lectures on Ethics*, Heath P, transl. Cambridge University Press, 210–213, p. 212.
47. Sorabji R, 2018. The One-Dimensionality of Ethical Theories. In Sorabji R, *Animal Minds and Human Morals*, 208–219. Cornell University Press.
48. Hume D, 2011 (1734). Of the Reason of Animals. *In A Treatise of Human Nature*, a public domain book, Amazon Standard Identification Number (ASIN): B004TRB7CU, 123–125, pp. 123–124.

49. Hume D, 2011 (1734). Of the Reason of Animals. In *A Treatise of Human Nature*, a public domain book, Amazon Standard Identification Number (ASIN): BOO4TRB7CU, 123–125, p. 124.
50. Bentham J, 1976 (1780). *Introduction to the Principles of Morals and Legislation*. Oxford University Press and the Liberty Fund, Kindle location 5973–5990.
51. Sorabji R, 2018. The One-Dimensionality of Ethical Theories. In Sorabji R, *Animal Minds and Human Morals*, 208–219. Cornell University Press, p. 210.
52. Singer P, 2015 (1975). *Animal Liberation*. Open Road Media.
53. Regan T, 1975. The Moral Basis of Vegetarianism. *Canadian Journal of Philosophy* 5(2): 181–214. DOI: 10.1080/00455091.1975.10716107.
54. Regan T, 1975. The Moral Basis of Vegetarianism. *Canadian Journal of Philosophy* 5(2): 181–214, p. 210. DOI: 10.1080/00455091.1975.10716107.
55. Perri AR, Feueborn TR, Frantz LAF, et al., 2020. Dog Domestication and the Dual Dispersal of People and Dogs into the Americas. *Proceedings of the National Academies of Sciences* (PNAS) 118(6): e2010083118. DOI: 10.1073/pnas.2010083118.
56. Gronewold N, 2020 (January 31). 'Unprecedented' Locust Invasion Approaches Full-Blown Crisis. *Scientific American*. https://www.scientificamerican.com/article/unprecedented-locust-invasion-approaches-full-blown-crisis/.
57. Cressman K, 2020 (January 31). Quoted in Gronewold N, 'Unprecedented' Locust Invasion Approaches Full-Blown Crisis. *Scientific American*. https://www.scientificamerican.com/article/unprecedented-locust-invasion-approaches-full-blown-crisis/.
58. Salih AAM, Baraibar M, Mwangi KK, Artin G, 2020. Climate Change and Locust Outbreak in East Africa. Nature Climate Change 10: 584–585. DOI: 10.1038/s41558-020-0835-8.
59. Nussbaum MC, 2006. Beyond Compassion and Humanity. In Nussbaum MC, *Frontiers of Justice*. Harvard University Press, 325–407.
60. Jecker NS, Forthcoming. Ubuntu Ethics and Climate Change: Standing in Solidarity with Future People. In Chitando E, Okyere-Manu B, Chirongoma S, Dube M, eds., *The Palgrave Handbook of Ubuntu, Inequality and Sustainable Development*. Springer Nature.
61. Eze MO, 2017. Humanitatis-Eco (Eco Humanism): An African Environmental Theory. In Afolayan A, Falola T, eds., *The Palgrave Handbook of African Philosophy*. Palgrave Macmillan, Kindle locations 15927, 15932.
62. Eze MO, 2017. Humanitatis-Eco (Eco Humanism): An African Environmental Theory. In Afolayan A, Falola T, eds., *The Palgrave Handbook of African Philosophy*. Palgrave Macmillan, Kindle location 16041.
63. Eze MO, 2017. Humanitatis-Eco (Eco Humanism): An African Environmental Theory. In Afolayan A, Falola T, eds., *The Palgrave Handbook of African Philosophy*. Palgrave Macmillan, Kindle location 16048.
64. Tangwa GB, 2010. African Bioethics and Sustainable Development. In Tangwa GB, *Elements of African Bioethics in a Western Frame*. Research and Publishing CIG, 39–48. Project MUSE at muse.jhu/book/16848.
65. Tangwa GB, 1996. Bioethics: An African Perspective. *Bioethics* 10(3): 183–200. DOI: 10.1007/s10892-015-9209-2.
66. Tangwa GB, 2019. *African Perspectives on Some Contemporary Bioethics Problems*. Cambridge Scholars Publishing. ADOBE DIGITAL.
67. Tangwa GB, 2000. The Traditional African Perception of a Person. *Hastings Center Report* 30(5): 39–43. DOI: 10.2307/3527887.
68. Burnett GW, wa Kang'ethe K, 1994. Wilderness and the Bantu Mind. *Environmental Ethics* 16(2): 145–160, p. 157. DOI: 10.5840/enviroethics199416229.

69. Murove MF, 2007. The Shona Ethics of *Ukama* with Reference to the Immortality of Values. *Mankind Quarterly* 48: 179–189. DOI: 10.46469/mq.2007.48.2.4.
70. Burnett GW, wa Kang'ethe K, 1994. Wilderness and the Bantu Mind. *Environmental Ethics* 16(2): 145–160, p. 156. DOI: 10.5840/enviroethics199416229.
71. Tempels P, 2010. *Bantu Philosophy*, transl. King C. HBC Publishing.
72. Dzobo NK, 2010. Values in a Changing Society: Man, Ancestors, and God. In Wiredu K, Gyekye K, eds., *Person and Community: Ghanaian Philosophical Studies, I*. Washington, DC, Council for Research in Values and Philosophy: 223–240. https://www.crvp.org/publications/Series-II/Series02-1.html..
73. Kasenene P, 1994. Ethics in African Theology. In Villa-Vicencio C, de Gruchy J, eds., *Doing Ethics in Context: South African Perspectives*. Orbis Books, 138–147, pp. 140ff.
74. Molefe M, 2015. A Rejection of Humanism in African Moral Tradition. *Theoria*, 62: 59–77.
75. Tangwa G, 1996. Bioethics: An African Perspective. *Bioethics* 10(3): 183–200. DOI: 10.1007/s10892-015-9209-2.
76. Tangwa G, 2004. Some African Reflections on Biomedical and Environmental Ethics. In Wiredu K, ed., *A Companion to African Philosophy*. Blackwell Publishing Ltd, Kindle locations 6430–6565.
77. Okafor SO, 1982. Bantu Philosophy: Placide Tempels Revisited. *Journal of Religion in Africa* 13(2): 83–100, p. 84. DOI: 10.2307/1581204.
78. Tempels P, 2010. *Bantu Philosophy*, transl. King C. HBC Publishing, p. 52.
79. Ekwealo C, 2013. African Environmental Values Expressed through Proverbs. In Appleton J, ed., *Values in Sustainable Development*. Taylor & Francis, 193–203, p. 268.
80. Senghor LL, 2016. Negritude: A Humanism of the Twentieth Century. In Hord FL, Lee JS, eds., *I am Because We Are: Readings in Africana Philosophy*, 2nd ed. University of Massachusetts Press, 55–64. p. 59.
81. Chemhuru M, 2019. The Moral Status of Nature: An African Understanding. In Chemhuru M, ed., *African Environmental Ethics*. Springer Nature, 64–95, p. 86.
82. Metz T, 2022. *A Relational Moral Theory*. Oxford University Press, p. 179.
83. Tempels P, 2010. *Bantu Philosophy*, transl. King C. HBC Publishing, p. 60.
84. Dzobo N, 1992. Values in a Changing Society: Man, Ancestors, and God. In Wiredu K, Gyekye K, eds., *Person and Community*. Ghanaian Philosophical Studies, I, Washington, DC, Council for Research in Values and Philosophy: 223–240, p. 229. https://www.crvp.org/publications/Series-II/Series02-1.html.
85. Kasenene P, 1994. Ethics in African Theology. In Villa-Vicencio C, de Gruchy J, eds., *Doing Ethics in Context: South African Perspectives*. Orbis Books, 138–147, p. 140.
86. Dzobo N, 1992. Values in a Changing Society: Man, Ancestors, and God. In Wiredu K, Gyekye K, eds., *Person and Community*. Ghanaian Philosophical Studies, I, Washington, DC, Council for Research in Values and Philosophy: 223–240, p. 229. https://www.crvp.org/publications/Series-II/Series02-1.html.
87. Tangwa G, 1996. Bioethics: An African Perspective. *Bioethics* 10(3): 183–200, p. 189. DOI: 10.1007/s10892-015-9209-2.
88. Tangwa G, 1996. Bioethics: An African Perspective. *Bioethics* 10(3): 183–200, p. 190. DOI: 10.1007/s10892-015-9209-2.
89. McClure MT, 1934. The Greek Conception of Nature. *Philosophical Review* 43(2): 109–124, p. 112. DOI: 10.2307/2179890.
90. McClure MT, 1934. The Greek Conception of Nature. *Philosophical Review* 43(2): 109–124, pp. 112–113. DOI: 10.2307/2179890.

91. Hesiod, 1988 (700 BCE). *Theogony*. In West ML, transl., *Hesiod: Theogony and Works and Days*. Oxford University Press, p. 6.
92. Amundsen DW, 1996. Tatian's 'Rejection' of Medicine in the Second Century. In Amundsen DW, *Medicine, Society, and Faith in the Ancient and Medieval Worlds*. Johns Hopkins University Press, 158–174, p. 169.
93. Hughes JD, 2014. Concepts of the Natural World. In Hughes JD, *Environmental Problems of the Greeks and Romans, 2nd ed*. Johns Hopkins University Press, 43–67.
94. Thommen L, 2009. *An Environmental History of Ancient Greece and Rome*, transl. Hill P. Cambridge University Press.
95. Fustel DC, 2000 (1874). *The Ancient City: A Study on the Religion, Law, and Institutions of Ancient Greece and Rome*, Small W, transl. Boston: Lee and Shepard, electronic text by the University of Michigan, Ann Arbor, p. 160.
96. Sorajbi R, 2018. Plants and Animals. In Sorabji R, *Animal Minds and Human Morals*. Cornell University Press, 97–104.
97. Kingsley K, Parry S, Parry R, 2020. Empedocles. In Zalta EN, ed., *Stanford Encyclopedia of Philosophy*. https://plato.stanford.edu/archives/sum2020/entries/empedocles/.
98. Carpenter AD, 2008. Embodying Intelligence: Animals and Us in Plato's Timaeus. In Carpenter A, Dillon J, Zovko J, eds., *Platonism, and Forms of Intelligence*, 39–58.
99. Carpenter AD, 2010. Embodied Intelligent? Souls: Plants in Plato's' 'Timaeus.' *Phronesis* 55(4): 281–303. DOI: 10.1163/156852810X523897.
100. Aristotle, 2007 (~fourth century BCE). *The History of Animals*, Thompson DW, transl. In *Aristotle: The Complete Works*. University of Adelaide, eBooks@Adelaide, 1376–1775, p. 1656.
101. Aristotle, 2007 (~fourth century BCE) *Animal Physics*, Thompson DW, transl. In *Aristotle: The Complete Works*. University of Adelaide, eBooks@Adelaide, 1375–2190, p. 1656.
102. Sorajbi R, 2018. Plants and Animals. In Sorabji R, *Animal Minds and Human Morals*. Cornell University Press, 97–104, p. 98.
103. McClure MT, 1934. The Greek Conception of Nature. *Philosophical Review* 43(2): 109–124, p. 115. DOI: 10.2307/2179890.
104. Singer P, 2015 (1975). *Animal Liberation*. Open Road Media, p. 143.
105. Aristotle, 2007 (350 BCE). *Politics*, Jowett B., transl. In *Aristotle: The Complete Works*. University of Adelaide, eBooks@Adelaide, 2785–3045, p. 2798.
106. Aristotle, 2007 (350 BCE). *Politics*, Jowett B., transl. In *Aristotle: The Complete Works*. University of Adelaide, eBooks@Adelaide, 2785–3045, p. 2799.
107. *The Holy Bible*, Douay-Rheims Version. Book of Genesis, Book 1, lines 26–27, p. 4. http://triggs.djvu.org/djvu-editions.com/BIBLES/DRV/Download.pdf.
108. White L, 1967. The Historical Roots of Our Ecological Crisis. *Science* 155(3676): 1203–1207, p. 1205. DOI: 10.1126/science.155.3767.1203.
109. Bacon F, 2015 (1620). *The New Organon*. Centaur Editions, p. 57.
110. Jecker NS, 1991. Knowing When to Stop: The Limits of Medicine. *Hastings Center Report* 21(3): 5–8, p. 6. Stable URL: http://www.jstor.org/stable/3563315.
111. Merchant C, 2020. *The Death of Nature: Women, Ecology, and the Scientific Revolution*, 40th Anniversary Edition. Harper One, p. 2.
112. Merchant C, 2020. *The Death of Nature: Women, Ecology, and the Scientific Revolution*, 40th Anniversary Edition. Harper One, p. 127.
113. Merchant C, 2020. *The Death of Nature: Women, Ecology, and the Scientific Revolution*, 40th Anniversary Edition. Harper One, p. 193.

114. Midgley M, 2007. Introduction: The Not-So-Simple Dearth. In Midgley M, ed., *Earthly Realism: The Meaning of Gaia*. Societas Imprint Academic, Kindle location 233.
115. United Nations (n.d.). What Is Climate Change? https://www.un.org/en/climatechange/what-is-climate-change.
116. Brennan A, Lo NYS, 2022. Environmental Ethics. In Zalta EN, ed., *Stanford Encyclopedia of Philosophy*. https://plato.stanford.edu/archives/sum2022/entries/ethics-environmental/.
117. Leopold A, 2020 (1949). *A Sand County Almanac*. Oxford University Press, p. 211.
118. Leopold A, 2020 (1949). *A Sand County Almanac*. Oxford University Press, p. 191.
119. Callicott JB, 1980. Animal Liberation: A Triangular Affair. *Environmental Ethics* 2(1): 311–338. DOI: 10.5840/enviroethics19802424.
120. Rolston H, 1975. Is There an Ecological Ethic? *Ethics* 85: 93–109. DOI: 10.1086/291944.
121. Stone CD, 2010. *Should Trees Have Standing? 3rd ed.* Oxford University Press.
122. Næss A, 1973. The Shallow and the Deep, Long-Range Ecology Movement. *Inquiry* 16(1): 95–100. DOI: 10.1080/00201747308601682.
123. Næss A, 1985. The World of Concrete Contents. *Inquiry* 28(1–4): 417–428, p. 427. DOI: 10.1080/00201748508602059
124. van Jaarsveld J, 2019. Expanding Nussbaum's Eighth Capability Using African Environmental Ethics. In Chemhru M, ed., *African Environmental Ethics*. Springer International Publishing, 369–395, p. 382.
125. Ridge M, 2017. Reasons for Action: Agent-Neutral vs. Agent-Relative. In Zalta EN, ed., *Stanford Encyclopedia of Philosophy*. https://plato.stanford.edu/archives/fall2017/entries/reasons-agent/.
126. McKeever S, Ridge M, 2006. *Principled Ethics*. Oxford University Press.
127. Ridge M, 2017. Reasons for Action: Agent Neutral vs. Agent Relative. In Zalta EN, ed., *Stanford Encyclopedia of Philosophy*. https://plato.stanford.edu/archives/fall2017/entries/reasons-agent/.

Chapter 7

1. Kaufman JA, Lenartz A, Floyd TE, 2022. An Interplanetary Land Ethics. *Sustainability* 15(1): 50–57. DOI: 10.1089/scc.2021.0068.
2. Parthemore J, 2013. The 'Final Frontier' as Metaphor of Mind. In Dunér D, Persson E, Holmberg G, eds., *The History and Philosophy of Astrobiology: Perspectives on Extraterrestrial Life and the Human Mind*. Cambridge University Press, 67–92.
3. Opata DU, 2008. Cultural Astronomy in the Lore and Literature of Africa. In Holbrook J, Medupe RT, Urama JO, eds., *African Cultural Astronomy: Current Achaeoastronomy and Ethnoastronomy Research in Africa*. Springer, 217–229, p. 217. DOI: 10.1007/978-1-4020-6639-9_16.
4. Billings L, 2020. The Social Construction of the Biosphere and the Expansion of the Concept into Outer Space. In Smith KC, Mariscal C, eds., *Social and Conceptual Issues in Astrobiology*. Oxford University Press, 239–261.
5. Billings L, 2020. The Social Construction of the Biosphere and the Expansion of the Concept into Outer Space. In Smith KC, Mariscal C, eds., *Social and Conceptual Issues in Astrobiology*. Oxford University Press, 239–261, pp. 240–241.
6. National Academies of Science, Engineering, and Medicine, 2007. *Limits of Organic Life in Planetary Science*. National Academies Press, p. 31. https://nap.nationalacademies.org/download/11919.
7. Weir A, 2021. *Project Hail Mary*. Ballantine Books, an imprint of Random House.

8. Snedegar K, 2016. Astronomy in Sub-Saharan Africa. In Selin H, ed., *Encyclopaedia of the History of Science, Technology, and Medicine in Non-Western Cultures*. Springer, 742–752. DOI: 10.1007/978-94-007-7747-7.
9. Library of Congress, 2003. *Ancient Manuscripts from the Desert Libraries of Timbuktu*. https://www.loc.gov/exhibits/mali/.
10. Chami FA, 2008. Evidence of Ancient African Beliefs in Celestial Bodies. In Holbrook J, Medupe RT, Urama JO, eds., *African Cultural Astronomy: Current Archaeoastronomy and Ethnoastronomy Research in Africa*. Springer, 121–130. DOI: 10.1007/978-1-4020-6639-9_10.
11. Chukwuezi B, 2008. Relationship between Human Destiny and the Cosmic Forces. In Holbrook J, Medupe RT, Urama JO, eds., *African Cultural Astronomy: Current Archaeoastronomy and Ethnoastronomy Research in Africa*. Springer, 209–215. DOI: 10.1007/978-1-4020-6639-9_15.
12. Opata CU, 2008. Cultural Astronomy in the Lore and Literature of Africa. In Holbrook J, Medupe RT, Urama JO, eds., *African Cultural Astronomy: Current Archaeoastronomy and Ethnoastronomy Research in Africa*. Springer, 217–229, p. 218. DOI: 10.1007/978-1-4020-6639-9_16.
13. Achebe C, 1964. *Anthills of the Savannah*. Heinemann Educational Books.
14. Liyong TL, 1976. The Sun Is My God and I Shall Worship Him When He Rises, Reaches His Zenith, and Reposes for the Night. In Liyong TL, *Ballads of UnderDevelopment*. East Africa Literature Bureau: 83-94.
15. Snedegar K, 2016. Astronomy in Sub-Saharan Africa. In Selin H, ed., *Encyclopaedia of the History of Science, Technology, and Medicine in Non-Western Cultures*. Springer, 742–752, pp. 744, 747. DOI: 10.1007/978-94-007-7747-7.
16. Behrens K, 2010. Exploring African Holism with Respect to the Environment. *Environmental Values* 19(4): 465–484, p. 476. DOI: 10.3197/096327110X531561.
17. Molefe M, 2020. *African Personhood and Applied Ethics*. Published on behalf of the African Humanities Program by NISC (Pty) Ltd.
18. Metz T, 2022. *A Relational Moral Theory*. Oxford University Press.
19. Gyekye K, 1995. *An Essay on African Philosophical Thought*, rev. ed. Temple University Press, p. 143.
20. Mbiti JS, 2015. *Introduction to African Religion*, 2nd ed. Waveland Press, Inc., p. 44.
21. Behrens KG, 2014. An African Relational Environmentalism and Moral Considerability. *Environmental Ethics* 36(1): 63–82, p. 65. DOI: 10.5840/enviroethics20143615.
22. Menkiti IA, 1984. Person and Community in African Traditional Thought. In Wright RA, ed., *African Philosophy: An Introduction*, 3rd ed. University Press of America, 171–181, p. 173.
23. Gyekye K, 2011. African Ethics. In Zalta EN, ed., *Stanford Encyclopedia of Philosophy*. https://plato.stanford.edu/archives/fall2011/entries/african-ethics/.
24. Molefe M, 2020. *African Personhood and Applied Ethics*. Published on behalf of the African Humanities Program by NISC (Pty) Ltd., p. 77.
25. Hutchinson L, 2021 (May 28). Science Is Better with Friends—Andy Weir's Project Hail Mary and the Soft, Squish Science of Language. *ARS Technica*. https://arstechnica.com/gaming/2021/05/andy-weirs-project-hail-mary-and-the-soft-squishy-science-of-language/.
26. Metz T, 2022. *A Relational Moral Theory*. Oxford University Press.
27. Behrens K, 2010. Exploring African Holism with Respect to the Environment. *Environmental Values* 19(4): 465–484, p. 478. DOI: 10.3197/096327110X531561.
28. Lindberg DC, 2007. *The Beginnings of Western Science*, 2nd ed. University of Chicago Press, p. 5.
29. Wright EJ, 2002. *The Early History of Heaven*. Oxford University Press, p. 110.

30. Hesiod, 1988 (700 BCE). *Theogony*. In West ML, transl., *Hesiod: Theogony and Works and Days*. Oxford University Press, pp. 6–7.
31. Vlastos G, 1952. Theology and Philosophy in Early Greek Thought. *Philosophical Quarterly* 2(7): 97–123, p. 99.
32. Lindberg, DC, 2007. *The Beginnings of Western Science*, 2nd ed. University of Chicago Press, p. 27.
33. US Library of Congress (n.d.). Ancient Greek Astronomy and Cosmology. In *Finding Our Place in the Cosmos: From Galileo to Sagan and Beyond*. https://www.loc.gov/collections/finding-our-place-in-the-cosmos-with-carl-sagan/articles-and-essays/modeling-the-cosmos/ancient-greek-astronomy-and-cosmology.
34. US Library of Congress (n.d.). Ancient Greek Astronomy and Cosmology. In *Finding Our Place in the Cosmos: From Galileo to Sagan and Beyond*. https://www.loc.gov/collections/finding-our-place-in-the-cosmos-with-carl-sagan/articles-and-essays/modeling-the-cosmos/ancient-greek-astronomy-and-cosmology.
35. National Air and Space Museum. Exploring the Planets: Ancient Times and the Greeks. https://airandspace.si.edu/exhibitions/exploring-the-planets/online/discovery/greeks.cfm.
36. Berryman S, 2016. Democritus. In Zalta EN, ed., *Stanford Encyclopedia of Philosophy*. https://plato.stanford.edu/archives/win2016/entries/democritus/.
37. Crowe MJ, 1999. *The Extraterrestrial Life Debate: 1750–1900*. Dover Publications, Inc., p 3, emphasis added.
38. Lovejoy AO, 2001. *The Great Chain of Being*. Harvard University Press, p. 52.
39. Plato 2023 (360 BCE). *Timaeus*. In *Plato: The Complete Works*. Pandora's Box, p. 1214.
40. Aristotle, 2023 (~350 BCE). *Metaphysics*. In *Aristotle: The Complete Works*. ATN Classics, Kindle location 12114.
41. Crowe M, 2008. The Debate in Antiquity. In Crowe M, ed., *Extraterrestrial Life Debate: Antiquity to 1915: A Source Book*. University of Notre Dame Press, 3–13.
42. Crowe M, Dowd F, 2013. The Extraterrestrial Life Debate from Antiquity to 1900. In Vakoch DA, ed., *Advances in Astrobiology and Biogeophysics, Astrobiology, History, and Society*. Springer-Verlag, 2–56, p. 4.
43. Oxford University Press, 2023. n., angel. *OED Online*. Oxford University Press.
44. Adler M, 1982. *Angels and Us*. Macmillan Publishing Co., Inc., Kindle location 209.
45. Crowe M, Dowd F, 2013. The Extraterrestrial Life Debate from Antiquity to 1900. In Vakoch DA, ed., *Advances in Astrobiology and Biogeophysics, Astrobiology, History, and Society*. Springer-Verlag Berlin Heidelberg, 2–56, p. 4.
46. Danielson D, 2013. Early Modern ET, Reflexive Telescopics, and Their Relevance Today. In Vakoch DA, ed., *Advances in Astrobiology and Biogeophysics, Astrobiology, History, and Society*. Springer-Verlag, 57–72, p. 57.
47. Knox D, 2019. Giordano Bruno. In Zalta EN, *Stanford Encyclopedia of Philosophy*. https://plato.stanford.edu/archives/sum2019/entries/bruno/.
48. Kepler J, 2008 (1610). *Kepler's Conversation with Galileo's Sidereal Messenger*. Reprinted in Crowe M, ed., *Extraterrestrial Life Debate: Antiquity to 1915: A Source Book*. University of Notre Dame Press, 53–64, pp. 60–61.
49. Pascal B, 2008 (1670). *Pensées*. In Crowe M, ed., *Extraterrestrial Life Debate: Antiquity to 1915: A Source Book*. University of Notre Dame Press, 69–71, p. 71.
50. Pascal B, 2008 (1670). *Pensées*. In Crowe M, ed., *Extraterrestrial Life Debate: Antiquity to 1915: A Source Book*. University of Notre Dame Press, 69–71, p. 71.
51. Kant I, 2008 (1755). *Universal Nature and Theory of the Heavens*. In Johnston I, transl., *Immanuel Kant, Universal Nature and Theory of the Heavens or An Essay*

on the Constitution and the Mechanical Origin of the Entire Structure of the Universe Based on Newtonian Principles. Richer Resources Publications, Kindle locations 1896–1907.
52. Kant I, 2008 (1755). *Universal Nature and Theory of the Heavens*. In Johnston I, transl., Immanuel Kant, *Universal Nature and Theory of the Heavens or An Essay on the Constitution and the Mechanical Origin of the Entire Structure of the Universe Based on Newtonian Principles*. Richer Resources Publications, Kindle location 1907.
53. Kant I, 2008 (1755). *Universal Nature and Theory of the Heavens*. In Johnston I, transl., Immanuel Kant, *Universal Nature and Theory of the Heavens or An Essay on the Constitution and the Mechanical Origin of the Entire Structure of the Universe Based on Newtonian Principles*. Richer Resources Publications, Kindle location 1930.
54. Kant I, 2008 (1755). *Universal Nature and Theory of the Heavens*. In Johnston I, transl., Immanuel Kant, *Universal Nature and Theory of the Heavens or An Essay on the Constitution and the Mechanical Origin of the Entire Structure of the Universe Based on Newtonian Principles*. Richer Resources Publications, Kindle location 1999.
55. Kant I, 1981 (1785). *Grounding for the Metaphysics of Morals*. In Ellington JW, transl., *Grounding for the Metaphysics of Morals*, 3rd ed. Hackett Publishing Company, Inc., p. 394.
56. Williams B, 2008. The Human Prejudice. In Moore AW, Moore AWW, eds., *Philosophy as a Humanistic Discipline*. Princeton University Press, 124–138.
57. Singer P, 2009. Reply to Bernard Williams. In Schafer JA, ed., *Peter Singer under Fire: The Moral Iconoclast Faces His Critics*. Open Court, 97–102, p. 102.
58. Singer P, 2009. Reply to Bernard Williams. In Schafer JA, ed., *Peter Singer under Fire: The Moral Iconoclast Faces His Critics*. Open Court, 97–102, p. 102.
59. Potthast A, 2020. Ethics and Extraterrestrials. In Smith KC, Mariscal C, eds., *Social and Conceptual Issues in Astrobiology*. Oxford University Press, 197–208, p. 200.
60. Williamson J, 1942. Collision Orbit. *Astounding Science-Fiction* July 85/2.
61. Pruchner J, 2007. v., terraform. *Brave New Worlds: The Oxford Dictionary of Science Fiction*. Oxford University Press.
62. O'Callaghan J, 2022 (January 2). NASA's Retiring Top Scientist Says We Can Terraform Mars and Maybe Venus, Too. *New York Times*.
63. McKay CP, 1982. On Terraforming Mars. *Extrapolation* 23(4): 309–314. DOI: 10.3828/extr.1982.23.4.309.
64. Sagan C, 1961. The Planet Venus. *Science* 133: 849–858. DOI: 10.1126/science.133.3456.849.
65. National Aeronautics and Space Administration (NASA), 2018 (July 30). Mars Terraforming Not Possible Using Present-Day Technology. https://www.nasa.gov/press-release/goddard/2018/mars-terraforming.
66. Day C, 2021. Terraforming Mars. *Physics Today* 74(7): 8–8. DOI: 10.1063/PT.3.4781.
67. National Aeronautics and Space Administration (NASA), 2020 (July 21). Cultivating Ideas for Mars. NASA Earth Observatory. https://earthobservatory.nasa.gov/images/147053/cultivating-ideas-for-mars.
68. Vaz E, Penfound E, 2020. Mars Terraforming: A Geographic Information Systems Framework. *Life Sciences in Space Research* 24: 50–63. DOI: 10.1016/j.lssr.2019.12.001.
69. Vaz E, Penfound E, 2020. Mars Terraforming: A Geographic Information Systems Framework. *Life Sciences in Space Research* 24: 50–63. DOI: 10.1016/j.lssr.2019.12.001.

70. Vaz E, Penfound E, 2020. Mars Terraforming: A Geographic Information Systems Framework. *Life Sciences in Space Research* 24: 50–63. DOI: 10.1016/j.lssr.2019.12.001.
71. Robinson KS, 1993. *Red Mars*. Penguin Random House.
72. Sullivan W, 2013. Planetocentric Ethics: Principles for Exploring a Solar System that May Contain Extraterrestrial Microbial Life. In Spitz IC, Stoeger W, eds., *Encountering Life in the Universe: Ethical Foundations and Social Implications of Astrobiology*. University of Arizona Press, 167–177, p. 172.
73. Behrens K, 2010. Exploring African Holism with Respect to the Environment. *Environmental Values* 19(4): 465–484, p. 476, emphasis added. DOI: 10.3197/096327110X531561.
74. Molefe M, 2020. *African Personhood and Applied Ethics*. Published on behalf of the African Humanities Program by NISC (Pty) Ltd., p. 90.
75. Metz T, 2022. *A Relational Moral Theory*. Oxford University Press, pp. 160–161.
76. Behrens K, 2014. An African Relational Environmentalism and Moral Considerability. *Environmental Ethics* 36(1): 63–82. DOI: 10.5840/enviroethics20143615.
77. White L, 1967. The Historical Roots of Our Ecological Crisis. *Science* 155: 1203–1207, p. 1205. DOI: 10.1126/science.155.3767.1203.
78. Callicott, JB 1999. Genesis and John Muir. In Callicott JB, *Beyond the Land Ethic: More Essays in Environmental Philosophy*. State University of New York Press, 187–219.
79. Newmyer ST, 2017. *The Animal and the Human in Ancient and Modern Thought*. Taylor and Francis, p. 48.
80. Aristotle, 2007 (~350 BCE). On the Parts of Animals, Ogle W, transl. In Thomas S, ed., *Aristotle: The Complete Works*. University of Adelaide, eBooks@Adelaide, 1776–1948, p. 1795.
81. Otto E, 2003. Kim Stanley Robinson's Mars Leopoldian Land Ethics. *Utopian Studies* 14(2): 118–135, p. 120.
82. Atuire CA, 2020. Philosophical Underpinnings of an African Legal System: Bulsa. *Nigerian Journal of African Law* 2: 62–78.
83. Otto E, 2003. Kim Stanley Robinson's Mars Leopoldian Land Ethics. *Utopian Studies* 14(2): 118–135, p. 120.
84. Robinson KS, 1993. *Red Mars*. Penguin Random House, p. 103.
85. Callicott JB, 2015. How Ecological Collectives Are Morally Considerable. In Gardiner SM, Thompson A, eds., *The Oxford Handbook of Environmental Ethics*. Oxford University Press, 113–124.
86. Singer P, 2015 (1975). *Animal Liberation*. Open Road Media, p. 23.
87. Rolston, H, 1988. *Environmental Ethics*. Temple University Press, p. 193.
88. Rolston, H, 1988. *Environmental Ethics*. Temple University Press, p. 195.
89. Rolston, H, 1988. *Environmental Ethics*. Temple University Press, pp. 196–197.
90. Callicott, JB, 1999. Intrinsic Value in Nature. In Callicott JB, *Beyond the Land Ethic: More Essays in Environmental Philosophy*. State University of New York Press, 239–261, p. 246.
91. Rolston H, 2016. The Anthropocene! Beyond the Natural? In Gardiner SM, Thompson A, eds., *The Oxford Handbook of Environmental Ethics*. Oxford University Press, 62–74, pp. 64, 65.
92. Rolston IH, 2011. Species and Biodiversity. In Rolston, IH, *A New Environmental Ethics*. Taylor and Francis Group, 126–157, p. 131.
93. Rolston H, 2014. Terrestrial and Extraterrestrial Altruism. In Vaockh DA, ed., *Extraterrestrial Altruism: Evolution and Ethics in the Cosmos*. Springer-Verlag: 210–222, p. 212.

94. Rolston H, 2014. Terrestrial and Extraterrestrial Altruism. In Vaockh DA, ed., *Extraterrestrial Altruism: Evolution and Ethics in the Cosmos*. Springer-Verlag, 210–222, p. 221.
95. United Nations, Office for Outer Space Affairs, 1967. Treaty on Principles Governing the Activities of States in the Exploration and Use of Outer Space, Including the Moon and Other Celestial Bodies. https://www.unoosa.org/oosa/en/ourwork/spacelaw/treaties/introouterspacetreaty.html.
96. US Congress, 2015. U.S. Commercial Space Launch Competitiveness Act. H.R.2262. https://www.congress.gov/bill/114th-congress/house-bill/2262.
97. Trump White House Archives, 2020 (April 6). Executive Order on Encouraging International Support for the Recovery and Use of Space Resources. https://trumpwhitehouse.archives.gov/presidential-actions/executive-order-encouraging-international-support-recovery-use-space-resources//.
98. Deloitte, n.d. Introducing See Yourself in Space. https://www.youtube.com/watch?v=CjhBkcQR3d8.
99. Mallick S, Rajagopalan RP, 2019. If Space Is the 'Province of Mankind,' Who Owns Its Resources? Observer Research Foundation (ORF) No. 182. https://www.orfonline.org/wp-content/uploads/2019/01/ORF_Occasional_Paper_182_Space_Mining.pdf.
100. National Aeronautics and Space Administration, 2023 (August 23). CoolCosmos: How Many Galaxies Are in the Universe? NASA. https://coolcosmos.ipac.caltech.edu/ask/240-How-many-galaxies-are-in-the-Universe-.

Epilogue

1. Goldin I, Mariathasan M, 2014. *The Butterfly Defect*. Princeton University Press, p. 10.
2. Scheuerman W, 2023. Globalization. In Zalta EN, Nodelman U, eds., *Stanford Encyclopedia of Philosophy*. https://plato.stanford.edu/archives/spr2023/entries/globalization/.
3. Scheuerman W, 2023. Globalization. In Zalta EN, Nodelman U, eds., *Stanford Encyclopedia of Philosophy*. https://plato.stanford.edu/archives/spr2023/entries/globalization/.
4. Heidegger M, 1971. The Thing. In Heidegger M, *Poetry Language and Thought*, Hofstadter A, transl. Harper & Row Publishers. Mod: 163–180, p. 163.
5. Heidegger M, 1971. The Thing. In Heidegger M, *Poetry Language and Thought*, Hofstadter A, transl. Harper & Row Publishers. Mod: 163–180, p. 163.
6. Heidegger M, 1971. The Thing. In Heidegger M, *Poetry Language and Thought*, Hofstadter A, transl. Harper & Row Publishers. Mod: 163–180, p. 163.
7. Heidegger M, 1971. The Thing. In Heidegger M, *Poetry Language and Thought*, Hofstadter A, transl. Harper & Row Publishers. Mod: 163–180, p. 163.
8. Heidegger M, 1971. The Thing. In Heidegger M, *Poetry Language and Thought*, Hofstadter A, transl. Harper & Row Publishers. Mod: 163–180, p. 163, 175.

Bibliography

Abate C, 2023. People and Their Animal Companions: Navigating Moral Constraints in a Harmful Yet Meaningful World. Philosophical Studies 180: 1231–1254. DOI: 10.1007/s11098-022-01852-z.
Abney K, 2011. Robotics, Ethical Theory, and Metaethics. In Lin P, Abney K, Bekey GA, eds., Robot Ethics. MIT Press: 35–52.
Achebe C, 1962. Things Fall Apart. Heinemann.
Achebe C, 1964. Anthills of the Savannah. Heinemann Educational Books.
Ad Hoc Committee of the Harvard Medical School to Examine the Definition of Brain Death, 1968. A Definition of Irreversible Coma. Journal of the American Medical Association 205(6): 337–340. DOI: 10.1001/jama.1968.03140320031009.
Ahiauzu N, 2006. Ubuntu and the Obligation to Obey the Law. Cambrian Law Review 37: 17–36.
Aidoo AA, 1977. Asante Queen Mothers in Government and Politics in the Nineteenth Century. Journal of the Historical Society of Nigeria 9(1): 1–13.
Allmark P, 2001. Death with Dignity. Journal of Medical Ethics 28: 255–257. DOI: 10.1136/jme.28.4.255.
American Veterinary Medical Association, 2008 (July 15). One Health: A New Professional Imperative. American Veterinary Medical Association. https://www.avma.org/resources-tools/reports/one-health-ohitf-final-report-2008.
Amundesn D, 1995. Medicine, Society, and Faith in the Ancient and Medieval World. Johns Hopkins University Press.
Amundsen DW, 1978. The Physician's Obligation to Prolong Life: A Medical Duty without Classical Roots. Hastings Center Report 8(4): 23–30.
Anderson E, 2004. Animal Rights and the Values of Nonhuman Life. In Sunstein C, Nussbaum M, eds., Animal Rights: Current Debates and New Directions. Oxford University Press: 277–298.
Anderson E, Willett C, Meyers D, 2021. Feminist Perspectives on the Self. In Zalta N, ed., Stanford Encyclopedia of Philosophy. https://plato.stanford.edu/archives/fall2021/entries/feminism-self/.
Anderson ES, 1999. What Is the Point of Equality? Ethics 109(2): 287–337. DOI: 10.1086/233897.
Annas J, 2017. Which Variety of Virtue Ethics? In Carr D, Arthur J, Kristjánnson, eds., Varieties of Virtue Ethics. Palgrave Macmillan: 35–51.
Aquinas T, 1947 (1265–1274) Summa Theologica. Fathers of the English Dominican Province, transl., digital edition. http://www.domcentral.org/summa/.
Arcas BA, 2022 (June 19). Artificial Neural Networks Are Making Strides Towards Consciousness, According to Blaise Agüera y Arcas. The Economist.

Aristotle 2000 (~340 BCE). Nicomachean Ethics. In Crisp R, ed. and transl., Nicomachean Ethics. Cambridge University Press. http://catdir.loc.gov/catdir/samples/cam032/99036947.pdf.
Aristotle, 2007 (~ fourth century BCE). On the Motion of Animals, Farquharson ASL, transl. In Aristotle: The Complete Works. University of Adelaide, eBooks@Adelaide: 1950–1966.
Aristotle, 1999 (~340 BCE). Nicomachean Ethics, Ross WD, transl. Batoche Books, Kitchener.
Aristotle, 1999 (350 BCE). Politics, Jowett B, transl. Batoche Books, Kitchener.
Aristotle, 2007 (~350 BCE). Metaphysics. In Aristotle: The Complete Works. University of Adelaide, eBooks@Adelaide: 2192–2526.
Aristotle, 2007 (~350 BCE). On the Parts of Animals, Ogle W, transl. In Aristotle: The Complete Works. University of Adelaide, eBooks@Adelaide: 1776–1948.
Aristotle, 2007 (~fourth century BCE) Animal Physics, Thompson DW, transl. In Aristotle: The Complete Works. University of Adelaide, eBooks@Adelaide: 1375–2190.
Aristotle, 2007 (~fourth century BCE) The History of Animals, Thompson DW, transl. In Aristotle: The Complete Works. University of Adelaide, eBooks@Adelaide: 1376–1775.
Aristotle, 2007 (350 BCE) Politics, Jowett B., transl. In Aristotle: The Complete Works. University of Adelaide, eBooks@Adelaide: 2785–3045.
Aristotle, 2007 (n.d.). Topics, Pickard-Cambridge WA, transl. In Aristotle: The Complete Works. University of Adelaide, eBooks@Adelaide: 320–505.
Aristotle, 2007. Logic (Organon). Edghill EM transl. In Aristotle: The Complete Works. University of Adelaide, eBooks@Adelaide: 6–575.
Aristotle, 2017 (~340 BCE). Nicomachean Ethics, Ross WD, transl. Enhanced Media.
Aristotle. *Rhetoric,* Roberts WR, transl., Dover.
Atuire CA, 2019. Humans, Persons, Personhood and Morality in African Communitarianism: Gyekye Revisited. Nigerian Journal of Philosophy 27: 19–38.
Atuire CA, 2020. Philosophical Underpinnings of an African Legal System: Bulsa. Nigerian Journal of African Law 2: 62–78.
Atuire CA, 2021. African Perspectives of Moral Status. BMJ Medical Humanities 48: 238–245. DOI: 10.1136/medhum-2021-012229.
Atuire CA, Kong C, Dunn M, 2020. Articulating the Sources for an African Normative Framework of Healthcare. Developing World Bioethics 20(4): 216–227. DOI: 10.1111/dewb.12265.
Augustine S, 2021 (430 CE). On the Soul and Its Origins. In Wallis RE, Holmes P., transl., The Complete Works of Saint Augustine: The City of God, On Christian Doctrine, The Confessions of Saint Augustine, On the Trinity and Others. Strelbytskyy Multimedia Publishing: 10496–10715.
Bacon F, 2015 (1620). The New Organon. Centaur Editions.
Barclay L, 2000. Autonomy and the Social Self. In Mackenzie C, Stoljar N, eds., Relational Autonomy: Feminist Perspectives on Autonomy, Agency, and the Social Self. Oxford University Press: 52–71.

Batterman R, 2020. Intertheory Relations in Physics. In Zalta EN, ed., Stanford Encyclopedia of Philosophy. https://plato.stanford.edu/archives/fall2020/entries/physics-interrelate/.

Battistuzzi L, Recchiuto CT, Sgorbissa A, 2021. Ethical Concerns in Rescue Robotics: A Scoping Review. Ethics and Information Technology 23: 863–875. DOI: 10.1007/s10676-021-09603-0.

Becker LC, 2017. A New Stoicism, revised edition. Princeton University Press.

Bedau MA, Humphreys P, 2008. Introduction to Philosophical Perspectives on Emergence. In Bedau MA, Humphreys P, eds., Emergence: Contemporary Readings in Philosophy and Science. MIT Press: 9–18.

Behrens K, 2010. Exploring African Holism with Respect to the Environment. Environmental Values 19(4): 465–484. DOI: 10.3197/096327110X531561.

Behrens K, 2011. Two 'Normative' Conceptions of Personhood. Quest: An African Journal of Philosophy 25(1/2): 103–117.

Behrens K, 2014. An African Relational Environmentalism and Moral Considerability. Environmental Ethics 36(1): 63–82. DOI: 10.5840/enviroethics20143615.

Behrens K, 2014. Toward an African Relational Environmentalism. In Imafidon E, Bewaji JAI, eds., Ontologized Ethics. Lexington Books: 55–72.

Behrens KG, 2017. A Critique of the Principle of the 'Respect for Autonomy,' Grounded in African Thought. Developing World Bioethics 18: 126–134. DOI: 10.1111/dewb.12145.

Belcher WL, 2015. Introduction to the Text. In Belcher WL, Kleiner M, transl., Galawdewos, the Life and Struggles of Our Mother Walatta Petros: A Seventeenth-Century African Biography of an Ethiopian Woman. Princeton University Press: 1–48.

Bell D, 2000. Communitarianism. In Zalta EN, ed., Stanford Encyclopedia of Philosophy. https://plato.stanford.edu/archives/sum2020/entries/communitarianism/.

Bentham J, 1976 (1781). Introduction to the Principles of Morals and Legislation. Oxford University Press and the Liberty Fund.

Berryman S, 2016. Democritus. In Zalta EN, ed., Stanford Encyclopedia of Philosophy. https://plato.stanford.edu/archives/win2016/entries/democritus/.

Bickhard M, 2009. The Interactivist Model. Synthese 166: 547–591. DOI: 10.1007/s11229-008-9375-x.

Bickhard MH, 2012. A Process Ontology for Persons. New Ideas in Psychology 20: 107–109. DOI: 10.1016/j.newideapsych.2009.11.004.

Bickhard MH, 2017. The Emergence of Persons. In Durt C, Fuchs T, Tewes C, eds., Embodiment, Enaction, and Culture: Investigating the Constitution of the Shared World. MIT Press: 201–213.

Billings L, 2020. The Social Construction of the Biosphere and the Expansion of the Concept into Outer Space. In Smith KC, Mariscal C, eds., Social and Conceptual Issues in Astrobiology. Oxford University Press: 239–261, pp. 240–241.

Bird-David N, 1999. 'Animism' Revisited: Personhood, Environment, and Relational Epistemology. Current Anthropology 40 Supp: S67–S91. DOI: 10.1086/20061.

Bittles AH, 2009. The Background and Outcomes of the First-Cousin Marriage Controversy in Great Britain. International Journal of Epidemiology 38: 1453–1458. DOI: 10.1093/ije/dyp313.

Blain-Moraes S, Racine E, Mashour GA, 2018. Consciousness and Personhood in Medical Care. Frontiers in Human Neuroscience 12: 306. DOI: 10.3389/fnhum.2018.00306.

Blay YA, 2017. Asamando. In Encyclopedia Britannica. Encyclopedia Britannica Inc. https://www.britannica.com/topic/Asamando.

Blumenthal-Barby J, 2023. The End of Personhood. American Journal of Bioethics 24(1): 3–12. DOI: 10.1080/15265161.2022.2160515.

Bondeson J, 2001. Buried Alive: The Terrifying History of Our Most Primal Fear. W.W. Norton & Company.

Bouchard CB, 2010. Those of My Blood. University of Pennsylvania Press.

Boxer J, Weddell S, Broomhead D, Hogg C, Johnson S, 2019. Home Pregnancy Tests in the Hands of the Intended User. Journal of Immunoassay and Immunochemistry 40: 642–652. DOI: 10.1080/15321819.2019.1671861.

Brandt R, 1987. The Morality and Rationality of Suicide. In Perlin S., ed., Handbook for the Study of Suicide. Oxford University Press: 61–75.

Brennan A, Lo NYS, 2022. Environmental Ethics. In Zalta EN, ed., Stanford Encyclopedia of Philosophy. https://plato.stanford.edu/archives/sum2022/entries/ethics-environmental/.

Brundage JA, 1987. Law, Sex, and Christian Society in Medieval Europe. University of Chicago Press.

Buber M, 1970. I And Thou. Charles Scriber's Sons.

Bucar EM, 2018. Islamic Virtue Ethics. In Snow NE, ed., The Oxford Handbook of Virtue. Oxford University Press: 206–218.

Burnett GW, wa Kang'ethe K, 1994. Wilderness and the Bantu Mind. Environmental Ethics 16(2): 145–160. DOI: 10.5840/enviroethics199416229.

Butler J, 1999. Gender Trouble: Feminism and the Subversion of Identity. Routledge.

Butler J, 2020. The Force of Nonviolence. Verso.

Calder T, 2020. The Concept of Evil. In Zalta EN, ed., Stanford Encyclopedia of Philosophy. https://plato.stanford.edu/archives/sum2020/entries/concept-evil/.

Callicott JB, 1980. Animal Liberation: A Triangular Affair. Environmental Ethics 2(1): 311–338. DOI: 10.5840/enviroethics19802424.

Callicott JB, 2015. How Ecological Collectives Are Morally Considerable. In Gardiner SM, Thompson A, eds., The Oxford Handbook of Environmental Ethics. Oxford University Press: 113–124.

Callicott, JB 1999. Genesis and John Muir. IN Callicott JB, Beyond the Land Ethic: More Essays in Environmental Philosophy. State University of New York Press: 187–219.

Callicott, JB, 1999. Intrinsic Value in Nature. In Callicott JB, Beyond the Land Ethic: More Essays in Environmental Philosophy. State University of New York Press: 239–261.

Carpenter AD, 2008. Embodying Intelligence: Animals and Us in Plato's Timaeus. In Carpenter A, Dillon J, Zovko J, eds., Platonism, and Forms of Intelligence. De Gruyter Akademie Forschung: 39–58.

Carpenter AD, 2010. Embodied Intelligent? Souls: Plants in Plato's' 'Timaeus.' Phronesis 55(4): 281–303. DOI: 10.1163/156852810X523897.

Chami FA, 2008. Evidence of Ancient African Beliefs in Celestial Bodies. In Holbrook J, Medupe RT, Urama JO, eds., African Cultural Astronomy: Current Archaeoastronomy and Ethnoastronomy Research in Africa. Springer: 121–130. DOI: 10.1007/978-1-4020-6639-9_10.

Chemhuru M, 2019. The Moral Status of Nature: An African Understanding. In Chemhuru M, ed., African Environmental Ethics. Springer Nature: 64–95.

Chilver EM, 1990. Thaumaturgy in Contemporary Traditional Religion: The Case of Nso' in Mid-Century. Journal of Religion in Africa 20(3): 226–240. DOI: 10.2307/1580885.

Christman J, 2020. Autonomy in Moral and Political Philosophy. In Zalta EN, ed., Stanford Encyclopedia of Philosophy. https://plato.stanford.edu/archives/fall2020/entries/autonomy-moral/.

Chukwu AO, 2017. A Bibliographic Report on African Philosophy. In Afolayan A, Falola T, eds, The Palgrave Handbook of African Philosophy. Palgrave Macmillan: 1393–1417.

Chukwuezi B, 2008. The Relationship between Human Destiny and the Cosmic Forces. In Holbrook J, Medupe RT, Urama JO, eds., African Cultural Astronomy: Current Archaeoastronomy and Ethnoastronomy Research in Africa. Springer: 209–215. DOI: 10.1007/978-1-4020-6639-9_15.

Churchland PS, 2014. The Neurobiological Platform for Moral Values. Behaviour 151(2/3): 283–296. DOI:10.1163/1568539X-00003144.

Clark SR, 2012. Animals in Classical and Late Antique Philosophy. In Beauchamp TL, Frey RG, eds., The Oxford Handbook of Animal Ethics. Oxford University Press: 36–60.

Clarke S, Savulescu J, 2022. Rethinking our Assumptions about Moral Status. In Clarke S, Zohny H, Savulescu J, eds., Rethinking Moral Status. Oxford University Press: 1–19.

Clarke S, Zohny H, Savulescu J, eds., 2021. Rethinking Moral Status. Oxford University Press.

Coeckelbergh M, 2010. Robot Rights? Toward a Social-Relational Justification for Moral Consideration. Ethics and Information Technology 12: 209–221. DOI: DOI 10.1007/s10676-010-9235-5.

Coeckelbergh M, 2012. Care Robots, Virtual Virtue, and the Best Possible Life. In Brey P, Briggle A, Spence E, eds., The Good Life in a Technological Age. Taylor & Francis Group: 281–292.

Coeckelbergh M, 2012. Growing Moral Relations: Critique of Moral Status Ascriptions. Palgrave Macmillan.

Coeckelbergh M, 2021. How to Use Virtue Ethics for Thinking about the Moral Standing of Social Robots. International Journal of Social Robotics 13: 31–40. DOI: 10.1007/s12369-020-00707-z.

Coetzee PH, 2003. Morality in African Thought. In Coetzee PH, Roux APJ, eds., The African Philosophy Reader. Taylor & Francis: 623–654.

Cohen J, 2020. Controversial 'Human Challenge' Trials for COVID-19 Vaccines Gain Support. Science 20 July. DOI: 10.1126/science.abd9203.

Collins E, Ghahramani Z, 2021. LaMDA: Our Breakthrough Conversation Technology. https://blog.google/technology/ai/lamda/.
Comaroff JL, Comaroff J, 2001. On Personhood: An Anthropological Perspective from Africa. Social Identities 7(2): 267–283. DOI: 0.1080/13504630120065310.
Cooley D, 2007. A Kantian Moral Duty for the Soon-to-Be Demented to Commit Suicide. American Journal of Bioethics 7: 37–44. DOI: 10.1080/15265160701347478.
Crowe M, 2008. Extraterrestrial Life Debate: Antiquity to 1915: A Source Book. University of Notre Dame Press.
Crowe M, 2008. The Debate in Antiquity. In Crowe M, ed., Extraterrestrial Life Debate: Antiquity to 1915: A Source Book. University of Notre Dame Press: 3–13.
Crowe MJ, 1999. The Extraterrestrial Life Debate: 1750–1900. Dover Publications, Inc.
Crowe MJ, Dowd MF, 2013. The Extraterrestrial Life Debate from Antiquity to 1900. In Vakoch DA, ed., Advances in Astrobiology and Biogeophysics, Astrobiology, History, and Society. Springer-Verlag Berlin Heidelberg: 2–56.
Curtis B, Savulescu J, 2022. Is Google's LaMDA Conscious? A Philosopher's View. The Conversation, 15 June.
Danaher J, 2020. Welcoming Robots into the Moral Circle: A Defence of Ethical Behaviourism. Science and Engineering Ethics 26: 2023–2049. DOI: 10.1007/s11948-019-00119-x.
Daniels N, 1985. Family Responsibility Initiatives and Justice between Age Groups. Law, Medicine and Health Care 13(4): 153–159. DOI: 10.1111/j.1748-720X.1985.tb00911.x.
Danielson D, 2013. Early Modern ET, Reflexive Telescopics, and Their Relevance Today. In Vakoch DA, ed., Advances in Astrobiology and Biogeophysics, Astrobiology, History, and Society. Springer-Verlag: 57–72.
Darwall S, 1977. Two Kinds of Respect. Ethics 88(1): 36–49. DOI: 10.1086/292054.
Darwall S, 2006. The Second Person Standpoint. Harvard University Press.
Davis W, 1988. Passage of Darkness: The Ethnobiology of the Haitian Zombie. University of North Carolina Press.
Day C, 2021. Terraforming Mars. Physics Today 74. DOI: 10.1063/PT.3.4781.
De Grazia D, 2005. Human Identity and Bioethics. Cambridge University Press.
Del Guercio G, 1986. The Secrets of Haiti's Living Dead. Harvard Magazine January–February: 31–37.
Deloitte, n.d. Introducing See Yourself in Space. https://www.youtube.com/watch?v=CjhBkcQR3d8.
Descartes, 1997 (1637). A Discourse on Method. In Veitch J, transl., The Project Gutenberg eBook of A Discourse on Method, by René Descartes.
Desmangles LG, 1992. The Faces of the Gods: Vodou and Roman Catholicism in Haiti. University of North Carolina Press.
Desmond W, 2014. A Life According to Nature. In Desmond W, Cynics. Taylor & Francis Group: 132–161.
Dillon RS, 2016. Respect. In Zalta EN, ed., Stanford Encyclopedia of Philosophy. https://plato.stanford.edu/archives/win2016/entries/respect/.

Dzobo NK, 2010. Values in a Changing Society: Man, Ancestors, and God. In Wiredu K, Gyekye K, eds. Person and Community: Ghanaian Philosophical Studies, I. The Council for Research in Values and Philosophy (Washington, DC): 223–240. https://www.crvp.org/publications/Series-II/Series02-1.html.

Edet MI, 2016. Innocent Onyewuenyi's 'Philosophical Re-Appraisal of the African Belief in Reincarnation.' Filosofia Theoretica 5(1): 76–99. DOI: 10.4314/ft.v5i1.6.

Ekwealo C, 2013. African Environmental Values Expressed through Proverbs. In Appleton J, ed., Values in Sustainable Development. Taylor & Francis: 193–203.

Elder A, 2017. Robot Friends for Autistic Children: Monopoly Money or Counterfeit Currency? In Lin P, Abney K, Jenkins R, eds., Robot Ethics 2.0. Oxford Scholarship Online. DOI: 10.1093/oso/9780190652951.003.0008.

Ellis N, Larsen-Freeman, 2006. Language Emergence: Implications for Applied Linguistics. Introduction to the Special Issue. Applied Linguistics 27: 558–559. DOI: 10.1093/applin/aml028.

Emilsson E, 2022. Porphyry. In Zalta EN, ed., Stanford Encyclopedia of Philosophy. https://plato.stanford.edu/archives/spr2022/entries/porphyry/.

Engelhardt HT, 1975. Defining Death: A Philosophical Problem. American Review of Respiratory Disease 112: 587–590. DOI: 10.1164/arrd.1975.112.5.587.

Ereshefsky M, 2022. Species. In Zalta EN, ed., Stanford Encyclopedia of Philosophy. https://plato.stanford.edu/archives/sum2022/entries/species/.

Escobar A, 2020. Pluriversal Politics. Duke University Press.

Eze MO, 2013. What Is African Communitarianism? South African Journal of Philosophy 27(4): 386–399, p. 396. DOI: 10.4314/sajpem.v27i4.31526.

Eze MO, 2017. Humanitatis-Eco (Eco Humanism): An African Environmental Theory. In Afolayan A, Falola T, eds., The Palgrave Handbook of African Philosophy. Palgrave Macmillan: 1066–1086.

Feinberg J, 1980. The Child's Right to an Open Future. In Aiken W, LaFollette H, eds., Whose Child? Whose Rights? Rowman and Littlefield: 124–153.

Ferrari PF, 2014. The Neuroscience of Social Relations. Behaviour 151 (2/3): 297–131. DOI: 10.1163/1568539X-00003152.

Fischer B, Palmer C, Kasperbauer TJ, 2023. Hybrid Theories, Psychological Plausibility and the Human/Animal Divide. Philosophical Studies 180: 1105–1123. DOI: 10.1007/s11098-021-01743-9.

Flack HE, Pellegrino ED, eds., 1992. African-American Perspectives on Biomedical Ethics. Georgetown University Press.

Flanagan O, Ancell A, Martin S, Steenbergen G, 2014. Empiricism and Normative Ethics: What Do the Biology and the Psychology of Morality Have to Do with Ethics? Behaviour 151(2/3): 209–228, p. 216–217. DOI:10.1163/1568539X-00003142.

Fletcher J, 1976. Four Indicators of Humanhood. Hastings Center Report 4(6): 4–7.

Flikschuh K, 2016. The Arc of Personhood. Journal of the American Philosophical Association 2(3): 437–455. DOI: 10.1164/arrd.1975.112.5.587.

Foot P, 2003. Morality, Action, and Outcome. In Foot P, Moral Dilemmas. Oxford University Press: Kindle locations 1153–1373.

Foster C, Herring J, 2017. Identity, Personhood and the Law. Springer International Publishing.

Fowler C, 2004. The Archaeology of Personhood. Routledge.
Frede D, 2017. Plato's Ethics: An Overview. In Zalta EN, ed., Stanford Encyclopedia of Philosophy. Stanford University Press. https://plato.stanford.edu/archives/win2017/entries/plato-ethics/.
Frow J, 2020. Personhood. Oxford Handbook of Law and Humanities. Oxford University Press: 273–288.
Fustel DC, 2000 (1874). The Ancient City: A Study on the Religion, Law, and Institutions of Ancient Greece and Rome, Small W, transl. Boston, Lee and Shepard, electronic text by the University of Michigan, Ann Arbor.
Gade CBN, 2011. The Historical Development of the Written Discourses on Ubuntu. South African Journal of Philosophy 30(3): 303–329. DOI: 10.4314/sajpem.v30i3.69578.
Gallois A, 2016. Identity over Time. In Zalta EN, ed., Stanford Encyclopedia of Philosophy. https://plato.stanford.edu/archives/win2016/entries/identity-time/.
Gardiner D, Shemie S, Manara A, Opdam H, 2012. International Perspective on the Diagnosis of Death. British Journal of Anaesthesia 108(S1). DOI: 10.1093/bja/aer397.
Gbadegesin G, 2002. Èniyàn: The Yoruba Concept of a Person. In Coetzee PH, Roux APJ, Philosophy from Africa. Oxford University Press: 175–218.
Gbadegesin S, 1991. African Philosophy: Traditional Yoruba Philosophy and Contemporary African Realities. Peter Lang
Gbadegesin S, 1993. Bioethics and Culture: An African Perspective. Bioethics 7(2/3): 257–262. DOI: 10.1111/j.1467-8519.1993.tb00292.x.
Gibert M, Martin D, 2021. In Search of the Moral Status of AI. AI & Society 37(10): 319–330. DOI: 10.1007/s00146-021-01179-z.
Gibson AB, 2016. The Philosophy of Descartes. Routledge.
Gill C, 2013. Cynicism and Stoicism. In Crisp R, ed., Oxford Handbook of the History of Ethics. Oxford University Press: 93–111.
Goh EZ, Ali T, 2022. Robotic Surgery: An Evolution in Practice. Journal of Surgical Protocols and Research Methodologies 2022(1). DOI: 10.1093/jsprm/snac003.
Goldin I, Mariathasan M, 2014. The Butterfly Defect. Princeton University Press.
Gordon J-S, 2021. Human Rights for Robots? A Literature Review. AI and Ethics 1(4): 579–591. DOI: 10.1007/s43681-021-00050-7.
Goren G, 2019. Social Behaviour as an Emergent Property of Embodied Curiosity: A Robotics Perspective. Philosophical Transactions of the Royal Society B: Biological Sciences 374: 1771. DOI:10.1098/rstb.2018.0029.
Gourevitch D, 1969. Suicide among the Sick in Classical Antiquity. Bulletin of the History of Medicine 43(6): 501–518.
Gouws A, van Zyl M, 2015. Toward a Feminist Ethics of Ubuntu. In Engster D, Hamington M, eds., Care Ethics and Political Theory. Oxford University Press: 165–186.
Graham DW, 2009. The Atomists' Reform. In Graham DW, Explaining the Cosmos. Princeton University Press: 250–276.
Gronewold N, 2020 (January 31). 'Unprecedented' Locust Invasion Approaches Full-Blown Crisis. Scientific American. https://www.scientificamerican.com/article/unprecedented-locust-invasion-approaches-full-blown-crisis/.

Gunderson M, 2004. A Kantian View of Suicide and End of Life Treatment. Journal of Social Philosophy 35(2): 277–287. DOI: 10.1111/j.1467-9833.2004.00232.x.

Gunkel D, 2013. Mark Coeckelbergh: Growing Moral Relationships: Critique of Moral Status Ascription. Ethics and Information Technology15: 239–241. DOI 10.1007/s10676-012-9308-8.

Gunkel D, 2018. Robot Rights. MIT Press. Kindle location 1169.

Gunkel DJ, 2014. A Vindication of the Rights of Machines. Philosophy and Technology 27: 113–132. DOI 10.1007/13347-013-0121-2.

Gunkel DJ, 2020. Perspective on Ethics of AI: Philosophy. In Dubber MD, Pasquale F, Das S, eds., The Oxford Handbook of Ethics of AI. Oxford University Press: 539–552.

Gyekye K, 1987. An Essay on African Philosophical Thought: The Akan Conceptual Scheme, Revised edition. Temple University Press.

Gyekye K, 1995. Akan Philosophical Thought. Cambridge University Press.

Gyekye K, 1995. An Essay on African Philosophical Thought, Revised Edition. Temple University Press.

Gyekye K, 1995. An Essay on African Philosophical Thought, revised edition. Temple University Press.

Gyekye K, 1996. African Cultural Values. Sankofa Publishing Company.

Gyekye K, 1997. Person and Community: In Defense of Moderate Communitarianism. In Gyekye K, Tradition and Modernity. Oxford University Press: 35–76.

Gyekye K, 1997. Tradition and Modernity. Oxford University Press, p. 65.

Gyekye K, 2002. Person and Community in African Thought. In Coetzee PH, ed., The Struggle for Reason in Africa, 2nd edition. Oxford University Press: 297–312.

Gyekye K, 2010. African Ethics. In Zalta EN, ed., Stanford Encyclopedia of Philosophy. http://plato.stanford.edu/archives/fall2010/entries/african- ethics/.

Haldane J, Lee P, 2003. Aquinas on Human Ensoulment, Abortion, and the Value of Life. Philosophy 78(304): 255–278. DOI: i:10.1017/S0031819103000.

Hallen B, 2009. A Short History of African Philosophy, 2nd edition. Indiana University Press.

Hanke L, 1949. The Spanish Struggle for Justice in the Conquest of America. University of Pennsylvania Press.

Harding S, 1987. The Curious Coincidence of Feminine and African Moralities. In Eze EC, ed., African Philosophy: An Anthology. Blackwell Publishers, Inc.: 360–372.

Hare HH et al., 1846. I-Testamente Entsha yenkosi yetu Ka-Yesu Kristu, Gowka-maxoosa. E-Newton Dale. Cited in Gade CBN, 2011. The Historical Development of the Written Discourses on Ubuntu. South African Journal of Philosophy 30(3): 303–329. DOI: 10.4314/sajpem.v30i3.69578.

Harris J, 1990. The Value of Life. Taylor & Francis Group.

Harris J, Anthis JR, 2021. The Moral Consideration of Artificial Entities: A Literature Review. Science and Engineering Ethics 27: 53. DOI: / 10.1007/s11948-021-00331-8.

Harrison P, 1992. Descartes on Animals. Philosophical Quarterly 42: 219–227. DOI: 10.2307/2220217.

Heidegger M, 1971. The Thing. In Heidegger M, Poetry Language and Thought, Hofstadter A, transl. Harper & Row Publishers. Mod: 163–180.
Henrich J, 2020. The Weirdest People in the World. Farrar, Straus & Giroux.
Hesiod, 1988 (700 BCE). Theogony. In West ML, transl., Hesiod: Theogony and Works and Days. Oxford University Press.
Hesiod, 1988 (700 BCE). Theogony. In West ML, transl., Hesiod: Theogony and Works and Days. Oxford University Press: 3–77.
Hill TE, 2012. Self-Regarding Suicide: A Modified Kantian View. In Hill TE, ed., Autonomy and Self-Respect. Cambridge University Press: 85–103.
Hobbes T, 2020 (1651). The Leviathan. Pandora's Box Classics.
Hoffman A, 2016 (March 31). The Lazarus Phenomenon, Explained: Why Sometimes, the Deceased are Not Dead, Yet. Smithsonian Magazine. https://www.smithsonianmag.com/science-nature/lazarus-phenomenon-explained-why-sometimes-deceased-are-not-dead-yet-180958613/.
Holm S, 2020. Wise Old Men (and Women). Recovering a Positive Anthropology of Aging. In Schweda, Coors M, Bozzaro C, eds., Aging and Human Nature. Springer: 233–240.
Holm S, 2022. Personhood across the Lifespan. In Wareham CS, The Cambridge Handbook of the Ethics of Ageing. Cambridge University Press: 105–117.
Horsthemke K, 2015. Animals and African Ethics. Palgrave Macmillan.
Horsthemke K, 2017. Animals and African Ethics. Journal of Animal Ethics 7(2): 119–144.
Horton R, 1974. Traditional Thought and the Emerging African Philosophy Department. A Comment on the Current Debate. In Wilson BR, ed., Rationality. Oxford University Press: 153–155.
Huffman C, 2009. The Pythagorean Conception of the Soul from Pythagoras to Philolaus. In Frede D, Reis B, eds., Body and Soul in Ancient Philosophy. De Gruyter, Inc.: 21–43.
Hughes JD, 2014. Concepts of the Natural World. In Hughes JD, Environmental Problems of the Greeks and Romans, 2nd edition. Johns Hopkins University Press: 43–67.
Hume D, 2011 (1734). Of the Reason of Animals. In A Treatise of Human Nature, a public domain book, Amazon Standard Identification Number (ASIN): BOO4TRB7CU: 123–124.
Hume D, 1755. *Of Suicide*. Hume Texts Online. https://davidhume.org/texts/su/.
Hursthouse R, Pettigrove G, 2018. Virtue Ethics. In Zalta EN, ed., Stanford Encyclopedia of Philosophy. https://plato.stanford.edu/archives/win2018/entries/ethics-virtue/.
Hutchings K, 2019. Decolonizing Global Ethics; Thinking with the Pluriverse. Ethics and International Affairs 33(2): 115–125. DOI: 10.1017/S089267941000169.
Hutchinson L, 2021 (May 28). Science Is Better with Friends—Andy Weir's Project Hail Mary and the Soft, Squishy Science of Language. ARS Technica. https://arstechnica.com/gaming/2021/05/andy-weirs-project-hail-mary-and-the-soft-squishy-science-of-language/.
Ikuenobe P, 2006. Philosophical Perspectives on Communalism and Morality in African Traditions. Rowman and Littlefield.

Ikuenobe P, 2006. The Idea of Personhood in Achebe's Things Fall Apart. Philosophia Africana 9(2): 117–131. DOI: 10.5840/philafricana2006924.

Ikuenobe P, 2017. The Communal Basis for Moral Dignity: An African Perspective. Philosophical Papers 45(3): 437–469 DOI: 05568641.2016.1245833.

Ikuenobe P, 2018. African Communal Basis for Autonomy and Life Choices. Developing World Bioethics 18: 212–221. DOI: 10.1111/dewb.12161.

Irenaeus 1857 (~180 CE). Adversus Haereses (Against Heresies), Harvey WW, ed., Volume 2, Book 4, Chapter 20. Section 7. Public Domain, Google-digitized. https://babel.hathitrust.org/cgi/pt?id=njp.32101074938968&view=1up&seq=231.

Ishiguro K, 2021. Klara and the Sun. Alfred A. Knopf.

Jaworska A, Tannenbaum J, 2021. The Grounds of Moral Status. In Zalta EN, ed., Stanford Encyclopedia of Philosophy. https://plato.stanford.edu/archives/spr2021/entries/grounds-moral-status/.

Jecker NS, 1989. Are Filial Duties Unfounded? American Philosophical Quarterly 26(1): 73–80. Stable URL: http://www.jstor.org/stable/20014269.

Jecker NS, 1990. Anencephalic Infants and Special Relationships. Theoretical Medicine 11(4): 333–342.

Jecker NS, 1991. Knowing When to Stop: The Limits of Medicine. Hastings Center Report 21(3): 5–8. Stable URL: http://www.jstor.org/stable/3563315.

Jecker NS, 2007. The Role of Standpoint in Justice Theory. Journal of Value Inquiry 41: 165–182. DOI: 10.1007/s10790-007-9091-7.

Jecker NS, 2014. Against a Duty to Die. American Medical Association Journal of Ethics 16(5): 390–395. DOI: 10.1001/virtualmentor.2014.16.05.oped1-1405.

Jecker NS, 2020. African Conceptions of Age-Based Moral Standing. Hastings Center Report 50(2): 35–43. DOI: 10.1002/hast.1100.

Jecker NS, 2020. Ending Midlife Bias. Oxford University Press.

Jecker NS, 2020. Nothing to Be Ashamed of: Sex Robots for Older Adults with Disabilities. Journal of Medical Ethics 47(1): 26–32. DOI: 10.1136/medethics-2020-106645.

Jecker NS, 2020. What Cares? In Jecker NS, Ending Midlife Bias. Oxford University Press: 213–238.

Jecker NS, 2020. You've Got a Friend in Me: Social Robots for Older Adults in an Age of Global Pandemics. Ethics and Information Technology 23(Suppl 1): 35–43. DOI: 10.1007/s10676-020-09546-y.

Jecker NS, 2021. Can We Wrong a Robot? AI & Society 13: 31–40. DOI: 10.1007/s00146-021-01278-x.

Jecker NS, 2021. My Friend, the Robot; An Argument for E-Friendship. Proceedings of the Institute of Electrical and Electronic Engineers (IEEE) Conference on Robot and Human Interactive Communications (RO-MAN): 692–697. DOI: 10.1109/RO-MAN50785.2021.9515429.

Jecker NS, 2021. The Time of One's Life: Views of Aging and Age Group Justice. History and Philosophy of the Life Sciences 43(1): 24. DOI: 10.1007/s40656-021-00377-8.

Jecker NS, 2022. African Ethics, Respect for Persons, and Moral Dissent. Theoria 88(3): 666–678. DOI: 10.1111/theo.12390.

Jecker NS, 2022. What Is 'Personhood'? The Ethics Question Needs a Closer Look in Abortion Debates. The Conversation. 13 May.

Jecker NS, Atuire CA, Ajei MO, 2022, The Moral Standing of Social Robots: Untapped Insights from Africa, Philosophy and Technology 35: 34. DOI: 10.1007/s13347-022-00531-5.

Jecker NS, Atuire CA, Ajei MO, 2022, Two Steps Forward: An African Relational Account of Moral Standing, Philosophy and Technology 35(2): 38. DOI: 10.1007/s13347-022-00533-3.

Jecker NS, 2023, Ubuntu and Bioethics. In Imafidon E, Tshivhase M, Freter B, eds., Handbook of African Philosophy, Springer. DOI: 10.1007/978-3-030-77898-9_6-1.

Jecker NS, Atuire CA, 2023. Personhood Beyond the West. American Journal of Bioethics 24(1): 59–62. DOI: 10.1080/15265161.2023.2278551.

Jecker NS, Atuire CA, Forthcoming. Personhood: An Emergent View from Africa and the West. Developing World Bioethics.

Jecker NS, 2024. A Relational Approach to Moral Standing for Robots and AI. In Gunkel DJ, ed., Handbook on the Ethics of Artificial Intelligence. Edward Elgar Publishing: 156–171.

Jecker NS, 2024. Ubuntu Ethics and Climate Change: An African Approach to Solidarity between Generations. In Chitando E, Okyere-Manu B, Chirongoma S, Dube M, eds., The Palgrave Handbook of Ubuntu, Inequality and Sustainable Development. Palgrave MacMillan.

Jecker NS, Ko A, 2022. The Unique and Practical Advantages of Applying a Capability Approach to Brain Computer Interface. Philosophy and Technology 35: 101. DOI: 10.1007/s13347-022-00597-1.

Jecker NS, Miwa E, 2019. What Do We Owe the Newly Dead? An Ethical Analysis of Findings from Japan's Corpse Hotel Workers. Bioethics 33: 691–698. DOI: 10.1111/bioe.12578.

Jecker NS, Nakazawa E, 2022. Bridging East-West Differences in AI and Robotics. AI 3: 764–777. DOI: 10.3390/ai3030045.

Jobin A, Ienca M, Vayena E, 2019. The Global Landscape of AI Ethics Guidelines. Nature Machine Intelligence 1: 389–399.

Johnson R, Cureton A, 2022. Kant's Moral Philosophy. In Zalta EN, ed., Stanford Encyclopedia of Philosophy. https://plato.stanford.edu/archives/spr2022/entries/kant-moral/.

Jones SF, Kessel AS, 2001. The 'Redefinition of Death' Debate: Western Concepts and Western Bioethics. Science and Engineering Ethics 7(1): 63–75. DOI: 10.1007/s11948-001-0024-8.

Kant I 1996 (1797). The Metaphysics of Morals. In Gregor M, transl. and ed., Immanuel Kant Practical Philosophy. Cambridge University Press, pp. 434–435.

Kant I, 1981 (1785). Grounding for the Metaphysics of Morals. In Ellington JW, transl., Grounding for the Metaphysics of Morals, 3rd edition. Hackett Publishing Company, Inc.: 1–62.

Kant I, 1996 (1785). Groundwork for the Metaphysics of Morals. In Gregor M, ed. and trans. Practical Philosophy. Cambridge University Press: 43–108.

Kant I, 1997 (~1760–1794). Of Duties to Animals and Spirits. In Kant I, Lectures on Ethics, Heath P, transl. Cambridge University Press: 210–213.

Kant I, 1997 (~1775–1780.). Of Care for One's Life. In Heath P, Schneewind JB, eds., Heath P, transl., Immanuel Kant: Lectures on Ethics: 149–151.
Kant I, 1997 (~1775–1780.). Of Suicide. In Heath P, Schneewind JB, eds., Heath P, transl., Immanuel Kant: Lectures on Ethics: 144–151
Kant I, 1997 (1793). Notes on the Lectures of Mr. Kant on the Metaphysics of Morals. In Heath P, Schneewind JB, eds., Heath P, transl., Immanuel Kant, Lectures on Ethics. Cambridge University Press: 249–452.
Kant I, 2008 (1755). Universal Natural History and Theory of the Heavens, Johnston I, transl. Richer Resources Publications.
Kant I, 2015 (1785). Fundamental Principles of the Metaphysics of Morals. In Abbott TK, Hastie W, transl., The Ethics of Immanuel Kant, e-artnow ebooks.
Kant I, 2017 (1785). Groundwork of the Metaphysics of Morals. In Bennett J, transl., Groundwork for the Metaphysics of Morals Immanuel Kant. Early Modern Texts.
Kasenene P, 1994. Ethics in African Theology. In Villa-Vicencio C, de Gruchy J, eds., Doing Ethics in Context: South African Perspectives. Orbis Books: 138–147.
Kätsyri J, Förger K, Mäkäräinen M, Takala T, 2015. A Review of Empirical Evidence on Different Uncanny Valley Hypotheses. Frontiers in Psychology 6(390): 1–16. DOI: 10.3389/fpsyg.2015.00390.
Kauffman S, 2010. Reinventing the Sacred: A New View of Science, Reason, and Religion. Basic Books.
Kaufman JA, Lenartz A, Floyd TE, 2022. An Interplanetary Land Ethics. Sustainability 15(1): 50–57. DOI: 10.1089/scc.2021.0068.
Kelley D, Atreides K, 2020. AGI Protocol for the Ethical Treatment of Artificial General Intelligence Systems. Procedia Computer Science 169: 501–506. DOI: 10.1016/j.procs.2020.02.219.
Kepler J, 2008 (1610). Kepler's Conversation with Galileo's Sidereal Messenger. Reprinted in Crowe M, ed., Extraterrestrial Life Debate: Antiquity to 1915: A Source Book. University of Notre Dame Press: 53–64.
Kilner J, 1984. Who Should Be Saved? Hastings Center Report 14(3): 18–22.
Kingsley K, Parry S, Parry R, 2020. Empedocles. In Zalta EN, ed., Stanford Encyclopedia of Philosophy. https://plato.stanford.edu/archives/sum2020/entries/empedocles/.
Kingwell M, 2020. Are Sentient AIs Persons? In Dubber MD, Pasquale F, Das S, eds., The Oxford Handbook of Ethics of AI. Oxford University Press: 325–342.
Kirk R, 2021. Zombies. In Zalta EN, ed., Stanford Encyclopedia of Philosophy. https://plato.stanford.edu/archives/spr2021/entries/zombies/.
Kittay EF, 2005. At the Margins of Moral Personhood. Ethics 115(1): 100–131. DOI: 10.1086/454366.
Kittay EF, 2019. Love's Labor, 2nd edition. Routledge.
Kleinschmidt S, Dugas JN, Nelson KP, Fekdnab HA, 2021. False Negative Point-of-Care Urine Pregnancy Tests in an Academic Emergency Department: A Retrospective Cohort Study. Journal of the American College of Emergency Physicians Open (JACEP Open) 2: e12427. DOI: 10.1086/454366.
Knox D, 2019. Giordano Bruno. In Zalta EN, Stanford Encyclopedia of Philosophy. https://plato.stanford.edu/archives/sum2019/entries/bruno/.

Koplin J, Carter O, Savulescu J, 2021. The Moral Status of Brain Organoids. In Clarke S, Zohny H, Savulescu J, eds., Rethinking Moral Status. Oxford University Press: 249–268.
Korsgaard C, 1983. Two Distinctions in Goodness. Philosophical Review 92(2): 169–195. DOI: 10.2307/2184924.
Korsgaard CM, 1996. Creating the Kingdom of Ends. Cambridge University Press.
Korsgaard CM, 2016. Kant's Formula of Humanity. In Korsgaard CM, Creating the Kingdom of Ends. Cambridge University Press: 106–132.
Korsgaard CM, 2016. The Right to Lie: Kant on Dealing with Evil. In Korsgaard CM, Creating the Kingdom of Ends. Cambridge University Press: 133–158.
Korsgaard CM, 2018. Fellow Creatures. Oxford University Press.
Kraut R, 2022. Aristotle's Ethics. In Zalta EN, Nodelman U, eds., Stanford Encyclopedia of Philosophy. Stanford University Press. https://plato.stanford.edu/archives/fall2022/entries/aristotle-ethics/.
Kroeger F, 1992. Buli-English Dictionary. Lit Verlag.
Kurki VAJ, 2019. A Theory of Legal Personhood. Oxford University Press.
Kwame S, 2017. Rethinking the History of African Philosophy. In Afolayan A, Falola T, eds, The Palgrave Handbook of African Philosophy. Palgrave Macmillan: 189–201.
Laguerre MS, 1980. Bizango: A Voodoo Secret Society in Haiti. In Tefft SK, ed., Secrecy: A Cross-Cultural Perspective. Human Sciences Press: 147–160.
Laitinen A, 2013. Solidarity. In Kaldis B, ed., Encyclopedia of Philosophy and the Social Sciences, Volume 2. Sage Publications, Inc.: 948–950.
Lawrence DR, Harris J, 2021. Monkeys, Moral Machines, and Persons. In Clarke S, Zohny H, Savulescu J, eds., Rethinking Moral Status. Oxford University Press: 289–304.
Lemoine B, 2018. Can AI Have a Soul? Stanford Artificial Intelligence Law Society, 30 October. https://www.youtube.com/watch?v=AhX7cBqc8_M.
Lemoine B, 2022. Is LaMDA Sentient? An Interview, emphasis added. https://cajundiscordian.medium.com/is-lamda-sentient-an-interview-ea64d916d917.
Leopold A, 2020 (1949). A Sand County Almanac. Oxford University Press.
Lerner A, 2023. The Procreation Asymmetry. Philosophical Studies 180: 1169–1195. DOI: 10.1007/s11098-023-01954-2.
Lewis A, Kumpfbeck A, Greer D, et al., 2021. Barriers to the Use of Neurologic Criteria to Declare Death in Africa. American Journal of Hospice and Palliative Medicine 39(2): 243–249, p. 246. DOIi:10.1177/10499091211006921.
Lewis A, Richard BJ, Pope T, 2020. It's Time to Revise the Uniform Determination of Death Act. Annals of Internal Medicine 179(2): 143–145. DOI: 10.7326/L20-0257.
Library of Congress, 2003. Ancient Manuscripts from the Desert Libraries of Timbuktu. https://www.loc.gov/exhibits/mali/.
Lindberg, DC, 2007. The Beginnings of Western Science, 2nd edition. University of Chicago Press.
Liyong TL, 1976. The Sun Is my God And I Shall Worship Him When He Rises, Reaches His Zenith, and Reposes for the Night. In Liyong TL, Ballads of UnderDevelopment. East Africa Literature Bureau: 83–94. Reprinted in Opata

DU, 2008. Cultural Astronomy in the Lore and Literature of Africa. In Hobrook J, Medupe RT, eds., African Cultural Astronomy. Springer: 217.
Locke J, 2004 (1690). An Essay Concerning Human Understanding, Volume 1, Kindle Location 5059–5060. Project Gutenberg, EBook #10615.
Lorenz H, 2009. Ancient Theories of Soul. In Zalta EN, ed., Stanford Encyclopedia of Philosophy. https://plato.stanford.edu/archives/sum2009/entries/ancient-soul/.
Lovejoy AO, 2001 (1936). The Great Chain of Being. Harvard University Press.
Loy H-C, 2014. Classical Confucianism as Virtue. In van Hooft, ed., The Handbook of Virtue. Routledge: 285–293.
MacKenzie M, 2018. Buddhism and Virtues. In Snow NE, ed., The Oxford Handbook of Virtue. Oxford University Press: 153–170.
MacWhinney B, Kempe V, Brooks PJ, Li P, 2022. Emergentist Approaches to Language. Frontiers of Psychology 12: 833160–833160. DOI: 10.3389/fpsyg.2021.833160.
Majeed HM, 2017. Reincarnation: A Question in African Philosophy of Mind, Unisa Press.
Makropulos E, Makropulos E, 2019. Immortality in Early Greek Poetry and Philosophy. In Long AG, ed. Death and Immortality in Ancient Philosophy. Cambridge University Press: 7–28.
Mallick S, Rajagopalan RP, 2019. If Space Is the 'Province of Mankind,' Who Owns Its Resources? Observer Research Foundation (ORF) No. 182. https://www.orfonline.org/wp-content/uploads/2019/01/ORF_Occasional_Paper_182_Space_Mining.pdf.
Mariscal C, Brunet TDP, 2020. What Are Extremophiles: A Philosophical Perspective. In Smith KC, Mariscal C, eds., Social and Conceptual Issues in Astrobiology. Oxford University Press: 157–178.
Martin J, Bickhard MH, eds., 2012. The Psychology of Personhood: Philosophical, Historical, Social-Developmental, and Narrative Perspectives. Cambridge University Press.
Masolo DA, 2004. The Concept of the Person in Luo Modes of Thought. In Brown LM, ed., African Philosophy: New and Traditional Perspectives. Oxford University Press: 84–106.
Masolo DA, 2017. Africanizing Philosophy: Wiredu, Hountondji, and Mudimbe. In Afolayan A, Falola T, eds., The Palgrave Handbook of African Philosophy. Palgrave Macmillan: 127–148.
Mathur MB, Reichling DB, 2015. Navigating a Social World with Robot Partners: A Quantitative Cartography of the Uncanny Valley. Cognition 146: 22–32. DOI: 10.1016/j.cognition.2015.09.008.
Matolino B, 2009. Radical versus Moderates: A Critique of Gyekye's Moderate Communitarianism. South African Journal of Philosophy 28(2): 160–170. DOI: 10.4314/sajpem.v28i2.46674.
Mawere M, 2009. The Shona Conception of Euthanasia. Journal of Pan African Studies 3(4): 101–116.
Mbiti JS, 1989. Africa Religions and Philosophy, 2nd edition. Heinemann.
Mbiti JS, 2015. Introduction to African Religion, 2nd edition. Waveland Press, Inc.

Mbombo O, 1996. Practicing Medicine across Cultures: Conceptions of Health, Communication and Consulting Practice. In Steyn ME, Motshabi KB, eds., Cultural Synergy in South Africa. Knowledge Resources: 109–117.

McAlister EA, 2022. Vodou. Encyclopedia Britannica. https://www.britannica.com/topic/Vodou.

McArthur N, 2017. The Case for Sexbots. In Danaher J, McArthur N, eds. Robot Sex. MIT Press: 31–45.

McClure MT, 1934. The Greek Conception of Nature. Philosophical Review 43(2): 109–124. DOI: 10.2307/2179890.

McGuffie K, Newhouse A, 2020. The Radicalization of GPT-3 and Advanced Neural Language Models. Cornell University, Computers and Society, arXiv:2009.06807 [cs.CY]. DOI: 10.48550/arXiv.2009.06807.

McKay CP, 1982. On Terraforming Mars. Extrapolation 23(4): 309–314. DOI: 10.3828/extr.1982.23.4.309.

McKeever S, Ridge M, 2006. Principled Ethics. Oxford University Press.

Menkiti I, 1984, Person and Community in African Traditional Thought. In Wright RA, ed., African Philosophy: An Introduction, 3rd edition, University Press of America: 171–181.

Menkiti IA, 1979. Person and community in African Traditional Thought. In Wright RA, ed., African Philosophy: An Introduction, 2nd edition. University Press of America: 157–168.

Menkiti IA, 2004. Physical and Metaphysical Understanding. In African Philosophy: New and Traditional Perspectives. Oxford University Press: 107–135. DOI:10.1093/019511440X.003.0007.

Merchant C, 2020. The Death of Nature: Women, Ecology, and the Scientific Revolution, 40th Anniversary Edition. Harper One.

Metz T, 2012. African Conceptions of Human Dignity. Human Rights Review 13: 19–37. DOI: 10.1007/s12142-011-0200-4.

Metz T, 2012. An African Theory of Moral Status. Ethical Theory and Moral Practice 15(3): 387–402. DOI: 10.1007/s10677-011-9302-y.

Metz T, 2018. What Is the Essence of an Essence? Synthesis Philosophica 65: 209–224. DOI: 10.21464/sp33113.

Metz T, 2020. Recent Work in African Philosophy. Mind 130: 639–660. DOI: 10.1093/mind/fzaa072.

Metz T, 2021. Recent Work in African Political and Legal Philosophy. Philosophy Compass 16: e12765. DOI: 10.1111/phc3.12765.

Metz T, 2022. A Relational Moral Theory. Oxford University Press.

Midgley M, 1983. Animals and Why They Matter. University of Georgia Press.

Midgley M, 2007. Introduction: The Not-So-Simple Death. In Midgley M, ed., Earthly Realism: The Meaning of Gaia. Societas Imprint Academic: Kindle location 132–226.

Mkhize N, 2018. Ubuntu-Botho Approach to Ethics. In Nortjé, N, De Jongh J-C, Hoffmann WA, eds., African Perspectives on Ethics for Healthcare Professionals. Springer Nature: Kindle location 752–1457.

Mnyandu N, 2018. Exploring the Concept of Ubuntu in Relation to Dying with Dignity in Palliative and Hospice Care. Obiter 39(2): 384–398. DOI: 10.10520/EJC-120d09205d.

Molefe M, 2014. A Report on Ubuntu, Leonhard Praeg: Book Review, Acta Academica 46(2): 157–164.

Molefe M, 2015. A Rejection of Humanism in African Moral Tradition. Theoria, 62: 59–77. DOI: 10.3167/th.2015.6214304.

Molefe M, 2019. An African Philosophy of Personhood, Morality, and Politics. Palgrave Macmillan.

Molefe M, 2020. African Personhood and Applied Ethics. Published on behalf of the African Humanities Program by NISC (Pty) Ltd.

Molefe M, 2020. An African Ethics of Personhood and Bioethics. Palgrave Macmillan.

Molefe M, 2020. Personhood and a Meaningful Life in African Philosophy. South African Journal of Philosophy 39(2): 194–207. DOI: 10.1080/02580136.2020.1774980.

Molefe M, 2022. Human Dignity in African Philosophy: A Very Short Introduction. Springer Nature.

Molefe M, Muade E, 2023. An Appraisal of 'African Perspectives of Moral Status: A Framework for Evaluating Global Bioethical Issues.' Arumaruka: Journal of Conversational Thinking 3(1): 25–50. DOI: 10.4314/ajct.v3i2.2.

Mori M, 2012 (12 June). The Uncanny Valley. IEEE Robotics & Automation Magazine.

Muhammad KG, 2019. The Condemnation of Blackness: Race, Crime, and the Making of Modern Urban America. Harvard University Press.

Murove MF, 2005. African Bioethics. Journal for the Study of Religion 18(1): 16–36, p. 28. DOI: 10.4314/jsr.v18i1.6163.

Murove MF, 2007. The Shona Ethics of *Ukama* with Reference to the Immortality of Values. Mankind Quarterly. 48: 179–189. DOI: 10.46469/mq.2007.48.2.4.

Næss A, 1973. The Shallow and the Deep, Long-Range Ecology Movement. Inquiry 16(1): 95–100. DOI: 10.1080/00201747308601682.

Næss A, 1985. The World of Concrete Contents. Inquiry 28(1–4): 417–428, p. 427. DOI: 10.1080/00201748508602059.

Nagel T, 1970. Death. Nous 4(1): 73–80. DOI: 10.2307/2214297.

Nagel T, 1970. The Possibility of Altruism. Princeton University Press.

Nagel T, 1974. What Is It Like to Be a Bat? Philosophical Review 83(4): 435–450. DOI: 10.2307/2183914.

Nagel T, 1986. The View from Nowhere. Oxford University Press.

Nagle DB, 2006. The Household as the Foundation of Aristotle's Polis. Cambridge University Press.

Naragon S, 1990. Kant on Descartes and the Brutes. Kant-Studien 81(1): 1–23. DOI: 10.1515/kant.1990.81.1.1.

Nathan MJ, 2023. Disembodied AI and the Limits to Machine Understanding of Students' Embodied Interactions. Frontiers in Artificial Intelligence 6:1148227. DOI: 10.3389/frai.2023.1148227.

National Academies of Science, Engineering, and Medicine, 2007. Limits of Organic Life in Planetary Science. National Academies Press. https://nap.nationalacademies.org/download/11919.

National Aeronautics and Space Administration (NASA), 2018 (July 30). Mars Terraforming Not Possible Using Present-Day Technology. https://www.nasa.gov/press-release/goddard/2018/mars-terraforming.

National Aeronautics and Space Administration (NASA), 2020 (July 21). Cultivating Ideas for Mars. NASA Earth Observatory. https://earthobservatory.nasa.gov/images/147053/cultivating-ideas-for-mars.

National Aeronautics and Space Administration, 2023 (August 23). CoolCosmos: How Many Galaxies Are in the Universe? NASA. https://coolcosmos.ipac.caltech.edu/ask/240-How-many-galaxies-are-in-the-Universe-.

National Air and Space Museum. Exploring the Planets: Ancient Times & the Greeks. https://airandspace.si.edu/exhibitions/exploring-the-planets/online/discovery/greeks.cfm.

Nelson HL, 1996. Death with Kantian Dignity. Journal of Clinical Ethics 7(3): 215–221.

Newmyer ST, 2017. The Animal and the Human in Ancient and Modern Thought. Taylor and Francis.

Niederbacher B, 2014. The Human Soul: Augustine's Case for Soul-Body Dualism. In Meconi DV, Stump E, eds., The Cambridge Companion to Augustine, 2nd edition. Cambridge University Press: 125–141.

Nkafu MN, 1999. African Vitalogy. Paulines Publications Africa.

Nkafu MN, 2022. 'Bantu Philosophy' by P. Tempels as the Expression of African Philosophy in Front of African Vitalogy. In Dokman F, Cornelli EM, eds., Beyond Bantu Philosophy. Taylor and Francis: 56–91.

Nkulu-N'Sengha M, 2009. Bumuntu. In Kefe M, Mazama A, Encyclopedia of African Religion, Volume 1. Sage Publications, Inc., pp. 142–147.

Noddings N, 1991. Comment on Donovan's 'Animal Rights and Feminist Theory.' Signs 16(2): 418–422. DOI: 10.1086/494674.

Noddings N, 2003. Caring: A Feminine Approach to Ethics and Moral Education, 2nd edition. University of California Press.

Noonan JT, 1970. An Almost Absolute Value in History. In Noonan JT, The Morality of Abortion: Legal and Historical Perspectives. Harvard University Press: 51–59.

Norlock K, 2019. Feminist Ethics. In Zalta EN, ed., Stanford Encyclopedia of Philosophy. https://plato.stanford.edu/archives/sum2019/entries/feminism-ethics/.

Nozick R, 1974. Anarchy State and Utopia. Basic Books.

Nozick R, 1997. Do Animals Have Rights? In Nozick R, Socratic Puzzles. Harvard University Press: 305–310.

Nussbaum MC, 2006. Beyond Compassion and Humanity. In Nussbaum MC, Frontiers of Justice. Harvard University Press: 325–407.

Nussbaum MC, Putnam H, 1992. Changing Aristotle's Mind. In Nussbaum MC, Putnam H, eds., Essays on Aristotle's de Anima. Oxford University Press: 27–56.

O'Callaghan J, 2022 (January 2). NASA's Retiring Top Scientist Says We Can Terraform Mars and Maybe Venus, Too. New York Times.

O'Connor T, 2021. Emergent Properties. In Zalta EN, ed., Stanford Encyclopedia of Philosophy. https://plato.stanford.edu/archives/win2021/entries/properties-emergent/.

O'Grady W, 2008. The Emergentist Program. Lingua 118: 447–464. DOI: 10.1016/j.lingua.2006.12.001.

Okafor SO, 1982. Bantu Philosophy: Placide Tempels Revisited. Journal of Religion in Africa 13(2): 83–100. DOI: 10.2307/1581204.

Olúwolé S, 2017. Socrates and Orunmila, 3rd edition. ARK Publishers.

Omelianchuk A, Bernat J, Caplan A, et al., 2022. Revise the Uniform Determination of Death Act to Align the Law with Practice through Neurorespiratory Criteria. Neurology. Ahead of Print, DOI: 10.1212/WNL.0000000000200024.

Omonzejele PF, 2004. African Ethics and Voluntary Euthanasia. Medicine and Law 23(3): 671–686.

Onarheim KH, Sisay MM, Gizaw M, Moland KM, Miljeteig I, 2017. What if the Baby Doesn't Survive? Social Science & Medicine 195: 123–130. DOI: 10.1016/j.socscimed.2017.11.003.

Opata CU, 2008. Cultural Astronomy in the Lore and Literature of Africa. In Holbrook J, Medupe RT, Urama JO, eds., African Cultural Astronomy: Current Archaeoastronomy and Ethnoastronomy Research in Africa. Springer: 217–229. DOI: 10.1007/978-1-4020-6639-9_16.

Otto E, 2003. Kim Stanley Robinson's Mars Leopoldian Land Ethics. Utopian Studies 14(2): 118–135.

Oxford University Press 2023 (March). n. person. In OED Online, 3rd edition. Oxford University Press.

Oxford University Press 2023 (March). n. relationship. In OED Online, 3rd edition. Oxford University Press.

Oxford University Press, 2023 (March). adj. and n., alien. OED Online, 3rd edition. Oxford University Press.

Oxford University Press, 2023 (March). adj. and n., dividual. In Oxford University Press, OED Online, 3rd edition. Oxford University Press.

Oxford University Press, 2023 (March). adj. and n., individual. In Oxford University Press, OED Online, 3rd edition. Oxford University Press.

Oxford University Press, 2023 (March). n, ubuntu. OED Online, 3rd edition. Oxford University Press.

Oxford University Press, 2023 (March). n. Logos. OED Online, 3rd edition. Oxford University Press.

Oxford University Press, 2023 (March). n., apotheosis. In OED Online, 3rd edition. Oxford University Press.

Oxford University Press, 2023 (March). n., interaction. In OED Online, 3rd edition. Oxford University Press.

Oxford University Press, 2023 (March). n., relationship. In OED Online, 3rd edition. Oxford University Press.

Oxford University Press, 2023 (March). n., zombie, OED Online, 3rd edition. Oxford University Press

Parthemore J, 2013. The 'Final Frontier' as Metaphor of Mind. In Dunér D, Persson E, Holmberg G, eds., The History and Philosophy of Astrobiology: Perspectives on Extraterrestrial Life and the Human Mind. Cambridge University Press: 67–92.

Pascal B, 2008 (1670). Pensées. In Crowe M, ed., Extraterrestrial Life Debate: Antiquity to 1915: A Source Book. University of Notre Dame Press: 69–71.

Pearce MJ, 2017. Art in the Age of Emergence, 2nd edition. Cambridge Scholars Publishing.

Pellegrino E, 2008. Personal Statement. In President's Council on Bioethics, ed., Controversies in the Determination of Death, A White Paper of the President's Council on Bioethics: 107–122.

Perri AR, Feueborn TR, Frantz LAF, et al., 2020. Dog Domestication and the Dual Dispersal of People and Dogs into the Americas. Proceedings of the National Academies of Sciences (PNAS) 118(6): e2010083118. DOI: 10.1073/pnas.2010083118.

Persson I, Savulescu J, 2012. Unfit for the Future: The Need for Moral Enhancement. Oxford University Press.

Plato 2023 (360 B.C.E.). Timaeus. In Plato: The Complete Works. Pandora's Box: 1199–1186.

Playford RC, Playford ED, 2018. What Am I? A Philosophical Account of Personhood and Its Application to People with Brain Injury. Neuropsychology Rehabilitation 28: 1408–1414. DOI: 10.1080/09602011.2018.1456939.

Poe EA, 2021 (1844). The Premature Burial. In Poe EA, The Works of Edgar Allan Poe, Raven Edition, Volume II. The Project Gutenberg, eBook #2148.

Pope Paul III, 1993 (1537). Sublimus deus. Quoted in Seed P, 1993. 'Are These Not Also Men?': The Indians' Humanity and Capacity for Spanish Civilization. Journal of Latin American Studies 25(3): 629–652. DOI: 10.1017/S0022216X00006696.

Potthast A, 2020. Ethics and Extraterrestrials. In Smith KC, Mariscal C, eds., Social and Conceptual Issues in Astrobiology. Oxford University Press: 197–208.

Praegh L, 2014. A Report on Ubuntu. KawZulu-Natal Press.

Presbey GM, 2002. Massai Concepts of Personhood: The Role of Recognition, Community, and Individuality. International Studies in Philosophy 34: 57–82. DOI: 10.5840/intstudphil200234244.

President's Commission for the Study of Medicine and Biomedical and Behavior Research, 1981. Defining Death: Medical, Legal, and Ethical Issues in the Determination of Death. Government Printing Office.

Pruchner J, 2007. Brave New Worlds: The Oxford Dictionary of Science Fiction. Oxford University Press.

Putnam H, 2002. The Collapse of the Fact-Value Distinction and Other Essays. Harvard University Press.

Ramsey P, 1970. The Patient as Person. Yale University Press.

Rawls TJ, 1971. A Theory of Justice. Harvard University Press.

Reed PD, 2017. Maroon Community. Encyclopedia Britannica. https://www.britannica.com/topic/maroon-community.

Regan T, 1975. The Moral Basis of Vegetarianism. Canadian Journal of Philosophy 5(2): 181–214. DOI: 10.1080/00455091.1975.10716107.

Regan T, Singer P, eds., 1989. Animal Rights and Human Obligations, 2nd edition. Prentice-Hall.

Rettersøl N, 1998. Suicide in a Cultural History Perspective, Part 1. Norwegian Journal Suicidologi 2, n.p.n. https://www.med.uio.no/klinmed/english/research/centres/nssf/articles/culture/Retterstol1.pdf.

Ridge M, 2017 Reasons for Action: Agent Neutral vs. Agent Relative. IN Zalta EN, ed., Stanford Encyclopedia of Philosophy. https://plato.stanford.edu/archives/fall2017/entries/reasons-agent/.

Rist JM, 1974. Aristotle: The Value of Man and the Origin of Morality. Canadian Journal of Philosophy 4(1): 1–21. DOI: 10.1080/00455091.1974.10716918.

Rist JM, 1982. Human Value: A Study in Ancient Philosophical Ethics. E.J. Brill.

Robert JS, Baylis F, 2014, Crossing Species Boundaries, in Sandler RL, ed., Ethics and Emerging Technologies. Palgrave Macmillan: 139–154.

Robinson KS, 1993. Red Mars. Penguin Random House.

Rolston H, 1975. Is There an Ecological Ethic? Ethics 85: 93–109. DOI: 10.1086/291944.

Rolston H, 2014. Terrestrial and Extraterrestrial Altruism. In Vaockh DA, ed., Extraterrestrial Altruism: Evolution and Ethics in the Cosmos. Springer-Verlag: 210–222.

Rolston H, 2016. The Anthropocene! Beyond the Natural? In Gardiner SM, Thompson A, eds., The Oxford Handbook of Environmental Ethics. Oxford University Press: 62–74.

Rolston IH, 2011. Species and Biodiversity. In Rolston, IH, A New Environmental Ethics. Taylor and Francis Group: 126–157.

Rolston, H, 1988. Environmental Ethics. Temple University Press.

Rosfort R, 2018. Personhood. In Stanghellini G, Broome M, Raballo A, Fernandez AV, Pusar-Poli P, Rosfort R, eds., The Oxford Handbook of Phenomenological Psychopathology. Oxford University Press: 335–343.

Ruddick S, 1995. Maternal Thinking. Beacon Press.

Ryder RD, 2004. Speciesism Revisited. Think 2(6): 83–92. DOI: 10.1017/S1477175600002840.

Sagan C, 1961. The Planet Venus. Science 133: 849–858. DOI: 10.1126/science.133.3456.849.

Salih AAM, Baraibar M, Mwangi KK, Artin G, 2020. Climate Change and Locust Outbreak in East Africa. Nature Climate Change 10: 584–585. DOI: 10.1038/s41558-020-0835-8.

Santos B, 2015. Epistemologies of the South: Justice against Epistemicide. Routledge.

Satz D, 1994. Rational Choice and Social Theory. Journal of Philosophy 91(2): 71–87. DOI: 10.2307/2940928.

Saygin AP, Chaminade T, Ishiguro H, Driver J, Frith C, 2012. The Thing That Should Not Be: Predictive Coding and the Uncanny Valley. Social Cognitive and Affective Neuroscience 7(4): 413–422. DOI: 10.1093/scan/nsr025.

Scheuerman W, 2023. Globalization. In Zalta EN, Nodelman U, eds., Stanford Encyclopedia of Philosophy. https://plato.stanford.edu/archives/spr2023/entries/globalization/.

Schneewind JB, 2010. Essays on the History of Moral Philosophy. Oxford University Press: 248–276.

Schneiderman LJ, Jecker NS, Jonsen AR, 1990. Medical Futility: Its Meaning and Ethical Implications. Annals of Internal Medicine 112(12): 949–954. DOI: 10.7326/0003-4819-112-12-949.

Schoeman F, 1980. Rights of Children, Rights of Parents, and the Moral Basis of the Family. Ethics 91(1): 6–19. DOI: 10.1086/292199.

Schott R, 1974. Traditional Law and Religion among the Bulsa of Northern Ghana. Journal of African Law 31(1/2):58–69. DOI: 10.1017/S0021855300009244.

Sebo J, 2023. Kantianism for Humans, Utilitarianism for Nonhumans? Yes and No. Philosophical Studies 180: 1211–1230. DOI: 10.1007/s11098-022-01835-0.

Sedley D, 2009. Three Kinds of Platonic Immortality. In Frede D, Reis B, eds., Body and Soul in Ancient Philosophy. De Gruyter, Inc.: 145–161.

See Gyekye K, 2010. Person and Community in African Thought. In Wiredu K, Gyekye K, eds., Person and Community: Ghanaian Philosophical Studies, I. Council for Research in Values and Philosophy (Washington, DC): 101–122. https://www.crvp.org/publications/Series-II/Series02-1.html.

Seed P, 1993. 'Are These Not Also Men?': The Indians' Humanity and Capacity for Spanish Civilization. Journal of Latin American Studies 25(3): 629–652. DOI: 10.1017/S0022216X00006696.

Senghor LL, 2016. Negritude: A Humanism of the Twentieth Century. In Hord FL, Lee JS, eds, I am Because We Are: Readings in Africana Philosophy, 2nd edition. University of Massachusetts Press: 55–64.

Service RF, 2018. Synthetic Nerves Can Sense Braille, Move Cockroach Leg. Science 31 May. DOI: 10.1126/science.aau3449.

Setta SM, Shemie SD, 2015. An Explanation and Analysis of How World Religions Formulate Their Ethical Decisions on Withdrawing Treatment and Determining Death. Philosophy, Ethics, and Humanities in Medicine 10(6). DOI: 10.1186/s13010-015-0025-x,

Sharkey A, 2020. Can We Program or Train Robots to Be Good? Ethics in Information Technology 22: 283–295. DOI: /10.1007/s10676-017-9425-5.

Shewmon DA, 2021. Statement in Support of Revising the Uniform Determination of Death Act and in Opposition to a Proposed Revision. Journal of Medicine and Philosophy 48(5): 453–477. DOI:10.1093/jmp/jhab014.

Shulman C, Bostrom N, 2021. The Moral Status of Brain Organoids. In Clarke S, Zohny H, Savulescu J, eds., Rethinking Moral Status. Oxford University Press: 305–326.

Shutte A, 1993. Philosophy for Africa. University of Cape Town Press.

Shutte A, 1995. Traditional African Thought. In Shutte A, Philosophy for Africa. University of Cape Town Press: 46–58.

Shweder RA, Bourne EJ, 1982. Does the Concept of the Person Vary Cross-Culturally? In Marsella AJ, White GM, Cultural Conceptions of Mental Health and Therapy. D. Reidel: 97–137.

Siedentop L, 2014. Inventing the Individual: The Origins of Western Individualism. Harvard University Press.

Sim M, 2017. Confucian and Daoist Virtue Ethics. In Carr D, Arthur J, Kristjánnson, eds., Varieties of Virtue Ethics. Palgrave Macmillan: 105–121.

Singer P, 2003. Voluntary Euthanasia: A Utilitarian Perspective. Bioethics 17(5/6): 526–541. DOI: 10.1136/jme.28.4.255.

Singer P, 2009. Reply to Bernard Williams. In Schafer JA, ed., Peter Singer under Fire: The Moral Iconoclast Faces His Critics. Open Court: 97–102.

Singer P, 2015 (1975). Animal Liberation. Open Road Media.

Singer P, 2018. The Challenge of Brain Death for the Sanctity of Life Ethics. Ethics and Bioethics 8(3/4): 153–165. DOI: 10.2478/ebce-2018-0012.
Singer P, 2020. Is Age Discrimination Acceptable? Project Syndicate 10 June. https://www.project-syndicate.org/commentary/when-is-age-discrimination-acceptable-by-peter-singer-2020-06/.
Singer P, What's Wrong with Killing? In Singer P, Practical Ethics, 2nd edition. Cambridge University Press: 83–109.
Singer PW, 2009. Wired for War. Penguin Group Inc.
Sinnott-Armstrong W, Conitzer V, 2021. Monkeys, Moral Machines, and Persons. In Clarke S, Zohny H, Savulescu J, eds., Rethinking Moral Status. Oxford University Press: 268–288.
Slote M, 1985. Obedience and Illusions. In Sommers CH, ed., Vice and Virtues in Everyday Life. Harcourt Brace Jovanovich.
Smith NK, 1963. New Studies in the Philosophy of Descartes, 2nd edition. Macmillan.
Smorholm S, 2016. Suffering Peacefully. Ethos 44(3): 333–351. DOI: 10.1111/etho.12126.
Snedegar K, 2016. Astronomy in Sub-Saharan Africa. In Selin H, ed., Encyclopaedia of the History of Science, Technology, and Medicine in Non-Western Cultures. Springer: 742–752. DOI: 10.1007/978-94-007-7747-7.
Sodi T, Nkoana S, Mokwena J, 2021. Bereavement Rituals and Their Related Psychosocial Functions in a Northern Sotho Community of South Africa. Death Studies 45(2): 91–100. DOI: 10.1080/07481187.2019.1616852.
Sorabji R, 2018. The One-Dimensionality of Ethical Theories. In Sorabji R, Animal Minds and Human Morals: 208–219. Cornell University Press.
Sorajbi R, 2018. Plants and Animals. In Sorabji R, Animal Minds and Human Morals. Cornell University Press: 97–104.
Sorrell T, Draper H, 2014. Robot Carers, Ethics, and Older People. Ethics of Information Technology 16: 183–195. DOI: 10.1007/s10676-014-9344-7.
Sparrow R, 2002. The March of the Robot Dogs. Ethics and Information Technology 4: 305–318. DOI: 10.1023/A:1021386708994.
Sparrow R, 2004. The Turing Triage Test. Ethics and Information Technology 6: 203–213. DOI: 10.1023/A:1021386708994.
Sparrow R, 2021. Why Machines Cannot Be Moral. AI and Society 36(3): 685–693. DOI: 10.1007/s00146-020-01132-6.
Sprinkle T, 2018 (August 20). Sensors Allow Robots to Feel Sensations. American Society of Mechanical Engineers. https://www.asme.org/topics-resources/content/sensors-allow-robots-feel-sensation.
Steinbock B, 1978. Speciesism and the Idea of Equality. Philosophy 53: 247–256. DOI: 10.1017/S0031819100016582.
Steinbock B, 2011. Life Before Birth, 2nd edition. Oxford University Press.
Stone CD, 2010. Should Trees Have Standing? 3rd edition. Oxford University Press.
Stringer R, 2018. Realist Ethical Naturalism for Ethical Non-Naturalists. Philosophical Studies 175: 339–362, p. 347. DOI: 10.1007/s11098-017-0870-0.
Stringer R, 2021. Ethical Emergence and Moral Causation. Journal of Moral Philosophy 4: 331–362. DOI: 10.1163/17455243-20213272.

Sullivan W, 2013. Planetocentric Ethics: Principles for Exploring a Solar System that May Contain Extraterrestrial Microbial Life. In Spitz IC, Stoeger W, eds., Encountering Life in the Universe: Ethical Foundations and Social Implications of Astrobiology. University of Arizona Press: 167–177.

Tang J, LeBel A, Jain S, Huth AG, 2023. Semantic Reconstruction of Continuous Language from Non-Invasive Brain Recordings. Nature Neuroscience 26: 858–866. DOI: 10.1038/s41593-023-01304-9.

Tangwa G, 1996. Bioethics: An African Perspective. Bioethics 10: 183–200. DOI: 10.1017/S0031819100016582.

Tangwa G, 2004. Some African Reflections on Biomedical and Environmental Ethics. In Wiredu K, ed., A Companion to African Philosophy. Blackwell Publishing Ltd.: Kindle location 6430–6558.

Tangwa G, 2017. African Philosophy: Appraisal of a Recurrent Problematic. In Afolayan A, Falola T, eds, The Palgrave Handbook of African Philosophy. Palgrave Macmillan: 60–84.

Tangwa GB, 2000. The Traditional African Perception of a Persons: Some Implications for Bioethics. Hastings Center Report 30(5): 39–43. DOI: 10.2307/3527887.

Tangwa GB, 2010. African Bioethics and Sustainable Development. In Tangwa GB, Elements of African Bioethics in a Western Frame. Langaa Research & Publishing CIG: 39–48.

Tangwa GB, 2010. Elements of African Bioethics in a Western Frame. Langaa Research & Publishing CIG, p. 41. Project MUSE at muse.jhu/book/16848.

Tangwa GB, 2019. African Perspectives on Some Contemporary Bioethics Problems. Cambridge Scholars Publishing. Adobe Digital.

Taylor C, 1985. Atomism. In Taylor C, Philosophy and the Human Sciences: Philosophical Papers 2. Cambridge University Press: 187–210.

Taylor C, 1985. The Concept of a Person. In Taylor C, Philosophical Papers 1: Human Agency and Language. Cambridge University Press: Kindle location 1917–2261.

Taylor C, 2011. Conditions of an Unforced Consensus on Human Rights. In Taylor C, Dilemmas and Connections. Harvard University Press: 105–123.

Tellkamp JA, 2012. Vis Aestimativa and Vis Cogitativa in Thomas Aquinas's Commentary on the Sentences. The Thomist: A Speculative Quarterly Review 76(4), 611–640. DOI: 10.1353/tho.2012.0003.

Tempels P, 2010. Bantu Philosophy, transl. King C. HBC Publishing.

The Epistle to Diognetus, 1908 (~130 CE). In Radford LB, ed., Early Church Classics: The Epistle to Diognetus. Society for Promoting Christian Knowledge, pp. 61–63. Digitized by the Internet Archive, 2011. https://ia600502.us.archive.org/9/items/epistletodiognet00just/epistletodiognet00just.pdf.

The Holy Bible, Douay-Rheims Version. http://triggs.djvu.org/djvu-editions.com/BIBLES/DRV/Download.pdf.

Thommen L, 2009. An Environmental History of Ancient Greece and Rome, transl. Hill P. Cambridge University Press.

Thompson RF, 1988. Foreword. In Davis W, Passage of Darkness: The Ethnobiology of the Haitian Zombie. University of North Carolina Press: xi–xiv.

Thomson JJ, 1971. A Defense of Abortion. Philosophy and Public Affairs 1(1): 47–66.
Tiku N, 2022 (June 11). The Google Engineer Who Thinks the Company's AI has Come to Life. Washington Post.
Tooley M, 1972. Abortion and Infanticide. Philosophy and Public Affairs 2(1): 37–65.
Trivedi D, Rahn CD, Kier WM, Walker ID, 2008. Soft Robotics: Biologic Inspiration, State of the Art, and Future Research. Applied Bionics and Biomechanics 5(3): 99–117. DOI: 10.1080/11762320802557865.
Trump White House Archives, 2020 (April 6). Executive Order on Encouraging International Support for the Recovery and Use of Space Resources. https://trumpwhitehouse.archives.gov/presidential-actions/executive-order-encouraging-international-support-recovery-use-space-resources//.
Truog RD, 1997. Is It Time to Abandon Brain Death? Hastings Center Report 27(1): 29–37. DOI: 10.2307/3528024.
Truog RD, Magnus DC, 2023. The Unsuccessful Effort to Revise the Uniform Determination of Death Act. Journal of the American Medical Association 330(24): 2335–2336. DOI: 10.1001/jama.2023.24475.
Turkle S, 2017. Alone Together. Basic Books.
US Congress, 2015. U.S. Commercial Space Launch Competitiveness Act. H.R.2262. https://www.congress.gov/bill/114th-congress/house-bill/2262.
US Library of Congress (n.d.). Ancient Greek Astronomy and Cosmology. In Finding Our Place in the Cosmos: From Galileo to Sagan and Beyond. https://www.loc.gov/collections/finding-our-place-in-the-cosmos-with-carl-sagan/articles-and-essays/modeling-the-cosmos/ancient-greek-astronomy-and-cosmology.
United Nations (n.d.). What Is Climate Change? https://www.un.org/en/climatechange/what-is-climate-change.
United Nations, Office for Outer Space Affairs, 1967. Treaty on Principles Governing the Activities of States in the Exploration and Use of Outer Space, Including the Moon and Other Celestial Bodies. https://www.unoosa.org/oosa/en/ourwork/spacelaw/treaties/introouterspacetreaty.html.
Van Gulick R, 2022. Consciousness. In Zalta EN, Nodelman U, eds., Stanford Encyclopedia of Philosophy. https://plato.stanford.edu/archives/win2022/entries/consciousness/.
Van Jaarsveld J, 2019. Expanding Nussbaum's Eighth Capability Using African Environmental Ethics. In Chemhru M, ed., African Environmental Ethics. Springer International Publishing: 369–3966.
Vaz E, Penfound E, 2020. Mars Terraforming: A Geographic Information Systems Framework. Life Sciences in Space Research 24: 50–63. DOI: 10.1016/j.lssr.2019.12.001.
Veatch RM, 1976. Death, Dying, and the Biological Revolution. Yale University Press.
Veatch RM, 2005. The Death of Whole-Brain Death. Journal of Medicine and Philosophy 30(4): 353–378. DOI: 10.1080/03605310591008504.
Véliz C, 2021. Moral Zombies: Why Algorithms Are not Moral Agents. AI & Society 36: 487–497. DOI: 10.1007/s00146-021-01189-x.

Vlastos G, 1952. Theology and Philosophy in Early Greek Thought. Philosophical Quarterly 2(7): 97–123.
Vlastos G, 1984. Justice and Equality. In Waldron J, ed, Theories of Rights. Oxford University Press: 41–76.
Vodou priest (unnamed), 1988. Quoted in Davis W, 1988. Passage of Darkness: The Ethnobiology of the Haitian Zombie. University of North Carolina Press.
Wareham CS, 2011. On the Moral Equality of Artificial Agents. International Journal of Technoethics 2(1): 35–42. DOI: 10.4018/jte.2011010103.
Wareham CS, 2020, Artificial Intelligence and African Conceptions of Persons, Ethics and Information Technology 23(2): 127–136. DOI: 10.1007/s10676-020-09541-3.
Warren M, 1973. On the Moral and Legal Status of Abortion. The Monist 57(1): 43–61. DOI: 10.5840/monist197357133.
Warren MA, 2004. Moral Status: Obligations to Persons and Other Living Things. Oxford University Press.
Waweru-Siika W, Clement ME, Lukoko L, Nadel S, Rosoff PM, Naanyu V, Kussin PS, 2017. Brain Death Determination: The Imperative for Policy and Legal Initiatives in Sub-Saharan Africa. Global Public Health 12(5): 589–600. DOI: 10.1080/17441692.2015.1094108.
Weir A, 2021. Project Hail Mary. Ballantine Books, an imprint of Random House.
Weisberg M, Needham P, Hendry R, 2019. Philosophy of Chemistry. In Zalta EN, ed., Stanford Encyclopedia of Philosophy. https://plato.stanford.edu/archives/spr2019/entries/chemistry/.
White L, 1967. The Historical Roots of Our Ecological Crisis. Science 155(3676): 1203–1207. DOI: 10.1126/science.155.3767.1203.
Wiggins D, 2009. Solidarity and the Root of the Ethical. Tijdschrift Voor Filosofie 71(2): 239–269. DOI: 10.2143/TVF.71.2.2038077.
Wilkinson G, 2020. Juana la Loca/ 'Joanna the Mad' (1479–1555): Queen of Castile and of Aragon—and necrophiliac? British Journal of Psychiatry 217: 449. DOI: 10.1192/bjp.2020.71.
Williams B, 1973. The Idea of Equality. In Williams B, Problems of the Self: Philosophical Papers 1956–1972. Cambridge University Press: 230–249.
Williams B, 2008. The Human Prejudice. In Moore AW, Moore AWW, eds., Philosophy as a Humanistic Discipline. Princeton University Press: 124–138.
Williamson J, 1942. Collision Orbit. Astounding Science-Fiction July 85/2.
Wingo A, 2017. Akan Philosophy of the Person. In Zalta EN, ed., Stanford Encyclopedia of Philosophy. https://plato.stanford.edu/archives/sum2017/entries/akan-person/.
Wingo AH, 2015. The Immortals in Our Midst. Journal of Ethics 19: 237–255. DOI 10.1007/s10892-015-9209-2.
Wiredu K, 1980. How Not to Compare African Traditional Thought with Western Thought. In Wiredu K, Philosophy and African Culture. Cambridge University Press: 37–50.
Wiredu K, 1992. The Moral Foundations of African Culture. In Flack HE, Pellegrino ED, eds., African-American Perspectives on Biomedical Ethics. Georgetown University Press: 80–93.

Wiredu K, 1996. Cultural Universals and Particulars: An African Perspective. Indiana University Press.
Wiredu K, 2004. A Companion to African Philosophy. Blackwell Publishing Ltd.
Wiredu K, 2010. Death and the Afterlife in African Culture. In Wiredu K, Gyekye K, eds., Person and Community: Ghanian Philosophical Studies I. Council for Research (Washington, DC). In Values and Philosophy: 137–152.
Wiredu K, 2010. Moral Foundations of an African Culture. In Wiredu K, Gyekye K, eds., Person and Community: Ghanaian Philosophical Studies, 1. Council for Research in Values and Philosophy (Washington, DC): 193–206. https://www.crvp.org/publications/Series-II/Series02-1.html.
Wiredu K, Gyekye K, eds., 2010. Person and Community: Ghanaian Philosophical Studies, 1. Council for Research in Values and Philosophy (Washington, DC). https://www.crvp.org/publications/Series-II/Series02-1.html.
Witherington DC, 2017. The Explanatory Significance of Wholes: How Exclusive Reliance on Antecedent-Consequent Models of Explanation Undermines the Study of Persons. New Ideas in Psychology 44: 14–20.
Witherington DC, 2017. The Explanatory Significance of Wholes: How Exclusive Reliance on Antecedent-Consequent Models of Explanation Undermines the Study of Persons. New Ideas in Psychology 44: 14–20. DOI: 10.1016/j.newideapsych.2016.11.009.
Woollard F, 2023. 'Utilitarianism for Animals: Deontology for People' and the Doing/Allowing Distinction. Philosophical Studies 180: 1149–1168. DOI: /10.1007/s11098-021-01745-7.
World Health Organization, 2012. International Guidelines for Determination of Death. Canadian Blood Services and World Health Organization.
World Health Organization, 2014. Clinical Criteria for Determination of Death: Working Document: WHO Technical Expert Consultation. World Health Organization. https://iris.who.int/handle/10665/254737. World Health Organization.
Wright EJ, 2002. The Early History of Heaven. Oxford University Press.
Yang Q, Miller G, 2015. East-West Differences in Perception of Brain Death. Bioethical Inquiry 12: 211–225. DOI: 10.1007/s11673-014-9564-x.
Young G, 2019. Personhood across Disciplines. Ethics, Medicine and Public Health 10: 93–101. DOI: /10.1016/j.jemep.2019.100470.
Younger SJ, Arnold RM, 2001. Philosophical Debates about the Definition of Death: Who Cares? Journal of Medicine and Philosophy 26(5): 527–537. DOI: 10.1076/jmep.26.5.527.3002.
Ypi L, 2013. What's Wrong with Colonialism? Philosophy and Public Affairs 41(2): 158–191. DOI: 10.1111/papa.12014.
Zachos FE, 2016. Species Concepts in Biology: Historical Development, Theoretical Foundations and Practical Relevance. Springer International Publishing AG.

Name Index

For the benefit of digital users, indexed terms that span two pages (e.g., 52–53) may, on occasion, appear on only one of those pages.

Tables are indicated by an italic *t* following the page number.

Achebe C, 91, 118, 136–37, 213–14
Ahiauzu N, 17
Ajei MO, 66–67, 158
Allmark P, 140–41
Amundsen DW, 92–93, 138, 198
Anderson E, 78, 130–31
Aquinas T, 62, 186
Arcas BA, 163–64
Aristotle, 40–41, 43, 62, 65–66, 92–95, 100*t*, 107–8, 121, 129*t*, 143*t*, 184–85, 186–87, 192*t*, 199–200, 202, 206*t*, 218–20, 222, 227*t*, 232, 233, 239*t*
Augustine S, 186

Bacon F, 200, 201, 206*t*
Behrens K, 109–10, 119–20, 137, 180–81, 182–83, 189, 192*t*, 193, 215, 216–17, 230–31, 233, 237
Bentham J, 21, 23, 106–7, 122–23, 156, 187, 188
Bird-David N, 2
Bouchard CB, 51
Bruno G, 220

Callicott JB, 234–36, 237
Chemhuru M, 196
Churchland PS, 107
Coeckelbergh M, 159–60, 175
Cooley D, 140–41
Copernicus, 220
Cressman K, 189–90
Crisp R, 40
Curtis B, 164–65

Danaher J, 160, 166–67
Daniels N, 55–56

Darwall S, 23, 53
Darwin C, 187, 188
Davis W, 150–51, 152, 154
Democritus, 218–20
Descartes R, 184–85, 186–87, 192*t*, 199–200, 206*t*
Draper H, 167
Dzobo, N, 195, 196

Elder A, 172–73
Empedocles, 199
Engelhardt HT, 123–24
Epicurus, 218–19
Eze MO, 29, 193–94, 206*t*

Feinberg J, 98–99
Flanagan O, 107
Fletcher J, 123–24
Foot P, 75, 86–87, 104–5
Francis of Assisi, 200
Fustel DC, 38, 120, 198

Gade CBN, 34–35
Galileo, G, 220
Garland A, 169
Gbadegesin S, 19, 137, 152–53
Gordon J-S, 160
Gunkel D, 158–59, 160
Gyekye K, 13n.ii, 17, 18–19, 22–23, 29, 32, 36, 37, 58n.v, 58–59, 76–77, 81–82, 92, 107–9, 116, 117–18, 178, 215–16

Harris J, 122–23
Heidegger M, 173, 243–44
Henrich J, 51

Hesiod, 198, 217
Hill TE, 140–41
Hippocrates, 138
Hobbes T, 17–18
Holm S, 98, 111
Hume D, 107, 141, 187, 188

Ikuenobe P, 16–17, 90–91, 114–15, 136–37
Ishiguro K, 66–67, 158

Jecker NS, 119–20
Jesus, 41, 122, 221
Jonze S, 166

Kant I, 5, 14, 17–19, 20–21, 20n.viii, 23, 25–26, 30t, 37, 41, 57n.iv, 81–82, 86–87, 96, 98–99, 100t, 101–2, 111–12, 122–23, 126–27, 129t, 129–30, 140–41, 143t, 147–48, 151, 155–56, 157t, 159–60, 161t, 171t, 187, 192t, 202, 204, 206t, 223–24, 226, 227t, 233–34, 239t
Kasene P, 195, 196
Kepler J, 221
Kilner J, 89
Kittay EF, 54–55, 78
Korsgaard CM, 15, 20–21, 140–41, 155–56
Kubrick S, 166–67

Lemoine B, 162–63
Leopold A, 202–3, 204, 206t, 233–34, 235–36, 237, 239t
Leucippus, 218–20
Lindberg DC, 218
Liyong TL, 213–14
Locke J, 17–18, 96, 97
Lucretius, 121n.iv, 218–19

Mandela N, 131
Masolo DA, 32–33
Mawere M, 136
Mbiti JS, 17, 28–29, 35, 179, 215
Mbomo O, 135
McArthur N, 158–59
McGuffie K, 176

Menkiti IA, 16–17, 19–20, 23–24, 27, 28–29, 35, 37, 44, 58, 59, 79, 81–82, 88–90, 107–9, 113, 114–16, 137, 215–16
Merchant C, 201–2
Metz T, 16–17, 19–20, 27, 35, 75–76, 82, 83n.ix, 89, 119n.iii, 182–84, 193, 196, 208–9, 215, 216–17
Midgley M, 69, 73, 74–75, 78, 202
Mill JS, 122–23, 156
Molefe M, 13n.ii, 15, 16–17, 135–36, 182–84, 193, 208–9, 215
Mori M, 168–69
Muade E, 13n.ii, 15
Murove MF, 135, 195

Næss A, 203–4, 206t, 234, 235–36, 237, 239t
Nagel T, 68, 69–70, 207n.iv
Nelson HL, 140–41
Newhouse A, 176
Newmyer ST, 185–86
Nkulu-N'Sengha M, 33–34, 36
Noddings N, 69
Noonan JT, 25–26, 51–52
Nozick R, 78
Nussbaum MC, 185, 190–91

Onarehim KH, 88
Otto E, 233–34

Pascal B, 221–22
Penfound E, 227–29
Plato, 40–41, 92–95, 100t, 121, 129t, 143t, 184–85, 192t, 199–200, 206t, 218–20, 222, 227t, 232, 239t
Poe EA, 132–33
Pope Paul III, 41
Potthast A, 226–27
Presby GM, 115
Putnam H, 185
Pythagoras, 121, 184

Regan T, 188–89
Rist JM, 94–95
Robinson KS, 227–39
Rolston H, 235–38
Romero G, 148–58

NAME INDEX

Rousseau J, 17–18
Ryder RD, 51–52

Savulescu J, 21n.ix, 25–26, 55n.ii, 164–65
Schneewind J, 20–21
Schoeman F, 55–56
Senghor LL, 199
Shutte A, 19, 35
Siedentop L, 122
Singer P, 22, 51–52, 71, 75, 97–98, 141, 184, 188–89, 199–200, 225–26, 234–35
Slote M, 55–56
Socrates, 32
Sorrell T, 167
Spielberg S, 169
Steinbock B, 54–55, 78, 84, 110–11
Stringer R, 65–66

Tangwa G, 31–32, 61n.vi, 92, 180, 193–94, 196–97, 215

Tempels P, 80, 195, 196–97, 206t, 230–31
Thomson JJ, 25–26, 82n.vii
Tooley M, 25

Vaz E, 227–29
Veatch RM, 127
Vlastos G, 43

Warren M, 20, 123–24
Weir A, 211–27
White L, 200, 232–33
Wiggins D, 104–5
Williams B, 70, 71, 78, 111, 225–26
Williamson J, 227–28
Wingo A, 81–82, 115–17
Wiredu K, 13n.ii, 117–18, 135–36, 179

Ypi L, 32–33

Subject Index

For the benefit of digital users, indexed terms that span two pages (e.g., 52–53) may, on occasion, appear on only one of those pages.

Tables are indicated by an italic *t* following the page.

abortion. *See* African personhood and ethics, disability; Emergent Personhood; Kantian ethics; utilitarian ethics; Western ethics

African ethics. *See* African personhood and ethics

African personhood and ethics. *See also* Emergent Personhood; Greek philosophy ancient; Kantian ethics; medieval Christian approaches to personhood; utilitarian ethics; Western approaches to personhood
    abortion in (*see* arc of personhood in; birth significance in; child moral status in)
    advantages/disadvantages of, 48–49, 56–61, 60*t*, 75–77, 100–6, 129–34
    aging in (*see* arc of personhood in; binary/scalar moral status in; child moral status in; elders in; equality of moral status in; incorporation and; ancestors in)
    ancestors in, 6, 104–5, 113, 114–21, 135–36, 196 (*see also* arc of personhood in; death of persons; elders in; soul and)
    anthropocentrism and, 116, 178–84, 193–97, 226, 227*t* (*see also* family/filiation)
    arc of personhood in, 22–25, 26–28, 30*t*, 45*t*, 87–92, 95, 100*t*, 115–16, 179, 215–17, 230–31 (*see also* ancestors in; binary/scalar moral status in; birth significance in; child death in; elders in; equality of moral status in; incorporation and; infant moral status in; assisted suicide in)
    artificial intelligence/AI and, 66–67, 158–76, 161*t*, 170*t*, 171*t* (*see also* consciousness in; zombies in)
    assisted death in, 135–36, 143*t* (*see also* end of life in)
    assisted suicide in (*see* assisted death in; end of life in; autonomy in; suicide in)
    binary/scalar moral status in, 3–4, 5, 23–28, 24n.x, 30*t*, 44–46, 45*t*, 60*t*, 88–92, 95, 114–21, 143*t*, 192*t*, 196, 215–16, 230–31 (*see also* arc of personhood; equal/unequal moral status in; intrinsic/extrinsic moral status in; stable/changing moral status in; derivative/nonderivative moral status in; equal/unequal moral status in)
    birth significance in, 88–95 (*see also* abortion in; binary/scalar moral status in; capacity for communal relationships and; child death in)
    capacity for communal relationships and, 2, 16–30, 33–37, 43–46, 45*t*, 64–65, 75–77, 87–95, 100*t*,

African personhood and ethics (cont.)
107–8, 114–20, 129t, 135–40,
143t, 149–55, 151t, 157–58,
157t, 159–60, 161t, 170–71,
170t, 171t, 180–83, 192t, 193–
97, 206t, 208–9, 215–17, 226,
227t, 229–31, 239t (see also
binary/scalar moral status in;
definition of persons in; family/
filiation in; feminist perspectives
and; incorporation and)
care ethics (see feminist
perspectives and)
child moral status in, 49–95, 82n.vii,
100t, 103, 107–10, 117–18 (see
also arc of personhood in; binary/
scalar moral status in; end of life
in; equality of moral status in;
incorporation and; stable/
changing moral status in)
colonial influences on, 31–33, 41,
116n.i, 136–37
consciousness in, 2, 6, 14, 20, 129t,
147–72, 176–77, 182–83,
192t, 227t (see also artificial
intelligence/AI and; disability and
zombies and)
death of 'persons' in, 114–21, 124, 127–
28, 129t, 135–36, 143t (see also
ancestors in; arc of personhood
in; assisted death in; child moral
status in; definition of 'person' in;
elders in; suicide in)
definition of 'African' in, 12, 12n.i
definition of 'person' in, 13n.ii
derivative/nonderivative moral status
in, 16–20, 28–30, 30t, 34–36,
44–46, 45t, 58, 60t, 64–65, 76–77,
88–95, 100t, 115–16, 119–20,
129t, 160, 171, 181–82, 192t,
206t, 215–17, 227t, 230–31,
239t (see also earned/unearned
moral status in; equal/unequal
moral status in; intrinsic/
extrinsic moral status in;
scalar/binary moral status in;
stable/changing moral status in)

disability and, 78, 79, 82n.vii, 84,
86–87, 92, 97, 99, 100t, 101–2,
110–11, 143t
disease/health in, 135–37, 139–40
earned/unearned moral status in, 5,
20–21, 22–23, 30t, 44–46, 45t,
60t, 81–82, 87–95, 100t, 114–20,
128, 129t, 129–31, 135–37, 142,
143t, 148–55, 157t, 158–72,
174–76, 178–84, 192t, 193–97,
205t, 206t, 213–17, 227t, 230–31,
239t (see also intrinsic/extrinsic
moral status in; scalar/binary
moral status in; stable/changing
moral status in; derivative/
nonderivative moral status in;
equal/unequal moral status in)
elders in, 87–95, 100t, 101–2, 108–
10, 114–20, 131–32 (see also
ancestors in; arc of personhood
in; binary/scalar moral status in;
equality of moral status in)
Emergent Personhood compared
to, 2–3, 5–6, 7, 47–84, 86–87,
100–6, 107–8, 109–10, 111–12,
113, 126–28, 129t, 129–31, 142,
143t, 143–44, 148, 156–58, 157t,
160–61, 161t, 164–72, 170t,
176–77, 178, 183–84, 189–90–,
192t, 192, 206t, 208–9, 210–11,
226, 227t, 229–30, 237, 239t (see
also Greek philosophy ancient
compared to, |Kantian ethics
compared to; utilitarian ethics
compared to; Western approaches
to personhood compared to)
end of life in (see ancestors in; arc of
personhood in; assisted death
in; child moral status in; death of
persons in elders in; infants moral
status in; suicide in)
equal/unequal moral status in, 2, 3–4,
16–30, 30t, 44–46, 45t, 58–59,
60t, 75–77, 81–82, 87–95, 100t,
101–2, 103–4, 107–10, 114–21,
128, 129t, 130–31, 135–37, 143t,
148–72, 178–84, 193–97, 205t,

SUBJECT INDEX 319

206t, 211–17, 226, 227t, 227–31, 239t (*see also* arc of personhood in; binary/scalar moral status in; earned/unearned moral status in)
euthanasia in (*see* assisted death in; end of life in; suicide in)
family/ filiation in, 16–17, 25, 64–65, 88–90, 104–5, 135–37, 180–81, 194–95, 216–17 (*see also* capacity for communal relationships and; feminist perspectives and; incorporation and)
feminist perspectives and, 36, 56–57, 58, 108–9 (*see also* capacity for communal relationships and; family/filiation in; incorporation and)
five features of (*see* binary/scalar moral status in; intrinsic/extrinsic moral status in; earned/unearned moral status in; stable/changing moral status in; derivative/nonderivative moral status in)
force theory and, 80, 151–52, 180, 193–94, 195–97, 204, 206t, 230–31 (*see also* ancestors in; definition of persons in)
Greek philosophy ancient compared to, 5, 44–46, 45t, 47–49, 56–61, 60t, 84–85, 87–95, 100t, 103, 107–8, 111–12, 120–21, 122–23, 126–27, 129t, 137–38, 139–40, 143t, 192t, 206t, 227t, 239t (*see also* Emergent Personhood compared to; Kantian ethics compared to; utilitarian ethics compared to; Western approaches to personhood compared to)
incorporation and, 2, 16–30, 59, 60t, 79–84, 86–92, 95, 100t, 103, 114–28, 129t, 147–48, 162, 168–70, 170t, 226 (*see also* arc of personhood in; binary/scalar moral status in; capacity for communal relationships; child moral status in; derivative/non-derivative moral status

in; relationships and; feminist perspectives and)
infant moral status in (*see* arc of personhood in; binary/scalar moral status in; birth significance in; child moral status in; incorporation and)
intrinsic/extrinsic moral status in, 5, 12–13, 14–15, 18–22, 30t, 44–46, 45t, 60t, 179, 182–83, 196, 230–31, 233 (*see also* force theory and; relational aspects of)
Kantian ethics compared to, 5, 18–19, 20–21, 57n.iv, 81–82, 100t, 122–23, 129t, 129–30, 139–40, 143t, 147–48, 151, 157t, 161t, 206t, 227t, 233–34 (*see also* Emergent Personhood compared to; Greek philosophy ancient compared to; utilitarian ethics compared to; Western approaches to personhood compared to)
machine ethics (*see* artificial intelligence/AI and; consciousness in; zombies in)
medieval Christian approaches to personhood compared to, 5, 48–49, 56–61, 60t, 92–93, 116–17, 135–36
ōkra (soul) and (*see* soul and)
ontological progression of (*see* arc of personhood in; binary/scalar moral status in; birth significance in; child moral status in; incorporation and)
precolonial views of (*see* Ubuntu and; Colonial influences on)
'presumption in favour of prosocial virtues' in (*see* prosocial virtues and)
prosocial virtues and, 16–17, 22–23, 36–37, 64–65, 84, 129–30, 131, 135–36, 143t, 147–72, 174–76, 227t (*see also* ubuntu and)
relational aspects of, 2, 16–30, 33–37, 56–57, 60t, 61t, 61–62, 75–76, 78–79, 89–90, 96–99, 100t,

SUBJECT INDEX

African personhood and ethics (*cont.*)
101–2, 108–10, 111–12, 119n.iii, 122–23, 126–28, 129*t*, 129–30, 135–37, 140–41, 143*t*, 147–48, 160, 161*t*, 170–71, 180–83, 192*t*, 206*t*, 207–8, 216–17 (*see also* Emergent Personhood compared to; Greek Philosophy ancient compared to; utilitarian ethics compared to; Western approaches to personhood compared to)
rights versus duties in, 31–46, 57, 57n.iv, 136–37 (*see also* prosocial virtues and; Kantian ethics compared to)
soul and, 19–20, 22–23, 34–35, 81–82, 116–17, 116n.i, 120–21, 151–53, 179, 209 (*see also* ancestors in; arc of personhood; death of persons in; elders and)
stable/changing moral status in, 5, 26–28, 30*t*, 44, 45*t*, 47, 59, 60*t*, 86–94, 95, 100*t*, 101–2, 111–12, 129–30, 131, 143*t*, 158, 160–61 (*see also* arc of personhood; binary/scalar moral status in; derivative/nonderivative moral status in; earned/unearned moral status in; equal/unequal moral status in; incorporation and; intrinsic/extrinsic moral status in)
suicide in, 136–37
Ubuntu and, 33–37, 58 (*see also* capacity for communal relationships and; prosocial virtues and)
utilitarian ethics compared to, 25–26, 30*t*, 86–87, 100*t*, 101–2, 103–4, 111–12, 122–23, 129*t*, 129–30, 139–40, 141, 143*t*, 147–48, 151, 151*t*, 157*t*, 159–60, 161*t*, 171*t*, 192*t*, 196, 206*t*, 207–9, 227*t*, 233–34 (*see also* Emergent Personhood compared to; Greek philosophy ancient compared to; Kantian ethics compared to; Western approaches to personhood compared to)
Vodou in (*see* zombies in)
Western approaches to personhood compared to (*see* Greek Philosophy ancient compared to; Kantian ethics compared to; utilitarian ethics compared to)
zombies in, 148–55, 151*t*, 157*t*, 157–61, 161*t*(*see also* artificial intelligence/AI and; consciousness in)

African philosophy. *See* African personhood and ethics

Emergent Personhood. *See also* African personhood and ethics; artificial intelligence; Greek philosophy ancient; Kantian ethics; medieval Christian approaches to personhood; utilitarian ethics; Western approaches to personhood
abortion and, 79–84
African personhood and ethics compared to, 2–3, 5–6, 7, 47–84, 86–87, 100–6, 107–8, 109–10, 111–12, 113, 126–28, 129*t*, 129–31, 142, 143*t*, 143–44, 148, 156–58, 157*t*, 160–61, 161*t*, 164–72, 170*t*, 176–77, 178, 183–84, 189–90–, 192*t*, 192, 206*t*, 208–9, 210–11, 226, 227*t*, 229–30, 237, 239*t*
aging in (*see* binary/scalar moral status in; disability and; stable/changing moral status in
anthropocentrism *See* humble anthropocentrism and; speciesism and)
artificial intelligence/AI and, 66–67, 158–76, 161*t*, 170*t*, 171*t* (*see also* consciousness in; zombies in)
assisted death in, 141–42, 143*t*, See also death of persons in
assisted suicide in (*see* assisted death in; death of persons in)
binary/scalar moral status in, 57–58, 61*t*, 72*t*, 77–79, 83, 84, 100*t*,

SUBJECT INDEX 321

126–28, 189–90, 192t, 205t, 225, 239t (*see also* equal/unequal moral status in; intrinsic/extrinsic moral status in; scalar/binary moral status in; stable/changing moral status in; derivative/nonderivative moral status in)

care ethics (*see* feminist perspectives and; family/filiation in; relational aspects of)

consciousness in, 63–64, 79, 84, 101, 126, 129t, 151t, 157t, 158–76, 161t (*see also* artificial intelligence/AI and; disability and; zombies and)

conundrum of personhood and, 52, 77–78, 141–42, 188–89, 209

death of persons in, 113, 126–28, 129t, 131–34, 141–42, 143t (*see also* assisted death in; definition of 'Emergent Personhood' in)

definition of 'Emergent Personhood' in, 71–135, 72t, 156–58, 161t, 191

derivative/nonderivative moral status in, 47–49, 53–54, 55–56, 60t, 61t, 61–84, 104–6, 126–28, 129t, 131, 134, 156–57, 157t, 160, 161t, 171, 189–90, 192t, 204–6, 205t, 206t, 225–26 (*see also* earned/unearned moral status in; intrinsic/extrinsic moral status in; scalar/binary moral status in; stable/changing moral status in)

disability and, 3–4, 62, 76–77, 79, 84, 86–87, 97, 99, 100t, 100–3, 106, 107–8, 110–11, 126, 129t, 129–30, 131, 133–34, 141–42, 143t (*see also* consciousness in; privation and; stable/changing moral status in)

earned/unearned moral status in, 16–30, 30t, 60–79, 89–92, 100–1, 116–17, 171–72, 192t, 205t, 240–41 (*see also* derivative/nonderivative moral status in; equal/unequal moral status in; intrinsic/extrinsic moral status in; scalar/binary moral status in; stable/changing moral status in)

emergentist and, 61–84

end of life in (*see* assisted death in; death of persons in)

end of personhood objection and, 3–4

equal/unequal moral status in, 3–4, 43–46, 45t, 59, 60t, 75–77, 81–82, 87–95, 100t, 101–2, 103–4, 107–10, 111–12, 114–21, 129t, 151–55, 157t, 170–71, 171t, 181–83, 192t, 193–97, 206t, 215, 227t, 230–31, 239t (*see also* arc of personhood in; disability and; earned/unearned moral status in; scalar/binary moral status in; speciesism and; stable/changing moral status in)

euthanasia in (*see* assisted death in; death of persons in)

family/filiation in, 55, 59, 64–65, 66–67, 75, 82–84, 104–6, 111, 143–44, 224 (*see also* feminist perspectives and; relational aspects of; speciesism and)

feminist perspectives and, 31–46, 48–79, 106–11 (*see also* family/filiation in; speciesism and; relational aspects of

five features of (*see* intrinsic/extrinsic moral status in; earned/unearned moral status in; scalar/binary moral status in; stable/changing moral status in; derivative/nonderivative moral status in)

Greek philosophy ancient compared to, 47–61, 65–66, 79, 84–85, 101–3, 104, 106, 107–8, 111–12, 126–31, 129t, 142, 143t, 174–75, 178, 192t, 192, 206t, 210–11, 226, 239t, 240–41 (*see also* African personhood and ethics compared to; Western approaches to personhood compared to)

humble anthropocentrism and, 67–71, 189–91, 206–8, 237–38, *See also* speciesism and

322 SUBJECT INDEX

Emergent Personhood (*cont.*)
  infant moral status in (*see* equal/unequal moral status in)
  intrinsic/extrinsic moral status in, 14–15, 48–49, 60*t*, 61*t*, 61–65, 66–67, 71, 75–79, 143–44, 151*t*, 157–58, 157*t*, 170*t*, 170–71, 171*t*, 189, 190, 192*t*, 205*t*, 206*t*, 225, 239*t* (*see also* derivative/nonderivative moral status in; earned/unearned moral status in; relational aspects of; scalar/binary moral status in; stable/changing moral status in)
  Kantian ethics compared to, 5, 81–82, 86–87, 96, 101–3, 111–12, 122–23, 126–27, 129*t*, 129–31, 140–41, 143*t*, 147–48, 151, 155–56, 157*t*, 161*t*, 171*t*, 171, 206*t*, 226, 227*t* (*see also* Western approaches to personhood compared to)
  machine ethics (*see* artificial intelligence/AI and; consciousness in; zombies in)
  medieval Christian approaches to personhood compared to, 77–78, 104, 192, 226
  prenatal human life and (*see* abortion and)
  privation and, 62, 76–77, 108 (*see also* disability and; medieval Christian approaches to personhood)
  relational aspects of, 55, 64–65, 70, 75–76, 77–78, 79–84, 83n.ix, 104–6, 107–8, 111, 160, 161*t*, 171, 204–5, 207–9, 225, 237 (*see also* family/filiation in; feminist perspectives and; solidarity in; speciesism and)
  solidarity in (*see* family/filiation in; relational aspects of; speciesism in)
  sophisticated cognitive capacities and (*see* consciousness in; disability and; privation and)
  soul and (*see* conundrum of personhood and)
  speciesism and, 5, 52, 55, 66–69, 71–75, 72*t*, 206–8, 225–26, 227*t*, 237–38 (*see also* family/filiation in; humble anthropocentrism and; relational aspects of; solidarity in)
  species significance and (*see* family/filiation in; humble anthropocentrism and; relational aspects of; solidarity in; speciesism and)
  stable/changing moral status in, 5, 47–67, 60*t*, 71, 72*t*, 77–79, 83–84, 86–87, 100–2, 111–12, 129–32, 141–42, 143*t*, 158, 160–61, 171–72, 189–90, 192*t*, 205*t*, 207–8, 225, 240–41 (*see also* binary/scalar moral status in; consciousness in; derivative/nonderivative moral status in; disability and; earned/unearned moral status in; equal/unequal moral status in; intrinsic/extrinsic moral status in)
  utilitarian ethics compared to, 71–75, 72*t*, 100–6, 110–12, 126–27, 129*t*, 129–31, 141–42, 143*t*, 147–48, 151, 155–57, 157*t*, 159–60, 161*t*, 162, 171*t*, 192*t*, 206*t*, 206–8, 224–26, 227*t* (*see also* Western approaches to personhood compared to)
  Western approaches to personhood compared to (*see* Greek philosophy ancient compared to; Kantian ethics compared to; medieval Christian approaches to personhood compared to; utilitarian ethics compared to)
  zombies in, 148–51, 151*t*, 156–61, 157*t*, 161*t* (*see also* artificial intelligence/AI and; consciousness in)

fact/value distinction
  African personhood and, 34–36, 103, 104, 106–7, 171
  Emergent Personhood and, 104–7, 134, 171

SUBJECT INDEX 323

Greek philosophy ancient and, 103
Kantian ethics and, 103–4
medieval Christian personhood and, 104
utilitarian ethics and, 103–4, 106–7
Western personhood and, 103–4, 106–7, 171

Greek philosophy. *See* Greek philosophy ancient

Greek philosophy ancient. *See also* African ethics and personhood; Emergent Personhood; Kantian ethics; medieval Christian approaches to personhood; utilitarian ethics; Western approaches to personhood
ancestors in, 6, 38–40, 94, 120–21 (*see also* death of persons in; soul and)
anthropocentrism in, 184–86, 199–200, 222, 227t, 232
apotheosis in (*see* soul and)
assisted death in, 137–40, 143t (*see also* death of persons in; soul and)
binary/scalar moral status in, 38, 40–41, 43, 45t, 49–50, 60t, 92–95 (*see also* derivative/nonderivative moral status in; equal/unequal moral status in; intrinsic/extrinsic moral status in; stable/changing moral status in)
child moral status in, 49, 53, 59, 92–94, 100t (*see also* equal/unequal moral status and; stable/changing moral status)
death of persons in, 120–21, 121n.iv, 127–28, 129t, 143t (*see also* ancestors in; soul and)
derivative/nonderivative moral status in, 41–44, 45t, 60t, 92–95, 100t, 120, 129t, 137–40, 143t, 184 (*see also* binary/scalar moral status in; earned/unearned moral status in; intrinsic/extrinsic moral status in; stable/changing moral status)
disability and, 41, 97, 99, 100t, 101–2, 129t, 143t

earned/unearned moral status in, 31–46, 45t, 94–95 (*see also* intrinsic/extrinsic moral status in; scalar/binary moral status in; stable/changing moral status in; derivative/nonderivative moral status in; equal/unequal moral status in)
Emergent Personhood compared to, 47–61, 65–66, 79, 84–85, 101–3, 104, 106, 107–8, 111–12, 126–31, 129t, 142, 143t, 174–75, 178, 192t, 192, 206t, 210–11, 226, 239t, 240–41 (*see also* African personhood and ethics compared to)
end of life in (*see* ancestors in; assisted death in; death of persons in; equal/unequal moral status in)
equal/unequal moral status in, 37–38, 40–41, 43–46, 45t, 48–50, 59, 60t, 92–95, 100t, 101–2, 103–4, 111–12, 120–21, 128, 129t, 184–86, 192t, 197–200, 206t, 222, 227t, 231–33, 239t (*see also* disability and; earned/unearned moral status in; scalar/binary moral status in; slaves' moral status in; stable/changing moral status in; stable/changing moral status in; women's moral status in)
five features of (*see* binary/scalar moral status in; derivative/nonderivative moral status in; earned/unearned moral status in; intrinsic/extrinsic moral status in; stable/changing moral status)
immortality in (*see* ancestors in; death of persons in; soul and)
intrinsic/extrinsic moral status in, 5, 14–15, 44–46, 45t, 92–95, 185, 233 (*see also* binary/scalar moral status in; derivative/nonderivative moral status in; earned/unearned moral status in; soul and; stable/changing moral status)
medieval Christian approaches to personhood compared to, 49–56

SUBJECT INDEX

Greek philosophy ancient (cont.)
person as *persōna*, 1, 40, 119–20
slaves' moral status in, 40–41, 49, 53, 59, 79, 93–94 (*see also* equal/unequal moral status in)
soul and, 38, 120–21, 122–23, 184, 185–86, 199–200 (*see also* ancestors and; death of persons in)
stable/changing moral status in, 5, 44, 45t, 47, 60t, 86–87, 92–95, 100t, 101–2, 111–12, 120–21, 143t (*see also* binary/scalar moral status in; derivative/nonderivative moral status in; disability and; earned/unearned moral status in; equal/unequal moral status in; intrinsic/extrinsic moral status in)
women's moral status in, 40–41, 53, 59, 79, 93–94 (*see also* equal/unequal moral status)

humble anthropocentrism. *See* Emergent Personhood

Judeo-Christian ethics. *See* medieval Christian approaches to personhood; Western approaches to personhood

Kantian ethics. *See also* African personhood and ethics; Emergent Personhood; Greek philosophy ancient; medieval Christian approaches to personhood; utilitarian ethics; Western approaches to personhood
anthropocentrism and, 202, 223–24, 227t (*see also* equal/unequal moral status in)
artificial intelligence/AI, 158–60, 162–71, 170t, 171t (*see also* consciousness in; zombies in)
assisted death in, 140–41, 143t (*see also* autonomy in)
assisted suicide in (*see* assisted death in)
autonomy in, 16–30

binary/scalar moral status in, 16–30, 30t, 98–99, 100t (*see also* derivative/nonderivative moral status in; earned/unearned moral status in; equal/unequal moral status in; intrinsic/extrinsic moral status in; stable/changing moral status in)
consciousness in, 61–79, 96, 122–23, 129t, 147–76, 151t, 157t, 161t, 187, 192t, 204, 233–34 (*see also* artificial intelligence/AI and; disability and; zombies and)
death of persons in, 122–23, 129t, 143t (*see also* suicide and; assisted death in)
derivative/nonderivative moral status in, 17–19, 20–21, 29–30, 30t, 122–23, 129t, 140–41, 143t, 187, 192t, 202–3, 206t, 227t (*see also* binary/scalar moral status in; earned/unearned moral status in; intrinsic/extrinsic moral status in; stable/changing moral status in)
disability and, 25–26, 41, 54–55, 72t, 97, 98–99, 100t, 101–2, 111–12, 122–23, 129t, 143t (*see also* consciousness in; equal/unequal moral status in)
earned/unearned moral status in, 16–30, 30t, 45t (*see also* binary/scalar moral status in; derivative/nonderivative moral status in; intrinsic/extrinsic moral status in; stable/changing moral status in)
Emergent Personhood compared to, 5, 81–82, 86–87, 96, 101–3, 111–12, 122–23, 126–27, 129t, 129–31, 140–41, 143t, 147–48, 151, 155–56, 157t, 161t, 171t, 206t, 226, 227t (*see also* African ethics and personhood compared to)
end of life in (*see* assisted death in; death of persons in; suicide and equal/unequal)
moral status in, 16–30, 30t, 31–46, 96–99, 100–6
equal/unequal moral status in, 41–44, 46, 52–53, 54–55, 60–61, 98–99, 100t,

101–2, 111–12 (*see also* binary/scalar moral status in; derivative/nonderivative moral status in; earned/unearned moral status in; intrinsic/extrinsic moral status in; stable/changing moral status in)
euthanasia (*see* assisted death in; death of persons in)
five features of (*see* binary/scalar moral status in; derivative/nonderivative moral status in; earned/unearned moral status in; intrinsic/extrinsic moral status in; stable/changing moral status in)
intrinsic/extrinsic moral status in, 5, 12–13, 14–15, 18–19, 20–21, 30*t*, 96, 98–99, 100*t*, 103–4, 122–23, 140, 143–44, 171 (*see also* binary/scalar moral status in; derivative/nonderivative moral status in; earned/unearned moral status in; equal/unequal moral status in; stable/changing moral status in)
machine ethics (*see* artificial intelligence/AI and; consciousness in; zombies in)
sophisticated cognitive capacities and (*see* consciousness in)
stable/changing moral status in, 5, 28, 30*t*, 86–87, 98–99, 100*t*, 101–2, 122–23, 129–30, 140–41, 143*t* (*see also* binary/scalar moral status in; consciousness in; derivative/nonderivative moral status in; disability and; earned/unearned moral status in; equal/unequal moral status in; intrinsic/extrinsic moral status in)
suicide and, 140–41 (*see also* assisted death in)
zombies in, 148–51, 151*t*, 155–56, 157*t*, 157–60, 161*t*, 170*t*, 171*t* (*see also* artificial intelligence/AI and; consciousness in)

medieval Christian approaches to personhood. See *also* Western approaches to personhood; Greek philosophy ancient
African philosophy compared to, 5, 48–49, 56–61, 60*t*, 92–93, 116–17, 135–36
angels and celestial beings in, 3–4, 49–50, 220
anthropocentrism in, 22, 49–50, 51–56, 186, 200, 222–23, 227*t*, 232–33 (*see also imago Dei* in)
binary/scalar moral status in, 26, 41–44, 49–50, 53, 61*t* (*see also* derivative/nonderivative moral status in; earned/unearned moral status in; intrinsic/extrinsic moral status in; stable/changing moral status in)
conundrum of personhood in, 49–50, 51–57, 188–89, 209 (*see also* soul and; Western approaches to personhood)
death of persons in, 122–23, 135–36 (*see also* soul and)
disability and (*see* privation and)
derivative/non-derivative moral status in, 5, 41–44, 50–54, 55–56, 61*t*, 206*t* (*see also* earned/unearned moral status in; equal/unequal moral status in; intrinsic/extrinsic moral status in; scalar/binary moral status in; stable/changing moral status in)
earned/unearned moral status in, 41–44, 61*t* (*see also* intrinsic/extrinsic moral status in; scalar/binary moral status in; stable/changing moral status in; derivative/nonderivative moral status in; equal/unequal moral status in)
Emergent Personhood compared to, 77–78, 104, 192, 226
equal/unequal moral status in, 30*t*, 41–46, 49–50, 52–53, 60–61, 61*t*, 77–78 (*see also* binary/scalar moral status in; disability and; earned/unearned moral status in; intrinsic/extrinsic moral status in; stable/changing moral status in)

medieval Christian approaches to personhood (*cont.*)
family/filiation in, 41, 49, 122 (*see also* individualism and)
five features of (*see* binary/scalar moral status in; derivative/nonderivative moral status in; earned/unearned moral status in; intrinsic/extrinsic moral status in; stable/changing moral status in)
Greek philosophy ancient compared to, 49–56
imago Dei in, 26, 31–46, 48–61, 222–23, 227t (*see also*; conundrum of personhood in; intrinsic/extrinsic moral status in; soul and)
individualism and, 41, 44–46, 48–52, 53–54, 55–56, 122 (*see also* family/filiation in)
intrinsic/extrinsic moral status in, 5, 14–15, 43, 61t, 122–23 (*see also* binary/scalar moral status in; derivative/nonderivative moral status in; earned/unearned moral status in; *imago Dei* in; soul and)
privation and, 62, 76–77, 108
soul and, 26, 41–43, 49–57, 77–78, 116–17, 122–23, 186, 188–89, 209, 239t (*see also* conundrum of personhood in)
stable/changing moral status in, 41, 49–50, 53, 61t, 77–78 (*see also* binary/scalar moral status in; derivative/nonderivative moral status in; privation and; earned/unearned moral status in; equal/unequal moral status in; *imago Dei* in; intrinsic/extrinsic moral status in; soul and)

rights versus duties in, 55–56
robots. *See* African personhood and ethics; Emergent Personhood; Kantian ethics; utilitarian ethics; Western approaches to personhood

soul. *See* African ethics and personhood; Greek philosophy ancient; medieval Christian approaches to personhood; Western approaches to personhood

ubuntu. *See* African personhood and ethics
utilitarian ethics. *See also* African ethics and personhood; Emergent Personhood; Greek philosophy ancient; Kantian ethics; medieval Christian approaches to personhood; Western approaches to personhood
anthropocentrism and, 187, 202, 224, 225–26, 227t (*see also* speciesism and)
artificial intelligence/AI and, 158–60, 162–71, 170t, 171t (*see also* consciousness in; zombies in)
assisted death in, 141, 143t (*see also* death of persons)
assisted suicide in (*see* assisted death in)
binary/scalar moral status in, 16–30, 30t, 98, 100t (*see also* derivative/nonderivative moral status in; earned/unearned moral status in; intrinsic/extrinsic moral status in; stable/changing moral status in)
consciousness in, 61–79, 122–23, 129t, 147–76, 151t, 157t, 161t, 192t, 204, 233–34 (*see also* artificial intelligence/AI and; disability and; zombies in)
death of persons, 122–23, 129t, 143t (*see also* assisted death)
derivative/nonderivative moral status in, 17–18, 20, 21–22, 29–30, 30t, 122–23, 129t, 140, 141, 143t, 188–89, 192t, 202–3, 227t (*see also* binary/scalar moral status in; derivative/nonderivative moral status in; earned/unearned moral status in; intrinsic/extrinsic moral status in; stable/changing moral status in)
disability and, 25–26, 55, 72t, 73–74, 86–87, 96–98, 100t, 101–2,

SUBJECT INDEX 327

110–12, 122–23, 129t, 143t (see also consciousness in)
earned/unearned moral status in, 16–30, 30t, 45t (see also binary/scalar moral status in; derivative/nonderivative moral status in; equal/unequal moral status in; intrinsic/extrinsic moral status in; stable/changing moral status in)
Emergent Personhood compared to, 71–75, 72t, 100–6, 110–12, 126–27, 129t, 129–31, 141–42, 143t, 147–48, 151, 155–57, 157t, 159–60, 161t, 162, 171t, 192t, 206t, 206–8, 224–26, 227t
end of life in (see assisted death in)
equal/unequal moral status in, 41–44, 46, 52–53, 55, 60–61, 71–75, 72t, 97–98, 100t, 101–2, 111–12 (see also binary/scalar moral status in; derivative/nonderivative moral status in; disability and; earned/unearned moral status in; intrinsic/extrinsic moral status in; stable/changing moral status in)
euthanasia in (see assisted death in)
five features of (see binary/scalar moral status in; derivative/nonderivative moral status in; earned/unearned moral status in; intrinsic/extrinsic moral status in; stable/changing moral status in)
intrinsic/extrinsic moral status in, 5, 12–13, 14–15, 21–22, 30t, 96, 97–98, 100t, 103–4, 122–23, 140, 143–44, 171 (see also binary/scalar moral status in; derivative/nonderivative moral status in; earned/unearned moral status in; equal/unequal moral status in; stable/changing moral status in)
machine ethics (see artificial intelligence/AI and; consciousness in; zombies in)
sophisticated cognitive capacities and (see consciousness in)
species and (see speciesism and; anthropocentrism and)
speciesism and, 51–52, 55, 55n.ii, 71–75, 72t, 206–8 (see also anthropocentrism and)
stable/changing moral status in, 5, 28, 30t, 86–87, 97, 100t, 101–2, 110–12, 122–23, 129–30, 141, 143t (see also binary/scalar moral status in; consciousness in; derivative/nonderivative moral status in; disability and; earned/unearned moral status in; equal/unequal moral status in; intrinsic/extrinsic moral status in)
Western ethics (see Greek personhood ancient; Kantian ethics; medieval Christian approaches to personhood; utilitarian ethics; Western approaches to personhood)
zombies in, 148–51, 151t, 155, 156, 157t, 157–60, 161t, 170t, 171t (see also artificial intelligence/AI and; consciousness in)

Western approaches to personhood.
See also Greek philosophy ancient; Kantian ethics; medieval Christian approaches to personhood; utilitarian ethics
ancestors in, 6, 38–40, 120–21 (see also death of persons; soul and)
anthropomorphism in, 22, 49–50, 51–56, 184–89, 199–204, 222, 223–24, 225–26, 227t, 232–33 (see also imago Dei in; speciesism and)
artificial intelligence/AI and, 158–60, 162–71, 170t, 171t (see also consciousness in; zombies in)
assisted death in, 137–41, 143t (see also death of persons; soul and)
binary/scalar moral status in, 5, 16–30, 30t, 31–46, 45t (see also derivative/nonderivative moral status in; earned/unearned moral status in; equal/unequal moral status in; intrinsic/extrinsic moral status in; stable/changing moral status in)

Western approaches to personhood (*cont.*)
  care ethics (*see* feminist perspectives and)
  consciousness in, 61–79, 122–26, 129*t*, 140, 147–76, 151*t*, 157*t*, 161*t*, 184–89, 202–4, 233–37 (*see also* artificial intelligence/AI and; disability and; zombies and)
  conundrum of personhood in, 48–61, 77–78, 188–89 (*see also* soul and; *imago Dei*)
  death of persons in, 120–28, 129*t*, 135–36, 143*t* (*see also* ancestors in; assisted death of persons in; soul and)
  definition of 'Western' in, 12
  derivative/nonderivative moral status in, 5, 17–19, 20–22, 28–30, 30*t*, 37–41, 44, 45*t*, 49–54, 60*t*, 61*t*, 122–23, 129*t*, 140–41, 143*t*, 187, 188–89, 192*t*, 202–3, 206*t*, 227*t* (*see also* binary/scalar moral status in; earned/unearned moral status in; equal/unequal moral status in; intrinsic/extrinsic moral status in; stable/changing moral status in)
  disability and, 25–26, 28, 41, 52, 54–55, 58, 84, 86–87, 96–99, 100*t*, 101–2, 122–24, 129*t* (*see also* consciousness in; equal/unequal moral status in; privation and; stable/changing moral status in)
  earned/unearned moral status in, 5, 16–30, 30*t*, 31–46, 45*t*, 86–87 (*see also* binary/scalar moral status in; derivative/nonderivative moral status in; earned/unearned moral status in; intrinsic/extrinsic moral status in; stable/changing moral status in stable/changing moral status in)
  end of life in (*see* death of persons in)
  equal/unequal moral status in, 37–38, 40–46, 45*t*, 48–50, 52–53, 54–55, 60–61, 60*t*, 61*t*, 92–95, 98–99, 100*t*, 101–2, 111–12, 128, 155–58, 157*t*, 170–71, 171*t*, 184–89, 192*t*, 197–204, 206*t*, 223–24, 227*t* (*see also* binary/scalar moral status in; disability and; earned/unearned moral status in; intrinsic/extrinsic moral status in; stable/changing moral status in)
  feminist perspectives and, 31–46, 48–79, 106–11
  five features of (*see* binary/scalar moral status in; derivative/nonderivative moral status in; earned/unearned moral status in; intrinsic/extrinsic moral status in; stable/changing moral status in)
  human dignity in (*see* intrinsic/extrinsic moral status in)
  imago Dei in, 26, 31–46, 48–61, 222–23, 227*t* (*see also*; conundrum of personhood in; intrinsic/extrinsic moral status in; soul and)
  individualism and, 41, 44–46, 48–52, 53–54, 55–56, 122 (*see also* conundrum of personhood in; medieval Christian approaches to personhood)
  intrinsic/extrinsic moral status in, 5, 12–13, 14–15, 18–19, 20–22, 30*t*, 43, 44–46, 45*t*, 60*t*, 61*t*, 92–96, 97–99, 100*t*, 103–4, 122–23, 140, 143–44, 171, 185, 202–4, 233–36 (*see also* binary/scalar moral status in; derivative/nonderivative moral status in; earned/unearned moral status in; equal/unequal moral status in; *imago Dei*; soul and; stable/changing moral status in)
  machine ethics (*see* artificial intelligence/AI and; consciousness in; zombies in)
  privation and, 62, 76–77, 108
  relational turn in, 78, 160
  rights versus duties in, 55–56
  sophisticated cognitive capacities and (*see* consciousness in)
  soul and, 26, 41–43, 49–57, 77–78, 116–17, 120–21, 122–24, 185–87,

188–89, 199–200, 209, 239t (*see also* conundrum of personhood in; *imago Dei*)
speciesism and, 51–52, 55, 55n.ii, 71–75, 72t, 206–8 (*see also* anthropocentrism and; *imago Dei*)
stable/changing moral status in, 5, 28, 30t, 44, 45t, 47, 49–50, 53, 59, 61t, 77–79, 86–87, 92–95, 97–99, 100t, 101–2, 110–11, 120–21, 122–23, 129–30, 140–41, 143t, 159–60 (*see also* binary/scalar moral status in; derivative/nonderivative moral status in; disability in; earned/unearned moral status in; equal/unequal moral status in; intrinsic/extrinsic moral status in; soul and)
zombies in, 148–51, 151t, 155–56, 157t, 157–60, 161t, 170t, 171t (*see also* artificial intelligence/AI and; consciousness in)